W9-CRM-411

The Evangelical Century

MCGILL-QUEEN'S STUDIES IN THE HISTORY
OF RELIGION

G.A. Rawlyk, Editor

Volumes in this series have been supported by
the Jackman Foundation of Toronto.

1 Small Differences
Irish Catholics and Irish Protestants, 1815–1922
An International Perspective
Donald Harman Akenson

2 Two Worlds
Protestant Culture of Nineteenth-Century
Ontario
William Westfall

3 An Evangelical Mind
Nathanael Burwash and the Methodist Tradition
in Canada, 1839–1918
Marguerite Van Die

4 The Dévotes
Women and Church
in Seventeenth-Century France
Elizabeth Rapley

5 The Evangelical Century
College and Creed in English Canada from the
Great Revival to the Great Depression
Michael Gauvreau

The Evangelical Century

College and Creed in English Canada from the Great Revival to the Great Depression

MICHAEL GAUVREAU

McGill-Queen's University Press
Montreal & Kingston • London • Buffalo

© McGill-Queen's University Press 1991
ISBN 0-7735-0769-8

Legal deposit first quarter 1991
Bibliothèque nationale du Québec

Printed in Canada on acid-free paper

This book has been published with the help of a
grant from the Social Science Federation of Canada,
using funds provided by the Social Sciences and
Humanities Research Council of Canada.

All illustrations are from The United Church of
Canada / Victoria University Archives, Toronto.

Canadian Cataloguing in Publication Data

Gauvreau, Michael, 1956–
The Evangelical century
(McGill-Queen's studies in the history of religion,
ISSN 1181-7445 ; 5)
Includes bibliographical references.
ISBN 0-7735-0769-8
1. Evangelicalism – Canada – History. I. Title.
II. Series.
BR570.G39 1990   260'.0971   C90-090417-8

Typeset by Typo Litho composition inc., Québec, in
10/12 Palatino.

For Nancy Christie
Friend, Companion, Fellow-Explorer

Can two walk together, except they be agreed? Will a lion roar in the forest, when he hath no prey? will a young lion cry out of his den, if he hath taken nothing? Can a bird fall in a snare upon the ground, where no gin is for him? shall one take up a snare from the earth, and have taken nothing at all? Shall a trumpet be blown in the city, and the people not be afraid? shall there be evil in a city, and the Lord hath not done it? Surely the Lord God will do nothing, but he revealeth his secret unto his servant the prophets. The lion hath roared, who will not fear? the Lord God hath spoken, who can but prophesy?

Amos 3:3–7

Contents

Illustrations following page x

Acknowledgments ix

Introduction 3

1 Between Awakening and Enlightenment: The Evangelical Colleges, 1820–1860 13

2 Authority and History: Evangelicalism and the Problem of the Past 57

3 Prophecy, Protestantism, and the Millennium: The Preaching of History 91

4 The Evolutionary Encounter: "Every Thought is to be Brought into Captivity to the Obedience of Christ" 125

5 History, Prophecy, and the Kingdom of God: Toward a Theology of Reform 181

6 The Paradox of History: College and Creed in Crisis 218

7 The Passing of the Evangelical Creed: War, the College, and the Problem of Religious Certainty 255

Conclusion: The Evangelical Mind and the Persistence of the Eighteenth Century 284

viii   Contents

Notes   293

Bibliography   369

Index   393

Acknowledgments

My interest in the thinking of English-Canadian evangelical clergymen began quite accidentally nearly a decade ago. While doing some preliminary research on English-Canadian academic thought in the inter-war years, I optimistically (some would say naïvely) attempted to treat in a short paragraph the impact of biblical criticism on the social and political thought of one prominent Presbyterian. Soon, the issues raised by the encounter of Victorian evangelicalism with various forms of "critical" thought drew me backwards from the 1920s to the late eighteenth century, when the evangelical creed was forged in the transatlantic crucible of revival, revolution, and Enlightenment. To my surprise and occasional bewilderment, religious history threatened to engulf an entire section of the original dissertation. Only then, after some salutary prompting from my thesis supervisor, did I reluctantly admit that religious history was my real interest.

Although my own foray into the history of evangelical religion can be likened to an intellectual blind man's bluff, I have been spared the worst consequences of my blundering by the consistent advice, scholarly assistance, and moral support of several people to whom I am deeply grateful. Like many other scholars who have laboured in the Gothic reading room under the admonitory gaze of Egerton Ryerson, my research was greatly facilitated by the knowledge and unfailing courtesy of the staff of the United Church of Canada Central Archives in Toronto. I thank them and their counterparts at the Public Archives of Canada, Queen's University Archives, the Ar-x Acknowledgments

chives of the Maritime Conference of the United Church of Canada in Halifax, the Public Archives of Nova Scotia, and the Mount Allison University Archives in Sackville, New Brunswick, for the effective preservation and accessibility of so much of our religious heritage.

I have greatly benefitted from the wise advice of three individuals, each of whom has provided a model of committed historical scholarship. Carl Berger at the University of Toronto supervised the original doctoral dissertation, which took on a shape very different from its original outline. It was he who was perceptive enough to channel my enthusiasm in the direction of religious history. Later, George Rawlyk, my series editor, provided a stimulating criticism of the manuscript, renewing my faith in the possibilities and potential of religion as a serious subject of study. Nancy Christie took time from her own work in Canadian cultural history to offer thoughtful criticism of each chapter, as well as the common-sense advice (not always followed) to avoid equating the religious experience with "high" intellectual history.

My colleagues Gerald Friesen, William Westfall, and Paul Wood read various versions and portions of the manuscript, offering sound criticism and constructive suggestions. Paul Wood, in particular, proved a most illuminating guide to the thorny question of the Scottish Enlightenment. Their suggestions have greatly improved the final product. Don Akenson and Peter Goheen of McGill-Queen's University Press provided sound advice and ensured that the manuscript cleared the various hurdles leading to publication. Lesley Andrássy performed the chore of copy editing with superb critical flair, substantially improving the text. Any remaining errors, omissions or infelicities of expression remain my own responsibility.

The research for this study was funded by the Government of Ontario, the Social Sciences and Humanities Research Council of Canada, and the University of Toronto.

Finally, this book is dedicated to Nancy Christie. From her unflinching scholarly integrity, intellectual challenge, and support I have learned the greatest lesson of all: that only through moral commitment does the study of the past become a worthy human endeavour. No ritual formula can repay this debt.

The Rev. Thomas Mc-
Culloch, founder of
Pictou Academy, first
president of Dalhousie
University

Below: *left* The Rev. William MacLaren, Charles
Hodge's leading Cana-
dian disciple, professor of
systematic theology and
later principal, Knox
College

right The Rev. Donald
Harvey MacVicar, princi-
pal, Presbyterian College,
Montreal, 1868–1902

The Rev. Egerton Ryerson, founder of Victoria College, architect of the Methodist synthesis of piety and learning

Below: *left* The Rev. Samuel Nelles, president of Victoria College, 1850–1887

right The Rev. William Caven, principal of Knox College, 1870–1903

Above: *left* The Rev. George Monro Grant, principal of Queen's University, 1877–1902

right The Rev. Salem Bland, professor of New Testament exegesis, Wesley College, Winnipeg

The Rev. Robert Burns, Free Church leader, professor of church history, Knox College

Upper Canada Academy, Cobourg

Victoria College, Toronto, showing the college motto, "The Truth Shall Make You Free," above the entrance

Wesley College, Winnipeg, the forum for the new theology of Salem Bland

Knox College, Toronto

The Rev. John Mark King, principal
of Manitoba College

Pine Hill Divinity Hall, the Presbyterian theological institution in
Halifax

Presbyterian College, Montreal

The Rev. Samuel Dwight Chown,
twentieth-century defender of the
Methodist synthesis of personal
evangelism and social action

The Evangelical Century

*The office of critic, useful as it may be in its place, is a very
cold one compared with that of Testifier.*

Henry Flesher Bland, "*Christian Experience*," sermon, 19 Nov. 1890

*Indeed, by the very intimate relation that subsists ... through-
out the English-speaking world, between the churches and the
theological colleges ... the breach between the Professor and
the pastor is never likely to be a very wide one. It is different
in Germany ... There theology is more likely to be studied as
a pure science. The gain is that theology learns to come to
terms with other sciences; the loss frequently is that the most
essential factor in theological investigation is ignored. The isolation of theology from the life of the Church is even more fa-
tal than the isolation from the sister sciences, because the
Bible is related to the life and faith of the Church.*

John Edgar McFadyen, *Old Testament Criticism
and the Christian Church*, 1903

Introduction

Goldwin Smith, Victorian Canada's pre-eminent man of letters, surveyed the turbulent Anglo-Saxon cultural life at the end of 1895 with
considerable foreboding. He believed that during the preceding half-
century the foundations of Protestant religion had been undermined
by the advance of evolutionary thought. Natural science and biblical
criticism had already eroded the strongest bulwark of Christianity,
"the cosmogonical and historical foundations" of traditional belief
contained in the Bible. Worse, complained Smith, the defenders of
the faith had surrendered to the enemy. Dubious theories of "semi-
inspiration" applied to the biblical record had led "liberal" theologians to give up "the authenticity and authority" of the Book of
Genesis. These thinkers, he wrote, compelled educated Christians
to relinquish their beliefs concerning the central doctrines of the Fall,
the Redemption, and the Incarnation. The one certain result of the
doubt created by the Protestant churches' abdication of authority
was intellectual, moral, and social anarchy. Smith and many of his
contemporaries feared that agnosticism and a secular outlook would
dominate twentieth-century culture.[1]

Though Smith was a former Regius Professor of History at Oxford
and a formidable literary figure, his exposure of the supposed contradictions of evolutionary theory and Protestant doctrine did not
go unchallenged. In *Queen's Quarterly*, April 1896, the Rev. Salem
Bland, a young Methodist preacher from Ontario, dismissed Smith's
indictment of contemporary theology on two counts. First, he
claimed that the methods of evolutionary science did not destroy
the faith of the Christian churches in the Bible. To soften the old

Protestant insistence on biblical "inerrancy" or verbal inspiration did not mean a complete denial of the Bible's authority. Rather, he asserted, "[t]he Higher Criticism and archaeological research of this generation are, probably, Moses-like, guiding to a truer theory and interpretation" of biblical literature. Of greater significance for understanding the attitude of the late nineteenth-century Protestant churches was Bland's questioning of the irrevocable opposition between Christian faith and evolutionary science. He maintained that evolution, "the divine method of development in nature and human history"[2] was a sacred and not a secular process. Fortified rather than undermined by alliance with the historical criticism of the Bible, Protestantism might retain its commanding position by Christianizing late Victorian thought, instead of declining into irrelevance.

The positions defended in this exchange between the professor and the preacher demand a reconsideration of a number of much-debated questions crucial to the understanding of the cultural history of English Canada. To what extent, historians have asked, were the tenets of Protestant religion, based on belief in an inspired and authoritative Scripture, displaced from the minds of educated people by the methods and assumptions of Darwinian science and historical criticism? Did increasing acceptance of the logic of evolutionary naturalism by many eminent figures in the late nineteenth century mean the denial of the right and competence of the Christian faith to guide, enlighten, and discipline human intellectual and cultural endeavour? Such questions point to the vexed and complex problem of secularization, defined by Owen Chadwick as a growing tendency to do without religion, a phenomenon both intellectual and social in its origins and implications, and particularly evident in Western Europe and North America.[3]

The process that dislodged Protestant religion from its central place in English-Canadian society and culture provides one of the most compelling questions for Canadian intellectual historians. During the past twenty years, most have come to agree on the main outlines and chronology of the development from a mid-nineteenth century culture dominated by the theological categories of religious "orthodoxy" to a secular society in the short space of two generations. It has become almost a truism among those who have examined the relationship between Protestant religion and English-Canadian culture that the impact of Darwin's theory in the years after 1859 was the central point of disjuncture, ushering in a battle between religion and science, in which Protestantism was the clear loser. Evolution, it is claimed, weakened the central tenets of Christianity and the intellectual life they sustained. The rapid course of this religious decline was punctuated in the 1880s by the rise of a "theological liberalism,"[4] heavily laced with naturalistic theory and philosophical idealism. Its transitory characters proved that contact between evolutionary modes of thought and Christianity could end only in the erosion of an explicitly religious worldview, and the adoption of a secular outlook by many Christian believers and clergymen. By 1900 the Canadian intellectual community, including many Protestant clergymen, had accepted the irrelevance of theology and had resolved its tenets into philosophy, the science of society, or forms of social criticism and reform. This was the penultimate step toward a "secular culture," a milieu from which Protestant religion had been displaced intellectually by the physical and social sciences.[5]

The question of whether secularization was a benign or a destructive process remains in dispute. Was the journey from religious "orthodoxy" through theological "liberalism" to the eventual "irrelevance" of Protestantism a largely progressive one, in which the evangelical religious vision premised on regeneration gave birth to the emerging social sciences and movements of social and political reform, thus preserving and enshrining religious values in the nation's culture?[6] Or was secularization a destructive process, in which the Canadian churches, in a frantic search for social relevance in the face of naturalistic explanations of individual and social behaviour, turned the emphasis on regeneration, which had previously been directed to other-worldly concerns, to the task of creating an earthly Kingdom of God? In so doing, did Protestant clergymen unwittingly capitulate to secularism and, by too easily resolving theology into social science and reform, ensure their own irrelevance by abandoning any explicit religious criteria they might have used to guide a society in the process of modernization?[7]

From the perspective of the late twentieth century celebrating or lamenting the secularization of English-Canadian life involves particular conceptual and methodological difficulties. The ever-present temptation is to pass over the tensions and ambiguities in the encounter of nineteenth-century religion with secular modes of thought, and to posit an irreversible and linear movement leading directly from a culture dominated by an inflexible religious "orthodoxy" to one characterized by the irrelevance of Protestantism. Though ostensibly concerned with nineteenth-century religion, those who have studied the secularization of English-Canadian thought and culture are in reality more interested in the origins of twentieth-century English-Canadian thought – an approach that wrenches the thought of the late nineteenth-century from its context and forces key elements of Victorian culture into a mould cast by the expectations and attitudes characterizing the modern relationship between religion and society. It glosses over the problem of identifying the elements of nineteenth-century Protestant theology and their meaning and function in the wider society.

This book consciously avoids both the progressive and the pessimistic interpretations of late nineteenth-century English-Canadian religion and culture, and endeavours to preserve an attitude of agnosticism concerning the so-called secularization of Protestant theology and its resolution into the modern social science temper. Implicit in this approach is an impatience with the opposition of "theology" and "secular thought" – an opposition that has obscured rather than explained the meaning and role of religion in the intellectual world of Victorian Canada. I have resisted, as far as possible, the formulation of comprehensive interpretations of the origin of twentieth-century English Canadian thought. In the absence of more detailed historical treatments of the nineteenth-century religious experience in English Canada, any such formulation would be premature.

This study attempts to explain why, in the 1890s, the young Methodist preacher Salem Bland found it possible to argue confidently with Goldwin Smith, a man with an international reputation, that the higher criticism of the Bible did not impair the central tenets of his evangelical faith. Could it be argued that, unlike late twentieth-century English Canadians, most late Victorian Christian believers did not automatically assume that the religious and scientific explanations of nature and human society conflicted? Yet how could traditional theology be anything more than a passive obstacle before the corrosive criticism of the modern intellect? Could any form of theology hope to preserve its position of authority in the face of this onslaught?

The central assertion of this book is that between 1850 and 1900 the theology of the Methodist and Presbyterian churches survived the encounter with various currents of secular thought through a flexibility[8] forged in the ambiguous evangelical encounter with the eighteenth century that permitted a constructive dialogue with certain modern thought. This enabled clergymen to preserve much of their status and intellectual leadership in the wider culture until the early twentieth century. For these clergymen, scientific evolutionary thought was not the major intellectual challenge. Their anxieties centred on the implications of higher criticism, historical scholarship, and the insights of the social sciences for their religious outlook. For them Darwinism was merely an undercurrent. When faced with these perplexing problems, clergymen found in their theology the resources to shape and direct these newer scientific, historical, and philosophical currents. Although this accommodation might be regarded as a sign of weakness, a prelude to the inevitable dominance of secular modes of social thought, another interpretation of the late Victorian cultural transformation is possible. Historians have been content to consider the impact of Darwinism on Protestant religion a defeat, and to confirm their arguments by pointing to the irrelevance of the churches in modern society. This was by no means clear to many Anglo-Canadians in the years between 1870 and 1930. To them the absorption of some elements of modern thought by theology indicated not irrelevance and futility but persistence and viability. So vital and culturally significant was this theology that its central beliefs and assumptions remained intact until the 1920s.

The persistence of theology in the Protestant church colleges and pulpits between 1870 and 1930 challenges the familiar shape of English-Canadian cultural history. The direct linear process of secularization, by which theology becomes first philosophy and then sociology, fails to explain why many Canadian clergymen resisted the resolution of their religious traditions into either philosophy or social science. The vitality of theology as an intellectual discipline in the church colleges also points to the need for a new understanding of how Protestant Christian thought became irrelevant to the intellectual and academic communities. Theology became redundant as a discipline within the colleges not because it had been absorbed into the new social sciences, but because it did not remain open to the questions of human nature and society that traditionally had informed the evangelical creed.

Given that the persistence of theology as well as the process of secularization must be understood in order to explain the development of Canadian cultural history a study of how that theology was formulated and communicated to the wider culture becomes imperative. To the modern mind, the term "theology" is redolent of the unworldly and the esoteric, and of a closed, inflexible system of dogmatic propositions comprehensible only to a small elite. In the nineteenth-century, the understanding of Protestant theology in English Canada was radically different. All Protestant denominations had been shaped to a greater or lesser extent by evangelicalism, the product of the great wave of religious revivals between 1780 and 1860. Under the influence of the religious experience of these revivals, theology was not so much a fixed philosophical system of doctrine as a much looser, and consequently more pervasive, body of beliefs and assumptions concerning God, the individual, and society. As Goldwin French argued nearly twenty years ago, the culture of the evangelical churches might best be termed a "creed" rather than a formal system of thought.[9] As products of this evangelical age, Anglo-Canadian clergymen would have scorned a theology that limited itself to speculative questions, or simply posited a basis for morality in reason. The persistent note of evangelical theology was biblical and activist, not metaphysical or theoretical. Theology said Principal John Mark King of Manitoba College, was "biblical" rather than systematic or speculative – sound doctrine was not the product of reason, but was derived from faith and from close study of the Scriptural record.[10] This body of beliefs was premised on a single truth – God's will, as revealed in the Bible, could sanctify and transform the human soul, human knowledge, and the community.

The very nature of this theology reflected the evangelical passion for the conversion and salvation of an entire society. These tenets were articulated by leading clergymen who believed that theology should not simply be studied by the learned few, but should be preached to a wider audience. They maintained that in order to animate and regenerate Canadian culture Christian doctrine must be intelligible, and applicable to the everyday life of the congregation. In its broadest sense, evangelical theology was democratic and popular. The doctrines contained in the Bible were the common heritage of all Protestants.

Although the evangelical creed was the common property of Anglicans, Baptists, Methodists, Presbyterians, and Congregationalists, this study does not pretend to be a comprehensive exploration of the experience of all Canadian Protestants. I have limited it to the Methodist and Presbyterian churches, which were the largest Protestant denominations in Canada between 1820 and 1920.[11] Despite sharp initial differences over questions of church polity, educational jurisdiction, and the thorny question of salvation, the fusion of the two groups in 1925 to form the United Church of Canada points to a broad area of theological agreement and common intellectual experience. Of greater significance for this study is the early and highly visible role of these two churches in the promotion of institutions of higher learning. These colleges formed the central components of the modern Canadian university system.[12] The most direct encounter between theology and the far-reaching transformation of thought represented by the new human sciences and the historical criticism of the Bible occurred in their classrooms.

As an intellectual and cultural history, this book does not offer a comprehensive regional treatment of the church colleges or the educational policies of the Methodist and Presbyterian churches. It concentrates on the oldest and largest of the colleges: Presbyterian College, Halifax; Presbyterian College, Montreal; Queen's University, Kingston; Knox College, Toronto; Mount Allison Wesleyan College; and Victoria College. This is not intended as a slight to the colleges of Western Canada. But until the years immediately before World War I, the western colleges functioned largely as offshoots of eastern institutions, and were designed primarily to train missionaries for the rapidly expanding western provinces. Wesley College, Winnipeg, and Manitoba College recruited their staff from Britain and from the older colleges, replicating the colonial relationship that characterized evangelical culture in English Canada. The rise of a distinctive theological emphasis at Wesley College, Winnipeg, between 1905 and 1914, as clergymen like Eber Crummy, Salem Bland, and A.J. Irwin preached an evolutionary "social gospel,"[13] coincided with, and was largely a symptom of, the final crisis of the evangelical creed.

The thought and experience of the clergymen-professors in the Methodist and Presbyterian church colleges provide an ideal point of entry for the study of the meaning and function of theology in the wider culture of English Canada. Their positions as professors led these clergymen to positions of prominence and power in their churches. Charged with the duty of training the next generation of clergymen and, in a broader sense, of educating an Anglo-Canadian elite in the precepts of liberal culture,[14] they conceived their principal mission as the elaboration and defence of a theological tradition that they believed guided and informed human intellectual endeavour. Only the continued existence and vitality of such a theology could, they held, assure the salvation of both man and society.

Although it might be tempting to dismiss these ideas as an attempt to perpetuate the influence of an elite academic clergy in an age of doubt and social transition, they possessed broader cultural significance in the nineteenth century when the importance of the clergymen-professors was far greater than their number. By 1900, they had trained the majority of the ministers in the Methodist and Presbyterian churches. But these professors did not simply train preachers. For more than a century they were themselves preachers. Nearly all had begun their careers ministering to congregations. In a land chronically plagued by a shortage of clergy, many continued to preach. This combination of careers ensured that their theology could never become simply an academic tradition. Rather, it was adapted to the changing needs of the congregation in order to establish harmony between piety and intellect. Between 1820 and 1920 the relationship of faith and reason was continually shaped by the needs of the preacher.

Among the most prominent of these figures were Thomas McCulloch, William Caven, Michael Willis, William MacLaren, George Monro Grant, and Robert Falconer of the Presbyterian church; and their Methodist counterparts, Egerton Ryerson, Samuel Nelles, Nathanael Burwash, Samuel Dwight Chown, and Salem Bland. These men ranked as major figures in the cultural world of English Canada. Their teaching on the inspiration and authority of the Bible, the relationship of religion and science, and the connections between church and society penetrated to the local congregations through the sermons of their numerous students. Furthermore, as active contributors to the religious press and to periodicals read by many educated Anglo-Canadians, they and less well-known colleagues achieved a forum for their theology beyond the confines of college and church. Their leadership not only directed the intellectual response of many Protestant Christians in the encounter with modern thought, but encouraged a distinctive spirit of harmony and accommodation between evangelical religion and the newer currents of thought. They endeavoured to perpetuate a body of religious beliefs, assumptions, and ideas, in a way that would secure the continued dominance of theology in intellectual life.

For the clergyman-professor, the vital task was the definition of a proper relationship between revelation, the Bible, and the products of the human intellect. Between 1820 and 1930 evangelical clergymen insisted on the sinful nature of humanity, and thus the necessity of revivalism and preaching to save souls. To these tenets, which formed the basis of the evangelical creed, must be added a set of related assumptions that conferred authority on the evangelical theology. In the Presbyterian and Methodist colleges, the Bible occupied the position of honour, its study forming the centre of the liberal arts curriculum. Reflecting this emphasis, clergymen-professors enjoined generations of students to preserve a balance between piety and intellect by subordinating critical reason to faith, urging them to avoid speculative hypotheses on the nature of religious truth, and to acquire both secular and theological knowledge through the sober accumulation of facts. Among these Canadian evangelicals, biblical study was informed by a particular concept of time and history that infused history, both sacred and secular, with a divine purpose. Through preaching and the proper use of reason, Christian believers might be encouraged to turn their energies to the building of the divine society on earth.

Any study of evangelical theology and its relationship to English-Canadian culture is, at the very outset, beset with a nagging difficulty. During the nineteenth century, Canada was a cultural colony of Great Britain and was also affected by intellectual currents from the United States. There is a natural tendency to look for direct replication in English Canada of patterns present in the two larger English-speaking societies. Canadian cultural historians have assumed that, because clergymen and ideas moved freely in the transatlantic world of nineteenth-century Protestantism, a version of the American pattern of intellectual history can best explain the interaction of religion and culture in English Canada. These historians have been content to describe a process that led from a rigid "orthodoxy," characterized by insistence on an inerrant Bible and the formulation of inflexible, systematic theologies, to the world of the Enlightenment, where these beliefs were modified by rationalism and natural theology. After 1860, it is claimed, the impact of evolution encouraged the rise of philosophical idealism, theological "liberalism," and secular forms of social thought. [15] Closer study of the Methodist and Presbyterian church colleges challenges this imported model of intellectual change advanced by historians anxious to place their culture within the framework defined by the ruling British and American ideas.

Two differences will immediately strike the student of the nineteenth-century religious scene in English Canada. The evangelical church colleges lacked the vibrant traditions of philosophical or speculative theology that informed religion and intellect in Britain and America. The observer looks in vain for the great debates on the issues of free will, divine sovereignty, and the fine balancing of will and intellect that agitated British and American clergymen from the seventeenth century to the advent of Darwin. English-Canadian church colleges lacked the commanding presence of philosophical theologians of the calibre of Jonathan Edwards or Charles Hodge. In biblical scholarship, the historian will not find Canadian counterparts of the great German and English scholars who were instrumental in fostering a new relationship between revelation and critical reason. [16] At the same time, English-Canadian evangelicals were not plagued by the widening gulf between religious modernists and antimodernists. According to the seminal study by George Marsden, [17] this division split American denominations between 1870 and 1930, and shaped the character of present-day American Protestantism.

Did the lack of speculative theology and the relative absence of religious controversy in the church colleges mean that English-Canadian Protestants existed in a religious backwater and that their theology was a derivative and stunted product? Or was there some deeper relationship between a missing tradition of systematic theology and the failure of a militant fundamentalist movement to find a congenial home in Canada? This book argues that the theological outlook that governed Canadian Methodists and Presbyterians was forged in a time of religious revolt against those very speculative theologies that defined the character of British and American Protestantism. Their theology united the passions and enthusiasms of the great religious revivals of the late eighteenth century with the practical reason of one strand of the Scottish Enlightenment. Entrenched in the colleges between 1820 and 1860, this type of religious thought played a crucial role in guiding the complex development of Protestantism and intellectual life in late Victorian English Canada.

From the foundation of the church colleges during the Great Revival to the ordeal of evangelical culture in the Great Depression, the primacy of biblical theology in the curriculum assured the integrity of the evangelical creed. Its very simplicity secured it against any particular system of philosophy, and gave it the flexibility to meet and absorb the shocks of secular thought and the historical criticism of the Bible. The wellsprings of this outlook lay not only in the academic teaching of the colleges, but also in the popular world of preaching and revival. The authority of evangelical theology in English-Canadian intellectual life weakened only after the turn of the century, when the relationship between college and pulpit broke down.

1 Between Awakening and Enlightenment: The Evangelical Colleges, 1820–1860

In the fall of 1819 a group of young men gathered outside a large white frame house in the little port town of Pictou, Nova Scotia. Dressed in the uniforms of Glasgow University scholars, they eagerly awaited the opening of the Pictou Academy, the first institution of higher learning sponsored by the Presbyterian Church in the provinces of British North America. For the founder and principal of the college, the Reverend Thomas McCulloch, it was a proud moment, the fulfillment of a vision that had fired him from the moment of his arrival from Scotland in 1803. Containing a small but valuable library, a laboratory complete with "philosophical apparatus," and a museum of the natural history of Nova Scotia, the academy was intended to provide a sound education founded on the traditional Scottish liberal arts curriculum.[1] Students completing the four-year program would graduate knowing the classical languages, moral philosophy, "natural philosophy" or science, and mathematics, and algebra.

McCulloch, the overworked principal who taught both philosophy and science, collected botanical and animal specimens for the museum, ministered to the Pictou congregation, and published both theological and literary works, was a Scottish missionary. Born in the Lowlands in 1776, he attended university in Glasgow and was ordained in 1799, quickly establishing a reputation as a forceful preacher.[2] On arrival in Nova Scotia, he had been profoundly moved by the religious destitution of his countrymen in the Pictou region. This part of the province was far removed from the seaport of Halifax, with its wider educational and social opportunities. The remedy he prescribed was the training of a provincial clergy, rather than reliance on the uncertain missionary efforts of the metropolis. To this end, in 1806 he opened a small grammar school, which secured a charter and grant as Pictou Academy in 1816. By 1820 McCulloch had realized his ambition. In that year, he established a private theological class, associated with the college, to train candidates for the Presbyterian ministry. Here, down to the smallest details, was ostensibly a miniature replica of a Scottish university.

Though linked to the parent culture by dress, curriculum, and ceremony, a spirit far removed from the eighteenth-century Scottish spirit of inquiry prevailed at Pictou. While Scottish education glorified scientific and moral improvement through the independent use of human reason and critical faculties, especially the discipline of moral philosophy,[3] McCulloch's ideal of education stressed the limits of reason and its inability to provide, unassisted by revelation, even a glimmering of what the human spirit craved. Speaking at the dedication of the new college building in 1819, McCulloch stated his views on the goals of education. First he reminded the students that man had been designed by the divine power for intellectual and moral improvement. But, he cautioned, the inspiration and end of education lay removed from the realm of human reason and attainment. "I do not pretend," he declared, "that any system of education will change the heart, or conform the actions of man to the standard of divine law. This is the prerogative of the gospel impressed upon the mind by the Holy Spirit." Christian faith and devotion must guide, inform, and validate any system of sound education. The goal of McCulloch's academy was eminently practical – the cultivation of self-knowledge, an ideal conducive both to good conduct and happiness in life and to the preparation, through the fostering of devotion and piety, of the human soul for a future life.[4]

Although it might be tempting to view McCulloch's exhortations as part of a linear process by which Scottish culture was transplanted in English Canada, his efforts must be understood against a more complex background of intellectual endeavour. His attempt to strike a balance between devotion and knowledge, faith and reason, reflects not simplicity but ambiguity. His weighting of the balance on the side of faith, with the suggestion that the truths of divine revelation must command and discipline human reason, marks the resolution of a creative moment of bitter contest between two rival cultures then striving for mastery in his homeland – Evangelicalism and Enlightenment. The battle lines were drawn over certain fundamental questions. The character of religious truth, human nature, and intellect, and the right relationship between human beings and the divine power agitated partisans in both camps. This debate informed and shaped the character of religion, education, and preaching among Methodists and Presbyterians in the Canadian colonies. It had, by the 1840s, provided a matrix that differentiated the culture of these northern provinces from those of the other English-speaking societies on both sides of the Atlantic.

THE CASE OF THE "MISSING ENLIGHTENMENT"

Defining the contours of intellectual and cultural life in English Canada in the formative years between 1780 and 1860 has proved a perplexing task for historians. Protestant Christianity provided a body of truths that underpinned a variety of beliefs and assumptions important to early nineteenth century Anglo-Canadians.[5] However, the relationship of English Canada to the late eighteenth-century world of enlightenment, revolution, and religious awakening – Thomas McCulloch's world – remains problematic. The great Canadian literary critic Northrop Frye, stating what many English Canadians have sensed concerning their intellectual origins, once said that unlike the older Atlantic societies, Britain and the United States, Canada experienced neither the Enlightenment nor the age of revolution. Propelled by a "foreshortening" of history, her cultural life leaped in a single bound from the seventeenth-century age of empire to the era of evangelical religion and romanticism. More recently, the historian Brian McKillop has disputed this notion of cultural change. He claims that during the crucial early decades of the nineteenth century, a close contact with the Scottish Enlightenment nourished English-Canadian clergymen, scientists, and literary figures, and provided the central pillars sustaining the Anglo-Canadian "mind."[6]

A perceived dichotomy between evangelicalism and Enlightenment has thus become the shorthand of historical debate. For Protestant Christians at the end of the eighteenth century these categories were not mutually exclusive.[7] Yet they did encompass a basic disagreement over the character of the Christian tradition on both sides of the Atlantic and its effect on both intellectual life and popular discussion. Was Christianity, educated men in Britain and America argued, a religion that exalted the revealed truths of Scripture over the achievements of the human intellect, and insisted on the sinfulness of the unredeemed soul and the perverted nature of reason divorced from divine revelation? Or was it a faith anchored on human benevolence, an optimistic creed preaching a rational epistemology, and a moral philosophy that set forth a precise calculus of duties and obligations?

It is easy, but simplistic, to moor English Canada more firmly within the cultural world of the Anglo-American Enlightenment, where the sufficiency of reason to illuminate the essential order in man and nature was an article of faith. After all, these convictions formed the staple of public discussion in early nineteenth-century British North America. The Enlightenment, however, must be viewed not only as an intellectual movement, but also as a social phenomenon. In England, Scotland, and America, it was the product of an urban culture, dependent for its propagation on a network of clubs, literary societies, coffee houses, taverns, and universities, where the canons of polite learning were discussed and codified by the literati.[8] There was no such Enlightenment in the newly-settled Canadian colonies. They lacked the institutions and amenities offered by urban centres such as Edinburgh, Boston, New York, and Philadelphia, which were necessary to sustain even a "provincial" version of the Enlightenment. And in the critical period between 1820 and 1840, when the social life of British North America began to take on a firmer shape, the Enlightenment had already been subsumed and redefined by a more powerful and popular current of ideas – evangelicalism.

The Methodist and Presbyterian educators and preachers of Thomas McCulloch's generation worked within a cultural climate defined by the evangelical awakening that swept the English-speaking world in the years after 1780. They did not subscribe to the polite learning or to the religion of the eighteenth century that emphasized the independent role of reason.[9] For these men, their students, and their congregations, Christianity was a passion, a living force, a pulsating energy infusing the individual soul and human society. Their descriptions of its power often took the form of medical analogies in which faith assumed the character of a "remedy" for the "disease" of sin. Theology, when explicitly stated, found its expression not in learned, systematic treatises, but in expositions of Scripture exhorting the achievement of faith through personal conversion and regeneration. Their doctrine centred on the sacrifice of Christ for the sins of a fallen humanity, as testified to by the undoubted, literal truth of the Bible. Here, with the cosmic drama of sin and salvation, lay the glowing core of the evangelical creed, a set of assumptions sustaining religious thought and action and the wider culture of English Canada. This evangelical current broke decisively with the reasonable, benevolent Christianity of the Enlightenment

by insisting on the importance of divine revelation in the apprehension of religious truth.

Even in the colleges, where professors strove for a balance between Christian piety and reason, ministers such as the Methodists
Egerton Ryerson and Samuel Nelles, or the Presbyterians James
George and William Lyall, were simply not interested in original
inquiry or contributions to the complex philosophical tradition of
Common Sense. This stood in marked contrast to the evangelical
denominations in the United States. By the early nineteenth century,
American Protestant churches had evolved a widespread network
of colleges and academies where the teaching of biblical studies and
theology was largely cast in terms of Common Sense philosophy.
According to the historian Mark Noll, "Common Sense" in the American context implied three distinct emphases: first, the epistemological, derived from the writings of the Scottish thinker Thomas Reid,
which posited that human perceptions reveal the world as it actually
is; second, the moral, which asserted that just as humans know
intuitively some basic realities of the physical world, so they know
by the nature of their own being certain fundamental principles of
morality; and third, the "methodological," or the scientific, closely
connected with an exaltation of Francis Bacon, which stated that
truths about consciousness, the world, or religion must be built by
a strict induction from irreducible facts of experience.[10]

Although the evangelical creed in English Canada was certainly
influenced by the Common Sense philosophy, the connection between the two was far less intimate. Far from being subservient to
the principles of the Enlightenment, evangelicals in British North
America drew heavily upon the "retort to reason" offered by the
eighteenth-century clergymen William Law and Bishop Butler, who
sustained a view anchored on the authority of revelation, and emphasized the limited province of the human intellect.[11] More importantly, Anglo-Canadian evangelical divines turned for inspiration
and intellectual sustenance to the great figures of the Awakening,
the Presbyterian Thomas Chalmers or the Methodist John Wesley,
rather than to the philosophers of the Enlightenment.

"Epistemological" Common Sense, which played a major role in
the shaping of American Protestant theology, received comparatively little attention in the Canadian colleges. While the works of
Scottish philosophers like Thomas Reid, Thomas Brown, Dugald
Stewart, and Sir William Hamilton were certainly read in Presbyterian and Methodist colleges, the fine distinctions between sense,
perception, and intellect were regarded as distractions from the
proper aims of Christian education. Nor did "moral philosophy"

ever assume the commanding position it enjoyed in the Scottish universities or American colleges. For Thomas McCulloch, Michael Willis, Egerton Ryerson, and Samuel Nelles, the study of ethics was not simply a rational discipline of precepts and obligations, but a much less specialized study of the human character, which they elucidated by reference to what they believed were the eternal laws of conduct explicitly set forth in the Scriptures, not by reference to the Scottish philosophers. Only "methodological" Common Sense, or Baconianism, ever became a staple of teaching in the English-Canadian colleges. And, as we shall see, this was the one element of the Common Sense program ultimately compatible with the evangelical insistence on the supremacy of the Bible and theology in education and culture.

This same Awakening, however, refused to tolerate religious obscurantism. In an address to a group of college students in 1857, the Rev. Samuel Nelles, Principal of Victoria College, reminded them that piety and intellect could not be divorced. Without education, religion degenerated into superstition, while learning, if deprived of the Christian faith, was apt "to grow proud, shallow, and unprofitable."[12] Ministers such as Nelles extolled the blessings of a reasonable faith and a faithful reason, a pairing suggestive not only of tension between revelation and the inquiring reason, but also of the little-appreciated flexibility and tolerance of the evangelical creed in its age of expansion.

Such statements point to another feature characteristic of the formative years of English-Canadian culture. The legacy of the Enlightenment, though rejected as a foundation of Christian inquiry, could not be completely dismissed. Although the criteria of theological discussion in the evangelical church colleges in British North America between 1820 and 1860 were fixed by the zeal of the Awakening, Anglo-Canadian clergymen appropriated those elements of the Enlightenment most amenable to a Christian interpretation.[13] Like many of their contemporaries, they subscribed to a vision of scientific and moral progress, with the proviso that such advances could only occur under the influence of biblical Christianity. Of equal significance for the culture of the early nineteenth century was the confident belief in a final harmony between faith and reason. Where intellect observed its proper limits and subordinated its claims to the higher knowledge of revelation, the Christian gospel could best accomplish its transforming and redeeming work in soul and society.

Despite the continued influence of their eighteenth-century inheritance on English-Canadian evangelical Protestants, they lacked exposure to the full range of cultural possibilities included under the rubric "Enlightenment." The northern provinces of British America did not enter the intellectual orbit of the British metropolis until the 1770s, and thus missed the sceptical and revolutionary phases of the Enlightenment that shaped the life of the infant United States. Certain tenets of the Anglo-Scottish Enlightenment reached the non-revolutionary colonies only in a vestigial, fragmentary form.[14] When they did, they were filtered through spectacles coloured by the evangelical Awakening. It was this blending of fragments of the Enlightenment and the eighteenth-century critique of rationalism with the evangelical creed that shaped the religion and culture of British North America during its early decades. Though it might be decried as intellectually shallow, it was, in fact, an attempt to encompass two worlds – the culture of scientific and social improvement, dominated by the vision of experiment and discovery, and the culture of religious revival, characterized by the theological priorities of original sin and God's saving grace freely given in Christ, doctrines accessible to all believers in an inerrant and fully inspired Scripture.

Within the limits of this creative tension, the missionary founders of the Anglo-Canadian evangelical church colleges developed a body of knowledge premised on theological priorities, especially the individual response to the word of God. In these colleges, the Bible occupied a central place as the guide and organizer of Christian life and thought. Scripture served as the foundation of doctrine and the fountainhead of devotion. More than this, evangelicals believed that people encountered God through the "word." Faith based upon the Bible was thus the precondition of learning. Philosophical speculation, historical study, the classical languages, and scientific thought must be ruled by its claims. At once reverent and practical, this outlook regarded intellectual systems, both philosophical and theological, as relative and secondary, useful only insofar as they contributed to fostering a Christian life. Pious learning bred sound preaching. If this equation were found wanting the evangelical impulse to convert the world would be rendered futile.

A PRESBYTERIAN OUTPOST: PICTOU

The complex fusion of the spirit of the Awakening and the Anglo-Scottish Enlightenment was most evident in the Presbyterian colleges. Four of these institutions were founded between 1820 and 1850: the Pictou Academy; Queen's University, Kingston; Knox College, Toronto; and Presbyterian College, Halifax.[15] Their purpose and curriculum reflected the shifting currents of religion and intellect in the Scottish metropolis. By the 1840s these had divided the Church of Scotland into warring camps and, in the process, had destroyed the cosmopolitan impulse that had been characteristic of the Enlightenment. To cross the Atlantic in the 1820s was, however, to enter a world that had never experienced the full flowering of the Scottish Enlightenment, a culture that felt the impact of the intellectual divisions within the parent society, but did not replicate them. Already solidly aligned in the camp of the Awakening, Presbyterians in British North America blended their old ideal of a learned ministry, the Calvinist theology, and the practical reason of the eighteenth century, and tempered them into a new alloy, the evangelical creed.

The Pictou Academy was the joint creation of the missionary impulse of the Awakening and the efforts of Thomas McCulloch. Pious zeal, not the independent spirit of inquiry, pervaded its goals and curriculum. McCulloch's own theology, though premised on a balance between piety and learning, imposed a severely practical scale of priorities determined by the concerns of Christian doctrine. Preaching, not inquiry, doctrine rather than philosophy, made up the intellectual fare of the Pictou students. Indeed, of the thirty-seven scholars enrolled in the early 1820s, no less than twelve had declared for the Presbyterian ministry as their vocation.[16]

McCulloch's religious outlook was founded on the traditions of Calvinist theology, which stretched back to the sixteenth century. Its grim insistence on original sin, human depravity, God's absolute sovereignty, and the apparent contradictions of predestination, free will, and divine grace formed the staple of theological education at Pictou. Through fortnightly lectures, McCulloch hoped to instil these values into the souls and preaching of his students. Calvinism, he declared in a work published posthumously in 1849, was the Christian system. Humanity's general tendency was toward moral evil, he stoutly maintained (in contrast to the benevolent optimism of the Enlightenment), an evil remedied only by God's grace, which awakened faith in Christ and brought salvation. Such views, he believed, were sanctioned by both revelation and reason, and marked the point of departure of the human search for redemption.[17]

Although cast in the mould of Calvinism, McCulloch's thought was not an atavism, or a late flowering of the seventeenth century in British North America. Calvinism in North America has usually been traced to its origins in Puritan New England. There, in the seventeenth century, Calvinist divinity functioned not only as the raw material for popular preaching, but also as the theological foundation of university education. It was a systematic, intellectual theology derived from the work of Calvin himself and from that of successive generations of interpreters. It sustained a body of moral philosophy and speculative theology that was often rational and legalistic in character. The great exemplars of the Calvinist tradition in America were the New England clergyman, Jonathan Edwards and, in the nineteenth century, Charles Hodge, the exponent of the Princeton theology. Their philosophical theology eagerly debated humanity's sinfulness, individual responsibility, the nature of grace, and human freedom in a world governed by law.[18]

When placed beside such giants, Thomas McCulloch seems a pale ghost. His Calvinism, devoid of philosophical discussion, had little in common with the great Edwardsean or Princeton systems of theology. McCulloch's religious thought grew out of a culture defined by a different intellectual dynamic. Between 1740 and 1840 American clergymen were challenged by a bewildering diversity of cultural and religious impulses. The First Great Awakening between 1740 and 1760 saw Calvinism, through the writings and sermons of Edwards and others, meet the intellectual challenge of a wave of emotional revivalism and the currents of the British Enlightenment. The influence of Edwards and George Whitefield enabled it to retain its dominant position. The decades between 1790 and 1840, however, brought increasing difficulties to American Calvinism. Under the impact of the Second Great Awakening, it had to justify its doctrinal inheritance in the face of the Methodists and others who stressed free grace over election and predestination, and espoused a radically simplified theology centred on the sacrifice of Christ. The issue of revivalism split American Presbyterians into two groups – the "Old School," who adhered to the traditions of systematic Calvinism, and the "New School," who desired compromise with certain tenets of the evangelical revival.[19]

Such cultural polarizations were muted in the Presbyterianism of the northern provinces. McCulloch and his contemporaries brought from the metropolis a Calvinism already modified by evangelicalism. Purged of much of its philosophical, rationalist, and legalistic baggage, it was a theology premised on compromise with the fervent revivalistic spirit of the Second Great Awakening. It offered the prospect of a warm, living faith confirmed by the evidence of the Bible rather than by intellectual criteria supplied by systematic metaphysics. It stressed missionary preaching and aimed at personal conversion through the appeal of God's will to the conscience.

Despite the presence of certain pessimistic tenets of the old Calvinism in his religious outlook, McCulloch's creed was founded upon the confidence of the Awakening. Like many British and American evangelical clergymen in the early decades of the nineteenth century, he believed that missionary endeavour could convert and Christianize entire societies,[20] and he looked to historical events to justify this optimism. In a sermon preached in 1814, McCulloch discerned even in the most calamitous events evidences of God's care for his church and people. The wars and revolutions plaguing Europe during the Napoleonic years were but the "times of trouble" that "an over-ruling Providence has marked out for the revival of the spirit of religion, for abundant enlargement of the prosperity of Zion." Signs of the great revival were everywhere – the spread of a spirit of benevolence, the abolition of slavery, and the growth of vital religion through social unions and educational societies.[21]

This fusion of Calvinism and the evangelical spirit was drawn not only from the general intellectual climate of the Awakening, but also from McCulloch's own religious roots. He was a minister, not of the established Church of Scotland, but of the smaller Secession Church that had split from the national church in 1733 over the question of church patronage. An influential force in the Glasgow region, the Secessionists stressed loyalty to the Calvinist traditions inherited from the political and religious struggles of the seventeenth century. For the Secessionist clergy, however, Calvinism was not the scholastic system of doctrine drawn from seventeenth-century divinity. John Brown of Haddington, the famous Seceder whose works McCulloch would have encountered during his theological course under the Rev. Archibald Bruce at the Seceder seminary at Whitburn, insisted not on the eternal decrees and sovereignty of God, but on God's activity in history. He turned the minds of his students directly to the Bible and to church history, tapping the rich wellsprings of Scottish popular tradition that dwelt on the sufferings of the Protestant religious martyrs.[22] This theological tradition stressed reverent Bible study over speculation, and the life of the ordinary Christian over the culture of an elite of clergymen and philosophers.

McCulloch's teaching, writing, and preaching shared the enthusiasms of both Seceder and evangelical. Like John Brown of Haddington, he was an avid student of church history and engaged with relish in anti-Catholic polemic. His literary ambition to write a three-volume series of Scottish historical tales extending to the Revolution of 1688 was realized in the 1820s with the completion of "Auld Eppie's Tales," a three-volume series of Scottish historical tales extending from Reformation times to the Revolution of 1688. Writing in reaction to Sir Walter Scott's interpretation of the past, McCulloch intended that his novel "deal with popery and the progress of Lollardism in the west of Scotland, not forgetting a due quantity of witches, kelpies and other gods whom our Fathers worshipped." In contrast to Scott's work, "Auld Eppie's Tales" contained little nostalgia for a lost past. McCulloch's Protestantism was evident in his portrait of the corrupt relationship between the pre-Reformation church and the Scottish people. William Blackweed, the Edinburgh publisher, while impressed with McCulloch's literary abilities, rejected the "Tales," claiming that the humour was too broad and would offend the more cultivated audience of Scotland.[23] Taken together with his explicitly theological writings, these works situate him firmly within the process of religious transformation then altering the balance of piety and intellect in the Scottish metropolis. At the time of his emigration to Nova Scotia, this blending of popular Calvinism and evangelicalism had just begun to penetrate the intellectual life of the Scottish universities. By 1850 this upsurge of evangelical energy had radically changed the balance between theology and inquiry.

The problem of salvation was central to the Presbyterian outlook in both Scotland and America. Like that of his contemporaries, the "New School" clergy of the United States, and Thomas Chalmers, leader of the evangelical movement in the Church of Scotland, McCulloch's theology sought a compromise between the old Calvinist system and the evangelical offer of free grace to all who would repent and believe. In a volume of moral tales published in 1826 he downplayed the traditional Calvinist concern with election and predestination. More important than these, he argued, was the biblical drama of salvation, which identified the Cross as the decisive fact in redemption and Christian belief. Humanity, he insisted, needed the saving grace of Christ in order to be saved from sin. With religion centred on Christ's sacrifice, the old Calvinist portrait of God as arbitrary sovereign was softened. God, McCulloch argued, was a just and merciful "moral governor" actively seeking the redemption and regeneration of fallen creation.[24]

McCulloch's balancing of Calvinist and evangelical outlooks was a vital determinant of the Presbyterian intellectual tradition in Canada. It was grounded on the central tenets of the Awakening, the all-encompassing character of Christ's sacrifice, and the reality of the great biblical doctrines of sin, salvation, and judgment. The culture of the revival, however, had an inherent tendency to devalue learning and systematic study, and to rely on emotion as the test of true conversion and piety. This raised the question of religious authority, which was exacerbated by the welter of millenarian and antinomian sects on the fringes of the revival. During McCulloch's early years in Canada, the religious scene in Britain had been disturbed by the adherents of Joanna Southcott, a prophetess who claimed authority through direct revelation from the Holy Spirit. In Nova Scotia itself, the religious enterprise of men like McCulloch was challenged by antinomian "New Light" preachers and congregations sustained by a powerful tradition of popular evangelism begun in the 1780s by Henry Alline. To belong to the evangelical movement without sacrificing a rich heritage of learning and theology posed a problem with serious implications for North American Presbyterians. The Presbyterian intellect in the provinces, as represented by McCulloch, resolved the conundrum by refusing to condone the emotional excesses of the sectarian piety then sweeping the United States and British North America,[25] and by insisting on the necessity of a ministry learned in biblical interpretation and theology.

McCulloch's theology, though popular and accessible in its appeal to Scripture and reference to the Scottish cultural heritage, endeavoured to strike a balance between feeling and intellect in the Christian's search for salvation, thus preserving the authority of the clergy as a professional class called and trained to expound the word of God. "Upon this continent," he warned his first theological class in 1820, "there is a considerable disposition to overlook religious truth, and to reduce religion itself to mere feeling and conduct ... Feeling and action man has in common with the inferior creation; but intelligence is the glory of his nature."[26] Conversion could only begin when the conscience and mind of the believer had achieved a rational understanding of the facts and doctrines contained in the Bible. Religious truth was thus not simply the province of private revelation. McCulloch's belief that the Spirit of God revealed no new doctrines enabled him to declare that faith must be tested through appeal to an unalterable body of certain truth, the Scriptures.

The students at Pictou were reminded not only of the compromise between their Presbyterian heritage and the evangelical Awakening and of the priority of understanding over mere feeling in the apprehension of religious truth, but also of their high calling and responsibility as Christian ministers. For McCulloch, the expansion of the Presbyterian religion and the continuance of its traditions were premised on the presence of a learned ministry, a clergy schooled in a definite set of religious principles derived from the testimony of Scripture. In quest of this ideal, he exhorted his charges to "attend to religion as a scientific pursuit." Until they had mastered its systematic structure, they were qualified "neither to instruct the ignorant nor to edify the intelligent."[27] For an evangelical armed with a passionate belief in the mission to convert and Christianize an entire continent, the scientific study of religion was not an injunction to an isolated life of scholarship or theological research. The minister, McCulloch believed, was above all a preacher, and his task the practical, almost utilitarian one of winning souls. "Religion," he declared, "is a practical system, and as closely connected with the present life, as with a future existence ... ministerial duty requires, not merely a statement of the general principles of religion, but the application of these to a life which prepares for a future existence ... you will perceive that he who is without knowledge of immediate utility, stumbles at the very threshold of religious improvement." Education, both liberal and theological, must ultimately be subordinate to the art of preaching. This, he maintained, was clearly the most useful in awakening the spirit of vital religion in the heart of the sinner.[28]

McCulloch's teachings, though firmly within the theology and culture of the Awakening, strove to preserve elements of the Presbyterian heritage. At a time when the claims of feeling and experience threatened to displace doctrinal traditions and the intellect, Calvinism, the Scottish historical legacy, and the insistence on a college-educated clergy acted as a stabilizer for evangelical piety. McCulloch's faith was both missionary and practical, accentuating the redemptive side of doctrine at the expense of election and predestination. Though insistent on the role of the intellect in the search for faith, he placed little weight on speculative traditions of theology, preferring to rely exclusively on the study and exposition of the Bible as the basis of preaching. He would have dismissed the formulation of a philosophical theology as a distraction from the important task of evangelizing a new continent. Although loyal to an earlier heritage of learning, McCulloch's evangelical creed modified vital elements of the Calvinist heritage. This blending of traditions accomplished at Pictou could be dismissed as of minor moment next to the achievements of the giants of American Calvinist theology. It was to prove, however, the forerunner of the main strand of Presbyterian theology in British North America, powerfully reinforced by the events of the 1840s.

EVANGELICALS AND THE TRANSFORMATION OF SCOTTISH CULTURE

The Calvinist evangelicalism imported from Scotland to Nova Scotia by McCulloch in the early years of the nineteenth century was planted in the provinces at the mid-point of a rancorous debate between the culture of the Awakening and the intellectual traditions of the Scottish Enlightenment. The issue hinged on the respective claims of human reason and revealed faith to dominate the universities and thus the national life of the metropolis. Was biblical revelation, partisans of each camp asked, superior to unaided human reason? How, in an age of scientific discovery, could the authority of the Bible be preserved without sacrificing its claims to contain a higher form of reason? The discussion over religious knowledge was equally serious. Could theology be regarded as the central science, a body of principles and facts that could organize, discipline, and legitimate human intellectual endeavour? Or was theology simply an adjunct of philosophy, founded on nothing more than feelings and beliefs possessing no inherent rationality, and no independent means of validation? Any answer to these questions by clergymen of McCulloch's generation in both Scotland and the colonies was fraught with implications for their efforts to convert human souls and build a Christian society.

The evangelical creed was premised on the essential harmony of revelation and reason. In colonial colleges such as the Pictou Academy, knowledge was respected as the foundation of sound preaching, and of piety in both clergy and congregation. McCulloch and his colleagues consistently admonished their students to tolerate "no system of religious opinions which indulges ignorance or inattention to duty."[29] Beneath the confident assertion of harmony, however, lay more ambiguous attitudes reflecting the continuing evangelical Presbyterian revolt against certain tenets of the Scottish Enlightenment. Such developments provided much of the energy animating the teaching of both theology and liberal arts in the colleges. Despite the reliance on the overt forms of university education in the metropolis, the colonial academies, shaped by evangelical missionaries, were in the process of rejecting or altering much of their intellectual legacy.

At the turn of the nineteenth century the dominant disciplines in the Scottish universities were the classics and, most significantly, philosophy, encompassing logic, rhetoric, moral philosophy, and the physical sciences. The reigning Scottish Common Sense Realism, Canadian historians have argued, formed an important component of the framework of ideas governing Anglo-Canadian thought in the years prior to 1860.[30] According to historian Richard Sher's account of the eighteenth-century Scottish religious environment, Common Sense was a late phase of the Scottish Enlightenment prominent in intellectual circles after the 1780s. In contrast to the older strand of moral philosophy, a form of moral preaching heavily influenced by Christian ethics prevalent in the universities and represented by William Robertson, Adam Ferguson, and Francis

Hutcheson, Common Sense offered an overtly philosophical, rather than a theological, grounding for human knowledge. It provided the key link between intellectual and moral convictions, and thus enabled many eminent thinkers to posit, through rational inquiry, laws of human mind and society. Its leading proponents, Dugald Stewart and Thomas Reid, contributed original and influential works on moral philosophy, epistemology, metaphysics, and political economy. Cosmopolitan, reasonable, and optimistic, Common Sense promoted a spirit of inquiry detached from the doctrinal constraints of the national church. It sought to replace the old Calvinism with a religion resolved into a benevolent moral philosophy of duty and obligation.[31]

Such independent philosophical inquiries failed to take root in the Scottish colleges in Canada. They did *not* arise from the late eighteenth-century spirit of cosmopolitanism and the application of Newtonian science to human society, but from the attempt of Scottish evangelicals to digest and Christianize this legacy. The years between 1820 and 1860 marked a period of acute tension in the metropolis. It concluded only with the victory of theology over philosophy, a triumph that indelibly marked Presbyterian religion in British North America. How to explain the absence of an intellectual tradition that so powerfully defined the cultural life of the United States?

The thought and experience of McCulloch and his missionary contemporaries can only be understood when related to the acute tension in Scotland. By the 1760s the tenets of the Enlightenment had penetrated the Church of Scotland. Ministers who had assimilated its tenets, and particularly its emphasis on polite learning, were usually described by their "popular" or "evangelical" opponents as "moderates," and held to the outward forms of the old Calvinism while preaching a supreme confidence in the powers of reason. These "moderates" controlled the church and the universities for much of the eighteenth century.[32] Between 1770 and 1786, however, their optimistic moral philosophy lost its hold. A large and vocal "evangelical" party accused the "moderates" of being in league with deists and infidels. It was widely believed the the "moderates" had abandoned far too much in accommodating Calvinist theology to the spirit of the Scottish Enlightenment, in some cases even discarding the biblical doctrines of the fall, original sin, grace, salvation, and the atonement.[33]

The majority of the Presbyterian clergy in Canada supported the efforts of the Scottish evangelicals to restore theology in the universities and the supremacy of Christian faith in the nation.

McCulloch, for example, equated "moderatism" with religious rationalism and dismissed it as infidel "sophistry," which he identified as the root of the revolutionary troubles then plaguing Europe.[34] By the 1820s the Scottish "moderates" were in retreat, and evangelicals were beginning to dominate church councils and university faculties. Their intellectual leaders had begun a task of reconstruction. By purging the Common Sense philosophy of its rationalist overtones clergymen could reshape it as a weapon in the arsenal of Christian apologetic. Evangelical professors such as Thomas Chalmers and James McCosh retained the outward forms of the philosophical legacy and the Enlightenment vision of scientific progress. The Common Sense epistemology, based on the primacy of conscience ar d the moral sense in the acquisition of knowledge, accorded perfectly with the Presbyterians' need for religious truth to appeal to the mind. But, these leaders maintained, intellect and inquiry must be informed and disciplined by Christian faith based on the living truths of Scripture. For the evangelical, Christ alone could redeem the human soul and assure the progress of civilization.[35]

This shift in the cultural balance between evangelicalism and Enlightenment was reflected in the concerns of Presbyterian educators in British North America. Unlike the United States, where a form of Common Sense Realism had flourished since the 1760s, the northern provinces received a Scottish philosophy already garbed in the livery of the Awakening. In America, Common Sense acted as a powerful subterranean stream, nourishing Protestant theology and providing an intellectual basis of religious apologetic.[36] In a recent study of early nineteenth-century Anglo-Canadian culture, Brian McKillop claims that the Scottish philosophy had a similar influence in Canada. It provided, he says, a buttress of reason that preserved the connection between God and mind, enabling educated Christians to withstand the assaults of infidelity on essential doctrines.[37] Common Sense epistemology and moral philosophy, by this account, dominated and informed theology, providing it with its basic intellectual categories.

While McKillop presents a lucid and compelling case for the continuity of Common Sense philosophy in all three Atlantic societies, he has reckoned without the historical reality of Scottish evangelicalism. Far from revealing a pattern of cultural continuity with the Enlightenment, the Presbyterian church colleges in Canada were shaped by one of the great discontinuities of Scottish intellectual history. To the Scottish minister Thomas Chalmers and to the Nova Scotian preacher Thomas McCulloch, Common Sense as a system of philosophy was already suspect and believed to be tainted with the cosmopolitan, tolerant creed of the eighteenth-century "moderates." These evangelicals realized that, despite its value as Christian apologetic, the Scottish philosophy could easily draw the human mind away from the Bible and sound theology to deism and infidelity.

The atmosphere of religious crisis during the 1840s reinforced the Presbyterian evangelicals' latent suspicion of philosophy . More importantly, these tensions destroyed the social and cultural foundations that, since the 1730s, had maintained the intellectual and institutional supremacy of certain tenets of the Enlightenment. In 1843 the Great Disruption splintered the national church. Led by Thomas Chalmers, numerous evangelical clergymen withdrew to found the Free Church. Edinburgh, once the citadel of the Enlightenment, was now the scene of an assault on its very principles. Chalmers, the evangelical chieftain and Professor of Divinity at New College, was the central figure in this intellectual reorientation. Beginning his career as minister to a rural parish, by 1820 he had evolved a new urban evangelism from his pulpit at the Tron Kirk, Glasgow. Appointed Professor of Moral Philosophy at St Andrew's University in 1823, he was called to the Chair of Divinity at Edinburgh in 1827, a position he held until his death in 1847. Such posts enabled him to exert profound influence on the religion and culture of Scotland. By the 1840s, he had personally trained a substantial number of the Scottish clergy. Chalmers's professorial career was dominated by his efforts to proclaim a hierarchy of revelation and reason based on the evangelical creed. This endeavour required nothing less than the elimination of Common Sense philosophy as the determining factor in Christian education and the formulation of theology.[38]

The Disruption of 1843, which further divided the partisans of evangelicalism and the Enlightenment, contributed in a very real sense to the demise of the exclusive dominance of Common Sense. Evangelicalism, committed to the centrality of the Bible and the supremacy of its doctrines of sin and atonement over the unaided exercise of reason, could not abide the independence of critical forms of inquiry. Although it might be argued that Chalmers and his supporters continued to use the categories of Common Sense to offer a reasoned defence of Christianity, this defence was characterized by a reluctance uncharacteristic of the old cosmopolitan ideal. Chalmers and John Cairns, a Professor of Divinity who likewise made the journey from philosophy to evangelical religion, both rejected reason as the arbiter of all things. That role was now filled by the higher reality of revelation. For these men the goal of moral philosophy was not epistemology or the elucidation of laws of social development, but a statement of Christian ethics ultimately drawn from Scripture.[39] Because reason was validated in revelation, morality was specifically grounded in the gospels. This intellectual position effectively subverted the Enlightenment and its claims to interpret, through reason, the data of religion. The evangelical counter-attack proclaimed that, unless based on a Christian revelation beyond the province of the human intellect, reason could not be dignified by that name.

The corollary to the evangelical victory in the universities was a scepticism regarding philosophical systems. By the mid-1850s professors loyal to the new emphasis on revelation, such as James McCosh, could insist that Christianity must never be joined inseparably to any particular philosophical system. McCosh's strictures were prompted by the increasing difficulty many Christians experienced in assimilating new developments in philosophy to sound doctrine.[40] They symbolized the deep fissure in the unity of the Common Sense philosophy caused by the Disruption, and revealed the existence of two distinct groups debating the validity of categories established by reason as the basis of inquiry.

One group, the cosmopolitan, was led by Sir William Hamilton, Professor of Logic and Metaphysics in Edinburgh, and his disciple J.F. Ferrier. Faithful to the spirit of the eighteenth-century enterprise, they developed the "philosophy of the unconditioned," an attempt to reconcile the epistemology of Common Sense with the insights of Immanuel Kant's idealism. Ostensibly, this was the old program of discovery, through reason, of the divine order in mind and nature. The logic of their inquiry led, however, to a species of agnosticism[41] unacceptable to the evangelical creed. They argued that the mind could attain no certain knowledge of God – a pessimistic conclusion divorcing reason and Christian faith, and resembling that advanced nearly a century before by David Hume, whose corrosive scepticism had furthered the advance of infidelity. Common Sense, the very philosophy designed to combat Hume, had given rise to an approach that could subvert religious certainty. Educated Christians were scarcely reassured by the publication, in 1858, of the *Limits of Religious Thought*, by Henry Mansel, a disciple of Hamilton. His central contention that God was unknowable to the human mind served only to further convince evangelicals of the suspect nature of the Scottish philosophy.[42]

This version of Common Sense, which assumed the priority of philosophy over theology, was no longer acceptable to the Scottish clergy. The inner dynamic of this system of inquiry led increasingly toward a narrow and esoteric course of speculation divorced from the concerns of Christian ministers and people. The survival of the evangelical creed as a cultural influence was premised on obtaining certain knowledge of God and the divine order. Evangelical professors such as Chalmers, Cairns, and McCosh proposed a remedy for the impotence of philosophy's search for the divine. In his *Institutes of Theology*, published in the late 1840s, Chalmers argued that theology, far from being a poor relation of Common Sense, had an independent ground of validation – the Bible, which he believed to be divinely revealed. By adhering closely to the plain meaning of the biblical text, rather than engaging in rational speculation, theology might furnish certain knowledge of the mind and activity of God.[43] This new hierarchy, in which theology founded on faith was identified as prior to and thus superior to philosophy, signalled the subordination of Common Sense to the evangelical creed. From the late 1840s the Scottish philosophy was accorded the status of method, not intellectual arbiter. Biblical study, not metaphysics, was the road to knowledge for the educated Protestant. Christian ethics derived the basis of conduct and obligation from Scripture, not moral philosophy.

The separation of Common Sense from Christian theology accomplished by Chalmers and his adherents between 1843 and 1855 has been condemned as the "provincialising"[44] of a rich intellectual tradition. To these clergymen, however, the issue was not the survival of a philosophical system, but the far more crucial preservation of the harmony between faith and reason, on which rested the evangelicals' attempt to construct a Christian civilization. The barrier that Chalmers's biblical theology raised between preachers and their congregations and the increasingly esoteric and irrelevant direction of philosophical inquiry significantly furthered this endeavour. By divorcing theology and metaphysical philosophy, and by founding theology on the empirical data of the Bible, these evangelicals could guarantee a continued relationship between faith and reason that would be both reverent and accessible. Philosophy without revelation could lead only to the morass of agnosticism. Only under the guidance of faith could reason perform its allotted task.

MISSIONARY COLLEGES

Far from being a stunted provincialism, the evangelical creed that now radiated from Scotland's capital was a transatlantic movement in scope. Its ability to shape religious and cultural life in the thinking of the Scottish colonies gave it the place occupied by Common Sense in the eighteenth century. Established already in the outpost of the Awakening founded by Thomas McCulloch at Pictou, the evangelical theology was powerfully reinforced in the early 1840s. The arrival of Free Church emissaries in British North America in 1844 opened a more aggressive phase of the Presbyterian endeavours. Two new institutions, Knox College, Toronto, and Free Church College, Halifax, were the fruit of these efforts. The founders of these colleges, the Rev. Robert Burns, Michael Willis, and Andrew King, were all disciples of Thomas Chalmers. Their ideal of learning had been forged against a background of cultural conflict in Scotland and spurred a campaign of energetic proselytizing by the Free Church in the colonies. By 1860, this denomination was the most powerful of all Presbyterian groups in British North America.[45]

The goals of these church colleges reflected not only the priorities of the Disruption, but also McCulloch's earlier experiment. The colleges, these colonial leaders maintained, must actively uphold the central Christian doctrines, and must be dedicated to the training of a professional body of missionary clergy. Such considerations imposed practical priorities for education. For a church devoted to evangelization, a learned ministry was not a cultural adornment – but its function was to preach the gospel in a simple, plain style comprehensible to all believers. "The pulpit," said one observer, was "the great centre of all religious instruction. The preacher brings all his study to bear on his sermon."[46] The college was not a hall of inquiry, but a great missionary institution devoted to the diffusion of Christian truth.

In his inaugural address, the Rev. Dr Michael Willis, who like McCulloch was a graduate of the University of Glasgow, testified to the missionary ideal in explaining the function of the college. "The door is indeed open to various walks of study," he told the students, "yet with us these are means to one recognized end – the accomplishing and qualifying the youth who resort hither for spiritual office, as expositors of the Word of God and missionaries of the Cross of Christ."[47] For this associate of Thomas Chalmers, who had been called to the principalship of Knox College in 1847, theological considerations governed all branches of study. As at the Pictou Academy, however, theology at Knox was a practical discipline that bore little resemblance to the speculative systems of earlier Calvinist writers. Willis, who stressed the close connection between learning and preaching, was not a systematic theologian in the technical sense. Rather, his addresses and exhortations to the students of Knox College, rigorously honed in the preaching culture of Seceder Scotland and in the battles of the Great Disruption of 1843, called for "more frequent exhibition of the Gospel" through preaching, which he defined as "clear expositions of the scriptural grounds on which the preacher rests his statements – all this, of course, with a practical view, and for the strengthening of appeals to conscience and affections."[48] Willis's Maritime colleague, the Rev. Principal Andrew King of Halifax, who emphatically stated that theology was, before all else, biblical, would have agreed. The principles of theological study were set forth in the Westminster Confession of Faith, the doctrinal standard of the Presbyterian Church. This document derived its authority not from reason, but from the Bible, which established the rules and assumptions underlying the exercise of reason.[49]

Only a sound theology could nourish piety and effective preaching and accomplish the work of conversion. The curriculum of the Free Church colleges was intended, above all, to teach students to interpret the Bible and, through a preaching based on the exposition of its central doctrines, to rebuke sin and awaken belief. Thus skill in the ancient languages, Hebrew and Greek, and familiarity with the historical background of Scripture were regarded as its "soul and substance." Although theological in orientation, these institutions did not neglect other branches of learning. Mental and Moral Science and Natural Theology were designed to enable the minister to "meet the various subtle forms of reasoning or sophistry which may be employed on the part of sceptics or infidels."[50] Learning was thus both offensive and defensive in purpose. Intended to propagate the gospel, it was also the minister's armour against infidelity and doubt.

Like their Scottish mentors, Presbyterian evangelicals in the Canadian church colleges were convinced that there must be harmony between revelation and reason. The generation of the 1840s, however, could not accept a facile identification of religion and philosophy. Theirs was an expansive faith, but also an embattled one, fully conscious of the perils of philosophical speculation. They noted the progress of the idealist school in Germany, and its attempt to read the Bible not as the literal truth but in terms of the rational categories proposed by Kant or Hegel.[51] Even the Scottish philosophy was an unreliable guide in religious matters. Did it offer sufficient guarantees for faith amidst a welter of potentially agnostic systems? Like Thomas Chalmers, Canadian Presbyterians were driven to the conclusion that no system of philosophy could provide this certainty. Only a rigorous limitation of the scope and method of philosophy could ensure that speculation did not usurp the central role of the Bible and faith as the dominant cultural influences.

Professors of philosophy in the Presbyterian colleges of British North America had a particular obligation to enforce the separation between theology and philosophy demanded by the Scottish evangelical creed. The exercise of reason was strictly bounded by the biblical doctrine of original sin. As early as 1819, McCulloch was informing his students that divine wisdom had placed humanity in a state of dependence. The very existence of a biblical revelation, he declared, "indicates the imperfection of human capacity for acquiring, by any other means, a correct knowledge of his will." The Rev. Andrew King of Halifax College was even more firm in his admonitions. The use of knowledge independent of Christian truth led to grave perils. Cultivation of the intellect at the expense of moral principle, King argued, was "only arming him with a more powerful instrument which he will employ for the accomplishment of evil. The depravity of his heart inclines him to do what is wrong." Mere reason, these educators insisted, could not serve as the basis of religion and morality. Only the living reality of the Christian faith could guide the search for truth. "Man must be taught," urged King, "to feel himself everywhere under the observation of Him whose eyes are in every place beholding the evil and the good, and who will render to every man according to his deeds."[52]

College clergymen admitted the importance of the study of philosophy, the chief discipline of the Scottish university tradition, if only in an auxilliary role. As one professor at Knox College said, "logic, which teaches the laws that ought to govern the human mind ... was indispensable to the students." The theologian, he stated, "ought to be well acquainted with the philosophy of mind."[53] At Knox College, it was treated as an external buttress of biblical revelation, but by no means as the key to Christian education. Despite attempts by the Rev. Robert Burns, the professor of church history, to place more importance on the teaching of philosophy, the missionary ideal continued to sustain the central position of biblical study. Far from being the master discipline, moral philosophy was encompassed and ruled by theology, its insights founded ultimately on the ethical precepts contained in the Scripture.[54] Professors of philosophy, themselves clergymen, accepted the bounds imposed by the need of the evangelical endeavour to propagate Christian ethics whose criteria lay beyond the scrutiny of the unaided reason rather than to encourage speculative inquiry.

The case of the Rev. William Lyall, professor of classics and mental philosophy at Free Church College, Halifax, between 1850 and 1863, illustrates the power of the limits imposed by the evangelical creed. The author of the essay *Strictures on the Idea of Power* (1842) and a philosophical treatise, *Intellect, the Emotions, and Man's Moral Nature* (1855), Lyall has been characterized as a "philosopher who happened to have been ordained."[55] He did not, however, conceive of his discipline in terms independent of theology. A preacher by training, he had absorbed the ideas and evangelical conviction of Thomas Chalmers during his education at Glasgow and Edinburgh universities. Though anchored within the Common Sense tradition, his outlook reflects the pull of the respective claims of Awakening and Enlightenment on Scottish culture. In a lecture entitled *The Philosophy of Thought*, delivered in 1853 to the students of Free Church College, Halifax, Lyall insisted on the creative power of the mind as the determining factor of human progress and advanced an interpretation of the development of civilization heavily indebted to that of the Scottish conjectural historians of the Enlightenment. The conclusion of his address, however, broke decisively with the Common Sense belief in the retreat of religion before the march of reason. "Revelation," Lyall proclaimed, "supersedes moral investigation" and "supplies the only key by which the mysteries of the moral world can be solved." "The spiritual" was "the highest part of man's nature, for which even the mental is subordinate."[56]

All reasoning, he declared in an 1858 address to the theological class, was founded on "Conviction and Expectation of order in the mind." Reason alone could not validate these convictions or essential principles of inquiry; this was the province of faith alone. These strictures on the province of reason served to confirm, not Lyall's wholesale importation of the Common Sense tradition, but his dissent from the program of the Enlightenment, which accepted as an article of faith the supremacy of the human intellect in discerning the laws of the physical world and humanity's moral nature. Thus Lyall introduced to his students the Scottish evangelical temper of the 1850s, which was intent on distancing itself from the increasingly irrelevant debates over the nature of metaphysics led by Sir William Hamilton and his circle. "Carlyle," Lyall stated in his philosophical treatise, "has regarded metaphysics as a science of doubt rather than a science of positive knowledge; and in one sense it is so. Doubt, not unbelief – ignorance, not scepticism. A science of doubt – a science of ignorance – might well seem a contradiction. But the doubt is the doubt forced upon us by the necessary limitation of our faculties – the ignorance is the ignorance necessitated by the limits set to our knowledge by the Creator."[57] Lyall traced the limits of human reason directly to the existence of sin and evil in the world, a mystery the human intellect could not explain. "In the Scripture account," he concluded, "we have the only – we have the authoritative – statement of man's apostasy." Philosophy may speculate – the Bible reveals.[58] The truly critical intellect existed only in harmony with the Christian religion.[59] Reason must draw upon biblical revelation for guidance and validation of its insights. Divine revelation, he stated in 1853, was "necessary to purge the intellectual vision,"[60] to remove from philosophy the effects of sin, and to provide a basis of belief as the precondition of inquiry in both natural science and the study of the human mind and society.

Lyall's views on the relation of philosophy to revelation are significant. He was the only professor in the Presbyterian colleges who can possibly be considered as an original contributor to philosophical discussion in English Canada. Was there a seminal intellectual tradition of moral philosophy emanating from Scotland and upheld by Lyall and others? Such a theory is invalidated by the markedly different emphasis in the stated goals of the missionary colleges. Common Sense epistemology and moral philosophy were certainly present, but as a strand of ideas overshadowed by the priorities of the evangelical creed in both metropolis and colony. Philosophy, even for Lyall, was a poor relation to theology, incapable of discerning the proper goals and direction of its inquiry through the independent exercise of reason.

The Rev. James George, professor of moral philosophy and logic at Queen's College, Kingston, was more typical of an evangelical professor of philosophy. A recent student of George's thought, attempting to place him within the vaunted Queen's University tradition of moral inquiry, has expressed some surprise that his works, a collection of sermons and addresses, make no reference to the great philosophers of the Common Sense tradition – Reid, Stewart, and Hamilton.[61] But George's lack of attention to Common Sense becomes more comprehensible when related to his intellectual background and the demands of Queen's College in the 1850s.

From his emigration to Canada in 1829 to his call to the chair of philosophy in 1853, George was a preacher. Like Lyall, he was a disciple of Thomas Chalmers, having attended St Andrew's University in the 1820s, when the great Scottish evangelical held the chair of moral philosophy. In contrast to his Halifax colleague, however, he did not join the Free Church during the Disruption of the early 1840s, preferring to remain within the Church of Scotland. It might be assumed that George was thus shielded from the tide of evangelicalism and, at least in theory, Queen's College did offer its students an ideal of education less overtly subservient to theological concerns.[62] Closer study reveals, however, that the cultural imperatives of the evangelical creed were as pervasive among the clergy of the Church of Scotland as among the more aggressively missionary Free Churchmen in Toronto and Halifax. In a sermon preached in 1837 George elaborated a high view of the substitutionary nature of the atonement.[63] In an 1854 address he sharply rejected the elevation of worldly knowledge as an end in itself, for human destiny lay beyond the visible world. This intrusion of theological categories in university study was reflected in the Queen's curriculum, where more than half the course of study in arts revolved around the Bible and theology.[64] Christian piety and the study of doctrine unmistakably set the tone of intellectual life.

Like his mentor Chalmers, George was concerned with the preaching of practical Christian ethics not with the cosmopolitan strand of moral philosophy that devoted itself primarily to epistemology. Conscience led the human mind, not to the categories of philosophy, but to the gospels.[65] For George, too, faith was superior to reason and biblical theology to philosophy. His 1859 address *What Is Civilization?* provided one of the most forceful statements by an evangelical clergyman-professor of the proper hierarchy of Christian revelation and philosophy. "Philosophy," he proclaimed:

may sit as a queen on her throne if she only teaches Science and Art, but if she attempts to be an instructress in ethics and to lay down principles for social life and civil government, she will utter nothing better than pretty rhetoric or feeble logical theories, to which men may listen, or on which they may curiously speculate; but from which they never can draw principles that shall bind their conscience or regulate their moral conduct. Philosophy has no Sinai, no Calvary, no Omnipotent Judge, and alas! in no sense any Saviour for men. If she works behind the Cross, and with her eye reverently fixed on the Bible, as well as on nature, she will do great things for the world. But, if she despises the Cross and casts away the Bible, she will only prate like a learned fool, or set the world on fire by her atheistical dogmas.[66]

Here, expressed in their starkest form, were the strictures imposed on the use of reason by the evangelical creed. Philosophy was subordinate to the central doctrines of the Bible, which were both the foundations of civilized life and the vital guarantees of the rationality of inquiry. Not only was reason deficient, but it might even challenge the principal tenets of Christianity. So feared the Scottish evangelicals in the 1850s, as they observed a growing disjuncture between piety and Common Sense philosophy. In this period of acute tension between philosophy and theology, Lyall and George enjoined the supremacy of revelation and thus subtly directed their students to a distrust of all philosophical systems.

The scepticism of these clergymen-philosophers sought to guard against the encroachments of agnostic modes of inquiry on the ter-

ritory of Christian faith, and foreshadowed a situation equally unpalatable to Presbyterian evangelicals. The struggle between
Awakening and Enlightenment that had fragmented the Scottish
intellectual inheritance held the potential for a divorce between revelation and all forms of human reason. To admit this dichotomy
meant conceding the defeat of the evangelical mission to Christianize
society and culture. It would reduce religion to irrational, irrelevant
outbursts of sectarian piety. How then, to preserve the harmony of
Scripture, science, and philosophy, while ensuring that reason
would not trespass on the domain of revelation? If, as evangelicals
maintained, theology was superior to philosophy as a form of knowledge, how could its insights be made accessible to the human mind?
And how, in an age of scientific discovery, could evangelicals demand that a faith based on the Bible constitute the basic assumption
of all inquiry, and the foundation of morality and civilization?

REVERENT REASON: THE BACONIAN IDEAL

In 1855 an anonymous Nova Scotia Presbyterian drew the attention
of his readers to the study of "Mental Science." This important discipline, he wrote, determined the "proper province of inquiry." Curiously, he made no attempt to equate mental science with the
epistemology or psychology of the Common Sense tradition, and
did not mention Scotland's great luminaries, Reid, Stewart, and
Hamilton. Rather, he invoked the name of Francis Bacon, the Eliz-
abethan philosopher and scientist. "It was with a fine knowledge of
our mental nature," he declared, "that Bacon laid down the laws of
Induction." To comprehend the order of the universe, philosophy
and science must found their principles upon this method, which
entailed the careful observation of phenomena. Although "generalization" was the goal, the "grand process" of the mind, it was only
valid and rational if based on careful induction.[67] This appeal to the
legacy of Francis Bacon, rather than to the luminaries of Scottish
Common Sense, reveals the atmosphere prevailing in the Presbyterian colleges of British North America. References to Bacon and
to the inductive method indicated that colonial clergymen, like the
influential communities of scientists and clergy on both sides of the
Atlantic, looked to scientific discovery as the proof and confirmation
of revelation.[68] Even more significant was the grafting of Baconianism onto the evangelical creed in the years after 1820, illustrating
how ambivalently English Canadians tried to assimilate yet distance
themselves from the traditions of Scottish Common Sense.

During the first five decades of the nineteenth century, the name of Francis Bacon underwrote a variety of religious, cultural, and scientific strategies in both Britain and America. The popularity of Baconianism was closely associated with the distinctive features of Scottish moral and natural philosophy. It was invoked by men such as Thomas Reid and Dugald Stewart because it appeared to successfully apply the methods of the physical sciences to investigation in the moral sciences. Leading English men of science such as William Whewell and Baden Powell sought to construct a philosophy of scientific discovery on the basis of Baconian induction.[69] These philosophic and scientific meanings of Baconianism, however, found few echoes within the Canadian Presbyterian colleges. Because clergymen-professors displayed a marked scepticism towards the epistemology of the Scottish philosophy and its claims to posit a system of reason and morality independent of revelation, Baconianism or "the inductive method" carried a meaning very different from the intentions of its Common Sense progenitors.

From the evangelical standpoint, the link with Baconian induction was not merely another intellectual tie binding parent society and colony. It offered other distinct advantages, particularly when understood against a background of cultural tension and change in the interconnected realms of theology, philosophy, and science. The easy identification of Protestantism and Common Sense characteristic of the thinking of many educated Christians had been shattered by the evangelical Awakening and by the attempt of philosophy to recast theology without reference to faith and scripture. Even science, the supposed partner of revelation, was often untrustworthy. By the 1830s geologists such as Charles Lyell had advanced theories at variance with the account of creation set forth in Genesis, while scientific popularizers such as Robert Chambers challenged prevailing clerical and scientific structures of intellectual authority. With the publication of *Vestiges of the Natural History of Creation* in 1844, Chambers boldly proclaimed a theory of evolution that raised the spectre of a world in which the harmony between religion and scientific inquiry had been shattered.[70] Evangelicals, particularly college clergymen, were faced with a dilemma. In affirming the rationality of their religion and its doctrines, they ran the risk of implicitly subjecting it to the scrutiny of an inquiry based on principles not derived from Scripture. Science, in the course of proving the truth of revelation, might also encourage a doubting or irreverent disposition. Here, they drew on the broader and more popular implications of the Baconian ideal. Because it emphasized careful methods of inquiry and a rigid attention to the collection of data, rather than to the formulation of hypotheses, both evangelicals and their utilitarian opponents lauded Baconianism as inculcating sound attitudes to knowledge and encouraging wide participation in science. In evangelical circles, Baconianism became a rhetorical structure promoting caution and reverence rather than a philosophical theory or a guide to scientific practice.[71] But even here it was used more as a buttress upholding the social and cultural supremacy of theology than as a tool to promote the harmony of science and religion.

Evangelical educators in all Atlantic societies pointed specifically to the human intellect as the disturbing factor in the delicate balance of science and faith. In a lecture to the students of Pictou Academy, Principal McCulloch reminded them that "preconceived opinions, and vicious modes of reasoning, and especially inaccurate methods of enquiry" had contributed to retarding the progress of knowledge. "Men evidently came to the Book of Nature, just as they came to the Book of Revelation," he cautioned them, "not to learn but merely to seek confirmation of their own preconceived opinions."[72] McCulloch's assumptions were twofold. First, his juxtaposing of nature and revelation maintained, implicitly, that a similar mode of inquiry could discover laws or principles underlying each. This looked to the preservation of a relationship in which revelation would guide scientific activity. Second, he drew a sharp distinction between "sound" and "unsound" modes of inquiry. Such views arose from a set of assumptions that evangelicals believed to be the foundation of civilization itself.

Speaking in 1854, George admonished his students at Queen's to remember that "civilization has ever sprung from morality, and ... a people becomes great and civilized just in proportion as they are intellectually moral and morally intellectual." These principles, however, were sanctioned not by reason or the Scottish epistemology, but by the revealed doctrines of Christianity. They were thus immutable and eternal.[73] This vision of civilization depended on the maintenance of the relationship between scientific progress and revelation. "Sound" reason would reverently work to promote and extend the alliance, while "unsound" reason would impiously disturb Christian faith through speculations that challenged the Bible. Sin would thus weaken the moral bonds of human society, and cause the decline of civilization.

A particular strategy of education and inquiry was required to avoid this perilous abyss. Presbyterian clergymen such as McCulloch devoted a great deal of energy to the proper definition of "sound" inquiry. In his 1817 lecture on the subject of liberal education, McCulloch looked to "the improvement of man in intelligence and moral principle." The acquisition of knowledge was, however, a rigorous process that resisted the impulse to dabble or speculate. It must begin with minute study of individual objects and circumstances and proceed, through comparison, to knowledge of abstract truths or principles. These principles, the fruit of inductive reasoning, acted as "the primary objects of science, which, in its various parts, constitutes the materials of a learned education."[74]

McCulloch's advocacy of the inductive method as the ideal of learning places him within a powerful early nineteenth-century intellectual movement. His enthusiasm was derived from his student days at the University of Glasgow, where his philosophical mentor, George Jardine, professor of logic and rhetoric, introduced the "inductive method" as the foundation of the mental sciences. With the application of induction, he declared, "Philosophy was now brought down to the level of the most Ordinary Abilities, and was Prosecuted according to the Natural Conceptions of Mankind."[75] In contrast to Jardine, who held a secular view of human progress, his pupil found induction perfectly compatible with the imperatives of his evangelical creed. Baconianism legitimated the scientific enterprise by insisting that its foundation be defined by the needs of Christian doctrine. McCulloch's own interests in science, medicine, religion, and education at Pictou reflected a firm belief in the ultimate harmony of these endeavours.[76] In no sense, however, can Baconianism be described as a philosophical system. Emerging with the beginnings of the evangelical rejection of the primacy of reason, so vaunted by the cosmopolitan culture of the Scottish Enlightenment, it encompassed attitudes particularly suited to the evangelical creed. First, the Baconian ideal was based on the inductive methodology of current science, which derived its general laws of nature from a meticulous survey of particulars. Second, exponents of the inductive method propagated an emphatically empiricist approach to all forms of knowledge and greatly preferred objective fact to theories or hypotheses. Finally, clergymen and scientists who subscribed to these beliefs indicated a distrust of hypotheses and even of reason itself.[77] Evangelicals in British North America would turn to this call for sound inquiry to confirm the supremacy of theology and the Bible in formulating the agenda and direction of scientifc and philosophical inquiry.

In the context of the Presbyterian revolt against the Common Sense Enlightenment, Baconianism assumed particular importance. In contrast to Britain and the United States, where both "epistemological" and "moral" versions of the Common Sense tradition acted on the evangelical tradition, "methodological Common Sense" operated as the sole strand of the Scottish philosophical tradition in English Canada.[78] Though grounded on certain assumptions of eighteenth-century Scottish epistemology, the Baconian ideal allowed clergymen to establish the limits of reason, particularly in the disputed borderland between religion and science. This cultural use of Baconianism differed from that of the scientists and philosophers, who sought in the inductive method the unity of the moral and the scientific. Such a goal could only be secondary to clergymen concerned with discerning a biblical and theological foundation to human conduct and social organization. For them Baconian induction provided the intellectual matrix of Christian revelation and theology, and, far from establishing science as the idiom of culture, offered the much-sought guarantee against "unsound" or impious research.

More significantly, as interpreted by Chalmers, the intellectual mentor of the Free Church missionaries, Baconianism provided theology with a method that rendered it apparently independent from and invulnerable to philosophy. Near the end of Chalmer's long career as professor of divinity at Edinburgh, his Baconian theology took on a more precise form. There were, he argued, mysteries that the progress of the intellect would never penetrate. Science, though it would improve human knowledge, could never reveal the whole of the divine plan.[79] For Chalmers, the inductive method established limits to theological inquiry. Research, he declared, should be founded not on the speculative formulations of philosophy, but on the careful study of Scripture. Only thus could the "facts" contained in the Bible be made clear. He limited the role of philosophy and reason to the collection and classification of scriptural facts, to explication, but not modification, of the content of revelation.[80]

The emerging alliance of Baconianism and the biblical emphasis of evangelical theology permitted Chalmers and his disciples to escape the influence of the Enlightenment, with its demands that all experience be interpreted according to categories established by human reason. Here at the cutting edge of science was a rational method that ostensibly acknowledged the supremacy of divine mystery. By enjoining care and caution in research, Baconianism urged due reverence for the biblical text. The inductive method decreed that the "facts" of the Bible, because they were divinely revealed, were superior to those of nature, philosophy, or science, which were discovered by human reason, not disclosed by God. The Bible and its doctrines were thus immune from alteration or criticism, and provided the immutable principles that validated all other forms of inquiry, and sustained progress and civilization.

The Baconian vision of theology as the master discipline was quickly enshrined in the missionary colleges of British North America. Speaking in 1847 to the students of Knox College, the Rev. Mr Robb advised a careful perusal of the writings of Chalmers. He likened the task of the systematic theologian to that of the natural philosopher – the same inductive method must be used to draw legitimate inferences from the facts of the Bible and exalt it as a "perfect and harmonious system of truth."[81] Despite its accessibility to the human mind, Scripture, for the clergyman-professor, was a repository of divine truth, mysterious and eternal. As one Nova Scotia Presbyterian declared, "New discoveries in matters of revealed truth I look not for ... Theological truth is not come at as other truth is." The "facts" of Scripture were not "the result of any long and laborious induction. It is not built up by any experiment. It is a science of pure revelation; and therefore must have existed in its perfection, from the date of the revelation. It cannot be affected, as the other sciences, by the march of mind, for it is the *human* mind that marches, not the *divine*. Now, theological truth is the expression of this mind, to which there can be no accession of new ideas."[82] This unchanging quality, possessed only by the revealed data of faith, offered the Christian mind a point of certainty in an age of troubling transformations in science and philosophy. To the adherents of the Baconian ideal, it served to establish religion as the sole guarantor of true reason.

The Baconian ideal drew upon and and reinforced another emphasis of the evangelical creed. Induction, with its demands for caution and reverence, accorded with the view of unaided human reason as limited and sinful. Presbyterian professors thus accepted that in relation to revelation, the exercise of reason must be constrained and subordinated. The inductive method became synonymous with the discipline of philosophy in the Free Church colleges, a development that explains, in part, the lack of reference to the great Scottish philosophers. Ruled by Baconian principles, philosophy, while preserving the outward form of Common Sense, became a pale shadow of its eighteenth-century progenitor. According to Principal Willis of Knox College, the science of philosophy must be joined with serious piety. He reminded the students that it "compares, generalises, divides, defines, so as to discriminate truth from fallacy; and especially in the spirit of the inductive philosophy collects data largely and patiently on which to found conclusions, and to establish principles – the data in this case being the various portions of one divine record."[83] Reason could neither alter nor transcend the data. Here was a central irony of the evangelical creed – a method of rational, inductive study was used to limit the exercise of reason. The Baconian ideal tamed reason, diverting it from the unprofitable and potentially agnostic course of speculative philosophy to the way of true piety – scientific discovery joined to biblical faith.

"The Christian philosopher," declared one Presbyterian minister in 1851, "has nothing to fear from the profoundest researches of science, properly so called. He believes that all Scripture is given by inspiration of God."[84] Thus the alliance of the inductive method and evangelical piety rendered the harmony of faith and science possible by enforcing the supremacy of theology. In so doing, Baconianism also supplied Protestant Christians with a ready-made method of theological and biblical research. Chalmers and his British North American disciples endeavoured, by applying the rules of induction, to make theology a science as precise as geology. As Principal Willis told the Knox College theological class at the opening of the 1857 session, "Theology was an inductive science like all other sciences." Willis's guiding assumption was that the "facts" of the Bible were readily observable, empirical realities. Just as the human mind could gather, arrange, and systematize the scattered facts of physical science, so should reason be applied to the study of theology, Willis urged. This "science," according to Presbyterian evangelicals, was a discipline likewise based on induction from the given "facts" of Scripture, and their classification and arrangement into more general categories, the principles or "doctrines" of the Christian faith.[85]

By harnessing the prestige of the scientific method, clergymen-professors hoped to establish the supremacy of theology in an early Victorian culture awed by rapid scientific progress. From the pioneer efforts of McCulloch, this need entrenched Baconian induction in the colleges as the buttress of the evanglical creed. An educational system that championed the primacy of biblical theology and preaching, yet was fascinated by scientific experiment, would naturally prefer the Baconian attitude to the potentially agnostic procedures of Scottish Common Sense. Practical, empirical, and anti-speculative, promoting a cautious and reverent use of reason in those areas of inquiry where the Bible or Christian doctrine were involved, Baconianism was the perfect justification. Christian reason could collect, classify, and draw inferences from facts both natural and revealed, but for the evangelical clergyman the theological priorities must be preserved. The understanding of God's will and purpose as revealed in the Bible was the goal of all knowledge and science. This biblical point of departure for all forms of inquiry confirmed the relationship between revelation and the human mind in which God was the "author and source," and man the "subject and percipient."[86]

The synthesis of Baconian inquiry and the evangelical creed emerging between 1820 and 1860 linked Canadian Presbyterians with a wider Atlantic culture. It also served as a bond within the developing Anglo-Canadian community, establishing an important point of intellectual contact with Methodism, whose theology and institutional structure differed in many respects. Founded in Canada in the 1770s, by 1830 the Methodist Church, through aggressive missionary efforts and evangelism, had become the largest of the Protestant churches in central Canada. Throughout this period the genius of Methodism lay in its preaching of vital religion to the scattered communities of British North America. This practical emphasis fostered a balance of faith and reason ostensibly different from that prevailing among Presbyterians, but equally congenial to the union of evangelical theology and the inductive method.

As with its Presbyterian rival, the intellectual traditions of Methodism emerged from a period of tension between Christian theology and the Enlightenment. Locating the Methodist church within such a pattern of cultural exchange, however, presents a problem. Its intellectual heritage is less institutionalized and more eclectic, and offers no moment comparable to the establishment of the Pictou Academy by the Presbyterian McCulloch. Since the mid-nineteenth century many historians have accepted that Methodism, unlike Presbyterianism, had no traceable intellectual lineage. Its founder, John Wesley, has been generally portrayed as a man almost exclusively concerned with Christian living and experience, and not interested in the formulation of a creed or theology that would appeal to the understanding. Methodism has often been dismissed as an antiintellectual, regressive, repressive religion with but a confused and inadequate theology.[87] Studies of Canadian Methodism in relation to its cultural setting have tended to perpetuate this harsh estimate. Methodism in British North America seems undefined, preoccupied either with enthusiastic camp meetings and revivals or with inflaming the politics of church and state.[88]

While there were many theological issues that divided Methodists and Presbyterians, the period between 1820 and 1860 witnessed the development of certain underlying points of similarity. Both churches were preoccupied with the evangelization of a new society undergoing rapid social change, and both saw the need for an immutable, certain body of truth that was accessible to the human mind and could act as the solid foundation of Christian civilization. More importantly, such a harmony between religion and reason must be accessible not only to an educated clergy, but also to the congregation. The Methodist leaders Egerton Ryerson and Samuel Nelles agreed with their counterparts in the Presbyterian colleges on the primacy of theology in education and culture, and on the premise that Christian belief functioned in a world defined by the advance of scientific knowledge.

Much of the historical confusion stems from the meaning of the term "experimental religion." Between 1820 and 1860 Methodists valued this concept above theological systems and church organization. It lay at the root of a democratic tradition of theology stemming from the writings of John Wesley. Together with the Bible, Wesley's sermons formed the basic intellectual equipment of the Methodist preacher. For Wesley, the value of theology was directly related to its degree of service to the Christian life. His work offered no precise system of theology, but posited guidelines on the nature of religious authority. The founder of Methodism championed the Bible as infallibly true, given by inspiration of God, and free from any real error. But he modified this position by allotting equal scope to experience, reason, and tradition. His concept of theological knowledge took the form of a quadrilateral.[89] This popular theology could be dismissed as simply an obscurantist revolt against the rationalist systems of religious thought devised by many Protestant churches during the Enlightenment. But, on the contrary, it did not represent a radical separation from the culture of the Enlightenment and the early nineteenth century. Like the Presbyterians, Wesley and his Canadian disciples proposed an intellectual alternative, at once Christian and evangelical, that they believed to be compatible with the scientific and social progress of the transatlantic Protestant world. Although involved in a debate with the Enlightenment, they incorporated some of its legacy into their theology. In anchoring religion on the data of feeling and experience, Wesley drew extensively on the empirical philosophies of John Locke and David Hume, who also distrusted the speculative reason and exalted experience. He diverged from them, however, in not drawing rationalist implications from the empirical view of reality. Wesley preserved his faith in a divine revelation that acted upon the conscience or spiritual sense, conferring assurance of divine grace.[90]

The belief that religious truth was tangible and accessible to the soul of the believer was the cornerstone of Methodist theology. As the Rev. Matthew Richey, principal of the Methodist Upper Canada Academy at Cobourg maintained, the proof of the gospel rested not only on logical systematic demonstration, but in the heart imbued with its spiritual influence. "'The truth as it is in Jesus,'" stated another prominent Methodist, "cannot be adequately understood without being felt."[91] Feeling, for Methodists in colleges and at revival meetings between 1820 and 1860, was paramount in the apprehension of religious truth. The gospel, often described as a "remedial scheme," contained the great drama of sin and salvation. The Bible thus appealed to the heart, mind, and soul of the believer, not simply to the intellect. Though there was widespread agreement that Christianity and reason could not be divorced, Methodists refused to countenance the reduction of evangelical religion to a simple comprehension of abstract doctrines or precepts. "A knowledge of Christianity, in the true sense," concluded one clergyman in 1854, "consists in something beyond a theoretical acquaintance with its principles and precepts. The way of salvation is comprehended only when an experimental knowledge of its doctrines is realized in the soul of the believer."[92] Although this approach to religious knowledge owed much to the empirical traditions of the Enlightenment, it diverged from its intellectual inheritance in its powerful critique of knowledge that relied exclusively on the rational intellect. Experimental religion, for the Methodist, meant not merely an antispeculative, intellectual empiricism, but a willingness to consider, weigh, and evaluate the validity of various sources of religious data in the light of faith anchored on Scripture and the practical test of a Christian life.

Because its theology lacked system, Methodism could be dismissed as an approach based on a simple reliance on the Bible and the experience of feeling, of little consequence for the traditions of learning and culture being forged in English Canada. Because they considered the Gospel as a remedy for sin, not as a set of intellectual principles, the early Methodists set little store by a college-educated ministry. They valued evangelical power in preaching, the winning of souls, and the "science of salvation" over intellectual refinement and the liberal arts. Where Presbyterians insisted, even in the colonies, on four years of preparatory training in arts prior to admission to a three-year theological program, the Methodist clergy until the 1870s was itinerant, a travelling ministry that could cope with the primitive transportation and communication systems, and the shortage of clergymen that plagued the religious life of early Canada. Methodism lacked the metropolitan university traditions that Presbyterians adapted to the Canadian setting. At that time all it required of its ministers was a basic level of literacy, supplemented by sound knowledge of the Bible and Wesley's works, experience in preaching, and a conversion experience.[93]

Between 1830 and 1860 Methodism was drawn into a wider world than that defined by camp meetings and revivals. Although nothing comparable to the Great Disruption troubled its intellectual life, Methodism, like other Protestant churches, had to accommodate biblical authority and scientific discovery in a matrix preserving the primacy of revelation and the supremacy of theology. By the 1850s the growth of an educated, urban society in central Canada imposed new demands on the Methodist clergy. While preaching power remained the crucial element of the itinerant's training, more rigorous courses of theological study were provided, stressing better preparation in systematic theology and church history. This emerging balance of Christian piety and learning drew its sustenance from the theological traditions of Methodism, and was not simply a reaction to changes in the social and cultural environment. Christian experience and the practical requirements of a Christian life shaped the Methodist ideal of learning in the colleges.

"Education," proclaimed the Rev. Samuel Nelles in 1857, "is the broad & symmetrical culture of the whole mind, and this embraces the conscience, the affections, the imagination, & the will, as well as the mere intellect. Active principles are to be inculcated ... the student is to be *prepared* for life."[94] Nelles, who became professor of moral philosophy at Victoria in 1850 and president of that institution in 1854, was a principal architect of the Methodist balance of faith and learning. It might be assumed, at first glance, that Nelles's ideal of education contained little of substance. Though it drew upon the thought of Francis Wayland, the famous American Baptist clergyman and moral philosopher,[95] this definition of the goals of college learning encompassed more than a simple extension and replication of an American ethic on Canadian soil. While Canadian Methodists such as Nelles drew from a less formalized theological heritage than did their Presbyterian counterparts, they too were faced with the difficult problem of harmonizing the demands of the evangelical creed for a culture based on the theological certainties of Scripture with the demands of society for an education combining the biblical and doctrinal traditions of Christianity with a vision of scientific and social progress.

Nelles proposed the term "character" to describe the goals of college education. Learning, he declared, involved not the mere cultivation of intellect, but the formation of "character," encompassing man's inward state, and his intellectual and moral development.[96]

In its lack of reference to the Bible and Christian doctrine, this statement might seem to advocate a pursuit of truth derived purely from criteria supplied by moral philosophy. Closer examination reveals, however, that Nelles's ideal of character was deeply informed by theological considerations. As a Methodist minister Nelles believed, like his Presbyterian counterparts William Lyall and James George, that Christian ethics, not philosophy, must supply the substance and method of the study of morals. His very description of what constituted "character" was derived less from the textbooks of the Common Sense moral philosophy than from Methodist views of the nature of "experimental religion," a harmonious blending of conscience, feeling, and intellect subordinate to and validated by divine revelation.

The theology underlying the concept of education at Victoria College was not introduced by Nelles, but rather inherited. It rested on a complex fusion of earlier Methodist traditions with the equally powerful current of Baconianism increasingly espoused by articulate clergymen in the years after 1830. Victoria College had been created through the efforts of Egerton Ryerson, perhaps the leading intellectual figure in Wesleyan Methodism in the decades between 1825 and 1860. Born in 1803 into a Loyalist family claiming Puritan ancestry, Ryerson derived much of his early education from the polite literature of Lord Kames and Hugh Blair, leading representatives of the Edinburgh Enlightenment. At the age of twelve he underwent a conversion experience, and soon forsook his family's Church of England leanings to join the Methodists.[97] Ryerson became, successively, a circuit-rider, founder and editor of the *Christian Guardian* in 1829, pastor of Newgate church, Toronto, principal of Victoria College in 1842, and superintendent of education for the Province of Canada, and his contributions to religion, society, and culture in English Canada were of immense and lasting significance.[98]

He secured the charter of Victoria College against a turbulent background of political radicalism and sectarian enthusiasm. Upper Canada in the 1840s was recovering from the aftermath of an abortive rebellion against British rule, and was establishing an infrastructure of educational and municipal institutions and services that was to give its political, social, and intellectual life a distinct and lasting shape.[99] Through the establishment of their own university, Methodist leaders hoped to share in this process of consolidation. For these men raised in the culture of intense religious revivalism, the creation of a college bore testimony to their efforts to temper a religion that often exalted the emotional moment of conversion, and to link the vital, but at times transitory, Christian experience of the revival to the more enduring structure of sound learning and moral conduct. It was an affirmation of the Methodist achievement of social and political respectability.[100] They were, however, confronted by circumstances that threatened to subvert their vision of a colonial culture premised on religious certainty.

The founding of Victoria College coincided with the rise of the Millerites, a radical millenarian sect powerful in upstate New York whose ideas found much sympathy in Upper Canada. Led by William Miller, adherents of this sect claimed that through study of the biblical prophecies contained in the Book of Revelation they could definitely fix the end of the world for the summer of 1844.[101] Loyal to their democratic traditions of theology, Methodists found it difficult to resist the millenarian challenge. Miller's biblical speculations called into question the need for an educated clergy and, indeed, for an institutional church, given the proximity of the Last Judgment. Worse, the Methodist theology, praising preaching power over learning and exalting "experience" and "feeling" over the intellectual apprehension of religious truth, might be claimed to be tainted with this popular religious radicalism. Opponents of Methodism might suggest that one of the central elements of its theology actually encouraged ordinary members of Methodist congregations to flirt with a sect subject to none of the moral and doctrinal constraints of the Christian tradition.

The problem was a serious one for Ryerson and other leading Methodists – as complicated as the attempt by Presbyterian evangelicals to separate their theology from the philosophy of Common Sense. Ryerson could not separate himself from Methodist origins and replace the old system of training preachers through conversion experience and biblical study with a system providing a college-educated elite buttressed by a formalized and abstract theology. But Millerism must be refuted if Methodism was to retain its position at the head of the evangelical endeavour. Ryerson's design for Victoria College envisioned a less tight but no less secure bond between evangelical theology and liberal education. While the college did not aim to train a class of clergy, as did the Scottish model, all branches of learning were pervaded by the insistence on biblical study and the practical application of Christian ethics to daily life. Ryerson's ideal stressed a broad exposure to English culture aimed at developing the powers of the mind. He divided the college course into five parts: ancient languages and antiquities; mathematics; moral science, with philosophy and logic directed to elucidating the evidences of Christianity; rhetoric and belles-lettres; and theology, which embraced the Hebrew and Greek languages, biblical criticism, sacred history, and doctrine.[102] This ideal of learning testified to the practical nature of evangelical theology in its application to Christian living. Like the Methodist preacher addressing the congregation, the college professor must appeal to human faculties, feelings, intellect, and will. Christian learning must lead the student to the perfection of character.

Ryerson's Victoria College was as insistent on theological priorities as were the Presbyterian colleges. Theological study, the Bible, the evidences, doctrine, and biblical languages formed the heart of its curriculum. At Victoria as in other evangelical colleges, moral philosophy, far from being fundamental to a liberal education, became a branch of Christian ethics designed "to explain our obligations and duties to ourselves, to our fellow-men, and to our Maker – to elucidate and apply the cardinal principles of the Scriptures to the various relations and circumstances of human life."[103] Ryerson's description of ethics as "moral science" rather than "moral philosophy" is significant. His teaching was closely patterned on that of Francis Wayland, the president of Brown University, whose influential work, *Elements of Moral Science*, published in 1835, formed the basis of philosophy teaching at Victoria College. For Wayland, "moral science," although based on certain canons of Common Sense epistemology, was less an independent inquiry than a loose, highly theological discipline, in which professor and student ranged widely over logic, literary criticism, political economy, and psychology.[104] Both Ryerson and Wayland saw philosophy as an adjunct providing an external buttress to the Bible and Christian faith, not as a scientific grounding for morality.

Fear of unbridled philosophical reasoning pervaded the teaching at Victoria College. Although Ryerson and the Methodist clergy were spared the fragmentation of Scottish culture and the separation of clergyman and philosopher, they too were exposed to the growing international tension that foreshadowed the shattering of the harmony between Protestant doctrine and scientific reason. Ryerson envisioned a clear separation between the respective claims of religion and philosophy, and left no doubt in the minds of his students as to which was to predominate. He forcefully refused to "make the House of God a philosophical Lecture-Room, or the Christian Minister a literary teacher or metaphysical disputant, or divert his chief meditations from the great truths of the Sacred Scriptures."[105] He drew no distinction between church and college, regarding both as the "House of God." His views on the subject of the biblical foundations of Christian education were forcefully echoed a year later by the Rev. Humphrey Pickard, the founding principal of Mount

Allison College, the Wesleyan Methodist institution at Sackville, New Brunswick. While insisting that sound training in the sciences and the classics was essential for a proper liberal education, Pickard told the students and clergymen at his inauguration that the "volume of Inspiration" was "infinitely our most valuable text book. Let any other be taken away," he declared, "but this must not be removed or our efforts will be fruitless. Lock up Homer and Pindar, Horace and Virgil, Demosthenes and Cicero, Zenophon[sic] and Livy, Socrates and Seneca ... but seek not to close the book of life! Forbid us access to the laboratory of nature – draw a curtain of impenetrable mystery over all her phenomena, but let us ever see this lamp of God, this light of Eternity!"[106] Students and ministers must be guided by the divine will in their thoughts and actions, not by the categories of human speculation.

The thinking of Ryerson and Pickard forcefully impressed the young Samuel Nelles, among the first group of graduates from Victoria. Writing in 1848, he declared: "We need not fear philosophy; but I do think that the great thing we have to dread and to guard against in this age is *Philosophy out of Christ*. Philosophy never regenerates society ...'Power from on high' – this alone can disenthrall man."[107] Like the Presbyterians Lyall and George, Ryerson and Nelles were committed to a defence of the ideal of evangelical faith as the basis of culture. Thus, from the outset, they were constrained to set the limits of reason, boundaries imposed by the needs of biblical inspiration, morality, and civilization. All three were intimately linked – their harmony preserved through the spread of a theology resting on the authority of the Bible, a body of thought accessible to both clergymen and people.

If Ryerson's concept of college education sought to establish the supremacy of theology in the building of Christian character, what was the substance and method of theological study? Ryerson's answer to this question reveals the mind of Methodism in a process of transition from the world of the camp meeting to a society committed to scientific progress and the rationality of both divine and human knowledge. The study of theology, he said, was premised on Methodist traditons concerning the wellsprings of religion. Faith involved far more than an intellectual assent to certain doctrines. It was based in personal experience of Christ, feeling, and conscience. As he explained in an 1848 address:

A person may spend the greater part of his life in investigating disputed doctrines of Theology, and litigated questions of polity and ceremonies, and terminate his investigations in greater doubt than when he commenced them; but being master, by *experience* and reading the Word of God for himself, of the doctrine that "being justified by faith he has peace with God through our Lord Jesus Christ, and the love of God shed abroad in his heart by the Holy Ghost given unto him," he carries abroad in his heart the true antidote for the symbolism of Italy, the rationalism of Germany ... the Puseyism of England.

By theology, Ryerson envisaged something practical and closely related to Christian life. He equated direct study of the Bible with theology. Theology involved no esoteric skills, merely the ability to read the Bible in the English language.[108] It was, therefore, no mere philosophical system or formalized doctrinal structure, but the vital union of biblical study and the personal experience of God's saving grace manifest in Christ. Such a discipline was popular and accessible, binding together college students, professors, itinerant preachers, and ordinary members of the congregation.

This definition of the practical nature of theology owed much to the traditions derived from John Wesley. Was an appeal to Methodist origins sufficient to resist the inroads of the Millerites as well as to institutionalize the experiential traditions of the revival and reconcile them with the early Victorian culture premised on the harmony of science, morality, and religion? Having renounced a philosophical foundation for Christian theology, Ryerson was forced, like Chalmers, to establish a rationale for theology by other means, if Methodism was to survive in a society that demanded an unshakeable conviction as a basis for valid inquiry in both natural and human sciences.

In his inaugural address Ryerson seems to have attempted to harmonize Methodist traditions with a second strand of ideas. Theology, he declared, was "the most extensive and important science in the world," a science above all other branches of college learning. The view of theology as a science imposed a subtle tension between the democratic character of Methodism and the intellectual needs of the generation of the 1840s. Ryerson strained to balance the pull of these demands. This definition of theology echoed that advanced early in 1838 in *The Christian Guardian* by an anonymous contributor who claimed that theology was a "moral and religious science," functioning as "the foundation, cement, pervading element, and key-stone of the whole arch of the Sciences. It renders every branch of Science subservient and contributory to its grand design." Doctrines, he concluded, "are not probable conjectures or fanciful representations, but *declarations* or *descriptions* of *facts* and *realities*, which are of the highest moment and admit of a satisfactory proof."[109]

The use of terms such as "facts" and "realities" underscored the rise of the Baconian ideal in Canadian Methodist circles. Ryerson's address mentioned with approval a second great intellectual figure of Methodist tradition, Richard Watson, an English Methodist clergyman whose *Theological Institutes*, published between 1823 and 1829, were required reading for Methodist probationers until 1876. Unlike Wesley, Watson interpreted revelation almost exclusively as the communication of divine truths or "propositions" to the mind. Scripture was the source and authority for the whole of theology, an infallible basis for every doctrine of the Christian faith. The Bible, as the unerring transcript of the divine mind, was therefore secure from all error. Watson barred humanity's limited and sinful reason from a major role in the discovery of religious truth, obliging it to proceed humbly in this area of investigation.[110] This position, informed by Baconianism, stressed the sinful nature and limits of human reason, the supremacy of the Bible as the inerrant revelation of the divine will, and the scientific character and independence of theology.

Watson's interpretation of the inductive method strongly influenced the teaching at Victoria College. As a form of practical reason based on minute observation not speculation, Baconianism was compatible with the empirical ideal of experimental religion inherited from the Wesleyan revival. It allowed clergymen-professors such as Ryerson to establish not only the independence of a theology founded on biblical data and personal experience, but also its superiority to science. At the opening of the college in 1842, Ryerson stated, "Science creeps, while religion expands the wing and soars. One passing pious thought, in a devotional moment, on the structure of a pebble, shall produce deeper piety of feeling than if, in scientific adoration, we bowed before the sticks and stones of geological theories."[111]

Through his choice of words, Victoria's founder implicitly defined the role of Baconianism in Methodism. It was to supply, not an intellectual, systematic theology, but a rational basis for an experimental religion anchored in part on the data of feeling. This marked the intersection of the passion of the revival with a powerful early Victorian intellectual current – a religion that appealed to the data of reason and justified Christian feeling and Christian living. Ignoring the fundamental irony invoked, Ryerson, like his Presbyterian counterparts Michael Willis and Andrew King, used the rational, empirical, and scientific Baconian method to reinforce and promote a realm of truth that lay beyond the scrutiny of human reason.

This alliance of Wesleyan theology and the inductive method was the most significant formative influence on the Methodist colleges in central Canada. Ryerson's view of the relations between theology and education was forcefully impressed upon the student body. In a valedictory address to the graduating class Samuel Nelles insisted that inquiry must avoid speculation and painstakingly collect the facts. All research into matters of revealed truth, a category including science and philosophy, must be guided by faith. Only thus, Nelles believed, could the spirit of investigation achieve true freedom. As a young minister, Nelles was again to remind himself that "it is a sin to speculate about what God does not permit us to know. Man has a passion for the marvelous ... he should learn to be humble and *do his duty* ... he who seeks to pierce through the darkness of Jehovah's pavilion will be shivered and blasted by the lightnings of his wrath."[112]

By 1850 the inductive method had assumed the status of *the* Christian philosophy among those influenced by Watson, especially the professors and students at Victoria College. Methodists welcomed as eagerly as their Presbyterian counterparts an ideal of knowledge based on the patient observation and collection of facts, and subsequent generalization. In a world they viewed as increasingly afflicted with competing philosophies, some with anti-Christian implications, Baconian induction appeared to be the only one that did not threaten to recast the central evangelical doctrines. It also justified the subordination of reason to revelation and Christian experience. It enabled Methodists to preach the union of the Christian religion and civilization, urging educated people to draw both their science and their philosophy from the Bible.[113] Baconianism thus helped to transform Methodism from a religion of revivals and camp meetings to the faith of a settled, commercial, and urbanizing society during the years between 1830 and 1860. In a world aware of the pace of scientific discovery, a religion based on the data of feeling appeared to lack authority and, in certain cases, failed to distinguish Methodism from millenarianism or antinomianism. The inductive philosophy, however, re-established the connection between evangelical piety and human reason, and insisted that doctrinal conviction was essential to the continued progress of culture and Canadian society.

In the 1850s the evangelical creed was a principal contributor to the intellectual life of English Canada. By incorporating Baconianism into this creed, Presbyterians and Methodists could offer a cultural alternative to the Enlightenment – a civilization that was founded on Christian reason and recognized the supremacy of the Bible and theology. Thomas McCulloch, Michael Willis, William Lyall, James George, Egerton Ryerson, and Samuel Nelles hoped that the colleges would engender a learned piety that would bind preachers and congregations through the study of the Bible and its doctrines. Though it restricted the intellect, especially in theological matters, the evangelical creed in its formative era was both flexible and pragmatic. Methodists and Presbyterians insisted on direct contact with the "facts" of revelation as the essential element of Christian living. Evangelization, not the rooting of an elite tradition of systematic theology on colonial soil, was their raison d'être.

The evangelical creed was, however, a delicately balanced structure, the result of an attempt to combine currents of thought drawn from the Awakening and the eighteenth-century Enlightenment. It depended, ultimately, on the ability to reconcile the need for an immutable and eternal basis of truth with the evidence of the social, moral, and scientific advances that educated Victorians regarded as equally essential to civilization. Baconian induction was a method, not a certainty, and involved a circular mode of reasoning in theological matters that led evangelicals back to the Scriptures. From a twentieth-century standpoint, Baconianism did not provide a final answer to the dilemma of faithful Christians in an age that witnessed rapid scientific progress and the clash of religion and philosophy. But for the professors in the colonial church colleges, the fusion of the evangelical creed and the Baconian outlook offered a dependable intellectual tool and, more importantly, the strongest defence of the Bible in an unsettled age.

2 Authority and History: Evangelicalism and the Problem of the Past

"Surely nothing can afford more pleasure to an enquiring mind," confided Egerton Ryerson to his diary in 1826, "than the perusal of documents relating to the ancient chosen people of God." For this young Methodist circuit-rider, it was simply marvellous that the Old Testament Israelites who "according to their legitimate records" had more than eight hundred thousand men of military age, "should slip from the records of men, hide themselves from human observation, and inhabit limits beyond geographical research." It was, Ryerson declared, "a phenomenon unprecedented in the world's history," and a compelling proof of "the wonderful government of Him whose ways are past finding out."[1] The belief that the Bible – the books of the Old and New Testaments – contained the absolutely certain record of God's dealings with the human race was fundamental to the culture of evangelicalism that shaped Ryerson's outlook. The Bible provided the unshakeable foundation of faith. It disclosed to the believer the doctrines of sin, salvation, and judgment, principles that, to evangelicals, possessed universal validity.

It also functioned as a source of authority on a second level. For clergymen such as McCulloch and Ryerson, as well as for their congregations, Scripture was also history. The Bible contained an account of the origins of the universe and humanity, provided an explanation of human sin, and disclosed the miracle of salvation. It also looked to the future. Through study of its prophecies, Presbyterian and Methodist ministers believed that they could discern the future of their own society and of the entire human race. These historical and theological levels could not be separated without irreparable damage to the position of the Bible. Students in the church colleges were constantly reminded that the religious value of the Bible depended on its accuracy and reliability as an account of human history.

Although it has become standard historical practice to place evangelicalism in an intellectual sphere defined by Common Sense philosophy and a body of natural theology, a closer examination of the writings of leading Presbyterian and Methodist clergymen in English Canada indicates that another, more powerful influence helped to shape the evangelical mind. In both Presbyterian and Methodist colleges, the human mind and conscience encountered revelation neither through the patient observation of the natural world nor through complex philosophical systems or codified statements of theological doctrine. The evangelical creed that arose between 1780 and 1830 identified the Bible as the sole source and guarantee of religious truth. With their intellectual roots located firmly in the twilight of the Anglo-American Enlightenment, the clergymen-professors of British North America insistently maintained that biblical revelation alone provided the basis of reason, understanding, and morality necessary for Christian faith and civilization. They viewed the equation of theology and history expressed in the Bible as the foundation of all education and culture.

The alliance of theology and history was thus the source of stability and religious certainty in the fledgling church colleges. History, a term that included not only the written records of earlier societies but also their interpretation through writing and preaching, was generally regarded as a source of stability and certainty in a world characterized by rapid social and intellectual change. For many prominent early Victorians, history was a source of certain knowledge concerning national origins, political behaviour, moral conduct, and the future of individuals and societies.[2] More importantly for evangelical Christians, history disclosed the irrefutable religious truth. History was not simply the record of secular achievement in politics, war, or the intellect, but also the record of God's miraculous intervention in human affairs. Evangelicals believed that biblical history conveyed a superior meaning, because of its miraculous character. The narratives spoke to the faith and conscience of the reader as well as to the intellect and the imagination. It can be said without exaggeration that the equation of theology and history was the chief mode of expression among English Canadian evangelicals, the very determinant of their creed and their efforts to build a Christian civilization.

The prominence of the historical element in both theological study and preaching distinguished the evangelical culture of English Canada from those of the older societies of Britain and the United States. In the United States, clergymen could draw upon well-established traditions of systematic Calvinist theology, and an institutional structure of Common Sense philosophy, in addition to the biblical history of salvation. British clergymen, too, were backed by a variety of systematic philosophical and theological traditions, as well as a culture of inquiry dominated by the study of natural theology – the attempt to find religious meaning in scientific endeavours. English-Canadian clergymen, however, functioned in a culture where the more static pre-evangelical traditions of philosophy and theology had been substantially dissolved by the ferment of the revival. Evangelicalism, in turn, committed them to a dynamic view of the operation of divine will and its relationship to the mind and society. Their more biblically centred theology was, therefore, informed less by inherited traditions of natural theology and systematic Calvinism than by the study of history, whose rise after 1780 was coterminous with the evangelical revival itself.

History offered stability and reassurance, but in the early nineteenth century it was also a source of ambiguity and perplexity. The formative years for the evangelical creed in British North America coincided with a serious challenge to the biblical account of human history and its religious authority. In Germany and England and, to a lesser extent, in the United States, Christians who held to the supremacy of the Bible were faced with the rise of competing secular or natural explanations of the origins, change, and decline of human societies. These rival interpretations of history threatened to deny or reduce the role of the miraculous in the human past. By questioning the record provided in the biblical narratives, they threatened to sever the connection between theology and history. For colonial evangelicals, the record of the past was thus problematic. Between 1820 and 1860 the defence of the Bible as both doctrine and history became all important and shaped both the college curriculum and the preaching of the Presbyterian and Methodist churches. This quest for certainty through the rationalization of the changing nature of historical studies decisively marked the intellectual life of the evangelical churches during their first century in British North America.

FROM NATURE TO HUMAN NATURE: EVANGELICALISM AND THE RECASTING OF NATURAL THEOLOGY

In June 1857 the following statement, explicitly condemning the tendency of natural theologians to depreciate evil and sin, and to imagine a benevolent design at work where the evidence should indicate otherwise, appeared in the *Ecclesiastical and Missionary Record*, the journal of the Free Church Presbyterians in Nova Scotia: "Very much that is written on natural theology proceeds on the ... sophistical method." The anonymous author cautioned that "any mere reduction in the quantity of evil does nothing to diminish the difficulty of accounting for its existence. The mystery is that it should exist at all, that it should find its way into God's empire."[3] Natural theology, according to this view, failed to explain the existence and reality of sin and the consequent need for redemption, one of the central concepts of the evangelical creed.

At the time of this stern rebuke, however, natural theology seemed well established in British North American culture. As Carl Berger has eloquently stated, the nineteenth-century study of nature involved more than the collection of facts and the promotion of science – it invoked a sense of wonder and a celebration of mystery, and Victorians believed that in the works of nature they discerned God's design.[4] In the Canadian evangelical colleges, Archdeacon William Paley's *Natural Theology*, written in 1802, was a basic component of the curricula of Victoria, Knox, and Queen's colleges.[5] So powerful was the early nineteenth-century evocation of the workings of the divine plan in nature that it has often been forgotten that "natural theology" implied a much wider scope for the operation of divine providence. Evangelical clergymen were the heirs of a much older tradition, which saw evidences of God's design not only in physical nature, but also in the human mind and society. "Natural Theology," according to one prominent English Methodist, "embraces those truths concerning God, His being, His perfection and His moral government which are deducible from the works of Creation and the works of Providence and from the constitution of human nature – more from the latter than from all the rest, because here we learn the unalterable distinction between moral good and evil."[6]

The importance attached to the study of the interaction between God's design and human nature, and its elevation above the contemplation of the divine plan in the natural world, testified less to the evangelical desire to appropriate and Christianize the rising prestige of the natural sciences, than to their ambivalent attitude to the cultural legacy of the eighteenth century. This ambivalence was reinforced by the very way in which Methodist and Presbyterian leaders sought to appropriate and redirect the legacy of the Enlightenment. As an influence in shaping the evangelical mind in its formative years, it both impoverished and liberated.

The culture of transatlantic Protestantism viewed the sciences and theological study as complementary. In the eighteenth century

Christians in the English-speaking world had developed a tripartite edifice of religious truth through which they hoped to accommodate Enlightenment reason and Christian tradition. In their view, humanity's knowledge of God rested on the evidence of reason, the argument of God's design manifest in the natural world, and on the direct communication of Scripture. Such a formulation easily led to a common context of understanding among clergymen and scientists. Protestant ministers claimed for theology the status of a science, and scientists professed the religious nature of their inquiries.[7]

Evangelicals, however, did not merely uncritically appropriate the legacy of the eighteenth century into their culture. The natural theology of William Paley rested upon a cosmic optimism that discerned in creation the perfect adaptation of organisms to environments. Through the detailed enumeration of examples of wonderful adaptations to nature, Paley connected the organic and inorganic worlds in such a way as to convince Christian believers that both the natural and human worlds were ruled by the design of a benevolent God. However, Paley's view of the natural world and of human society presented in *Principles of Moral and Political Philosophy* displayed an implicit utilitarianism. Evil and suffering were merely effects and did not mar the beneficial design of creation. Wherever possible the Deity preferred to use pleasure rather than pain to accomplish the divine purpose. Thus evil and suffering were explained away as part of a greater good.[8]

The theology of the evangelical movement, with its insistence on the direct, inward, personal contact of Christ and the sinner, questioned Paley's tendency to seek, through the contemplation of nature, an external, rational argument to support the idea of divine revelation. For the evangelical, only the personal bond between God and the individual, forged by Christ's atonement, could convey assurance of the divine presence in the world. Evangelicalism also insisted on the absolute nature of ethics and morals, because they were revealed in the Bible, and from this standpoint many nineteenth-century Christians came to see Paley's utilitarianism as intensely selfish and relativistic, as the product of a desire to substitute the canons of expediency for the ultimate standards of Scripture. For this reason, they more readily took up idealist arguments for design which identified divine purpose in the general patterns, or archetypal plans, detected in creation – an emphasis wholly consistent and easily reconcilable with Christian belief.[9]

While a few evangelical clergymen, such as Thomas Chalmers and James McCosh, played a central role in the continuing debate over the supremacy of religion or science,[10] evangelical culture was responsible for an even more profound revision of the eighteenth-century tradition of natural theology. Where Paley looked to external nature for evidence of design, evangelicals sought the divine presence in the doctrine of the atonement, the personal bond between sinner and Redeemer. And here, Paley's argument, based on the utilitarian principles of expediency, was deeply offensive to the whole tenor of evangelicalism and could be of little use in conveying rational assurance of God's presence in the world. For preachers and professors in the transatlantic world of early nineteenth-century evangelicalism, the problem lay less in the relationship of religion and scientific discovery than in the search for a rational explanation of the evidence of God's presence and purpose in the even more dynamic and complex world of human will, behaviour, and social life.

Their solution was to renew the emphasis on another part of the eighteenth-century legacy. The works of the Anglican bishop Joseph Butler, the *Sermons* and *The Analogy of Religion Natural and Revealed to the Constitution and Course of Nature*, written in the 1730s, which predated the better-known treatises of William Paley, enjoyed a marked revival in the early nineteenth century. Not coincidentally, Butler's popularity was largely at the expense of Paley's.[11] Butler's views neatly dovetailed with the theological requirements of the rising evangelical movement. In contrast to Paley, who viewed the human mind as a passive agent acquiring knowledge through sensations, Butler, like the Common Sense philosophers upon whose psychological and epistemological ideas evangelicals relied, believed that the mind was active, endowed with various faculties as well as intuitive knowledge. His emphasis on conscience as the source of all ethical judgments showed how natural theology could be extended from the physical to the human world.[12] Although Butler and his devotees affirmed the harmonious connection between "Nature, Providence, and Revelation,"[13] they believed that the indissoluble link between the natural and moral governments of the world indicated the clear supremacy of supernatural purposes and moral laws over natural processes. Butler denied that a universe ruled by general laws had constrained human freedom or banished a personal God. "God's miraculous interpositions," he claimed, "may have been, all along in like manner, by *general* laws of wisdom."[14]

Butler's *Analogy* also called into question Paley's cosmic optimism, which many evangelicals found at odds with a theology that emphasized the fundamental fact of sin. In an age of social and ideological upheaval, Christian believers looking for precise assurance of salvation could take comfort from Butler, who stressed that absolute certainty was less important than the acceptance of the world as imperfect, as an arena of probation and moral trial. The *Analogy's* injunction was to follow the dictates of conscience or the moral faculty, which was, for early nineteenth-century Christians, the focal point where God's grace encountered human will.[15] Thus Butler's natural theology accounted not only for the paradox of sin in a world created by God, but also for the sudden irruptions and infusions of grace that alone could transform the sinner's life. As Boyd Hilton has explained in his study of evangelical social thought, "natural theology was thus transferred from the physical to the mental world and applied to the relations between men."[16]

Colonial evangelicals shared fully in this reorientation of natural theology, drawing directly on the promotion of Butler by English and Scottish clergymen. Thomas Chalmers, the intellectual mentor of the Free Church Presbyterians in English Canada, was a key figure in the encounter of evangelical theology and eighteenth-century thought. While reaffirming the solidity of the Protestant triad of religious certainty, his contribution to *The Bridgewater Treatises* and his work *On Natural Theology*[17] contained not only a subtle but effective criticism of Paley's reliance on the evidence of nature to prove the truth of Christian doctrine, but also an appeal to Butler's insistence on conscience and probability in seeking a new relationship between biblical revelation and natural theology.

Natural theology, Chalmers reminded his readers, was of great value in stimulating the human search for religious truth. His work denied, however, any logical relationship between Christian truth and the light of nature. Christianity, he wrote, rested "on its own proper evidence, and if, instead of this, she be made to rest on an antecedent natural religion, she becomes weak throughout, because weak radically."[18] Breaking with the Paleyite belief in the continuity of natural and revealed theology, Chalmers criticized the outlook of natural theology as useless at precisely the point of greatest importance for evangelicals: the existence and nature of sin, and the human need for redemption. With its praise of benevolent design in creation, the utilitarian natural theology could neither posit a cause nor suggest a remedy for sin. This, Chalmers believed, could be supplied only by the Cross and the Incarnation as revealed to the mind and conscience in the Bible and by the personal contact of the sinner and Christ.[19]

In his criticisms, Chalmers tended to lump together Paley's version of natural theology, Common Sense philosophy, and Scottish "moderatism" as opponents of evangelical religion. His modification of Protestant intellectual traditions stemmed, however, from attitudes that drew extensively from prevailing emphases in Scottish culture. Natural theology, in the generally accepted sense of the contemplation of the natural world and its divine design, had never secured wide currency in Scottish intellectual circles. The popularity of Paley's works in the years after 1780 coincided with the rise of the evangelical movement. With its emphasis on revelation and biblical study, the evangelical tendency in Presbyterianism curbed, in both pulpit and university, the appeal to the reverent mind to contemplate God's works in nature.[20] Of equal significance in the Scottish failure to develop this strand of natural theology was the orientation of Scottish inquiry in the eighteenth century. The prominent thinkers of the Scottish Enlightenment devoted themselves to interpreting the phenomena of the human realm – the movements and changes of mind and society – rather than to uncovering hidden geological strata or the laws governing the properties of chemical substances. Men such as Francis Hutcheson, William Robertson, Adam Smith, and David Hume focused on the study of human behaviour, the elucidation of laws governing the individual mind, and the development and progress of society.[21] The Common Sense philosophy, represented by Thomas Reid, Dugald Stewart, and Sir William Hamilton, was decidedly humanistic in its orientation. Linked to the eighteenth-century inquiry, it dwelt on man's moral sense, the conscience, and individual and social obligation. While evangelical leaders such as Chalmers sharply rejected the supremacy of reason over faith implicit in the creed of the Scottish Enlightenment, their theology preserved its focus on the human and the ethical. The evangelical life was directed not so much to science or to the pious contemplation of nature as to building a "godly commonwealth," a perfected human society constructed on Christian ethics drawn from the Gospels.

The appeal to the primacy of revelation and the moral sense so ably encouraged by Butler's *Analogy* thus easily displaced the older Paleyite natural theology among Scottish Free Church Presbyterians. In the context of Scottish religious discussion it distanced the evangelicals from the structures of certainty so characteristic of eighteenth-century Protestant Christians. Transferred to the colonial Presbyterian colleges by Free Church missionaries in the 1840s, Chalmers's human-centred "natural theology" reminded professors and preachers that only Scripture provided the authority for the exercise of the moral faculty. The turning from the contemplation of physical nature to the more troubling attempt to understand human nature was not merely an alternative within a wider culture, but the central strand of thinking in the attempt to define the relationship between theological and scientific inquiry.

Like their Scottish mentors, Canadian Presbyterians began with the insistence on the facts of human "death, sorrow, and fear, the dark progeny of sin" and the reality of redemption by the power of the Gospel.[22] While respecting the continued connection between science and religion represented by natural theology, Presbyterians shifted the position of this discipline in the hierarchy of knowledge. Natural theology, they claimed, was insufficient to ground faith or to redeem the sinner, for it was unable to realistically describe the human condition. To the evangelical, the central belief of theology was that God in his grace and mercy had ordained the law and redemption as revealed in the Bible to remedy humanity's fallen state.[23] In both college and pulpit, the evangelical creed stressed that the inner witness of faith was the beginning of knowledge, thus demoting the external and rational arguments offered by natural theology to the level of a secondary proof.

Criticized for failing to anchor Christian theology on biblical reality, the argument from design was open to objections on other grounds. Paley used evidence drawn from man's physical nature alone to anchor his harmony of religion and science. Such a definition failed to convince the Canadian disciples of Chalmers who, like their mentor, still adhered to vestiges of the moral and ethical emphasis of the Scottish inquiry. They looked to human character, not the natural world, for proof of God's design, and forcefully dismissed the Paleyite implication that man was merely a mechanism. Like their Scottish counterparts, while they criticised Paley they lauded Butler's humanistic natural theology. The *Analogy* was regarded as the key to a Christian education, and was praised by an anonymous Presbyterian as "a golden currency" that survived the assaults of rationalism and infidelity. "Butler's argument," he said, "is impregnable."[24] At this point, the Presbyterians of English Canada had already broken with a powerful current of ideas that led from the Anglican clergymen William Paley and Thomas Malthus through nineteenth-century British natural theology to Charles Darwin. The common strand uniting these diverse thinkers was the belief that mind and body were mechanisms, a conviction that placed humans within the bounds of the natural world. The evangelical legacy of Chalmers, however, insisted that humanity stood not within but above the rest of the natural order. Human nature was a trinity – physical, intellectual, and moral. Through the study of humanity, the reverent student might discern evidences of the character of God.[25]

The combined effect of evangelical passion and the optimistic, ethical, humanistic currents of Scottish university culture ensured that the Bible would dominate the curriculum in the colonial colleges. For the Presbyterian missionaries, the moral emphases of sin and redemption formed the basis of the relationship between God and humanity. The study of Scripture and the human character was of primary importance in the apprehension of religious truth. Butler's arguments appealed because while they placed natural theology in a human context, as a description of the workings of the moral faculty in both individuals and society, they also insisted that natural theology was secondary to revelation. Paley's intricate theory of God's design in physical nature failed to answer the most perplexing issues of sin, grace, and human conduct that preoccupied the teaching and preaching in evangelical colleges and pulpits. Thus it became but a faint echo of an eighteenth-century world largely left behind.

In the Methodist colleges a similar displacement of Paley by Butler supported the primacy of biblical over natural theology, and a corresponding interest in the paradoxes of human nature, as opposed to the ordered harmony of physical nature. John Wesley, the founder of the Methodist theological tradition, had written little on the subject of the argument from design. Wesley's emphasis on Christian experience, perfection, and the holy life placed him, like the Presbyterian evangelicals, squarely within a current of thought critical of certain aspects of the Protestant Christianity of the Enlightenment. The Wesleyan quadrilateral of Bible, reason, experience, and tradition focused attention on the human – on the decisive issues of sin and redemption, rather than on the orderly, mechanistic precepts of British natural theology.

By the 1840s Wesley's Canadian disciples had modified the original character of Methodist theology. Clergymen-professors like Egerton Ryerson, anxious to promote the harmony of science and religion, enlisted the aid of natural theology, admitting that it testified to Christian truth. By demonstrating that the "God of grace is also the God of nature," Christian apologists might, he declared, deny the field of inquiry to sceptics and infidels.[26] However, this implied no commitment to accord natural theology a separate status within the quadrilateral of religious knowledge. Rather, Ryerson expressed a ritual concern for the harmonious relations of religion and reason that denied an independent function to natural theology in the curriculum. Significantly, Ryerson's curriculum at Victoria College contained no course in "natural philosophy," the discipline that, in the late eighteenth century, most clearly directed the student to search the external world for evidence of God's design. Of even greater importance for the shaping of the Methodist intellectual tradition was Ryerson's definition of "natural theology":

The philosophy of mind inquires into the nature of those spirits of which we have any certain knowledge, or which it concerns us to know – the

Deity and the soul of man. The former branch of the inquiry is termed Natural Theology; the latter has sometimes been termed Psychology, or the philosophy of the human mind. The latter prepares the way for the former. From the knowledge of ourselves and our Creator arise our duty to both. This is the province of *Moral Philosophy*, – to explain our obligations and our duties to ourselves, to our fellow-men, and to our Maker – to elucidate and apply the cardinal principles of the Scriptures to the various relations and circumstances of human life.[27]

Natural theology was thus included under the general rubric "moral science." It was more concerned with the realm of individual and social conduct with the external world of physical nature – the sphere of scientific questions. Its starting-point was the human mind, and its proper role was to describe the relationship between God and the moral faculty, not the mechanisms of Newtonian physics or geology.

Such a definition indicated Ryerson's own intellectual pilgrimage within evangelicalism's eighteenth-century legacy. In 1841 he declared that "before I was twenty years of age I had read Paley's Political Philosophy, including his chapters on the British Constitution and a Church Establishment." From Paley he learned that "a Church Establishment is no part of Christianity, but a means of supporting it, and a means which should be used only when the majority of the people are of the religion thus supported."[28] Ryerson's account of his life frequently refers to Paley's textbook on moral philosophy, but only in a clearly limited sense, as a weapon in the controversy over the establishment of the Church of England in Upper Canada. Ryerson's evangelical convictions were unquestionably at odds with the utilitarian emphasis of Paley's teaching.[29] To him, "moral science" encompassed mental philosophy, natural philosophy, moral philosophy, and logic. This definition owed less to Paley than to the American Baptist educator Francis Wayland. Wayland himself had written his celebrated *Elements of Moral Science* out of a desire to replace the utilitarian ethics of Paley in the college curriculum. His emphasis on the insufficiency of natural theology as a source of religious knowledge, and his conviction that natural theology must deal with the bond between the believer and God, the primacy of conscience, and the supremacy of Scripture as the source of human conduct, made Wayland one of the most forceful American champions of Butler.[30]

Like Butler and Wayland, Ryerson broke with Paley by according natural theology a role strictly related to revelation, the authoritative record of the interaction between God and conscience. This implicitly barred it from serving as the discipline mediating faith and inquiry.

Natural theology, in the Butlerian-evangelical scheme, was useful for defending Christianity from the assaults of impious research, but the central insights regarding God and the human character remained the preserve of reverent inquiry into the biblical record. Generations of students at Victoria College were thus instructed that although the truths of natural and revealed religion harmonized perfectly, the former was vitiated by "necessary and inherent defects" that were only remedied by the knowledge of the character of God as disclosed in the Old and New Testaments. [31]

Ryerson and other Methodists displayed a further ambivalence toward the religious value of Paley's natural theology. Clergymen and their congregations were often reminded that the utilitarian notion of contrivance was alien to the culture of the evangelical Awakening. This strand of natural theology was criticized for its association with the Anglican establishment, and was equated with the hierarchical, orderly, external religion against which Wesley had led a revolt. According to one comment in *The Christian Guardian*, the argument from design had proved a useful weapon in the early eighteenth-century battle against David Hume and the English Deists. Unfortunately, the resort to such a method of proof had harmed English theology for, "in the anxiety to strengthen its defences the garrison not only declined to attempt new conquests, but withdrew from much of their ancient dominion. In this its apologetic age, English theology was distinguished by a wonted timidity and coldness." [32] With its metaphor of order, natural theology was suspect in the eyes of many Methodists – an undemocratic vestige of subservience to bishop and Establishment, an attempt to deny the popular character of religious truth by placing it in the hands of a cultured elite.

Even in those Methodist circles most willing to promote the partnership of theology and inquiry in the natural sciences, there was a clear sense of priorities. In his inaugural address at Victoria College in 1842, Ryerson left no doubt that he intended natural theology, like moral philosophy and the other liberal arts, to function as an adjunct of biblical study. [33] Samuel Nelles, Ryerson's student and eventual successor, defended the study of the evidences of nature and praised the argument from analogies. However, in a sermon preached in 1851 he declared that these were powerless to confer the assurance of grace, which came only through the mediation of Christ. The atonement, he informed the student congregation, was "the great fact in the history of our Race. It is the chief thing in the affairs of our world. He who would read aright the story of man or the character of God must learn to read them through the work of him who was God manifest in the flesh and who came both to maintain the divine glory and to reveal it."[34] Nelles's juxtaposition of "the story of man" and "the character of God" was a clear statement of the ethical and human assumptions of the evangelical creed. It directed preachers, students, and ordinary believers to the Bible in quest of the authoritative evidence and experience of faith. The most compelling proofs of Christianity, Nelles believed, were biblical and moral rather than natural. His elevation of the moral and the human over the natural in the quest for religious certainty placed evangelical theology at a critical juncture in the transformation of early Victorian thought.

Protestant Christianity in the eighteenth century relied on the evidence of reason, nature, and Scripture to support religious faith. Such an approach to theology, based upon the use of analogies, conflated the moral and the natural. This equation was the distinctive feature of both British and American Protestantism in the early nineteenth century. Clergymen such as the Presbyterian scholars James Thornwell and Charles Hodge drew no clear distinction between natural, social, and psychological phenomena. On the strength of the old transatlantic alliance of Baconianism and natural theology, they claimed scientific status for their systems of theology.[35]

Though paying lip-service to this unitary structure of truth, Canadian Methodists and Presbyterians stood on the other side of a theological watershed. The place accorded to natural theology by Ryerson, Nelles, and the missionary disciples of Chalmers was determined by their desire to explain the stark paradox of human depravity and Christ's redemption, not by a wish to participate in the common culture of religious and scientific discussion represented by the Paleyite inheritance. Much has been made of the enthusiastic promotion of "science" and the collection of natural history specimens by Presbyterian and Methodist clergymen such as McCulloch and Ryerson. In their enthusiastic addresses, however, they did not refer to the practice of "science," but to the "scientific" way of thinking, which they equated exclusively with the Baconian method. And their Baconianism meant nothing less than the supremacy of their creed over all other forms of human intellectual endeavour.[36] These colonial clergymen participated in the institutionalization of a rival strand of the eighteenth-century tradition, one that looked to the sciences of human behaviour – psychology, political economy, and especially history – rather than to physics, chemistry, or geology for evidences of God's design. The Butlerian-evangelical alliance clearly foreshadowed the separation of the moral and the natural, as well as the identification of the ethical element, or conscience, as superior because its data and imperatives were grounded more firmly in a biblical revelation than were other branches of knowledge.

From their beginnings, the evangelical colleges of English Canada functioned in an intellectual environment clouded by doubts concerning the maintenance of the eighteenth-century harmony between religion and culture based on the unity of reason, religion, and nature. The coincidence of internal and external developments can explain the growing gulf between the data of morality and science, and of the Bible and nature. Like their British and American counterparts, clergymen-professors in English Canada were surrounded by plentiful evidences of nature. However, they could not trust this natural world to exhibit the wisdom, power, and benevolence of God. In the 1830s and 1840s much of Canada was still a pioneer society, opening settlements and creating social institutions. Unlike British and American clergymen, Canadian evangelicals could not afford the leisurely contemplation of natural processes, and the collection and classification of geological and botanical specimens. They were compelled to concentrate on the definition of the human character of English Canada – the building of communities and institutions necessary to a settled existence.[37] The coincidence of the theology of evangelicalism with the need to define the emerging community directed clergymen to search for the ties between the individual, God, and human society, rather than to consider the relationship of God, humanity, and nature. Projects of moral and social reform – camp-meetings, conversion experiences, church building, schools, temperance, Bible societies – characterized the evangelical culture.

Despite the use of Paley's *Natural Theology*, the elaborate appeals to the evidence of nature as a source of religious truth characteristic of British and American religious and scientific communities were muted in the Presbyterian and Methodist colleges of British North America. Evangelical theology was anchored on the overriding sufficiency of God's revelation in the Bible, and emphasized the salvation of the individual and the building of a Christian civilization. Unlike their Anglican counterparts James Beaven and James Bovell of Trinity College, Toronto, Presbyterian and Methodist clergymen-professors felt no need for a precise, external, reasonable justification of Christian truth. Nor did they need reassurance concerning the pious nature of geological and biological inquiries, as did McGill University's Principal William Dawson, Victorian Canada's pre-eminent man of science.[38] Though conscious of the growing tension between religion and science, Presbyterians and Methodists in Canada stood at one remove from the issues dividing clergymen and scientists in the 1850s. Their evangelical theology had invested little in the maintenance of the Paleyite tradition. Even before the publication of Darwin's *The Origin of Species*, the intellectual leaders of the evangelical churches in both Britain and the Canadian colonies had quietly but effectively shifted the relationship between belief and knowledge from the natural to the human world. True Christian inquiry, they held, involved the study of God's revealed word and its saving power in human conscience and society, not the construction of elaborate theodicies and harmonies. Certainty lay in the relationship between humanity and God. The move from Paley to Butler impelled a renewed emphasis on the Bible and human conduct as guides to the ultimate truth. This approach enabled Canadian evangelicals to survive the initial shocks caused by the encounter of Christianity and evolutionary theory in the 1860s. Their biblical and humanistic biases ensured that there would be few lamentations for the shattered unity of revelation and the physical universe.

EVANGELICALS AND THE HUMAN WORLD: THE CONVERGENCE OF THEOLOGY AND THE HISTORICAL

By 1860 evangelical clergymen in British North America had both questioned and revised the intellectual structures of Enlightenment Christianity. Despite a vestigial presence, neither the philosophical enterprise of Common Sense nor the search for God's design in nature shaped the teachings in their colleges. Methodist and Presbyterian leaders stood at a distance from the supposedly universal early Victorian genteel ramble through the geological and botanical record in search of the footprints of the Creator.[39] For McCulloch, Ryerson, and Nelles, Christian inquiry was not furthered through the study of natural history. These men, their students, and the wider culture of evangelicalism did not reject the idea of God's design and activity in the world, but they believed that God's purpose was revealed in the living word of the Bible and in the past record of human societies, not in the inanimate strata of rocks. They studied these sources for proof of their doctrinal convictions as painstakingly as an Anglican clergyman-geologist might have collected plants or fossil specimens.

In distancing themselves from the religion and culture of the eighteenth century, English-Canadian evangelicals exposed themselves to a dilemma. Both Common Sense philosophy and natural theology sought to interpret the divine will to the human mind, to preserve the link between Christianity and inquiry. By abandoning these to exalt a theology drawn exclusively from the Bible, they risked separating doctrine and intellect, and thus weakening their attempt to forge a Christian culture in British North America. Methodist and Presbyterian clergymen resolved this problem by linking their theological enterprise to the more recent and equally powerful early nineteenth-century concern for "the historical."

The study of history – the attempt to find a meaning for human activity in the present through knowledge of past civilizations – represented the meeting-place of conscience, mind, and the divine purpose. The crucial early years of both the evangelical creed and the colleges that sustained it were marked by the growing commitment of men of letters, clergymen, and social thinkers in the English-speaking world to the study of human history. For evangelicals, the writing of history presented itself as a useful discipline, defined by the Rev. James Narraway as "philosophy teaching by example," where the student's "mental powers" and "moral faculties" were "called into vigorous action."[40] History's significance as a field of study, however, extended far beyond the precincts of the college. In eighteenth-century England, political and religious arguments were conducted through rival interpretations of the past concerning questions of church government, theological orthodoxy, the claims of Protestantism and Catholicism to greater antiquity, and, most importantly, whether the biblical story of humanity embodied the true intellectual and cultural life.[41] By the mid-nineteenth century, the movement toward "the historical" contributed to the shaping of the new human sciences, anthropology, archaeology, and a popular, diffuse interest in the life of primitive peoples and ancient societies.[42]

The relationship between Protestant religion and nineteenth-century historical modes of expression in English Canada involved more than a chronological coincidence between the emergent ideals of the colonial evangelical colleges and the rise of those human sciences that drew upon the study of the past. The formative cultural process in Canada between 1820 and 1860 cannot be interpreted as the imposition of a more varied metropolitan culture on an intellectually impoverished and subservient colony. Nor could it have been as one-dimensional as historians of secularization suggest when they posit a discontinuity and opposition between historical science and Christian faith. The eminent English historian Owen Chadwick, so aware of the affinities between historical study and Christianity, saw the key to the relationship as the impinging of a dynamic force, the new awareness of "the historical," on a relatively static body of religious beliefs and traditions.[43] This analysis fails to account for societies such as English Canada, whose founding intellectual ex-

perience was not defined by the traditions of centuries of ecclesiastical organization, systematic theology, and precise statements of
doctrine. Intellectual life in English Canada was shaped by the evangelical Awakening, one of the most important movements for cultural change between 1780 and 1860.

Although evangelicalism was the dominant form of religious
expression in Canada, it was not a static, intellectual system, nor
did it depend on the authority of the religious establishments or
institutional hierarchies that were seriously troubled by revolutions
in Europe and America. The evangelical creed's affinity with early
Victorian historical thought was of prime importance in the shaping
of Canadian intellectual life. Like the study of history, the evangelical
movement was a force transforming the culture of the English-speaking world. Both challenged and undermined the authority of the
elaborate formal theological systems of Enlightenment Protestantism
and the institutional structures of philosophy and natural theology
that sustained them.

From different premises, evangelicalism and the early Victorian
study of history stressed activity, ethics, and human behaviour over
the quest for dogma – the statement of immutable precise categories
of belief and knowledge.[44] More completely than the older societies
of Britain and America, English Canada experienced the convergence
of the evangelical Awakening and the early nineteenth-century
awareness of "the historical." This marked a boundary between the
colony and its British and American parent societies, where evangelicalism was shaped by its encounter with the religious traditions
of the seventeenth and eighteenth centuries. In this encounter between evangelicalism and history an enduring synthesis of religion,
education, and culture was forged in the northern provinces.

Though its concerns were more narrowly theological, evangelicalism had some common ground with early Victorian historical
writing. In seeking the redemption of individuals and the Christianization of society, evangelicalism bred in its adherents an almost
exclusive preoccupation with human behaviour as the evidence of
faith. More significantly, higher education in British North America
owed little to Calvinist theology and lacked institutions devoted to
the defence and elaboration of the relationship between philosophy
and religion. Evangelicalism in English Canada, lacking the comforting landmarks of Common Sense philosophy and natural theology, required some other means of communicating the central
insights of Christian belief to the community.

The shaping of the evangelical creed required the expression of
its theological traditions in terms accessible to a society in which

history was becoming the pre-eminent human science. The Methodist and Presbyterian colleges did not treat theology as a store of hoary doctrines passively awaiting dilution and transformation by the challenge of the early Victorian study of history. Rather, historical writing and the study of the past were moulded by a vital and culturally central evangelical theology. Clergymen-professors thus not only drew intellectual sustenance from the new awareness of the human past, but helped to define the nature, scope, and method of historical study in their colleges.

Unlike natural science, which educated Christians suspected of subordinating the moral nature of man to impersonal, mechanistic physical laws, history dealt with the human world. In contrast to philosophy, history formulated its conclusions only on the basis of all available "facts," and avoided the speculative conclusions so abhorred in the classrooms of the evangelical colleges. The early Victorian study of history skirted the abyss of materialism and moral anarchy that evangelical clergymen increasingly associated with the unbridled pursuit of philosophic wisdom or scientific discovery. Even in its secular forms, it elevated humanity and human achievements, and insisted on the supremacy of the moral element in shaping individual and social behaviour.

For the evangelical promoters of a Christian education, the great advantage of historical study was its compatibility, in both method and outlook, with the reign of theology. Historians claimed for their discipline the status of a science, since it entailed the painstaking study of "facts" drawn from the records of past civilizations, and the formulation of principles and laws governing human behaviour. This empirical tendency of early Victorian historical writing accorded well with the Baconian approach to inquiry dominant in the evangelical colleges. The respect for "facts" and observable data and the belief that these should lead to the inductive formulation of firm principles to guide human conduct and behaviour provided a common context for both theological and historical endeavour in the British metropolis and in the colonial churches and societies.

Because it dealt with humanity, history was a moral discipline as well as scientific one. For the early Victorians historical "science" was a moral exercise rather than an ideal of scholarly research into the original sources of the human past. It was widely believed that the past provided a source of lessons for human conduct in the present and future, and thus history fulfilled a prophetic function in nineteenth-century culture. This use of history as a source of prophecy and prediction reached its zenith between 1830 and 1850. The eminent British historians Thomas Carlyle, Thomas Arnold,

James Anthony Froude, and Thomas Macaulay all used imagination and narrative power to draw political lessons from the records of past civilizations. Their ability to mediate the Victorian needs for both moral certainty and scientific discovery accorded them the status of prophets and placed them at very heart of Victorian culture.[45]

By uniting the moral and scientific on evidence drawn from the behaviour of individuals and societies, the study of history led educated Christians toward the restoration of the harmony between religion and inquiry that had been threatened by the Common Sense philosophy and the agnostic direction of the natural sciences. Among colonial evangelicals, history functioned as the crucial moral discipline, a key component of the Christian culture that their colleges promoted. The historical record could allow professors and students to discern with inductive certainty the principles governing human conduct. In his 1842 inaugural address to the faculty and students of Victoria College, Ryerson said that the study of history "ought also to be employed, to impress both the mind and the heart of the pupil with the conviction of the dignity and the duty of uniting personal industry and enterprise with genius and learning."[46] The study of history could only serve to remind preachers and students of the importance of character as the visible sign of Christian experience. Similarly, the Rev. Robert Burns told the theological class at Knox College that a great deal of valuable history might "be gathered from the practical study of your own characters, and from judicious observation on the characters of others." He defined history as "not merely a record of facts; it ought to be made a repository of principles."[47]

The insistence of Ryerson and Burns on the firm moral direction that could be found through the study of the past testified to the importance accorded to history in the colonial colleges – it had assumed the status of a moral philosophy. It precisely and empirically described the relationship between God and humanity, while avoiding the speculative, anti-theological assumptions of philosophy.[48] History offered the sanction of science as the basis of moral action to a culture committed to authority and certainty. Clergymen-professors believed that the records of the past would elucidate the moral and social ideals their colleges were designed to inculcate – the harmony between Scripturally-based Christian ethics, learning, and scientific discovery.

But before the convergence of evangelical Christianity and historical study could be achieved, Presbyterians and Methodists had to determine how the study of the past could be made to testify explicitly to the central tenets of their theology. Could nineteenth-

century historical scholarship be reconciled with the miraculous redemptive power of God and the vital doctrines of sin, salvation, and
judgment? The decisive issue was the question of prophecy, of how
the meaning of the present might be found in the record of the
human past. Macaulay and Carlyle, the celebrated historians of Victorian Britain, believed that narrative power, imagination, and empirical study of documents conferred special insight into the meaning
of the past. Here was the point of peril for Protestants. For the
faithful Christian to accept this would mean the denial of the connection between religion and the human mind. History would displace theology as the central category of inquiry, and act not as an
inductive science, but as speculative philosophy under another
name. This would perpetuate rather than resolve the intellectual
confusion occasioned by the weakening of Common Sense, and
Paleyite natural theology.

For the evangelical, the moral insight necessary to civilization
could not be found in the interaction of the unaided reason and the
historical record. It was provided by an external sanction, the action
of reverent faith in awakening the moral sense of believers. Belief
conferred the prophetic power required to link the records of the
past to the lives of individuals and societies in the present and future.
The tension between evangelicalism and the currents of historical
writing in the English-speaking world thus arose over the nature of
prophecy, an issue involving the status of history in relation to
theology and Christian education. Baconian induction and the early
Victorian commitment to understanding the human world provided
a common context of discussion between the evangelical creed and
the historical enterprise. But evangelicals who aspired to create a
culture structured on belief and theology could not admit that historical reasoning was able, independently, to define either the content or the meaning of Christian faith.

In the evangelical colleges, faith was legitimated by Scripture
alone. It was precisely at this point that clergymen-professors articulated what they considered the right relationship between theology
and history. Presbyterians and Methodists held as an article of their
creed that the Bible was, in the words of a prominent citizen of
Upper Canada, "a Divine Revelation," inspired in its language and
invested with the full authority of God.[49] They also believed, however, that Scripture also contained a history of the human race, and
that this biblical history, written under the authority of divine inspiration, was superior to all other histories, which were the merely
the product of unaided human reason or observation. The Bible's
special "sacred" strand of history illuminated the inner character and

meaning of all other histories.[50] This meaning of history, directly founded upon faith and traditions of theology, was validated by the miraculous intervention of God in human affairs attested to by the biblical narratives.

For Presbyterians and Methodists, the Bible provided the only reliable expression of the theology that underlay and informed human history and reason itself. Scripture contained a record of God's dealings with the human race. It revealed the reality of sin and human free will. More importantly, it manifested God's redemption in Christ as the crucial event in the history of the world. These were not simply moral truths. Both before and after the Reformation, Christian traditions held that the Old and New Testaments accurately described events that had actually taken place.[51] For evangelical Christians, theology and history were indissolubly linked. They held that the theological teachings of the Bible were true because they were also literally true as history.

The equation of theology and history in the study of the Bible resolved the intellectual problem of colonial evangelicalism by enabling clergymen-professors to assert the supremacy of theological knowledge over historical reason. To understand the biblical record was to understand the meaning of all human history. In contrast to their secular Victorian contemporaries who used reason and imagination to discern the moral principles underlying past, present, and future human experience, evangelicals were explicit in their belief that such canons of morality must be derived from the specific doctrines of Christianity expressed in the historical record of the Bible. As a part of college education, history must promote not only a moral code, but also the more vital theological foundations of individual and social existence. In contrast to the more varied intellectual world of Victorian Britain, where history had by 1840 claimed its independence from theology, the evangelical churches of early nineteenth-century Canada were marked by the identity of theology and historical study. But the history was constrained and tamed by the primacy of the Bible in college and congregation, and defined by the need for abiding criteria of religious certainty.

If belief established the bond between the biblical narratives, theology, and history, evangelical clergymen faced another source of perplexity. Though purporting to describe doctrines and realities valid for all times, places, and forms of human experience, the historical elements of Scripture referred only to a tiny portion of the human race, the nation of Israel. How could the theology of history be accepted as normative for individuals and societies whose historical experience was not referred to in the Old and New Testaments? The entire cultural and educational enterprise of evangelical Christianity as well as the moral and spiritual value of the Bible were threatened. Any challenge to the historical validity of the Bible would weaken its sanction of religious certainty to the mind and conscience.

The task of relating theology and history through the study and interpretation of the Bible marked the most sustained strand of religious thought and education in English Canada's evangelical church colleges. Both Britain and America had more elitist and scholarly traditions of systematic theology, philosophy, or natural theology dating from their synthesis of religion and knowledge in the seventeenth and eighteenth centuries. Evangelicals in the older English-speaking societies had to contend with the continued intellectual and institutional power of these theological traditions. The evangelical theology of history depended not on the mediation of science or philosophical wisdom, but on the direct contact between the Bible and the mind of the believer. Unlike philosophy or natural theology, it required no scholarly abilities or training in esoteric skills. Rather, it was based on the idea of the Bible as accessible and self-explanatory, through faith.

The theology of history was thus a popular, unsystematic, expansive set of beliefs uniting preacher and professor, college and congregation. It derived its power from the ease with which it could be preached. It expressed a religious outlook appropriate to the education and Christianization of a newly settled society with a nascent institutional life, and to churches that valued missionary endeavour and popular preaching over intellectual theologies. To colonial congregations, this concept of history, infused with an eternally valid theology, empowered their clergy to discern the destiny of their new country through the study of the past – a powerful source of cultural authority in an era of bewildering social and intellectual change.

THE PROBLEM OF BIBLICAL CRITICISM: THE LIMITS OF HISTORY

The unity of theology and history, the value of Scripture in understanding the past, present, and future – these central convictions bound Presbyterians and Methodists in the early years of their endeavours in British North America. They also linked colonial clergymen, colleges, and congregations to the culture of the evangelical Awakening in Britain and the United States, and to a body of religious thought extending backwards to the early Christian centuries. The ability of this theology of history to inform education and culture rested upon the inspiration of the Bible as a body of truth divinely revealed. Despite the affinities between evangelicalism and the early nineteenth-century study of the past, leading colonial clergymen like Ryerson and McCulloch lived within an international Protestant culture where the equation of theology and history could not be taken for granted. The Canadian colleges were founded at a time of intellectual and cultural change in the Atlantic world. The Awakening was only one element. Their theology of history was thus defined in relation to rival beliefs concerning the proper relationship between the Bible and historical knowledge.

Between 1820 and 1860 Protestant Christians faced, in the words of the great English historian Owen Chadwick, "the question whether historians, by probing the moments of time associated with religion, could affect its meaning."[52] Methodists and Presbyterians in the British North American colonies recognized, albeit reluctantly, the secularizing implications of the early nineteenth-century discovery of the past. The rising culture of evangelical Protestantism, itself in the process of definition, also felt the impact of modes of thought inspired by the German philosophers Kant and Hegel.[53] Under the general rubric of "idealism," these currents challenged the emerging evangelical approach. German idealism most directly influenced the English-speaking world under the guise of "historicism," a current of thought subversive of the theology of certainty taught in the evangelical colleges.

"Historicism" was best represented by the prominent biblical critics W.M.L. de Wette and David Friedrich Strauss, and by the historian Leopold von Ranke. Its stress on process and change in the world directly questioned the adherence of evangelical clergymen to the principles of fixity and universality implicit in the alliance of their creed and the Baconian outlook. Most troubling, the German scholars were deeply religious men, convinced of the presence of the divine spirit in the world, and yet they denied the normative value assigned by Christian tradition to the Bible and its doctrines. German critics and historians maintained more consistently than their English counterparts that although Scripture and human history manifested the divine spirit, these records should be interpreted through reason and intuition, not from the standpoint of faith or theology.[54] "Historicism" thus reversed the evangelical Christian subordination of reason to faith, and located the meaning of human history not in revelation or miracle, but in the historical process itself. German thought affirmed the power of the human mind, acting without reference to belief or tradition, to discern the mind of God.

German historicism and Christian tradition had some common ground. Both were prophetic, holding that individual historical phenomena conformed to a larger pattern of meaning. They disagreed over the fundamental question of where the power to interpret the value of the past was to be found. For the evangelical, this could only be provided by faith and doctrine; for the advocates of "historicism," it lay in the sphere of reason and intuition. Despite these differences, between 1820 and 1860 clergymen in Britain and America became familiar with elements of German philosophy. They seized upon the connection between history and prophecy in an attempt to reconcile German scholarship and Christian theology. The "Liberal Anglicans" Thomas Arnold and Julius Hare, and the American evangelicals Horace Bushnell and Henry B. Smith all stressed the gradual unfolding of revelation in its historical context. Though interpreting Scripture through the eye of faith, they had discarded the Baconian outlook which considered the Bible an immutable body of facts and doctrines. "Christian historicism" was an organic approach to the past that discerned a continuous process of revelation in general history, and dispensed with the idea of a "sacred" history specially recorded in the Bible. They regarded all history as sacred, and viewed it as a process corresponding to the stages of growth in the natural world.[55] God, humanity, and nature were thus united, all were part of a purposive, rational, unfolding spiritual world.

Idealism and historicism, with their emphasis on process and development, challenged the eighteenth-century modes of reasoning, Common Sense and natural theology. This opposition set the tone of international religious discussion between 1820 and 1860. But British North America, alone among the English-speaking Atlantic societies, did not experience this creative dialectic of historicism and traditional theologies. No Horace Bushnell or Thomas Arnold graced English-Canadian colleges in the early Victorian period, nor did the evangelical culture of English Canada produce a defender of the old intellectual world of the calibre of Charles Hodge. This was less a consequence of cultural impoverishment than the result of the evangelical Awakening, which preserved only tenuous links between the Methodist and Presbyterian churches and the older religious atmosphere of the Anglo-American Enlightenment.

In both Britain and America, German thought was introduced through two main conduits. Both societies already had well-established traditions of philosophical speculation and literary expression. The "romantic" movement in literature was represented by Samuel Taylor Coleridge in Britain and by Ralph Waldo Emerson in the

United States. It powerfully shaped religious discussion in both of the older societies in the 1830s and 1840s. Of greater importance was the existence of a tradition of historical writing independent of overt theological constraint. The major early Victorian historians, Arnold, Macaulay, Carlyle, Bancroft, and Parkman introduced to a wide audience certain tenets of organicism and historicism developed by Ranke and other German scholars. Though the Protestant Christian bias of these writers muted the secularizing impact of German thought, by 1850 important intellectual communities in Britain and America were considering philosophy, historical writing, and religious thought in a new light.[56] Defenders of the Common Sense tradition who believed in fixed and certain modes of belief responded promptly. Charles Hodge of Princeton developed an entire body of systematic thought intended to combat the inroads of "romanticism" in philosophy, history, and religion, and to reassert the cultural authority of Calvinism and Common Sense.[57]

English Canada in 1820 lacked the network of institutions and literary and scholarly communities needed to introduce and mediate the new currents of thought. Only the clergy, through their control over the fledgling colleges, could have done so, but their adherence to the evangelical creed precluded any flirtation with its German rival. The Rev. Thomas Jackson urged his theological students to "Avail of the help afforded by Critics and Commentators." Of these, he rated John Wesley's Notes written in 1751 as "best," followed by the Methodist apologists Dr Adam Clarke and Richard Watson. He warned them, however to "avoid the German critics – even the best."[58]

Canada's Methodist and Presbyterian leaders had abandoned all vestiges of eighteenth-century thought apart from a diffuse Baconianism that, unlike the formal doctrinal system of Charles Hodge, merely buttressed the biblical and anti-elitist biases of the evangelical creed. But, it might be claimed, this Baconianism placed them within a tradition of thought close to that of the defenders of the old Calvinism. Was not their outlook premised on a fixed, miraculous revelation from God? Did not their doctrine of sin and salvation establish a clear separation between the human and the divine, that could be bridged only through divine miracle, the act of faith, and the subordination of reason?

Despite these links to older theological traditions, the same opposing camps were not present in religious discussions in the English-Canadian evangelical colleges. Neither Ryerson nor his Presbyterian counterparts looked to formal creeds or theological systems to defend their beliefs. The Bible itself was sufficient. They felt no call to accommodate elements of German "historicism" into their creed, as did the British "Liberal Anglicans." As the repository of their theology, the Bible also contained the central elements of their historical vision. The identification of the theological and the historical in the evangelical colleges of British North America compelled clergymen-professors to reject the central assumptions of "historicism." Although their creed was anchored on the premise of action, ethics, and behaviour and stressed moral insight, they refused to subordinate the activity of God or their ideas concerning the individual and society to the rational and natural logic of the historical process.

Deprived of the intellectual supports of formal creeds, Common Sense philosophy, and the easy harmony of physical and moral laws implicit in natural theology, Canadian clergymen defended their theology by appealing to the historical reliability of Scripture. Rejecting the philosophical and natural explanations of religious certainty, they sought to prove the certainty of their creed on grounds chosen by the idealist historians and critics. The colonial encounter with German thought took place not in the realms of philosophy, literature, or historical writing, but in the study of the Bible. In a culture where Scripture provided the essential theological and moral foundations of civilization, there was only one possible response to the new views of the relationship between the Bible and human reason.

Colonial evangelicals observed with alarm that the aim of the new historical approach was to establish a tradition of biblical study fundamentally at variance with the evangelical creed, which held that the Bible was an indivisible unity as well as the veritable truth both theologically and historically. In the words of Henry Flesher Bland, a young immigrant Methodist preacher, scripture was "without seam – woven throughout of precisely the same materials." It could be compared to "the garment worn by the Saviour."[59] By 1820, when evangelicalism in British North America was in its infancy, German scholars were investigating questions of authorship and sources of the books, and unity of the text of the Bible without the constraints of traditional or doctrinal opinions.[60] Their research led to the fragmentation of the biblical books into strands of narrative, called into question the authorship of the Pentateuch by Moses, and even cast doubt on the reliability of the biblical writings as historical documents, which were said to have been written, in many cases, centuries after the events they described, as compilations of earlier sources.

The historical criticism of the Bible raised a series of problems for a culture bereft of the intellectual resources available to the older Atlantic societies. British and American evangelicals could draw on many years of reasoned debate between Calvinist and Arminian, and between advocates of the covenant of grace and advocates of the covenant of works, as well as on the traditions of Common Sense philosophy and the harmony of theology and scientific endeavour. But the harmony of religion and knowledge in English Canada depended on the maintenance of an unassailed theology of history. Thus the clergymen-professors' most important intellectual endeavour was to defend biblical preaching against the inroads of German historical thought.

In refuting the assumptions and methods of German historical criticism, colonial evangelicals drew upon a limited arsenal supplied by their Baconianism. They condemned, not the commitment of the German scholars to empirical research, but their links to the idealist philosophical tradition. Baconian induction applied to theology fostered a suspicion of the independent exercise of philosophical reason, and it was from this premise that Methodists and Presbyterians dismissed German criticism as "almost universally characterized by a spirit of lax speculation on the canon of scripture and its inspired authority."[61] Principal Willis of Knox College declared in 1857 that "philosophy would never make an enlightened critic." He specifically warned the incoming students against the "German theory of intuitional consciousness," which he defined as a "rash deduction" from partial or limited premises. Such procedures of biblical study could only prove disastrous to Christian faith for they could only supersede the canon of Scripture as the ultimate rule of reason and conscience.[62]

Willis's equation of German criticism with speculative philosophy served both as a warning and as a reinforcement of the Baconian cast of the evangelical creed. Thus evangelical educators hoped to fortify their theology of history against the inroads of "historicism." The inductive outlook enabled them to claim affinity with the culture of empirical research so vital to nineteenth-century science and the historical enterprise. The difficulty for clergymen-professors lay in separating historical research from the secularizing implications of historicism. This required the promotion of a method of biblical study compatible with human reason yet able to maintain the dominance of Christian belief and doctrine.

The Rev. Albert Carman, a minister of the Methodist Episcopal Church and professor of mathematics at Albert College in Belleville, defined the limits of human reason in biblical study. "Criticism," he preached, "has to do with authenticity, genuineness, interpolations, corruptions, translations, &c: not the facts and doctrines."[63] When he delivered this sermon, Carman stood at the threshold of a long career as preacher, professor, and general superintendent of the Methodist Church. This early statement accurately reflected the spirit and method of biblical study practiced in the Methodist and Presbyterian church colleges before 1860. It stressed the main concerns of the evangelical creed – the integrity and authority of the Bible, and the subordination of reason to revelation. It also underlined other fundamental assumptions of evangelical educators. Sound reason was based upon Bible study, and it was thus the duty of professors, students, and preachers to understand Scripture in order to relate its doctrines to mind and conscience.

In his opening address to the theological students at Pictou, McCulloch noted that some elements of Scripture were not easily understood. These he described as details of national or natural history, allusions, and prophetic hints. To properly comprehend these elements, he said, the Old and New Testaments should be read in their original languages.[64] In the interests of explaining the Bible to the wider congregation, evangelical leaders were prepared to accord a place in the college curriculum to what they termed "criticism."

But what was meant by emphasis upon this discipline? The statements of Methodist and Presbyterian leaders on the subject of biblical study before 1860 revealed a far more limited scope for critical and historical study than had been achieved in Germany and in certain circles in Britain and America. Professors in all the colonial colleges would have accepted Carman's limitation of the function of critical reason. "Facts and doctrines" lay in the province of faith. It was the role of reason to clarify and verify, not to question or alter the given data of the biblical text.

The practice of biblical "criticism" among colonial evangelicals was an attempt to bridge the growing gap between the nineteenth-century discovery of the past and time-honoured Protestant traditions of interpreting and explaining Scripture. Since the Reformation a form of "textual" criticism had been practiced in colleges and seminaries in both Britain and Europe. This method involved the study and comparison of all available ancient manuscripts of the Old and New Testaments in order to determine the original or "pure" text of the biblical writings. The main purpose was to assure accuracy, to eliminate errors that had supposedly crept into Scripture over the course of many centuries.[65]

Textual or "lower" criticism accorded well with the main emphases of the evangelical creed. It did not, like the German historical or "higher" criticism, question the inspiration or reliability of the biblical text. Rather, it placed the "facts and doctrines" in the realm of faith, removed from the challenge of human reason. This type of biblical study was thus eminently compatible with the Baconian matrix of evangelical learning. By encouraging preachers and students to patiently collect and compare the words and phrases of the biblical text, "lower" criticism implicitly directed the future leaders of the church away from speculation or theorizing on the subject of the authority of the Bible, which was always assumed as a central article of faith. Both Methodists and Presbyterians turned to the widely-used Bible commentary written by the English clergyman Thomas Hartwell Horne in the early 1820s, the four-volume *Introduction to the Critical Study and Knowledge of the Holy Scriptures*. Horne was prepared to allow the exercise of reason where necessary to amend the text to secure a plain reading. He assumed, as did his evangelical readers, the unity of the Bible narratives and their plenary inspiration. Unlike scholars influenced by German idealism, Horne constrained the exercise of historical reason by placing it firmly under the supervision of traditional doctrines concerning the Scriptures.[66]

If anything, clergymen in the colleges of British North America were even more disposed than their English mentor to limit the application of historical criticism in biblical study. To admit the competence of human reason to determine the historical reliability and the moral and theological value of the events and doctrines in the books of the Bible would impair the concept of a sacred history and the theology of history upon which their cultural enterprise rested. Among evangelicals, adherence to the inductive method subordinated critical study of Scripture not only to faith, but also to an ideal of education that belittled the importance of research.

The alliance of theology and Baconianism suited churches preoccupied with evangelization and the creation of institutions and social life in a new country. Clergymen-professors reminded their students Christianity should be applied through missionary work and preaching, not simply studied with detachment . They accented the practical rather than the scholarly aspects of a college education. Though central to the curriculum, Bible study was no exception to the pervasive demands of the evangelical creed. Biblical study and criticism in the colleges were treated not as ends in themselves, but as means to the awakening of faith. As McCulloch warned his students in 1820, mere critical erudition was not enough. The democratic theology of evangelicalism assumed the accessibility of the Bible to the ordinary reader, and the principal of Pictou would not countenance the idea of the clergy as a scholarly elite. He asserted that plain statements of biblical truth were often the most valuable for purposes of faith. The mark of the evangelical clergyman, he concluded, was not profound research, but eloquent preaching.[67]

A similar distinction between ends and means marked the approach to "criticism" at Knox College, where Principal Willis gave an address stating its educational concerns. Though intended to guide the church during an age of revival, it was destined to become the standard to be applied by evangelicals in defining the relationship between biblical study, human reason, and the act of preaching. He was not, Willis declared,

disposed to admit that a minute attention to exegetical theology, or the niceties of philological criticism, is more important than an enlarged and comprehensive acquaintance with divine truth in its great outlines, and internal relations and harmonies ... there is, we think, a danger of magnifying hermeneutical science to the depreciation of theological systems – of attaching far too much importance to the assaults of modern infidelity, or neology, and letting ourselves down from the tone of confidence with which we are entitled to speak of long-established truths; as if the whole of Christianity were yet a question, and the very safety of the citadel were compromised by some small affair of a various reading, or some conjectural emendation of occasional clauses.[68]

The principal's address clearly separated faith and criticism, which he reduced to the level of technique. A sound understanding of the Bible was not promoted by the mere act of criticism. Rather, he decreed, reverent faith and acceptance of the saving doctrines must inform and set the standard of criticism itself.

Thus evangelicals did not embrace the assumptions of German critics and Christian "historicists" in Britain and America in their practice of biblical study. Both these groups admitted a large sphere of activity for the historical reason in determining the value of the content of the Bible, and thus the nature of Christian faith itself. "Higher" criticism implied a new understanding of the Old and New Testaments. It raised the problem of the relative value of certain portions of the Bible, and of the nature of truth itself. Could a series of events that were not literally true express permanent truths of moral or doctrinal value? To admit the independence of history and critical reason, as did the Germans, would be to destroy the unity of evangelical culture by impairing the ability of preachers and people to arrive at a common understanding of the Bible on the basis of faith. "Historicism" threatened to remove the Bible from its status as the common property of all Christians, and make it accessible only to those scholars trained in the new historical disciplines, an elite accountable to no standard of faith or authority.

This problem became most acute in the 1840s with the publication in English of David Friedrich Strauss's *Life of Jesus*. Strauss denied the validity of the miraculous events in the Gospels, but applied a theory of "myth" derived from the Hegelian philosophy to argue that the stories surrounding Christ expressed the desires of the early Christian communities for continued contact with so impressive a personality.[69] Such views of the nature of truth were unacceptable to evangelical faith. A religion based on the principle of immutable certainty could not countenance such subjective views of religious truth. For evangelical educators in the colonies, there could be no half measures. Any impairment of the historical reliability of Scripture would shake the foundations of theological and moral certainty. As Henry Flesher Bland reminded his congregation, Christian belief could not be a half-way house. Only one possible attitude regarding the Bible existed for the evangelical Christian – it had to be accepted as "a Divine Revelation."[70]

While this attitude interposed a barrier between the mind of the believer and inquiries guided by the philosophical assumptions of Strauss and other German critics, a serious question remained. How could one determine whether or not Scripture was a revelation of the divine will and purpose? The survival of the evangelical creed depended on providing a convincing answer that would prevent faithful interpreters of the Bible from turning to the insights of historical reason, which accorded belief no superior or normative status.

McCulloch, Willis, and Ryerson suggested that the answer lay in the internal evidence of the text itself. Interpretation of the Bible was thus a function of the prior possession of Christian faith. Professors and students relied upon two eighteenth-century works, Butler's *The Analogy of Religion* and Paley's *The Evidences of Christianity*. According to Principal MacNab of Victoria College, Paley's text was in constant use in the classroom, and no student was permitted to graduate without having mastered its contents. The appearance of the Anglicans Paley and Butler in the curricula of the colonial colleges illustrated the ambiguous nature of the evangelical encounter with the eighteenth century. While distancing themselves from the implications of Common Sense and natural theology, evangelicals had fully assimilated the arguments of these Enlightenment Christians concerning biblical inspiration and authority.

The writings of these English clergymen were not designed, however, to solve the intellectual problems raised by the "historicist" outlook of the German biblical critics. Their works dated from an earlier period of religious controversy and responded to the English Deists' assault on miracles and the reliability of the biblical text. In answering these objections, Butler and Paley adopted a double line of defence. They pointed to the Old Testament prophecies and to their fulfillment in the words and actions of Christ as evidence of the internal consistency and integrity of the biblical text. Butler's *Analogy* provided, for professors, students, and preachers, an almost foolproof method of dealing with objections to the plenary inspiration and historical accuracy of Scripture. Butler proclaimed that although the Bible contained many diverse elements it was authentic and genuine history: "prophecy is nothing but the history of events before they come to pass; doctrines also are matter of fact; and precepts come under the same notion." Scripture, he said, gave an account of the world as "God's world," and this inspired quality distinguished it from all other books.[71] The questions that agitated biblical critics were, for Butler and his followers, simply irrelevant for "neither obscurity, nor seeming inaccuracy of style, nor various readings, nor early disputes about the authors of particular parts; nor any other things of the like kind could overthrow the authority of the Scripture."[72] But they also used a more rational argument, based on the reliability of the "testimony" of the biblical authors. By proving the "honesty" and good intentions of these "eyewitnesses," Butler and Paley believed that they had established the truth of miracles and thus the inspiration of Scripture.[73]

By 1860 this argument was widespread among colonial evangelicals. Professors, students, and preachers in a new land could summon the aid of the well-tested methods of the British eighteenth century to buttress traditional beliefs concerning biblical authority. More importantly, Paley and Butler lent their immense prestige to the alliance of the Baconian method, the theology of history, and the evangelical creed. The work of the Anglican divines had established, in advance, a rational method of assessing the truth of the Bible without resorting to the German alliance of historical research and a speculative philosophy hostile to the traditional doctrines. Having proved the reliability and internal consistency of the biblical record, evangelicals could maintain, without violating the harmony of faith and reason, that the Bible was a divine revelation. Further criticism of the text was unnecessary and, from the point of view of faith and theology, could only harm the religious certainty that sustained evangelical culture in the northern provinces.

Criticism of the Bible, like human reason itself, was barred from an independent function in matters of religion. Such a solution was prompted by both the evangelical belief in the superiority of faith and theology, and the intellectual difficulties of post-Enlightenment Protestantism. Living in an age dominated by historical study, evangelicals sought, like many of their early Victorian contemporaries, to use this discipline as a source of stability and authority. For colonial clergymen, the task was even more compelling. Far more was at stake than maxims of political behaviour or the moral character of nations. In an age of competing philosophical and scientific currents, their task was to locate and defend the permanent, immutable elements of Christian belief, which alone could provide intellectual and moral certainty.

Faced with the denial of permanence inherent in the German biblical criticism, Methodist and Presbyterian clergymen subordinated historical study to the literal, unerring inspiration and authority of the biblical text. In case of conflict between historical reason and Christian doctrine, McCulloch reminded his students, "Christianity demands absolute submission to the veracity of God in his word; and, respecting those particulars which he has not been pleased to explain, man must walk by faith ... Besides, man, by weakness of intellectual capacity, tendencies of constitution, and acquired prejudices, is destitute of that accuracy and enlargement of view, which constitutes the perfection of reason ... It becomes not reason, so defective in all ... to accommodate revelation to its own standard."[74] This outlook claimed the alliance of faith and reason but was in fact founded on a relationship of inequality. Any suggestion of greater independence in the application of criticism to the Bible carried with it the hints of rationalism or infidelity.

Historians of religion in both Britain and America have pointed to attempts made by Protestant Christians after 1830 to reaffirm the eighteenth-century structures of religious truth in the face of historical and scientific challenges to the Bible. The fruit of these endeavours was the construction of systematic theologies premised on the notion of biblical infallibility. At Princeton the great Presbyterian scholar Charles Hodge drew on the inheritance of Calvinist theology and the Common Sense philosophy to defend the literal truth of Scripture in its scientific, historical, and theological aspects. In Britain the millenarian clergymen John Nelson Darby and Edward Irving drew many adherents by adopting a similar view of theology. Such attempts, it is claimed, served as the intellectual forerunners of the Fundamentalist movement that greatly influenced American culture and religion after 1870.[75]

The pervasive character of the evangelical theology of history, and the Baconian educational ideal that sustained it, precluded Canadian participation in this transatlantic movement. McCulloch, Ryerson, and Willis also founded their views of truth on an uncompromising absolutism, and assumed the infallibility of Scripture in the realm of faith and morals.[76] They were, however, the products of a movement that, in the interests of the supremacy of theology, had detached Baconianism from the philosophy of Common Sense and the old Paleyite natural theology.

In the colleges of English Canada, Baconianism was not merely one element shaping religious thought, it was the *only* one considered compatible with the supremacy of biblical religion and the activist task of evangelization. The inductive method was not used or intended to give rise to an intellectual or scholarly culture devoted to the systematizing of truth. Rather, it anchored a theology of history regarded as popular and diffuse, and served as the tool of clergymen who considered themselves preachers and missionaries above all.

The belief in the concept of biblical inerrancy and in a biblical theology detached from systematic intellectual or institutional defences was characteristic of the colonial churches whose formative years were between 1820 and 1860. Canadian Methodists and Presbyterians moved uneasily between the world of the late Enlightenment and an early Victorian milieu whose intellectual life was defined by the application of historical reason to human experience. Circumstances forced the theology of the evangelical churches into a perpetual state of tension. Clergymen-professors had to affirm religious certainty as the basis of education and culture in a transatlantic world that had adopted the language of process, change, development, and transformation, concepts that fundamentally challenged the metaphors of order and stability implicit in Christian doctrine. With their allegiance to Christian traditions reaffirmed by the evangelical revival, Presbyterians and Methodists were unable to accept the claims of biblical criticism to reinterpret the historical and doctrinal content of Christianity. At the same time, their defence of certainty was based on the identification of theology with the historical reality of biblical events not with philosophy or discoveries in the natural sciences. Colonial clergymen-professors might fear the clash of their creed with the rising culture of historical study, but they were faced with the task of defining firm and abiding religious tenets in a recently settled society. Having abandoned the Common Sense equation of morality, nature, and religion characteristic of the eighteenth century, they could neither avoid the theological implications of history nor deny its explanatory power.

3 Prophecy, Protestantism, and the Millennium: The Preaching of History

In a Sunday sermon, the Rev. Henry Flesher Bland reminded his congregation that even in a new land, the past was an ever-present reality. He urged them to consider the great events and heroic acts that marked the history of Christianity, and referred them to the spiritual transformation of the Roman Empire by the Church, the bold resistance and reforming zeal of John Wycliffe and Oliver Cromwell, and the "leaven of evangelism" injected by the preaching of John Wesley in the eighteenth century. All these, Bland declared, presented a clear and unequivocal message to the Christian believer. God's hand was evident in all history, both national and individual. The facts of history could not fail to indicate the activity of an overruling Providence.[1]

Bland and his family had emigrated from Yorkshire to Canada in 1858, from the England of the industrial revolution to a society still in the process of intellectual and institutional consolidation. His outlook had been shaped by the vibrant metropolitan evangelical culture of political reform and self-improvement, which sought the advancement of the individual and society through the network of mechanics' institutes, temperance organizations, and lobbies such as the Anti-Corn Law League.[2] This confidence in moral reform and improvement found expression in his Canadian sermons. The frequent references to the heroes of English history made his congregation feel that, even in a distant colony, they were witnessing the triumph of political liberty and social progress, a movement he identified particularly with the expansion of the Anglo-Saxon peoples.

Bland's address indissolubly linked a self-conscious Anglo-Saxon superiority to the passion of the evangelical creed but, beyond the expression of the aggressively Protestant outlook of the small farmers, skilled tradesmen, and businessmen of British North America, Bland and other preachers firmly articulated a set of beliefs that sustained the cultural life of college and congregation in the Canadian colonies. These nineteenth century ideas of liberty, individualism, and progress were ultimately derived from an explicit view that human history was infused with the presence of a divine purpose, that the human world contained evidences of God's design.

More revealingly, Protestant clergymen also claimed that divine activity was no mere metaphor, it was conscious and miraculous. It was the role of ministers to identify particular instances of this providence, the coupling of divine purpose with specific events in the past. Between 1820 and 1860 Methodist and Presbyterian clergymen claimed to discern a single inner meaning and value in past events. The delicately balanced cultural authority of the evangelical churches rested on this foundation. This theology of history offered a vision of the past that sustained the doctrines and efforts of the evangelical churches in a world lacking the certainties of age-old traditions and the institutional comforts of philosophy.

Both college and pulpit were united in their insistence that in the drama of sin and salvation lay the meaning of biblical history. But the evangelical creed depended for its authority on the ability of professors and preachers to predict the future course of events, to link the occurrences of the past to a meaningful sequence of trends and portents. The bond between past, present, and future, they declared, was provided by the prophetic elements of Scripture. Did not the Bible, evangelicals asked, contain the mysterious Book of Daniel and the Revelations of Saint John? These oracles offered to the believer the power to foretell the exact fate of nations and empires, and their role in the divine plan. In the rising evangelical culture of the northern provinces, history was nothing less than the fulfillment of prophecy.

Such beliefs functioned below the level of a formal theology. Ryerson, Nelles, McCulloch and Willis, the pioneers of evangelical education, wrote no church history, nor did they formulate their ideas in a scholarly fashion.[3] Nonetheless, the sense of history in the Methodist and Presbyterian colleges emerged clearly from the sermons, articles, and college addresses that characterized the missionary spirit of the early Victorian age. It was a history that was meant to be preached in the church, not merely studied in the classroom. In the absence of philosophical theology or reliable evidence

of God's design in nature, the preaching of history, which emphasized the relationship of God and the human world, served as the
sole basis of religious and moral authority.

Both clergymen and congregations in the newly settled society
drew comfort and reassurance from the knowledge that both past
and future were in the hands of God. Methodist and Presbyterian
leaders were compelled to posit a continuity with the past, and to
identify traditions appropriate to the shaping of religion and culture
in British North America.[4] Even more important was the careful
search through the Bible and the chronicles of the Christian past for
indications of God's providence manifest in the human world. These
records, they believed, were comprehensible to the human mind
and witnessed the active moral energy of faithful Protestants.

REDEMPTION AND PROPHECY: THE ROLE OF THE CLERGYMAN-HISTORIAN

In 1850 Nelles, soon to become professor of moral philosophy at
Victoria College, stated that there was "no right study of history
except along the line of Redemption." He sharply criticized those
students of history who mistakenly undertook "to find order or end
in the march of time without reference to the great economy and its
destined consummation."[5] This firm declaration, as well as his warning against agnostic accounts of the human past, revealed a fundamental approach to intellectual life in the evangelical colleges and
congregations. The expression "right study" exalted the place of
history as the principal means by which theology, morality, and the
intellect were harmonized in the Methodist and Presbyterian colleges.

For the propagators of evangelical culture in the colonies, the
study of the past held more than ethical implications. They universally maintained that history had explicitly religious overtones. It
not only articulated the doctrine of salvation, the dominant element
of the evangelical creed, but implicitly subordinated knowledge of
the past to specific theological assumptions. For colonial evangelicals, unlike other communities of educated Victorians, history possessed a sacred character. This they preached as an article of faith
– the record of the past provided certain evidence of the workings
of providence. More importantly, as faithful Christians, they believed that God had actually entered history to redeem humanity
from sin.

Nelles's reflections, however, contained a disturbing note. His
reference to histories written without the illumination of doctrine

indicated the delicate balance of evangelicalism's intellectual endeavour. It served as both reminder and warning fact that in the 1840s and 1850s educated Christians were confronted with a variety of interpretations of human origins and the progress of human societies.[6] Many of these were actively agnostic in their rejection of the Bible as the basis of history and of Christianity as the central factor in the progress of civilization. More problematically for evangelicals, these historical works appropriated the language of science and reason to promote their claims. In an age devoted to the quest for certainty, a pursuit fully shared by Presbyterian and Methodist educators, Christian culture would not survive if clergymen-professors failed to offer a defence of the Christian vision of history to their students and congregations. Their theology of history must advance a more authoritative dynamic of human origins and the development of human societies than those of its competitors.

The vision of history expounded by Nelles and preached by so many Methodist and Presbyterian ministers was already deeply rooted in the popular traditions and scholarly discussion of Protestant Europe when it was transplanted in British North America during the evangelical Awakening. Nineteen centuries of theological discussion on the human past had contributed to the evangelical Christian outlook. The Bible, both as theology and as a certain record of past events, was central to this vision of history. The Bible, evangelicals believed, displayed God's providence actively exercised for human salvation. The doctrine of divine providence thus served as a philosophy of history, and performed several vital functions in the intellectual world of the evangelical clergy.

Appealing to both faith and intellect, this theology of history posited that the cause of all historical events lay outside the human world, in the will of God. By rejecting chance or contingency as a feature of historical reality, it enabled evangelical clergymen to assert that all events were meaningful. In churches founded on the central doctrines of sin and salvation, this interpretation of history maintained God's active role in history by denying the power of the human will except as an instrument of divine purpose. Finally and most importantly, it guaranteed that history had an overriding purpose and shape – the divine order displayed in the revealed words of Scripture was ultimately reflected in human affairs.[7]

The events of the Reformation had sharpened and revitalized this theology of history by linking it specifically to attempts to interpret the rise of Protestantism, and to the liberty and expansion of the English-speaking peoples in Britain and America. Strongly influenced by the Puritan writer John Foxe, whose widely-read *Book of*

Martyrs was published in the 1550s, clergymen in the sixteenth and seventeenth centuries married the Protestant cause to an intense British nationalism and sense of mission. Britain, they believed, was the custodian of the pure word of God, which had sustained the "saints" against sixteen centuries of assault by the papal "Antichrist." The divine mission of Britain and her people was to lead humanity to God's Kingdom by propagating the doctrines and extolling the benefits of the Protestant religion. In the words of the eminent historian Peter Gay this vision of the human past "gave God his glory, man his place, events their meaning – and England its due."[8]

Protestants saw history as a sacred study closely akin to preaching. Because it taught God's will and his redemptive purpose displayed in the lives of individuals and communities, it revealed the inner meaning of human life as much as did prayer and self-examination. The vocations of clergyman and historian were thus interchangeable in the transatlantic Protestant culture, a bond reinforced by the insistence on the importance of Scripture in the awakening of faith. The task of the historian, constant and didactic, was to assure believers that the divine design was evident not only in the rise and fall of nations, but also in the smallest events in the lives of ordinary people.

Although important in defining the popular culture and preaching of post-Reformation England, the Protestant vision of history as providence competed with versions of the past that assigned greater prominence to independent human will and action. From the early sixteenth century, England had nurtured a tradition of historical writing that ignored religion and theology, and treated secular affairs and human politics as independent of an active, conscious providence.[9] In Puritan New England, however, the Protestant theology of history became a virtual cultural paradigm, informing the historical accounts written by clergymen such as William Bradford, Cotton Mather, and Jonathan Edwards, as well as the sense of mission and social cohesion of an entire society striving to place itself intellectually in a newly settled continent.[10]

The unity of theology, history, and nationalism sustaining the cultural enterprise of Protestantism remained the common coin of popular discussion in both Britain and America until the mid-nineteenth century. But among educated men, it was seriously challenged after the mid-eighteenth century. Scepticism concerning the miracles of the Bible led to the questioning of providential interventions in human history, and threatened to disrupt the biblical certainty that sustained the old theology of history. At the same time, the Scottish political economists Adam Smith, Adam Fergusson, and

James Millar, and the French thinkers Turgot and Condorcet advanced accounts of human progress fundamentally at variance with the biblical narratives and notions of an active providence. Progress, they argued, depended on human intellect and social organization, effectively limiting providential design as the sole factor of causation in the human world.[11]

The years between 1750 and 1830 witnessed dramatic changes in the Western interpretation of the past. The Industrial Revolution and the consciousness of rapid change bred competing visions of origins and progress, many of which assigned prominence to human or secular causes, rather than to the will of God. Implicit in the new study of history in the intellectual and scientific communities of Britain, France, and Germany was the separation of theology from history. By the early nineteenth century historians in these older societies accorded a wide sphere to human action and decision. Those influenced by late eighteenth-century social theory argued that it was possible to discern precise natural laws governing human behaviour. In the view of the Protestant clergy, if the existence of these laws could be demonstrated the need for faith would be obviated, and worse, unbelievers would have the power to gain insight into the inner meaning of history.

The origins of the evangelical endeavour in British North America coincided with this transatlantic challenge to Christian thought. Although Ryerson, Nelles, and McCulloch preached the old vision of history with the same intensity as their Protestant predecessors, their fledgling society lacked the intellectual and social cohesion of Puritan New England. As the beneficiary of Victorian culture, English Canada even in the 1840s had traditions of historical writing that had discarded overt theological imperatives in favour of the study of human social and political activities. The stress of these works was on secular explanations of origins and progress, not on the divine will.[12] Even in the religious sphere, the evangelical vision of the past competed with a well-established and equally expansive Catholic rival. The existence and strength of these competitors imperilled the convergence of theology and history that sustained the Canadian evangelical churches.

The problem was exacerbated by the close relationship between evangelical religion and the surrounding culture of early Victorianism. Like their clerical contemporaries, the secular historians Carlyle, Macaulay, Parkman, and Bancroft shared the Baconian insistence on inductive certainty. Though their claim was questionable by twentieth-century standards, these writers believed that through the empirical study of original documents they could discern the moral and natural laws governing individuals and societies.

Colonial evangelicals could not agree even with this limited research ideal. [13] They were constrained by the outlook of their colleges, which subordinated all knowledge, including history, to the training of preachers. Symptomatic of the dominance of doctrine and theology in the intellectual world of Methodists and Presbyterians, this view dictated that the study of history must be guided by biblical faith if it were to provide the final answers concerning human behaviour or shed light upon the "ways of God to man." [14]

If evangelical clergymen could not match secular historians in founding their claims to authority on empirical research, how could they impress their historical vision on the emerging culture of English Canada? In stating their claim, Protestant clergymen did, however, have certain clear advantages over their rivals. First, given the importance of the Bible in their society, a majority of their contemporaries probably sympathized with their views of progress, order, and human destiny. Second, Methodist and Presbyterian ministers occupied a position between the worlds of "high" and "popular" culture. The Sunday sermon and church newspapers gave them an audience that might have been envied by the men of letters who had captured the imagination of educated Victorians. [15] Finally, Ryerson, Nelles, and McCulloch were not plagued by doubts. They were conscious of their participation in a revitalization and reassertion of Christianity, which was in the process of triumphing over the agnostic tendencies of the Enlightenment, and they were confident that their theology could subordinate and Christianize the historical enterprise.

The evangelical view of the proper relationship between theology and the writing of history was most fully articulated in the addresses and writings of the Rev. Robert Burns, professor of church history at Knox College, between his arrival in Canada in 1844 and his death in 1869. For more than a quarter of a century, this Presbyterian minister, who doubled as pastor of Knox Church, Toronto, set forth clear guidelines for young preachers on the nature, role, and limitations of historical study. He began the college session of 1848 by telling his class that history assumed a central place in Christian experience and thought because it provided the only sure record of the divinely ordained scheme of salvation. It was, he declared,

the history of God's arrangements with our world, for displaying his own glory, and securing the salvation of his people: the history of successive dispensations of grace in behalf of guilty man: the history of the doctrines, the worship, the institutions of the visible Church: the history of the effects of true religion on the literature, the arts, the civilization of the species: the history of the relations established betwixt truth and error for the mastery.

On such a history much precious instruction may be grafted, and the historian and herald of the Churches, may become also the minister of God for the salvation of his people.[16]

History, Burns maintained, was above all concerned with the problem of salvation. The study of the human past was thus broader than the academic horizons of the colleges. The belief that history fulfilled God's design elevated historical study to the level of prophecy.

The final sentence of Burns's address was crucial. He clearly regarded the historian, the preacher, and the prophet as synonymous roles, an equation that attempted to resolve the early Victorian tensions between the evangelical theology of history and the more secular history of British and American writers. The difference, Burns believed, lay in method rather than in outlook. The study of history informed by Christian doctrine was "a solemn and a spiritual exercise." Because it attempted to "follow out the agency of the Redeemer ... on the scale of the world's history," the Christian vision of history was superior to "the temperament of the mere civil historian." The latter was animated by "a low and dwarfish aim," namely, the gathering of facts and "the chronicling of them for curiosity."[17]

Burns implied that, because it was concerned with the most vital questions of human existence – redemption, immortality, and a future life – the theology of history taught in the evangelical colleges was superior to other versions of history. Secular historians might stake their claims to authority on research and imagination, but Burns summarily dismissed these as inferior to the insights provided by faith. Because they possessed this faith, only clergymen could legitimately don the mantle of "historian." This was no idle dispute over professional boundaries. In a new society lacking both evidence of an ancient past and firm traditions of philosophy or education, the power to interpret history was regarded as essential to the survival of civilization. Only the doctrine of redemption, evangelical clergymen affirmed, and not critical erudition,[18] provided the mental and moral bond needed to shape a Christian civilization. And such power could not be resigned to those who attempted to study human behaviour without firm and explicit faith.

Redemption and prophecy were the central pillars of the vision of history preached in the evangelical colleges. They were fundamental to the evangelical creed and, clergymen believed, to human understanding itself. Both the doctrine of salvation and the prophetic role of the clergyman-historian were universally accepted by Presbyterians and Methodists. They linked the churches ostensibly competing for cultural leadership in the formative decades of British North American society. The Rev. Samuel Nelles provides an example. Beginning as a local preacher in the late 1840s, Nelles had by the mid-1850s emerged as president of Victoria College and the chief exponent of the ideals of education in the Methodist church. While his language was less overtly theological than that of his Presbyterian counterpart, Robert Burns, he was equally devoted to articulating the central tenets of the theology of history in the evangelical colleges.

According to Nelles, the study of history involved far more than the recording of human annals and chronicles. History, he declared, must reach "out to infinity." By connecting "with a past eternity we cannot here discover" the student of history bore witness to order and the rule of law.[19] To a superficial observer, this resembled the belief, current among the eminent historians of early Victorian Britain and America, that the essential truths of man's past were spiritual and moral in nature. But Nelles worked within an older tradition that stressed the separate and superior nature of biblical history, and used history explicitly to promote and enlarge faith. The pattern of "order and law" that Nelles and other clergymen discerned in the historical record was thus firmly doctrinal in character, its intellectual and moral certainty confirmed by the evidence of the Bible, which disclosed the inner meaning of all events.[20]

Colonial clergymen-professors such as Samuel Nelles and Robert Burns, then, remained on the periphery of the historical "revolution" shaping the intellectual life of Victorian England. Their theology was cast in historical terms, and history even acted as the principal "moral" discipline in their college curricula, but this history was ruled by the canons of the evangelical creed. Although much of the British scholarly and intellectual community acknowledged an independent role for history, in the evangelical circles of the Canadian colonies different emphases prevailed – history remained dominated by the biblical categories of sin and salvation and by the educational imperative furnished by Baconianism. These restricted and constrained the intellect, and firmly barred historical study from independent critical scrutiny of the biblical text and from the application of the unaided reason to the records of the human past.

THE BIBLE AND UNIVERSAL HISTORY: THE STRUCTURE OF THE PAST

By advancing the idea of redemption as the key to all human history, clergymen-professors insisted on their vocation as historians. Their possession of a certain and infallible body of doctrinal truth, they argued, afforded them superior prophetic insight into the meaning of the past. In an age when history had emerged as the central organizing discipline in the transatlantic intellectual world, such claims bolstered the authority of evangelical theology and the aspirations of Presbyterian and Methodist clergymen to cultural leadership. However, their insistence that "theology of history" was fundamental to knowledge of the past raised their most serious intellectual difficulties – how to defend the superior accuracy of biblical history in the face of competing naturalistic explanations of the human past, and to affirm a convincing connection between the Bible and "ordinary" human history.

"Scripture history," preached Nelles in 1848, "is God teaching by Providence. Scripture history is an unfolding to some extent of the divine administration toward a part of the human race. And from a part we learn the whole."[21] This statement indicates two important assumptions underlying evangelical study and preaching. Nelles assumed that the history as recorded in the Bible was, because of its sacred origins in divine revelation, superior to all other forms of historical writing. Ryerson, Nelles's mentor, took a similar position in a series of addresses to the students of Victoria College. Sacred history, Ryerson declared, was accurate down to the smallest detail, and explained to the believer "what all profane historians were ignorant of." These elements were crucial to the understanding of human behaviour, and included "the origins of nations ... an account of the peopling of the earth after the deluge, as no other book in the world ever did give; and the truth of which all other books in the world, which contain anything on the subject, confirm."[22]

Although these prominent Methodists affirmed the separation of "sacred" and "profane" history, they clearly assumed the existence of a link between the biblical history and what they termed "universal history." For clergymen whose creed was premised on God's activity in the world, no final separation was possible. Although the Bible was more reliable and superior because of its divine origin, Presbyterians and Methodists maintained that the entry of Christ into history had widened the sphere of redemption, and united all humanity in a common salvation. But how to find a link that was comprehensible to human reason, one that buttressed the evangelical theology of miraculous providence against a growing body of evidence that cast doubt on the traditional biblical account of human origins and development?

The survival of the evangelical creed as an intellectually respectable and coherent body of beliefs underpinning the transatlantic culture of the English-speaking world depended upon the resolution of this difficulty. Clergymen-professors in British North America could point with confidence to the march of vital Christianity as proof of the legitimacy of the biblical account of human history. A recent account of early Victorian social thought has argued that the years between 1820 and 1860 were marked by a reassertion of biblical views of the origins of man and his place in the universe. According to this scheme, all humanity was presumed to be descended from the one original pair formed by the final act of creation, to whom God had revealed the one true religion and certain other fundamental institutions of civilization. Central to the biblical paradigm was the degeneration, rather than the progress, of non-Christian peoples, both past and present, and a sharp distinction between man and other animal forms. [23]

Though acceptable to many educated Christians, this vision was increasingly beleaguered in the 1840s and 1850s by a growing body of historical and archaeological evidence. Expeditions to Palestine and Egypt cast doubt on the Old Testament narratives relating to human origins and Hebrew history. The discovery of ancient civilizations with historical traditions clearly older than the biblical chronology of four millennia led the American sceptics George Gliddon and Josiah Nott to play gleefully on the inability of Christian believers to reconcile "sacred" and "secular" chronology. Worse, these social thinkers used this discrepancy to justify the theory of "polygenism," the belief that the human race was in fact several races. They contradicted the biblical account by positing the multiple origin of humanity, and based an entire pseudo-science of racial types and craniometry on the deficiencies of Christian chronology. [24]

The growing popularity of the idea of development and organic views of human society was even more damaging to the traditional theology of history. By 1840 historians and social inquirers in Britain were applying so-called uniformitarian ideas drawn from geology to posit the gradual evolution of human society through "social laws." Such notions cast doubt on the validity of the Book of Genesis and implicitly denied the miraculous intervention of God in the creation of man and the validity of the idea of redemption as the key to explaining human history. [25] Upholders of Christian tradition faced two equally unpalatable alternatives involving the delicate issue of the intellectual authority of the Bible.

Christian believers might, like the English "Liberal Anglican" scholars Thomas Arnold, Julius Hare, and Arthur Stanley, make concessions to the new historical outlook and its discoveries. Between 1830 and 1860, these clergymen developed a mixture of German "historicism," uniformitarianism, and a view that societies were also governed by moral and natural laws. They used these arguments against any appeals to the "sacred" character of the Bible in theological discussion. Scripture, they maintained, should be judged by the criteria applied to other ancient books. Thus the biblical record of events and the history of the Hebrew people might be ruled by the same laws that governed the development of other peoples. At the same time, Arnold and his followers preserved the link between the biblical history and "universal history." No longer was it a matter of simply contrasting "sacred" and "profane." They argued that while the Israelites might possess special insights into the workings of providence, the entire historical process had a sacred character. Indeed, all nations had participated in a "divine education."[26] Though this might appear to be a restatement of the old idea of redemption, it had largely discarded traditional notions of miraculous and transcendent intervention. God's design was evident in history, but it was immanent, operative through social and moral laws evident not merely in the Bible, but in the records of all human societies.

For evangelicals, such a solution, while preserving the connection between the Bible and universal history, emptied their theology of history of its explicitly Christian content. To admit the free exercise of historical reason in the study of the biblical text would seriously impair the quest for intellectual and moral certainty, which alone could anchor a Christian civilization. But a withdrawal from the attempt to harmonize the biblical record with secular histories and chronologies would be to concede the cultural bankruptcy of Protestant Christianity, to admit that the doctrines and ethics of Scripture had no application to human societies either past or present and that the evangelical mission in a new land was without justification or foundation.

The years between 1840 and 1860, marked by the triumph of the historical outlook, the futility of Paleyite natural theology, and the decline of Common Sense philosophy, confronted educated Christians with the prospect of a divorce between religion and intellect. In the British North American colonies, evangelicals had created a structure of education premised on the connection between theology and history, a link that afforded both moral and empirical or scientific certainty to Christian doctrine. When clergymen-professors affirmed the existence of a connection between biblical and universal history, they testified to the role of theology as a central category of intellectual endeavour.

In a lecture to the Fredericton Athenaeum in 1857, the Rev. John Brooke, a New Brunswick Presbyterian, declared that "Secular and

Sacred History are like two rivers that run parallel, and that may thus sometimes even meet in the same channel; or, at least, some portion of the stream may occasionally pass reciprocally from one to the other."[27] In suggesting the influence of the sacred upon the secular, colonial clergymen such as Brooke faced the most nagging problem in their attempts to relate religion and intellect. They were compelled to posit some method of historical study that appealed to human reason and yet safeguarded the doctrinal and historical integrity of the Bible from the critical scrutiny of history as practiced by secular advocates or by Christians who attempted to reconcile doctrine and the new scholarship. The Baconian outlook that sustained the evangelical creed and the insistence on the absolute inerrancy of the Bible at a theological and historical level barred evangelical clergymen-professors from the "Liberal Anglican" solution. Divine revelation was unique, miraculous, and unchanging. The Bible could not be interpreted as the record of a process in which God and humanity were linked through the development of Christianity from lower to higher forms of religious understanding and experience.

It was at this point, the meeting-place of biblical and universal history, that the evangelical theology of history was strained to breaking-point. Here, the traditional theology of history encountered the new historical and archaeological insights that bade revision and reconstruction of the central canons of Christian faith. Having refused to accommodate the idea of development into their theology, clergymen were compelled to constrain the new knowledge within the bounds of older traditions that attempted to connect the Bible and human history.

For the evangelical, a legitimate concept of history had to be founded on the superiority of the Bible as an inerrant record of past events, both to remove the Bible from the improper exercise of reason, and to affirm that the same principles applied to sacred and universal history. The belief that sin and salvation were characteristic of all times, places, and cultures was fundamental to the evangelical creed. God's grace, clergymen-professors reminded their students, was operative not only in the Bible, but throughout the rest of human history. Having established that God's activity dominated all facets of human history, evangelicals then asserted a corollary. United by divine grace, the Bible and universal history also exhibited a common periodization or structure of time. This division they termed a "dispensation."

Speaking to the students of Victoria College in one of his Sunday lectures on biblical topics, Ryerson preached the unity and harmony of the divine purpose. He described history as a single grand system of grace, and divided it into Patriarchal, Levitical, and Christian dispensations. From Knox College, his Presbyterian counterpart, Robert Burns proclaimed a similar message. *"The close relationships,"* he reminded his class, "which connect the *four dispensations* of God to men and the *Christian* are too remarkable to have been the result of human ingenuity."[28] Though individuals might differ over the number of dispensations, Methodists and Presbyterians maintained that although each of these periods differed from the preceding one, all were characterized by the same principles: the conflict between sin and salvation, the persecution of the true church by the enemies of the faith, and the decline and revival of religion.

The organization of history into dispensations accorded well with the central tenets of the theology of history taught in the colonial colleges. Because each period flowed from God, this scheme of history preserved the vital belief in divine transcendence. Furthermore, it provided evangelicals with an explanation for the degeneration and decay of human societies in all ages: sin and defection from the true faith. This view suggested that the evangelical theology of history had cyclical implications. A Nova Scotian Presbyterian noted in 1849 that the whole history of the church displayed "a succession of ebbings and flowings, of declinings and revivings, of barrenness and fruitfulness."[29] In the years after 1870 certain British and American Protestant groups seized upon this cyclical pattern to evolve an entire theology of "dispensationalism." Extrapolating from this interpretation of the Bible and the catastrophic theories of premillennialism, they posited the inevitable decline of both church and civilization.[30]

Canadian Methodists and Presbyterians, however, did not draw pessimistic or catastrophic implications from the dispensational vision. Each dispensation, they believed, was more inclusive and universal than the one before. God's first promise, they maintained, was made to the original human pair, and the workings of grace had progressively extended that promise. Redemption would ultimately triumph over sin. By the nineteenth century, evangelicals could confidently look forward to the Christianization and salvation of the entire world. In his lectures on biblical topics, Robert Burns stressed the "gradual manner" in which the divine providence had unfolded.[31] By 1860, evangelicals such as Burns and Ryerson saw no final separation between sacred and universal history. The end of what they termed the "Christian" dispensation would see the final absorption of the secular by the sacred, and the establishment of Christ's rule over all humankind.

PROPHECY, CHRONOLOGY, AND THE
"REVOLUTION IN HUMAN TIME": THE
CRISIS OF THE 1850S

The evangelical enterprise sought the triumph of the sacred over the secular. Its religious, intellectual, and educational imperatives were premised on the act of preaching. While the dispensational structure of time provided a basic framework for understanding the connection between the biblical and universal histories, clergymen-professors constantly sought more explicit and empirical links between the two records. The preacher's ability to convince his congregation of the authority of Christian doctrine and biblical ethics depended on his ability to interpret the seeming chaos of the present in the light of the immutable, certain account of events contained in Scripture. Barred from the independent exercise of reason in theological matters by the inductive outlook and by the subordination of research to preaching, Methodist and Presbyterian clergymen in both college and church relied on the assertion of faith and the inherited "prophetic" traditions of religious discussion in their attempt to impose the order of doctrine on the flux of human time.

In answer to the "Liberal Anglicans" and the German critics, who reduced the Bible history to dependence on secular laws of change, evangelical educators promoted other methods of harmonizing sacred and secular chronologies. One of these appealed to the old popular tradition of figural or literal interpretation of Scripture, which established a link through time of Old Testament "type" or prophecy and New Testament "antitype" or fulfillment. [32] In addition to being deeply rooted in the art of preaching and the minds of Christian believers, figural interpretation confirmed the evangelical sense of history as prophecy, and reinforced the superiority of the Bible as the key to historical knowledge and interpretation.

The figural method was very much alive in the church colleges of English Canada between 1820 and 1860. Thomas Horne's widely used textbook of Scriptural commentary devoted an entire section to figural prophecy. Among Canadian Methodists who stressed the democratic nature of their theology, this old prophetic method assumed particular importance in the subordination of history to theology. God's revelation in Christ, which evangelicals identified as the central event in the world's history, furnished the key for the figural interpretation. As one Methodist author stated, "The process of recovery is made to go on from the first." The completion of the revelation in Christ, he declared, could be read both backwards and forwards: through faith in the divine promises, the power of redemption rendered "temporarily effectual that whose primary significance and design were to foreshadow and prepare the way for Him who should come."[33]

The dialectic of figure and fulfillment constituted, however, a source of grave difficulty for Methodist educators. The logic of figural prophecy maintained that the Old Testament "type" was a distinct and complete entity, and not a "germ" destined to "develop" into its New Testament "antitype." Any link between the two was established by an act of faith rather than by historical insight or critical skill. In a culture that increasingly demanded for its beliefs the sanction of prophecy founded on the certainty of empirical research, a theology of history anchored on this popular but hardly scholarly basis might appear tenuous.

The attempt to apply the notion of figure to universal history could, on occasion, lead evangelicals into uncertainty and confusion. Speaking in 1842 Ryerson stressed the inerrant nature of biblical revelation, and insisted that Scripture contained reliable historical documents, universally valid and unchanging at the level of both theology and history. His address concluded with the firm statement that "the doctrine of human redemption was preached and believed from Adam downwards." At the same time Ryerson assured the students of Victoria College that the religious knowledge of the Old Testament patriarchs was the same as that of nineteenth-century Protestants.[34] This denial of religious development accorded with the inherited theology of history, but could only confuse educated Christians who were aware of the new trends in early Victorian historical scholarship.

A few years later Nelles, one of the students who had heard Ryerson's lecture, risked a question that implicitly revealed the contradictions of his mentor's prophetic method, raising an issue that was potentially devastating for the evangelical linkage of faith and reason. He questioned the ability of the preacher to link past and present through the idea of redemption in a manner acceptable to human reason:

Did the Old Testament saints believe in Christ? Did they have an idea of justification by faith? Some will think strange of such a question, but there is a difficulty in this region. In Dr. Chalmers' Pastoral Address on the "Duty of diligence in the Christian life", I find it asserted that "the doctrine of justification by the righteousness of Christ" had not yet been revealed to the disciples of John. And in the same discourse it seems to be intimated that in the Old Test. saints were all in the same condition. How is this? Abraham had faith – but what was its kind?[35]

Such queries indicated the nagging problems afflicting evangelicals by the late 1840s. If the biblical text were infallible as history, it contained illogical elements difficult to reconcile with the exercise of reason. But to admit a larger role for critical reason in biblical and historical study would deny the primacy of faith, and would draw Christian students towards the abyss of theological and moral chaos.

These difficulties were symptoms of a shift in religious attitudes as historical study became the central mode of understanding in the 1840s. Though reluctant to abandon the rich popular strand of figural prophecy, Nelles was far less confident than Ryerson in its intellectual strength. His self-conscious questioning marked the dawn of a new mood in colonial evangelical circles. Nelles realized that the old theology of history was fraught with difficulties – most importantly, it could not address the intellectual needs of educated Christians in the changing culture of transatlantic Protestantism. Their faith required that, in addition to traditional doctrines, Christianity seek some moral and scientific support from the new historical disciplines. Only thus could theology face the challenge provided by ideas of natural and social development.

In contrast to the Methodists Ryerson and Nelles, Presbyterian clergymen possessed a longer tradition of academic biblical study. Their college ideal urged the training of ministers in the technique of "expository preaching," which combined textual commentary and analysis with a belief in an inerrant Scripture. Such studies were ably promoted at Knox College in the 1850s by the Rev. George Paxton Young, a student of Chalmers. Young arrived in Canada in 1849, accepting a call to the pulpit of Knox Church, Hamilton. Impressed by his intellectual abilities, his Free Church colleagues appointed him professor of logic, mental and moral philosophy, and the evidences of christianity at Knox College in 1853. Young's first book was a collection of sermons entitled *Miscellaneous Discourses and Expositions of Scripture*, published in 1854. It contained superb examples of "expository preaching," the statement of firm belief in the infalliblity of the word of God, and clear warnings of the awful facts of death and judgment, doctrines supported by examples drawn from the Bible and human history. [36]

Such preaching placed importance on the minister's ability to relate historical events to the central doctrines of Christianity. Because colonial Presbyterianism was dominated by the inductive Baconian ideal, it encouraged direct attempts to harmonize the "sacred" and "secular" chronologies at the level of individual events and to reduce through the exercise of reason the inconsistencies and conflicts between the two records. This method was at once more precise and more difficult than the typology practised at Victoria College. Since the seventeenth century this had been an all-consuming activity among many educated Christians. Respected clergymen such as the American Puritans Cotton Mather and Jonathan Edwards had attempted to decipher biblical accounts and to relate them to events in the secular world.[37] Although the technique differed from the Methodist reliance on figural interpretation, the scope and intent were similar: to prophetically discern the course of the drama of salvation and to interpret God's will to the congregation.

The harmonization of "sacred" and "secular" chronologies, the Rev. John Brooke declared, afforded "additional proof" to a number of positions central to evangelical theology, particularly "the credibility of Revelation" in an international religious climate increasingly hostile to the literalism and absolutism taught in the evangelical colleges. Deriving their arguments from the works of Butler and Paley, Presbyterian clergymen stressed that "the fulfillment of prophetic declarations" confirmed the inspired and infallible nature of the Bible.[38] In attempting to determine the relationship between history and prophecy, clergymen-historians required a minute, empirical acquaintance with both biblical and universal chronology. Founded on Butler's statement that "prophecy is nothing but the history of events before they come to pass,"[39] the study of chronology appeared to offer to the evangelical theology of history the certain sanction of both faith and reason.

By the time of Young's arrival at Knox College the attempt to reconcile supernatural and secular time through the study of chronology had encountered serious difficulties. At the heart of the problem was the reliability of the Old Testament events as the "key" to understanding the origins and histories of other ancient peoples. A growing body of scientific evidence, founded on the uniformitarian principles enunciated by Lyell, greatly extended the age of the earth and cast doubt on the story of creation in the Book of Genesis.[40] Although not directly subversive of the evangelical theology of history, these developments coincided with the introduction of a series of new researches in history and archaeology to scholarly and popular audiences in Britain and America.

On one level, evangelical clergymen could rest content in the belief that this was merely another infidel assault on the Bible. After all, did not the names of the American sceptics, Gliddon and Nott, feature prominently in the debate surrounding human origins? Had not the Christian concept of time and history successfully asserted itself against this shallow speculation? Beneath this outward show of confidence, however, lay the realization that these developments in the study of human culture held more serious implications. They challenged the Christian claim that the origins and destiny of man could be explained through theological evidence and the biblical framework.

Educated Protestants would have observed from a cursory reading of the periodical literature of the 1850s that the new study of man was not simply a plaything of agnostics or enemies of Christianity. Figures as respected as Baron Christian Bunsen, the pious German scholar and diplomat, were central to the changing views of the place of ancient peoples in universal history. Bunsen's main contribution, *Egypt's Place in Universal History*, published in 1853, argued for the existence of an original human race in China. He dated the beginnings of this race at about 20,000 B.C., well before the widely-accepted biblical date of 4004 B.C. Furthermore, Bunsen's researches implicitly downgraded the importance of the Hebrew people in the development of human religion for, he contended, Egypt was the principal bridge between the original human race and later ages.[41]

Though obscure and irrelevant to modern students of the Bible, Bunsen's efforts were part of a wider movement of intellectual change in the 1850s. He and his younger disciple Max Muller, a student of comparative philology, studied ancient chronology in an attempt to cope with the "revolution in human time," the realization that human societies were of greater antiquity than had been traditionally believed.[42] This movement had been launched by the impact of uniformitarian geology on the natural sciences in the 1830s. Given the close relation between religion, geology, and the emerging "human sciences," it was not surprising that the logic of scientific law was increasingly applied to the study of human societies. British scholars and social thinkers such as Sir Henry Maine drew from this the corollary that the progress of diverse cultures could be discerned not by the dialectic of sin and salvation or by the interposition of divine miracle, but by natural and social laws of development accessible to human reason, and operative in Christian and non-Christian societies alike.

Such attitudes toward the study of ancient peoples marked a significant shift in the intellectual framework of Victorian scholarship. In many respects the 1850s were transitional, marked by both the persistence of older concepts of time and the advance of social progress advocated by men such as Bunsen, Muller, and William Whewell, the prestigious clergyman-scientist who was master of Trinity College, Cambridge. These thinkers belonged to the last generation that attempted to harmonize and balance the biblical data of theology with the evidence of science. Despite their respect for the Christian account of human origins, they played an unintentional yet significant role in separating the study of human culture from the constraints of theological tradition. By the late 1850s the discipline of "anthropology" was taking shape in the writings of social thinkers such as Maine and Herbert Spencer.[43] This new science did not refer to Old Testament categories or to the dynamic of supernatural providence. Its radically different explanation of human behaviour was founded on the search for natural "laws" of cultural and social change.

Against this background clergymen-professors in the colonial Presbyterian colleges pursued their traditional task of harmonizing sacred and secular chronologies. Their long-standing commitment to the elaboration of doctrine founded upon empirical accuracy made them more vulnerable than their Methodist colleagues to the separation of the human sciences from the guidance and discipline of theology. By calling into question the inductive certainty of events that sustained the evangelical theology of history, the new anthropology and social thought threatened the factual basis of "expository preaching," the medium of communication between college and congregation and, in their estimation, the foundation of knowledge itself.

Not surprisingly Canadian Presbyterians were alarmed by the newspaper reports of expeditions to distant biblical lands and the reviews of the latest literature on universal history. They eagerly seized on any fresh evidence that seemed to confirm the truth of the biblical chronology and traditional concepts of time. Their basic assumption concerning the problem of human origins was stated by the Rev. Robert Burns of Knox College in a lecture to his students: only the Bible "proposes to give the genuine history of the origin of the human race." He contrasted the biblical account with "the fictions of profane writers," and stressed that "nothing in historic annals has yet appeared that is conclusively at variance" with Scripture.[44]

Despite this note of confidence, clergymen such as Burns sensed the vulnerability of their attempts to relate biblical and human time. Holding to an outlook that stressed the harmony of the biblical record with historical evidence, they refused to separate the two in the interests of preserving intact a body of theological truth. They hoped that these scientific discoveries could be wrested from the infidels and turned to the fortification of Christian doctrine and preaching. Canadian Presbyterians were greatly interested in the archaeological researches of the British traveller, Austen Henry Layard, at Nineveh, the ancient capital of Assyria. These were widely reported in Canadian religious journals and were promptly enlisted as external evidence of the truth of Scripture.[45]

"Among the more modern sources of evidence confirmatory of the historic facts narrated in the Bible," crowed the editor of the Halifax *Presbyterian Witness* in 1854, "are those subterranean discoveries which have recently been made." This prominent clergyman believed that archaeology reinforced not only the doctrinal bonds of Scripture, but also its claims to be considered accurate and reliable "chronological and historical data."[46] Though confidently proclaimed, this statement betrayed a fundamental misconception of the new "human sciences." Evangelicals espoused Baconianism, which placed great importance on the truth of individual "facts." Thus they considered the new evidence brought to bear by anthropology, archaeology, and biblical criticism to be the most serious challenge to their faith. In arguing for a continued harmony between theology and science, clergymen-professors often failed to understand that the perspective and method brought to bear upon the past by these new disciplines were no longer conditioned by theological criteria.

The Babylonian discoveries held the threat of a divorce between theology and history in the name of empirical research, and the subordination of the inspired record of the Bible by secular dynamics of time and social change. For evangelical clergymen this was the crux of the problem: how to relate a presumably static body of truth to a culture thinking in terms of progress from lower to higher forms of intellectual experience and social organization, and turning to secular reasons to explain these changes? If clergymen-professors were to promote their creed as the central body of unifying beliefs in Canadian culture, they needed a convincing answer to this question.

THE PROTESTANT DISPENSATION: THE PRINCIPLES OF HISTORY

Clergymen-professors were compelled to refute the claims of early Victorian social thinkers to discern rational or natural "laws" of change and development in human culture. In this debate, evangelical preachers were not completely bereft of weapons. They believed that the tradition of prophetic analysis in their theology of history was more reliable than reason or criticism in the study of the Bible and the human past. The belief in the superiority of the Bible as history and the related "dispensational" structure of time provided Methodists and Presbyterians with a ready set of principles or patterns that would allow the Christian believer to predict the future course of events. As the church historian Burns declared, the study of history testified to the existence of constant elements governing individuals and nations in all ages: "a common faith; a system of truths in which the great mass of Christian professors have concurred ... the particular scheme of Revelation or the peculiar doctrines of Christianity" writ large in human history.[47]

In the evangelical colleges the study of history was explicitly ruled by Christian doctrine and biblical concepts of time premised on the active guidance of providence. Professors such as Burns viewed universal history as a battleground where sin and salvation, truth and error warred for mastery. Their lectures were neither objective nor impartial. Evangelicals were certain both of the meaning of truth and salvation and of the source of error and sin. Methodist and Presbyterian ministers read into past, present, and future the doctrines of Protestantism, and equated these with liberty and progress. "Protestant" history was closely tied to those notions of Anglo-Saxon superiority and mission widespread in Britain and North America. Evangelical spokesmen distilled a heady theology of religion, history, and rabid nationalism for their congregations.

If colonial evangelicals identified "Protestant" doctrines and values with providence and salvation, they were equally specific in attributing the source and persistence of evil and sin in human societies to the Roman Church and its papalism, ritual, and cult of the saints, elements implacably opposed to the "true" or biblical faith preached in the evangelical churches. Methodists and Presbyterians frequently used terms like "Antichrist" or "Man of Sin" interchangeably with "Rome," a term the evangelical creed considered synonymous with ignorance, decadence, and corruption. In their equation of Romanism and sin, clergymen-professors could draw upon a rich body of popular tradition dating back to the Reformation. Works like Foxe's *Book of Martyrs* luridly detailed the threat of Roman Catholicism to civil and religious liberty and dwelt lovingly on the sufferings of Protestant martyrs as the defenders of true religion.[48]

Beneath this monotonous and often repellent catalogue of the persecution of the "true" faith by the Roman agents of "Antichrist" lay a crucial question for evangelical Protestants on both sides of the Atlantic. Methodists and Presbyterians posited a cyclical structure of time in which each dispensation was characterized by similar conflicts between sin and salvation. But such a view of past and future could lead ordinary Christians to inertia and despair, to a belief that the cosmic struggle would go on eternally without resolution or progress. Thus the attempt to prove the superiority of Protestantism involved impressing upon students and congregations that with the Reformation, the universal struggle between truth and error had been resolved. Evangelicals constantly reminded their congregations that Romanism was at long last in decline, and that the long cycle of persecution had finally ended. They believed that the last centuries of the Christian dispensation would witness the resolution of the cyclical pattern of warfare into a linear and final unfolding of the true faith.

In the evangelical colleges "Protestant" history and its corollary, anti-Catholicism, served far more than a rhetorical function. By providing the reassurance of ultimate success, they offered a guarantee that history was in the final analysis predictable and amenable to human effort. This dynamic enabled the evangelical creed to resist the inroads of the secular and natural explanations competing for the allegiance of educated Christians. It was crucial in shaping the harmony of faith and knowledge encompassed by the dominant theology of history. The enlistment of history in the struggle with Rome also bound colonial evangelicals in the northern provinces to a long British and American Protestant tradition of historical discussion and speculation seeking a providential mission and destiny for their churches and societies by identifying their nations as guardians of the "true faith." Since the seventeenth century, New England Puritan spokesmen such as Cotton Mather, William Bradford, and Jonathan Edwards, in their providential vision of history, had identified the rising fortunes of the Protestant cause with the success of their own social experiment.[49]

Between 1820 and 1860 the evangelical colleges were particularly anxious to embrace these traditions of historical thought. These years of definition for evangelicalism in English Canada coincided with a more acute phase of hostility between Protestantism and Roman Catholicism. In England the 1851 crisis over "Papal Aggression" raised fears for the survival of the constitution, fears exacerbated in both popular and educated circles by the earlier defection of John Henry Newman and a number of highly placed Anglican clerics to Rome. Papal power was regarded as an expansive and inexorable force directed to the subversion of the liberty, religion, and national character of the Anglo-Saxon peoples.[50] Methodists and Presbyterians in British North America regarded their own situation as far more tenuous. They believed that Romanism in North America was also on the move. The rise of ultramontanism in French Canada, the large body of Catholic adherents in the colonies, and the demand by the Catholic hierarchy for publicly supported separate schools[51] posed a pressing problem greater than that faced by the Puritan clergy in seventeenth-century New England. The character and destiny of the evangelicals' emerging institutions and society were at stake.

The study of history was all-important to the outcome of the battle with Rome. Protestant ministers employed both biblical and universal history to reassure their congregations as to the final outcome of the struggle. Lessons from the past were used to exhort Protestant effort and vigilance. These reaffirmed the culturally vital bond between Protestantism, AngloSaxon nationalism, and what clergymen saw as liberty and progress. Writing in 1858 an anonymous Methodist touched on all these themes. Protestantism and Popery were, he stated, "antagonist systems," precluding all compromise. The first tended to the "elevation" and "honour" of individual and nation, while Romanism led inevitably to "degradation and ruin."[52]

The identification of Protestantism with liberty and progress and Romanism with sin and decay was drawn directly from a reading of history. It was prevalent among even "secular" historians in both Britain and America in the early nineteenth century. The historians James Anthony Froude and Francis Parkman both used a "Protestant" dynamic to explain the rise and progress of their nations.[53] But for Protestant clergymen the appeal to the historical record was a double-edged sword. While they could find plenty of evidence to justify their views of Roman sin, cruelty, and oppression, they were aware that both the Bible and church history seemed to attribute a greater antiquity to the Roman claims of an apostolic succession of bishops as the basis of the "true" church. Again, the history that evangelical clergymen ransacked for proof might in the end imperil the link between their theology and the institutions and ideals of an emergent colony.

Clergymen-professors thus embarked on a forceful and consistent campaign to appropriate the past and to ensure that it testified explicitly to Protestant doctrines of authority and church government. First, Roman Catholicism was linked to heresy and paganism. According to the Rev. Andrew King of Presbyterian College in Halifax, a crucial function of historical study was to illuminate "the origins and progress of defections from the truth." King and his colleagues tirelessly repeated that such errors could be traced to a single source: the pretensions of the Roman Church to exclusive supremacy, based on fraudulent claims of an apostolic succession of bishops.[54]

Both Methodist and Presbyterian professors taught from texts more noted for their firmness in promoting Protestant doctrine than for their claims to an impartial rendering of the past – German scholar

Johann Lorenz von Mosheim's *Ecclesiastical History*, for example, first published in 1755. Burns based his entire course of lectures in church history on this venerable standard. Following Mosheim's outline closely, Burns went far beyond the refutation of Roman claims to apostolic succession to an implicit denial of the Christian lineage of the Roman Church. In a lecture on "Popery" delivered to his theological class, Burns argued that the rise and progress of this system of error could be traced to "the introduction at an early period of the strange errors and practices connected with what has been termed the 'oriental philosophy.' That philosophy was blended with many parts of the systems of the Greek schools and with much of the Jewish 'cabbala'; and issued in the monstrous system known by the name of 'Gnosticism'; a system which laid the foundations of nearly all the errors which have troubled the Church of God down to the present day."[55] Burns thus reminded the students of two lessons central to their careers in the church. First, there could be no possible grounds of accommodation between the "true" faith of Protestantism and the "paganism" of Catholicism. Second, evangelical faith required a consistent engagement with human history. The preacher must act as a guardian of the past, to ensure that history testified to the doctrines of Protestantism. Only in this way could Christian ministers offer an authoritative message to their congregations and shape the destiny of their emerging community.

The equation of paganism and Roman Catholicism in the evangelical church colleges represented far more than the scoring of debating points against an aggressive rival. The claims of Protestant clergymen-professors demanded the appropriation and reshaping of the evidence of history for an English-speaking culture that revered the authority of the past. Ironically, this respect actually worked to the detriment of Protestant claims to superiority. Unless evangelical clergymen could prove that their churches were of greater antiquity than Roman Catholicism, they risked losing a powerful sanction for their theology. But how to demonstrate convincingly that they, and not their Roman adversaries, were faithful to the forms and spirit of the ancient church?

This problem had confronted Protestant ministers since the time of the Reformation. In resisting the division of Western Christendom, Catholic priests and historians characterized the Protestants as recent innovators who had forsaken the traditions handed down from Christ himself.[56] Nineteenth-century Protestants countered this logic with the dispensational organization of biblical and universal history then prevalent in their church colleges. With its cyclical structure and emphasis on decline and recovery, dispensationalism allowed for breaks in the continuity of Christianity, and permitted Protestants to assert their adherence to the faith and practice of the apostolic age.

In one of the first Presbyterian theological works written in Canada, McCulloch set forth an outline of the past that was to dominate the study of history in the evangelical church colleges for over a century. McCulloch's own religious thought was firmly rooted in the popular piety of Scotland, a Presbyterianism replete with nationalistic references to Reformation martyrs and the Covenanters of the seventeenth century. He did not hesitate to ascribe the doctrines and outlook of these Protestant champions to the apostles and church fathers. From his research, McCulloch concluded that Protestantism was of greater antiquity than Romanism. Its origins, he maintained, could be traced to the Old Testament itself, to "the exhibition of the first promise of mercy." Such investigations clearly had but one purpose, to prove that the evangelical faith was the true church, the only one sanctioned by the word of God.[57]

The principal aim of history, as taught in the evangelical colleges, was to reclaim the heritage of the apostolic age for "Protestant" doctrines and forms of worship. Confident of the purity of their origins, clergymen-professors constructed their scheme of universal history around the pattern of religious revival and decline posited by the dispensational ideal. This view was powerfully stated in the Methodist *Christian Guardian*, in a reprinted article by the theologian Richard Watson on the origin of the Methodist Church. This eminent English clergyman declared that "The Church of the times of Titus and Timothy, a time immediately succeeding the death of the Scriptural writers was conformed in faith and practice to the Scripture, but in succeeding ages, that conformity was lost."[58]

Prominent evangelicals such as McCulloch pointed specifically to the rise of "Anti-Christ" or the power of the papacy as the central cause of this decline. They held that from the second century of the Christian era to the sixteenth-century Reformation the church was an institution in decay. But despite persecution the "true faith" of the apostles was kept alive by men such as Wycliffe, Hus, and the Waldenses, to revive once again through the efforts of Luther, Calvin, and the English Puritans.[59]

The Protestant pattern of history was best summarized by the Methodist *Christian Guardian* in 1856. "Every reformation is a restoration, and every restoration has the Divine sanction," declared the writer, articulating the dominant assumption in the teaching of biblical and universal history in the evangelical colleges.[60] Clergymen believed that in all ages human history was controlled by an active providence, with the fate of individuals and nations explained by the ongoing dialectic of sin and salvation. This view firmly linked Methodists and Presbyterians to the traditions of historical thought rooted in the Protestant churches of Britain, the United States, and Western Europe, giving them an all-important sense of origins.

The "Protestant" history taught in the colleges did more than cement the bond between colony and metropolis. Through the medium of historical study, the Old Testament and apostolic past legitimated the doctrines and church polity of the evangelical churches, which had rejected both hierarchical concepts of authority and traditional approaches to theological discussion. The belief that the church of the apostles was a "pure" church enabled colonial clergymen to refute the charges of their Roman adversaries that the Reformation heritage had abandoned tradition and continuity in the name of innovation.

The dispensational structure of history was even more important to the cultural life of the evangelical churches. Although McCulloch the professor and Bland the preacher both described their past as a cyclical rhythm of revival and decline of religion, they did not pessimistically conclude that this process was deterministic or eternal. They believed that the Reformation had accomplished something crucial to the historical process. By returning to the "purity" of the apostolic past, the Protestant reformers had moved universal history to a higher plane in the story of salvation. Heroic individuals such as Wycliffe, Luther, Calvin, Knox, and Oliver Cromwell had freed the "true church" from papal power, and had linked Protestant Christianity to the rising Anglo-Saxon empires of Britain and America.

By the early nineteenth century Protestant ministers confidently reminded their congregations that they had inherited the mantle of these heroes. Methodists and Presbyterians living in an age of religious revival believed that their own era had produced individuals of the calibre of Wesley and Chalmers, worthy successors of the Protestant reformers, Christian apostles, and Old Testament prophets. Appeals to this legacy served as a claim that history itself bound Protestantism, nationalism, and liberty and endowed their fledgling colonial society with a divine mission in the scheme of salvation. This heady mixture of optimism, expectation, and religion imposed upon the past liberated evangelicals from any fear that the cycle of rise and decay would repeat itself. The Protestant vision of history resolved the cyclical pattern of time into an upward spiral, a process by which all individuals and nations would eventually experience the working of God's redemption in history.

THE EVANGELICAL MILLENNIUM: TOWARD
A THEOLOGY OF PROGRESS?

The view of history taught in the evangelical colleges was never precisely codified by its chief exponents, McCulloch, Ryerson, Burns, and Nelles. But it was based nonetheless on a remarkably consistent and coherent body of assumptions, governed by the idea that the central determining "facts" in the life of individuals and in the unfolding of universal history were founded on the biblical theology of divine activity, human sinfulness, and redemption in Christ. But beyond legitimating the present through the study of the past, the preaching of history was used to bolster the clergy's claim to authority through prophecy, the ability to discern the shape of future events and the destiny of their emergent society.

Despite their view that history was governed by a cosmic struggle between good and evil, evangelicals firmly believed in the eventual triumph of God's design over sin. Furthermore, they maintained that the struggle would be resolved in earthly time, not in a heavenly realm removed from history. Between 1820 and 1860 they looked with confidence to the future. Their vision of the past suggested a spiral unfolding of universal history, and they believed the union of the sacred and the secular, the moral and the scientific appeared on the verge of consummation in their own culture in this era characterized by religious revivals, social and intellectual improvement, and a rising tide of discovery in science and technology.

College professors reminded their students that these phenomena were interconnected and testified to the activity of God in the lives of individuals and societies. However, the course of these events could be accurately predicted because the Bible, the inerrant key to both sacred and secular history, had hinted at their unfolding. They believed that the specifically prophetic Book of Daniel and the Revelation of Saint John provided a literal description of the end of history: the return and final victory of Christ and his saints over sin and the transformation of the human world into the Kingdom of God.

The reciprocal influence of evangelical religion and British North American culture was marked by a powerful conjunction of prophecy and history. In this respect, the colonial clergy reflected the expectations and speculations concerning the future that were rife in the churches of both Britain and North America. These beliefs have been grouped by historians under the term "millennialism," a body of assumptions identified as the crucial religious and intellectual foundation of the interaction between church and society. Scholars have credited millennial aspirations with an influence extending beyond the realm of theology. The stirring of the impulse for reform among Christian clergymen and believers, the peculiar sense of messianic nationalism that emerged in pre-Civil War American society, and the articulation of the republican political tradition itself have been traced to the concepts of time and history preached in the Protestant churches during the evangelical Awakening.[61]

Although the intersection of millennial beliefs and the wider culture reached its zenith in the world of transatlantic Protestantism between 1800 and 1860, theologies of the future had existed within the churches from the early Middle Ages. Christian believers had inherited Old Testament traditions of apocalypse – prophetic hints and predictions concerning the time of the end. Prior to the seventeenth century, these traditions were associated with the dispossessed in mediaeval and early modern European society. In times of social tension many ordinary Christians held that the return of Christ was imminent. Outbursts of popular piety and even violent unrest directed at the church hierarchy and the privileged classes were premised on the belief that on Christ's return the earthly order would be swept away in a fiery catastrophe, an earthly kingdom would be established that would endure for a thousand years, and the faithful would be rewarded for their perseverance.[62]

Such cataclysmic views of the end of the world persisted until well into the nineteenth century in the Protestant culture of Britain and North America. The British followers of the prophetess Joanna Southcott and the disciples of the American visionary William Miller preached fantastic visions of Christ's imminent return and the subsequent establishment of the millennial kingdom. Such beliefs classified these groups as "premillennialist" or "millenarian." Clergymen in the organized churches would certainly have observed that both Millerites and Southcottians rejected the authority and the ability of a trained clergy to interpret the prophecies of the Bible. Worse, their excesses threatened the fragile balance of piety and learning fostered by the evangelical churches. Their dissent struck at the principal buttress of preaching and education in the Presbyterian and Methodist churches. In a wider sense, the fervour and spiritual excesses of the millenarian sects challenged the inherent notions of order and education in early Victorian culture.[63]

It was not enough for professors and preachers to dismiss as idle fulminations the catastrophic shape of the future disclosed by the revival sects. Premillennial beliefs were not restricted to elements on the fringe of the institutional churches. Many respected Protestants within the evangelical churches held similarly pessimistic views. It might be argued that the dispensational structure of time taught in the evangelical colleges carried with it implications of cataclysm and catastrophe, which some Christians considered the inevitable judgment on human sin and defection from the ways of God.[64]

More directly subversive of the efforts of McCulloch, Ryerson, and Nelles, the pessimism of the premillenialists imperilled the vision of the evangelical commonwealth, by implicitly despairing of the power of human institutions to accomplish the divine will. Premillennial speculation could lead to inactivity. It was easy to conclude that if Christ's return and the destruction of all churches and societies were imminent, there was no point in working for conversion and salvation. Premillennialism negated the missionary impulse vital to the evangelical creed.

Worse, the premillennial position directly subverted the Baconian ideal that dominated the evangelical mind. Premillennialists' concept of time was founded on the same links between prophecy and history taught in the church colleges. Their warnings of a cataclysmic millennium employed the same literal interpretation of the Bible and the same linkage of past and future, sacred and secular. The pages of Methodist and Presbyterian journals were replete with denunciations of the mistakes made by sectarian visionaries in interpreting biblical prophecies. According to the editor of *The Presbyterian Witness*, "Nothing has tended more to create a distaste to the study of prophecy than the fanciful and arbitrary manner in which it has been frequently handled." In response to the premillennial challenge clergymen urged upon their congregations the evangelical ideal: the application of sober caution and sound judgment in the interpretation of Scripture.[65]

But it was not enough for clergymen to simply identify the errors of their opponents. Their claim to authority rested on their ability to offer a convincing alternative vision of the future to their congregations, one compatible with their own optimistic theology of history. In a sermon entitled "The Millennium" preached in 1864 the Rev. Henry Bland directed his Methodist audience to the Bible in discerning the shape of the future. While agreeing with his opponents that the millennium was an earthly kingdom realized in time, he rejected the notion that it meant the coming of Christ. Rather, he declared, it would be achieved gradually as the *"full development of the kingdom of grace in its present form."*[66]

Bland's idea of gradual growth signalled the transition from pessimism to optimism in millennial thought. The advent of the kingdom of God would involve no fiery cataclysm or destruction of earthly society. Of greater consequence for the evangelical view of time and history was the recession of the miraculous implied in Bland's sermon. Although the millennium was equated with the kingdom of God, it would not be achieved by direct divine intervention, but by providence working through human agencies and institutions. Leaders such as Nelles and his Presbyterian counterpart the Rev. William Snodgrass, who served as principal of Queen's University from 1864 to 1877, believed that the evangelical efforts to convert the world would hasten the advent of the millennial kingdom. Their optimistic vision of a blissful future contained a powerful injunction to "preach on, and pray on, and labour on" to embed the vital union of religion, character, and morality more firmly in both individual and society.[67]

This outlook reflected a significant shift in Protestant thought that began after 1750. Millennial expectation ceased to be simply a characteristic of fringe elements within Western Christendom. Impressed by the political, social, and religious liberty and stability of Britain and her American colonies, respected clergymen-scholars removed the cataclysmic, fantastic, and catastrophic speculations from the millennial legacy, and replaced them with a hopeful vision. Jonathan Edwards and other leading clergymen drew from a wide range of research in biblical and secular chronology, to convince their readers and congregations that the millennium did not lie in a preposterous dreamland, and would not involve the overturning of property or social relations. The establishment of God's kingdom, they maintained, would be gradual rather than cataclysmic. It would require no miraculous intervention, but would issue from the religious revivals and the extension of political liberty already at work in human society.[68]

Like its premillennial counterpart, the postmillennial vision that dominated the Methodist and Presbyterian churches rested on the expectation that the world was experiencing its "last days." Henry Bland and his colleagues assured their congregations that this prospect should be welcomed not feared. The end of history would mean not destruction but progress to a higher civilization characterized by the subordination of political authority to spiritual ends, the overthrow of "false systems of religion," the unity of the Christian churches, and "universal peace and temporal prosperity."[69] Because postmillennialism also drew upon the common evangelical belief in the literal fulfillment of prophecy, such men as the Presbyterian Rev. Alexander Forrester searched out the connections between biblical history and contemporary events as eagerly as those who foretold the end of the world in a fiery cataclysm. Upon the outbreak of the Crimean War in 1854 he assured his congregation that "it is the decided opinion of the great body of the interpreters of prophecy that we are living near the close of the last of the four empires which Daniel saw in vision, before the kingdom on earth was given to Messiah and the saints of the Most High."[70]

Despite their denominational differences, Bland and Forrester were united in their conviction, based on a mixture of theology and politics, that the events of the nineteenth century were ushering in a new age, the millennial dawn itself. The streams of biblical and secular history tenuously connected by a theology of history founded on prophecy were at last converging through the alliance of divine providence and the actions of individuals and nations. By the early nineteenth century this postmillennial outlook reflected the Methodists' and Presbyterians' belief in the ultimate harmony of Protestant religion and the emerging culture of science and discovery. For Bland, Snodgrass, Nelles, and McCulloch, the convergence of religious revival, scientific and social progress, and the rising power of the Anglo-Saxon nations of Britain and America was no mere coincidence, but a sign that the final union of sacred and secular in the perfect evangelical commonwealth was about to be realized. The millennium represented the triumph of the evangelical creed, the redemption of both individual and society.

Millennial optimism, the visible symbol of the marriage of evangelical doctrine to messianic nationalism, characterized the spirit of an address delivered by Nelles to Hamilton merchants in 1851. Taking as his theme the celebration of the Great Exhibition in London's Crystal Palace, he confidently asserted the superiority of Anglo-Saxon civilization. "The highest and best Civilization," he proclaimed, "will be found in Christendom – will be found in that part of Christendom which is Christian to the fullest extent and in the most proper sense – will be found in Great Britain and Great America." The achievements of these empires in culture, literature, science, and industry, he believed, stemmed from one critical factor: the Bible, the foundation of Protestant Christianity.[71]

Religious revival, moral and social improvement, scientific discovery, and the identity of Protestant Christianity and nationalism defined the millennial vision, the capstone of the theology of history taught and preached by evangelicals in British North America. This utopian optimism could be equated with the philosophies of progress formulated by British and European historians and social thinkers since the 1780s. Canadian preachers and clergymen-professors saw the steady advance of Protestant religion and the Anglo-Saxon nations since the time of the Reformation as inevitable. But did this emphasis on human effort imply a removal of divine providence from conscious activity in the historical process, and an emphasis on human intellect or natural forces as the motive power governing the developments of human societies?

Like many of their early Victorian contemporaries, evangelicals welcomed and revered the evidence of improvement in their own society. Their millennial theology consecrated and elevated these events as presaging the emerging kingdom of God. But their belief in the Bible as the key to understanding the past, present, and future excluded them from the search for social "laws" that characterized the work of Victorian historians, political economists, social thinkers, and even Christian reconcilers like the "Liberal Anglicans." The vital issue was the activity of providence in human affairs.

In an editorial in *The Christian Guardian*, Ryerson denounced the rising secular theories of progress as "directly at variance with the faith of any believer in the Divine Origin of the Christian Religion." Progress, he contended, could not be explained through rational or mechanical "laws." The primary and most effective cause of advance in human society was the power of religion.[72] Sermons, lectures, and articles by Methodist and Presbyterian clergymen reminded congregations that the progress that characterized the English-speaking nations, depended on the power of external supernatural forces acting on the course of history. They claimed that this was the only interpretation sanctioned by the inerrant authority of Scripture. Biblical history taught them that progress was neither indefinite nor automatic. The dynamic element was the divine will, not intellectual or material factors.[73]

The biblical paradigm governing the evangelical clergy's view of history also imposed a more sobering consideration on any attempt to identify progress as automatic or inevitable. The Bible asserted that sin was still present in human individuals and societies, and pointed to the fate awaiting nations that strayed from the path of grace. Burns, for example, assumed the inevitable degeneration of all non-Christian societies. He reminded his theological class that the law of progress functioned only insofar as a nation followed the laws of Christ. Not only the Bible, but also archaeological discoveries, he believed, confirmed that civilization would decay into barbarism and savagery through sin: "The Nineveh marbles confirm and illustrate most strikingly the Bible account of man's gradual degeneracy. There is abundant evidence in those sculptures to prove that the older forms of worship were comparatively pure. The earliest false religion [is] the worship of heavenly bodies. Star-worship rapidly degenerated into nature-worship ... the N. Sculptures illustrate the progress downward."[74] Here was an urgent admonition to college and congregation. Despite the wonders of the age of improvement, professors and preachers maintained, human life was still governed by the theological realities of sin and salvation. Only through conformity to the divine law would the millennial spiral continue, and history fulfill prophecy.

For Burns and his contemporaries fear of degeneration was the counterpoint to millennial optimism, serving as a reassertion of pessimism but as a warning to a culture devoted to secular and scientific pursuits that the value of these depended on the spiritual power of both individuals and nations. Though theological considerations governed their view of the historical process, colonial clergymen were not atypical early Victorians. Like the great narrative historians of the early nineteenth century, they used their authority to assert the primacy of the moral and the spiritual in the human realm.[75] They hoped that immutable theological and moral principles could anchor society against unrest and decay.

On this particular point the evangelical creed faced another serious challenge. Its theology of history was dynamic and optimistic. Its intellectual structure depended on the maintenance of an impregnable doctrine of the Bible as the source of fixed and eternal truths beyond the grasp of human reason. The attempt to ground the millennial vision of a dynamic society on a static principle of biblical authority was contradictory, and in the late 1850s it was subjected to a series of assaults. If evangelical Christianity aspired to retain its cultural primacy in British North America, it must accommodate, or offer an intellectually respectable alternative to the new concepts of time and history.

4 The Evolutionary Encounter: "Every Thought is to be Brought into Captivity to the Obedience of Christ"[1]

"The doctrine of Evolution," the Rev. S.H. Janes wrote in 1877, "when kept within certain bounds is quite consistent with a belief in an intelligent First Cause; and we think it is one of the ways in which God has proceeded in the preparation of the earth for man."[2] After nearly two decades of heated debate among evangelicals on both sides of the Atlantic concerning the implications of evolution for Christian thought, Janes, a Methodist, found it possible to reconcile the concept of evolution with the fundamental tenets of the evangelical creed: the activity of God in the world, and the rule of divine providence over the actions of both individual and society. Nor was he alone. From his pulpit at Queen's University, Canadian Presbyterianism's most formidable intellectual figure, George Monro Grant, insisted that "Christ's Kingdom is subject to the law of growth or to what is in the language of today the law of development or evolution."[3]

Historians commonly assert that the publication of Charles Darwin's *The Origin of Species* in 1859 marked the great disjuncture in the intellectual life of the nineteenth-century churches. Darwinism, it is claimed, shattered the system of beliefs termed "Christian orthodoxy" and precipitated religion into an inexorable, irreversible decline. "Darwinism" not only displaced the churches from their dominant position in the intellectual life of English Canada, but caused a debilitating internal disarray, dividing the churches into warring theological camps. "Conservatives" opposed any accommodation to the tenets of evolution, while those variously termed "liberals" or "modernists" sought to resolve the crisis of faith by abandoning theology for philosophical idealism or the practical concerns of social science and reform.[4]

But did those Protestant clergymen who experienced the encounter between evolutionary modes of thought and Christian beliefs between 1860 and 1890 see the process as one of decline and loss? If the concerns articulated by Janes, Grant, and others are taken into account, the clash of Darwinian science and Christian belief appears more ambiguous. Their idea of evolution "kept within bounds" and applied to the doctrines of Christianity suggests that many evangelical Christians regarded the meeting of their creed with the tenets of evolution positively, not as a threat to their theology, but as an opportunity to enrich and extend their thinking and widen the influence of their churches. It could be argued that these clergymen were simply misguided in teaching and preaching the affinities between Christian theology and modern thought, unaware of the inexorable secularizing imperative underlying evolutionary science.[5] But Nelles, the president of Victoria College, clearly recognized the disturbing implications of Darwinism. It was not, he declared, "more evolutionary than revolutionary, and all modern thinkers must adjust their teaching to this marvellous hypothesis." Nelles told his students that because Darwin's concepts pervaded so many facets of life, "we must breathe it, more or less, either as a new principle of life or a newly engendered poison." Despite the difficulties scientific discovery represented for believers, Nelles struck a positive note, refusing to despair or to abandon the idea of a world ruled by the divine will.[6]

This optimistic resolution of the problem of evolution was not unusual in the Victorian evangelical churches. Even clergymen whom the twentieth century might cast as "conservative" or "orthodox" spoke with considerable ambiguity on the issue. The Rev. Albert Carman, general superintendent of the Methodist Church after 1884, has been called an uncompromising advocate of biblical literalism, an old-style revivalism, and the pre-1860 doctrines of evangelicalism, and yet he used evolutionary metaphors and assumptions freely. Carman's university lectures exhorted students to study "*life*, and *growth*, the proof of life," and the progression from "the *lowest* to the *highest* organism" as the key to understanding human behaviour and society. Thus, for many Protestant clergymen, acceptance of evolutionary theories did not mean the surrender of the central doctrines of the faith: an inspired Bible, miracles, and a divine providence active in human culture and history.[7]

That so many shades of opinion within Canada's Presbyterian and Methodist churches found Darwinism a troubling but by no means devastating problem for their evangelical creed suggests that the relationship between the evangelical creed and intellectual life between 1860 and 1890 should be recast. The experience of the Victorian churches in English Canada vividly illustrates what historian James Moore has termed "the Protestant struggle to come to terms with Darwin." Moore's remarkable and seminal analysis of the debates over the implications of Darwinism has undermined the traditional notion of an irreconcilable opposition between evolution and Christian theology. The dominant response of transatlantic Protestant opinion was acceptance of at least some of Darwin's tenets, rather than outright opposition. Furthermore, the process of accommodation did not involve an absolute surrender by the churches. Clergymen looked to those doctrines of evolution that were most compatible with their religious outlook. Although Christianity was altered by the impact of evolution, its fundamental tenets survived and even proved able to transform some of the basic assumptions of the Darwinian study of natural science and society.[8]

The relationship between evangelical thought and evolution in English Canada not only confirms the general validity of Moore's insights, but adds a triangular dimension to his bipolar view of transatlantic science and religion. Even before the rise of Darwin, the participation of Canadian Methodists and Presbyterians in transatlantic Protestantism differed from that of their counterparts in Britain and America. History, rather than natural science or philosophy, provided the matrix for theology. This earlier emphasis of the evangelical creed determined the grounds of encounter between evolution and theology, and dictated the strategy clergymen followed in their thirty-year conversation with Darwinism.

For both Methodists and Presbyterians, the church college was the crucible in which the response was shaped. A generation of clergymen-professors, led by Nelles, Burwash, Grant, Caven, MacLaren, and Donald Harvey MacVicar, were able to draw on both their evangelical inheritance and the new possibilities of evolution. They produced a theology that, while abandoning the absolute insistence on biblical literalism characteristic of the formative years of the evangelical mind, was neither the fruit of defeat nor simply a system of evolutionary social ethics devoid of doctrinal content. Rather, their religious thought in these three decades combined the biblical and Baconian requirements of their creed with notions of historical development drawn from the application of evolutionary science to the study of human society.

THE AMBIGUOUS ENCOUNTER: THE
MISSING DARWIN DEBATE AND THE
IMPACT OF SOCIAL EVOLUTION

A puzzling cultural landscape confronts those who explore the relationship between the evangelical churches and evolutionary thought in Canada. In religious circles in Britain and America, Darwin's theory opened a great debate that raged for nearly three decades. By contrast, the Presbyterian and Methodist churches of English Canada did not have a single major contributor to the transatlantic discussion. The historian must search diligently through sermons and the evangelical press of the 1860s to find even the mention of Darwin's name.

Sir William Dawson, a prominent Presbyterian geologist and principal of McGill University, was a leading participant in the international scientific debate on the validity of the Darwinian hypothesis. Dawson's opinions, elaborated in works such as *Archaia*(1860), *Story of the Earth and Man*(1873), *Origin of the World*(1877), and *Modern Ideas of Evolution*(1890), established him as one of the most forceful and consistent opponents of the Darwinian view of evolution, and a defender of the correspondences between Genesis and geology.[9] So great was Dawson's prestige in the spheres of science and education that it might be tempting to regard his outright opposition to evolutionary science as typical of the evangelical churches as a whole. But Dawson's critique of Darwinism stemmed less from his religious or theological beliefs than from his scientific methodology, and his fears regarding the separation of science and religion in modern culture.[10] Although Dawson occasionally offered a course of six lectures on "Creation and the Deluge" to the students of Presbyterian College, Montreal, his views were even more atypical of evangelical attitudes toward modern thought than of the scientific reaction to Darwinism.[11] An overriding concern for sound scientific methodology was not the preoccupation of most Presbyterian and Methodist clergymen, who rarely shared the Victorian fascination with the natural world.[12] Evangelical thought was directed more to an understanding of the human world than to external nature.

The link between Darwinism and the eighteenth-century world of Paleyite natural theology provides the clue to the Canadian evangelical churches' lack of response to the theory of natural selection, which is even more puzzling when Canadian evangelicalism is contrasted with its American neighbour. There, the Presbyterian clergymen Charles Hodge and James McCosh each wrote an influential treatise on the implications of Darwinism for Christian doctrine.

Since the 1840s, these men had been trying to defend the central elements of the natural theology and Common Sense philosophical traditions being challenged by a culture defined by revivalist religion, idealist philosophy, and more dynamic notions of organic process derived from the prestige of history in Germany and England. Historians have argued that despite the inroads of these new currents of thought, the American evangelical colleges defined the integrity of their intellectual enterprise with reference to the legacy of natural theology and Common Sense.[13] Though they also adhered to the Baconian method, Canadian clergymen stood on the other side of a theological watershed. The life of their colleges was shaped more directly by the evangelical revolt against the intellectual and institutional tenets of eighteenth-century religion. Their Baconian definition of the unity of theology and the sciences was characterized by the analogy between Scripture and history not between revelation and natural science. Hodge and McCosh, scientists such as Asa Gray, and their Canadian counterparts Sir William Dawson and Sir Daniel Wilson directly experienced the impact of Darwin through their commitment to the formal harmony of theology and natural science.[14] By contrast, since the 1840s Canadian Methodist and Presbyterian clergymen-professors, influenced by Butler, had oriented themselves toward the "probabilities" and paradoxes of the human conscience, toward history and the human sciences. Thus the controversy embroiling Darwinians and those natural theologians committed to an explicit harmony between Scripture and science affected them less directly, and was seen in a different light, as involving issues far removed from the reconciliation of the fine points of systematic theology and formal scientific theory.

The problem of evolution was but a part of a larger problem facing evangelical culture. In the 1860s Canadian evangelicals found the tenets of their faith more disturbed by a series of perplexing issues grouped together under the rubric "infidelity." In 1865 an anonymous contributor to the Methodist oracle, *The Christian Guardian*, warned of the growth of a dangerous aspect of "infidelity" in the mother country – such ideas were no longer confined to educated circles or to the studies of sceptical professors. Even factory workers had "formed habits of reading," and were acquainting the British working class with the central tenets of infidelity – "objections to the Bible" advanced by "Colenso, Straus[sic], Lyell, or Darwin."[15] The placing of Darwin's name after the names of the celebrated biblical critics Bishop Colenso and David Friedrich Strauss is significant, implying that in evangelical circles, the challenge posed by natural science was in some respects felt as less severe and more indirect than the application of a critical outlook to the very sources of Christian life and doctrine.

According to the standard interpretation of nineteenth century religion, the appearance of *The Origin of Species* in 1859 triggered a period of tension for the theology taught in the Methodist and Presbyterian church colleges. But Darwin's theory was not the crucial issue facing professors and preachers. Since the 1840s clergymen-professors had defined their theology of history and the relationship between faith and reason against a background of biblical criticism and historical inquiry insistently demanding a greater role for reason in formulating Christian doctrine and, in extreme cases, denying the miraculous nature of the biblical revelation. A principal function of the church college had been the maintenance of the Bible, in the face of this challenge, as the foremost and immutable standard of evangelical faith and practice.

At the outset of the 1860s evangelicals felt the impact of evolutionary science as a subset of a more urgent and compelling problem: the application of historical criticism to the records of the Christian faith. In 1860 the bombshell of *Essays and Reviews* burst on the British intellectual scene and occasioned an immediate response in British North America. This collection of essays by clergymen in the Church of England was informed throughout by a common outlook. Benjamin Jowett's "On the Interpretation of Scripture" concerned most Canadian evangelicals. Jowett, a classicist and the future master of Balliol College, Oxford, challenged the foundation of the evangelical creed – the concept of the Bible as a separate, "sacred" history. He struck at the roots of both Baconianism and the all-important theology of history taught in evangelical colleges by suggesting that the truth of Christianity should not be tied to the maintenance of the literal truth of the events recorded in the Bible, and argued for a wider sphere for critical reason in relation to faith. By forcefully urging that the same rules of textual study applied both to Scripture and to other ancient documents, Jowett indicated that rather than determining the province of reason, doctrine must conform to the data and insights furnished by history and science.[16]

Essays and Reviews, Bishop Colenso's critical study of the Pentateuch published in 1863, and the lives of Jesus written by the French scholar Ernest Renan and the English historian J.R. Seeley, in particular, threatened the harmony of theology and history. These critics incurred the suspicion and hostility of evangelicals not only because they popularized the insights of German biblical scholars and philosophers, but because many of them were clergymen, ostensibly dedicated to upholding the supremacy of doctrine and the

Bible, and evangelicals felt they had betrayed their calling. Historians of the churches in Britain and America have often treated the debate launched by these "higher critics" as a footnote to the more general impact of Darwin and the natural sciences on religious faith. Even the great English scholar Owen Chadwick, who recognized historical scholarship as the main factor in the unsettlement of faith in the early 1860s, subsumed the challenge of history under the more general impact of "science."[17]

From the perspective of churches possessing well-established intellectual and institutional traditions of the harmony of theology and the natural sciences, such an interpretation holds considerable weight. For Canadian Methodists and Presbyterians, however, the Bible was not primarily a book of science, but a key to individual life, the formation of societies, and human history. For colonial clergymen-professors, their students, and their congregations, historical criticism had been for decades *the* pivotal problem. They realized that historical study could undermine, in ways that the investigation of natural phenomena could not, the biblical statements of fact and doctrine central to the evangelical creed. At issue was not merely the validity of the Bible, but the intellectual structure of evangelicalism. Clergymen-professors believed that the task of preaching and conversion and the link between college and congregation rested on their ability to draw from the Bible precise and predictable laws of human and divine behaviour true as theology, history, and moral precepts. Any weakening of the certainty of the "facts" revealed in the Bible would displace theology from its status as both history and science. Because theology and history formed an interlocking whole, any divorce between the two would shake the conviction of ordinary evangelical Christians in the Canadian provinces that their religion was the key to understanding and shaping both the past and the future of their society. This viewpoint explains both the hostile reaction to the popularization of German criticism in England and the relative neglect of Darwin and issues raised by the natural sciences.

The Methodist and Presbyterian response to the challenge of biblical criticism drew on Baconian notions of the proper place of criticism in relation to revelation and on tactics forged in English evangelical circles in the 1830s and 1840s to counter the impact of German historical criticism. The issue was bluntly stated by the editor of the *Christian Guardian*, who used notions of biblical authority drawn from Paley and Butler to stress the literal truth of the Bible. He reminded his readers that "the question between the believer and the infidel is this: were the original documents the revealed word of God?" The usual method employed in refuting the critics was to undermine their scientific pretensions. Accusing one's opponent of "metaphysics" or "speculation," claiming that the English critics had not arrived at their conclusions empirically or through practical study had the greatest impact on an evangelical audience.[18]

Evangelicals appealed insistently to the Baconian legacy in their attempt to contain the spread of "infidelity." Baconianism laid great stress on the accuracy of the "testimony" of the biblical writers, who lived at the time of the events and miracles described and therefore reliable. Critics such as Colenso and the "Essayists" misrepresented the office of reason by trying to arrive at religious truth without the aid of revelation. According to most Canadian clergymen, they opposed the attested "facts" of the Bible with mere hypothesis and conjecture. "Common sense," declared the editor of the *Presbyterian Witness*, "demands that any fact be admitted on sufficient human testimony; common sense will compel the thoughtful to accept the testimony of Christ and his disciples … rather than the theories of Infidels."[19]

The focus on the problem of historical criticism of the Bible in Canadian evangelical circles and the uncompromising defence of the Baconian view of religion and reason were not merely directed at the infiltration of German ideas into the British churches. Presbyterian and Methodist clergymen and their congregations viewed the work of Jowett and the "Essayists" as one aspect of a larger and more troubling problem. In the early 1860s a second current of English thought, more widespread and more subversive of the intellectual authority of the evangelical theology of history, intersected with the work of the critics. The Rationalist historians Henry Thomas Buckle and William Lecky, in a manner reminiscent of the great eighteenth-century sceptics, appealed to both educated and popular audiences by denying that the Bible and theology were the prime movers of intellectual and social progress. Characterizing theology or "dogmatism" as irrational and morally bankrupt, their histories expressed the concerns of a small but articulate group of Victorians who, following Leslie Stephen, claimed the moral superiority of agnosticism over Christian belief and did much to foster a climate of "doubt" in the universities.[20]

By denying the status of "knowledge" to theology, the writings of Buckle, Lecky, and the agnostics posited an alternative interpretation of progress for an age eagerly searching for predictable laws governing mind and society. From the standpoint of clergymen-professors in the church colleges, their works enlisted the historical method to subvert, rather than reinforce, the supremacy of revelation and theology. As McCulloch warned in an 1868 sermon, "*The religion of Jesus Christ* tolerates no free thought independent of revelation,"[21] thus forcefully asserting the central position of Scripture and theology in the hierarchy of knowledge. For churches where the unity of preaching and intellectual endeavour was premised on the close harmony of revelation, theology, and history, the popular works of Buckle and Lecky undermined the foundation supporting the authority of the evangelical creed.

The hostile treatment accorded Buckle and Lecky by evangelical clergymen and publicists echoed in one respect an old rivalry between Christian religion and eighteenth-century scepticism. The influence of these two men however, rested, not merely on their links to an earlier climate of Rationalism. In the cultural climate of the 1860s, their claim rested more on their position that human intellectual and social development was based on natural, evolutionary laws that could be discovered scientifically through historical research. Although rooted in the popular preaching and culture of the late eighteenth-century revival, evangelicalism as an intellectual force was shaped by a dialogue with the infant "human sciences," which arose in Germany, Britain, and the United States between 1780 and 1850. By seeking to account for human development without prior reference to Christian belief or to the data of the Bible, these branches of study questioned the foundations of the evangelical movement. Despite this rivalry, the generation of clergymen-professors represented by Ryerson and McCulloch had been able to reconcile religious imperatives and the culture of inquiry through the medium of their theology of history, a body of beliefs accepted by most educated Methodists and Presbyterians between 1820 and 1850.

In the two decades after 1870 the conversation between evangelical religion and the infant human sciences was transformed by a new factor. The second generation of evangelical educators sensed that they could no longer rely exclusively on their creed to provide a comprehensive synthesis of revelation, morality, and science acceptable to the wider culture. Between 1859 and 1871 the theory of evolution gave greater weight to explanations of human origins and progress drawn from the natural sciences, and particularly biology, rather than theology. Evolution became, in the words of a celebrated historian of the Victorian church, "axiomatic, or probable, or tolerable" to many educated Englishmen. In both the United States and British North America, evolution was rapidly adopted as the common coin of literary, historical, and philosophical discussion.[22]

Educated Christians on both sides of the Atlantic encountered the impact of "Darwinism" not primarily at the level of biology or scientific theory, but in the application of naturalistic explanations of development to human history and culture. By 1890 this strand of evolutionary thought supplied both the method and the governing assumptions of inquiry for historians, anthropologists, political economists, and philosophers. The evolutionary outlook provided the necessary impetus for the rise of the new social sciences. With its search for predictable "laws" of behaviour and development, the evolutionary method altered the balance between the evangelical creed and the human sciences by conferring upon late Victorian social thinkers the cachet of scientific certainty.

The cultural prestige of evolutionary methods and assumptions was so powerful that even the data of the Christian faith could not be spared. It was here, in the convergence of biblical criticism and the logic of the evolution of human societies, that Nelles, Burwash, Grant, and Caven faced the most urgent challenge to their religious and intellectual authority. The British social thinkers Herbert Spencer, Edward B. Tylor, and Max Muller applied the tenets of evolution in their attempts to discern natural "laws" of mental, moral, and social development. Their theories owed little or nothing to Darwin,[23] but drew on the rising prestige of evolutionary science in constructing interpretations of human culture sharply at variance with Christian tradition.

Tylor, for example, whose *Primitive Culture* was published in 1871, sought to account for the development of every civilization through the working of uniform causes. Religion, as but one element of culture, he considered subject to the same processes of natural development.[24] His conclusions threatened traditional Christian beliefs by denying that Christianity was a special, miraculous revelation. The laws governing "heathen" religions applied equally to the development of Christian doctrine and practice. All religions were products of stages of natural growth, subject to laws that reason might discern. More troubling for evangelicals, Tylor and other social inquirers reinforced the conclusions drawn by Victorian rationalists and agnostics with the prestige of their research into human origins. By characterizing nineteenth-century Protestantism with its rituals and dogmatic systems as but the "survival" of more "primitive" forms of belief, Tylor concluded that religion would inevitably fall before the march of reason.[25] Following this logic, the origins of Christianity were not to be found in a divine revelation given to the Chosen People of Israel or in doctrines founded on notions of divine miracle. Rather, the evolutionary method could locate the beginnings of Christian belief in a savage tribal desert community little different in culture and religion from the surrounding "heathen" peoples. At the same time, any advance in religious consciousness could be ascribed, not to the cosmic drama of sin and redemption, but to improvements in material culture and intellectual life as man moved from "savagery" to a more "civilized" state.

Given the prestige of evolutionary ideas in Victorian culture, it was only a matter of time until the new study of society was applied directly to the study and interpretation of the records of the Christian faith. After all, did not the Bible contain an explanation of the origins, development, and decline of society? For centuries, Christians had accepted the biblical narratives as reliable historical documents – the events of universal history unfolded in the sequence described by the authors. Furthermore, because Scripture was a divine revelation, it was more reliable than other histories and contained the prophetic key to universal history. By the 1870s, however, adventurous German critics challenged the vital equation of history and prophecy by using evolutionary naturalism to explain the origins and growth of the Hebrew religion, an approach directly at variance with Christian traditions regarding the Old Testament.

The most exciting and revolutionary of these attempts was Julius Wellhausen's *Prolegomena to the History of Israel*, published in 1878. At a stroke, Wellhausen apparently destroyed the factual basis of the evangelical theology of history. Drawing on the insights of ethnology, comparative religion, and a long tradition of German criticism, Wellhausen concluded that the books of the Old Testament were not accurate contemporary historical records. He argued that they consisted of three layers of tradition dating from different periods of Israel's national and social development. Where church historians such as Burns of Knox College would have posited a special, divine, or "theocratic" presence elevating Jewish history over that of all other nations, Wellhausen's researches indicated something quite different. Over time, he declared, the history of the Jews had been "clericalized" – the characteristics of the society that arose after the Babylonian Exile in the sixth century BC had been read back into the age of the patriarchs and Moses.[26]

There appeared little room for compromise between Wellhausen's conclusions regarding the Old Testament and the central tenets of the evangelical theology of history. The application of the tenets of evolutionary naturalism to the Bible was premised on the notion that the logic of historical method, rather than doctrine or tradition, could determine the actual content and religious and moral value of Scripture. Discarding the idea of the Bible as a "sacred" or universal history, Wellhausen and other critics argued that the natural laws of social development applied equally to Israel and other primitive peoples. By reducing the biblical narratives to layers of tradition, the "documentary hypothesis" posited by Wellhausen questioned the accuracy of the historical basis of faith. And because evangelicals made no separation between theology and history, this raised the possibility that the central doctrines of the Christian faith and the moral law that drew its authority from the Bible were not immutable and eternal, but were themselves the products of natural laws of social and intellectual development. If the history disclosed in the Old and New Testaments was not literally true, could clergymen continue to attempt to transform the individual and society through preaching?

Historians studying the impact of these currents on the Protestant churches have claimed that by 1880 the intersection of the study of history, higher criticism, and evolutionary naturalism confronted Victorian clergymen and the educated members of their congregations with the spectre of moral relativism and anarchy.[27] From the perspective of Canadian clergymen and their educational enterprise, the application of the evolutionary outlook and methods to the study of human history and society was an important and troubling problem, particularly since the rising prestige of evolutionary explanations meant that in the wider culture, theology had lost some of its pre-eminence in relation to the "human sciences." For the first time since the creation of their colleges in the age of revival, clergymen were forced to share some of their authority with philosophers, historians, and political economists.

Leading Presbyterian and Methodist clergymen, however, did not feel that the alliance of evolutionary naturalism and historical criticism of the Bible compelled a surrender of the central beliefs of their creed. Nor did the acceptance of certain elements of the new critical thought force an entire restructuring of their intellectual universe. In 1896 the Rev. W.S. Blackstock defined "higher criticism" as a method of investigation, a means to an end. More significantly, he declared that it involved nothing more than "the Baconian method applied to a most interesting and important branch of biblical inquiry." He urged his readers to take a confident attitude, reminding them that fear "may lead us to see hobgoblins where there are none, and to mistake the friends of the Bible for its enemies."[28]

Although from the perspective of the late twentieth century Blackstock's conflation of higher criticism and "the Baconian method" can be dismissed as mere wishful thinking, symptomatic of a failure in the evangelical churches to perceive the secularizing implications of historical study, it raises more fundamental questions concerning the relationship between evangelicalism and evolution in late Victorian Canada. Were the intellectual foundations of the evangelical creed completely at variance with the currents of evolutionary thought so readily adopted by historians and social thinkers? And was the expression of confidence by Blackstock and other clergymen based on something more than the simple capitulation of Christian doctrine to evolution?

PRESBYTERIANISM, BACONIANISM, AND THE SEARCH FOR A "HISTORICAL THEOLOGY"

The difficulties raised by the convergence of the historical criticism of the Bible and the methods of evolutionary naturalism touched the very core of evangelical belief. Was there not an absolute gulf between the idea of history ruled by an active divine providence manifested in a special strand of historical experience and an interpretation stressing not divine intervention, but the rule of uniform, natural "laws" governing human development? By its use of criteria supplied by the assumptions of social evolutionists, historical criticism subverted the insistence on factual certainty that shaped the intellectual life of college and congregation. It was thus particularly surprising that some preachers could equate the new higher criticism and the Baconian method they had traditionally used to study the Bible and theology.

At first sight, it might be thought that Baconianism and higher criticism belonged to two different worlds. As the American historian George Marsden has aptly observed, the division between the two expressed in very direct terms the difference between "liberals" and militant "conservatives" in American denominations. Protestants faithful to the Baconian approach drew upon eighteenth-century Common Sense epistemology in arguing that the "facts" of Scripture were certain and immutable realities, guaranteed by supernatural inspiration. The Bible was a unity governed by exact laws that could be discovered by careful analysis and classification. The crucial point was the idea of history. History was understood not as the operation of social laws but, according to the biblical picture, as a cosmic struggle between good and evil. By contrast, Marsden argues, those who applied historical criticism to the Bible assumed that human and natural forces shaped history.[29] Between 1870 and

1890 many influential American clergymen accepted that natural development and the idea of process supplied the key to understanding human culture, including Scripture itself.[30]

So deep was the division between the Baconian ideal and the new interpretation of the Bible that in the thirty years after 1860 the opposition between the two opened serious rifts among some evangelical denominations in the United States. So-called "Modernists" such as Henry Ward Beecher and the advocates of the "New Theology" preached accommodation and adjustment of Christian doctrine to some of the claims of science and biblical criticism. According to one historian, there was a connection between the abandonment of Baconianism and the Common Sense tradition and the renunciation of evangelical conviction. Bushnell and the Yale Congregationalist theologians advanced criticisms of Common Sense philosophy and downgraded the importance of revivalism in favour of "Christian nurture."[31] An increasingly militant group of "conservatives" loyal to the Baconian tradition drew on the Princeton theology of Hodge, the new revivalism of Moody, and the pessimistic, premillennial interpretations of history already present among some evangelical groups to construct a powerful rival to "modernist" currents within the Protestant churches.[32] The divisions between "modernists" and "conservatives" affected most profoundly those churches loyal to Calvinist theological traditions.[33] When transferred to the thought and experience of Canadian Presbyterians, however, the two-dimensional American categories of "modernist" and "conservative" have little meaning. The absence of noisy controversy and the infrequency of heresy trials dictates a revision of the model of intellectual change employed by American historians when applied to the experience of English-Canadian Presbyterians.[34] Between 1860 and 1890 Grant, Gordon, Caven, MacLaren, Snodgrass, and MacVicar, the colonial clergymen-professors who shaped and directed the theological training and preaching of the Presbyterian church, not only avoided splitting their congregations over theological questions, but also were able to achieve what their American counterparts were largely unable to do. By combining Baconian traditions and the main tenets of the evangelical creed with elements of the higher criticism they preserved the centrality of theology in their educational and cultural endeavours. As befitting its origins in a world suspended between revival and the Enlightenment, their religious outlook bridged the gap between the eighteenth-century world of order and immutable certainty and the new vision of historical process and human evolution.

The explanation of this remarkable development hinges on the position of the Canadian Presbyterian church held within the wider world of transatlantic Protestantism. To understand how these clergymen encountered evolutionary thought and the new biblical criticism one must, in the words of William George Jordan, journey "back again to Scotland and through Scotland to Germany."[35] For this eminent preacher and biblical scholar the currents of theology persisted in their traditional channel between 1860 and 1890. Despite the powerful influence of Hodge and Princeton on many young Canadian ministers and theological professors,[36] the Scottish universities retained their primacy as the institutional and intellectual models of the colonial church colleges. More importantly, an entire generation of the most prominent intellectual leaders of Canadian Presbyterianism learned to resolve the tensions between their evangelical inheritance and the varieties of evolutionary thought at these Scottish universities.[37]

Colonial Presbyterians who attended the Scottish universities between 1850 and 1890 encountered a culture in a state of flux. The antagonisms of the Great Disruption of 1843 fractured the intellectual unity of Scotland and ended the supremacy of Common Sense philosophy. Though the separation of the Church of Scotland and the Free Church might be interpreted as a source of religious and intellectual futility, the slow decline of Common Sense after 1843, and its resolution into a mediating, personal idealism that sought to straddle idealism and empiricism,[38] led to the forging of a new relationship between evangelical theology, historical study of the Bible, and Christian life. In this process of adjustment, the Free Church colleges played a crucial role, particularly in the sensitive area of biblical criticism. The "biblical revolution"[39] wrought in the classrooms of the Free Church divinity halls transformed Scottish religious thought and powerfully influenced the Presbyterian intellect in British North America.

Founded after the Disruption of the 1840s, the Free Church colleges drew their views on the relationship of revelation and reason from the writings of Chalmers, whose theology was strongly cast in Baconian terms. Asserting the independence of theology from philosophical speculation, Chalmers stressed the importance of the "facts" of biblical revelation and human conscience. Given this emphasis, Chalmers's successors Robert Candlish and William Cunningham were compelled, in defence of the Scriptural basis of religious knowledge, to face in most acute form questions raised by German biblical critics. By 1864 Candlish, principal of New College,

Edinburgh, had already retreated from an uncompromising biblical literalism. While declaring that the Bible was an infallible record of an infallible revelation, he argued that diversity of views in relation to doctrine was to be tolerated and encouraged. In particular, he argued that because the Spirit of God worked "in accommodation to and co-operation" with "human forces" of individual and social life, Scripture therefore contained a substantial human element. Thus the Bible could be interpreted in accordance with historical and scientific knowledge without sacrificing its infallible or authoritative character.[40]

A new generation of Free Church professors soon recognized the value of this "reverent" or "believing" criticism. By 1870 A.B. Davidson, professor of Hebrew and Oriental Languages at New College, Edinburgh, Principal Robert Rainy, Candlish's successor at New College, and the most famous Scottish critic, Robertson Smith, among others, had incorporated into biblical study and theology certain insights of the German critics. The central premise of the new relationship of revelation and reason was that theology must be made historical. As early as 1861, Davidson wrote that "revelation is a thing given by God to man, but given so as to work itself out through men, and it conforms rigidly to the usual laws of history and progress."[41] But certain basic premises governed the place of historical criticism in the Scottish colleges. First, scholars such as Davidson refused to banish God from the Bible and fought to retain the idea of Scripture as a sacred history ruled by an active and independent Deity. Second, they were loyal to the Baconian premises of Chalmers's theology, and urged their students to remain close to the "facts," structure, and traditional meaning of the biblical text. "Believing" or "reverent" criticism was thus the foundation of historical theology. Historical criticism, these Scottish clergymen maintained, preserved the inductive method in theology, and reinforced, rather than subverted the evangelical insistence that any expression of theology depend directly on the "facts" of revelation.

The definition of "historical theology" took shape against a background of heated religious debate in Scottish intellectual circles. The two decades after 1850 witnessed the introduction of Hegelian idealism to the Scottish universities by the brothers John and Edward Caird. These men sought to bridge the gulf they perceived between science and religion by claiming that both were really part of a higher unity. In rescuing Christianity from materialism, however, the Hegelian philosophy demanded a high price. The basis of the Cairds' synthesis required the acceptance of an evolutionary, naturalistic view of religion. Christianity, argued Edward Caird in 1893, had developed from a "germ" of primitive animism to its modern form in a series of stages, ruled not by supernatural revelation, but by some inner dynamic or logic.[42]

This denial of the biblical picture of Christian origins and development raised troublesome questions for many Presbyterian clergymen. Idealist philosophers, unlike the "reverent critics" of the Free Church, denied the doctrine of an eternally valid word of God as the basis of theology. "Historical theology" was far more acceptable than this idealism because it did not dispense with doctrine but sought to anchor it more firmly on the evidence of Scripture, thus preserving the intellectual structure of revelation, history, and prophecy. It was faithful to the evangelical heritage in two respects: first, theology and doctrine remained the ultimate ends of the wise exercise of reason; second, because the task of biblical interpretation was dominated by faith and not by mere adherence to critical methods or canons of evolutionary science, the close links between college and pulpit were preserved.

By 1875 the work of Principal Rainy and Robert Flint, professor of divinity at the University of Edinburgh, crystallized these emphases as the dominant synthesis of theology and critical thought in the Scottish church colleges. Both these clergymen proceeded from the assumption that doctrines had been progressively revealed in the Bible. Although pressing the case for a theology faithful to the claims of science and history, they were by no means radicals. Flint strongly disapproved of those who would discard the creeds and systems that the piety, scholarship, and reflection of earlier ages had elaborated. Far from abandoning the old verities of the faith, progress was "the continuous and consistent development which brings the new out of the old instead of parting with the old for the new."[43] But progress or development, these clergymen maintained, was not the same thing as the naturalistic evolution espoused by German critics and idealist philosophers. Human history was ruled by the conscious guidance of a divine purpose. While warning against the transfer of physical laws to the moral world, Flint and Rainy were able to enlist progress as part of the divine law, rendering the Christian outlook compatible with the central dynamic of nineteenth-century historical scholarship.[44]

Thus these Scottish clergymen defined "evolution" as a process "at once conservative and progressive" in which "all that is essential in the old is retained and perfected, while the form is altered to accord with new circumstances and to respond to new wants."[45] Such a formulation encouraged evangelicals in a confident belief that while the outward expression of their doctrines might change from age to age, the essential principles and the "facts" on which they were based would remain true to the original revelation. "Historical theology," like the older theology of history, viewed the past as largely shaped by the great doctrines and moral verities of the Christian tradition, a position that combined historical criticism with older evangelical notions of preaching and prophecy. The enlistment of the Baconian heritage as the foundation for the new "historical theology" legitimated historical criticism in Scottish church colleges. A true philosophy of history, claimed Flint, flowed from the "facts" themselves, from "the meaning, the rational interpretation, the knowledge of the true nature and essential relation of the facts." Because historical research would ultimately testify to the activity of God in the world, it would confirm and reinforce the historian's prophetic role.[46]

The teachings of Flint and Rainy on Christian doctrine and development corresponded closely to the dominant Protestant response to the challenge of evolutionary theory between 1870 and 1900. As the historian James Moore has argued, many evangelicals could not surrender their theology of history premised on an optimistic vision of God active in transforming human conscience and culture. They could not tolerate a theory such as Darwin's, which removed the sense of providence from creation. They adjusted evolutionary theory to the requirements of their theology by exploiting divisions within the evolutionist camp. In the writings of the British philosopher Herbert Spencer, either the originals or the popularized form, they found many affinities with the fundamental tenets of their creed. Prominent Scottish evangelicals drew eclectically upon such evolutionary thinkers to legitimate their theology of history.[47]

Such formulations offered a redoubt against the inroads of evolutionary naturalism and speculative idealism. Deriving divine law from the old inductive method that they equated with the methodology of historical research, Flint and Rainy anchored the essential doctrines of Christianity in an independent body of data, the Bible, whose factual accuracy could be verified through the historical method, a procedure distinct from the speculative hypotheses of scientists and philosophers. While making theology dependent on historical evidence, the main emphases of the evangelical theology of history were preserved. The role of historical criticism was carefully circumscribed by the professor's continuing vocation as a preacher and the insistence on faith as an *a priori* of sound scholarship. "Historical theology" fused evangelicalism and evolution, and cast them in an approach to learning that preserved the supremacy of faith and theology in inquiry.

THE PRESBYTERIAN COLLEGES:
HISTORICAL THEOLOGY, BIBLE STUDY,
AND PREACHING

Young Canadian Free Churchmen such as Andrew Browning Baird, Robert Falconer, and Clarence Mackinnon, who attended the Scottish universities and church colleges in the 1870s and 1880s recalled with excitement the impact of the new climate on their religious outlook. They took eager note of the "historical theology" taught by Flint, Davidson, and Rainy, and they listened with enthusiasm to the preacher Henry Drummond, who found no difficulty in combining sympathy for evolutionary science and association with the American evangelist Dwight Moody. Mackinnon was especially impressed by Drummond's ability to enlist evolution as a divine process, to preach that "even in the grimy depths of some stagnant pool there was a Divine agency at work."[48] Where American Presbyterians found themselves increasingly divided by the claims of evangelicalism and evolution, the churches of the Scottish metropolis offered an appealing alternative, a theology that strove to reconcile elements of the new critical thought with the traditions of the revival.

The continued influence of Scottish culture encouraged a tolerance and even acceptance of the idea of evolution in the colonial colleges, all founded under the auspices of the Free Church. In 1877 John Campbell, recently appointed professor of church history at Montreal College, drew a careful distinction between "development" and "Darwinian evolution." While Darwin's theory banished God from nature and society, the idea of evolution when kept within proper limits did not necessarily subvert the evangelical creed, which posited the idea of a Creator and an over-ruling Providence.[49] The imposition of limits, the hedging of evolution, was the key to the Presbyterian accommodation. In the *Knox College Monthly* in 1886, W. Dewar maintained that evolution was a purely scientific question. When "restricted to its proper region of science, and shown that it can only become at most a 'law,' and therefore a mode of creation, and not a 'cause'," evolution would not threaten Christian doctrine.[50]

These attempts to accommodate evolution and the main doctrines of the evangelical creed depended on the ability of clergymen-professors to keep theology and natural science in separate compartments. Their success reflected their pre-Darwinian rejection of natural theology as the harmonizer of faith and intellect. But the term "evolution" confronted Protestant Christians in the 1870s and 1880s with a far more serious problem, a difficulty that could not be masked by the mere assertion of a distinction between "evolution" and "Darwinism." The application of the idea of evolution to human history threatened the foundation of evangelical thought, the belief that a precise connection existed between divine and human activity, between a miraculous biblical revelation and the origins and progress of society. The use of insights derived from historical scholarship and the new human sciences to interpret the Bible directly challenged the evangelical assertion that Scripture be studied through the eye of faith. To argue that evolution characterized the human past threatened the dissolution of the Baconian certainty that anchored the life of Presbyterian colleges and preachers.

The thorny issue of the place of higher criticism in the Free Church colleges was fraught with the potential for debilitating conflict between advocates of a rigid biblical literalism and those who accepted at least some of the insights offered by the new critical thought. But the American-style polarization of "modernist" and "antimodernist" theological parties did not occur on Canadian soil, largely because traditionalists employed the Baconian outlook as a vehicle of accommodation. MacLaren, whose career as a preacher began in the 1850s, is an example. A devotee of the Princeton theology of Charles Hodge, his views on plenary inspiration were so widely respected that in 1903 he was invited by the American Bible League to join the editorial board of the *Bible Student and Teacher*.[51] In 1873, newly-appointed to the chair of systematic theology at Knox College, he defended his discipline as an "inductive science." He reminded his students that it was "by the Baconian method alone that a reliable Systematic Theology can be reached."[52] MacLaren fully accepted Hodge's stern advocacy of an uncompromising biblical literalism and the doctrines of Calvinism, and until the end of his career he insisted on the plenary inspiration of the Bible, which, he maintained, was explicitly taught by Christ.[53] The Princeton theology, although a minority tradition in late nineteenth-century Canadian Presbyterianism, was nevertheless an insistent presence. MacLaren succeeded Caven as principal of Knox in 1904, and he and his disciples powerfully resisted concessions to the evolutionary theory as applied to theology.[54] He spoke not only for those who accepted Hodge's formulations, but for Presbyterians uneasy with what they considered the division between evangelical belief and the methods of higher criticism.

In 1894 an anonymous Presbyterian attempted to summarize the principal objections to the historical criticism of the Bible felt by many shades of opinion within the church. "We are convinced," he wrote, "that if there is one thing more than another that makes the modern criticism distasteful, it is the attitude which its followers are too prone to assume." He charged that the attitude of biblical critics was often patronizing, and that their worst offence was to "state their wildest conjectures with a certitude that hardly admits of a doubt. They enter the field with a 'theory' and everything must of necessity fall into line."[55]

MacLaren was directly expressing the gulf that lay between the cautious inductive Baconian method that supported the intellectual life of the church and the outlook of the higher critic. Many clergymen and other believers held that the new historical scholarship simply ignored the "facts" contained in the biblical text so that its conclusions could rest on speculation. They implicitly recognized that the divorce between the old knowledge and the new held the seeds of cultural conflict. If clergymen-professors became higher critics and subordinated faith to the critical method, they would at once sever their connection with the wider world of the pulpit and the congregation. The evangelical endeavour required preachers to adhere to a certain body of truth that could ensure the redemption of individual and society. The loss of inductive certainty in the Bible would sunder intellect and Christian living, thus imperilling the structure of evangelicalism.

Despite these fears, MacLaren refused to simply abandon the dialogue with critical thought. Like his mentor Hodge, he drew explicit limits around the doctrine of plenary inspiration, limits that allowed him considerable flexibility and tolerance in his approach to modern thought. In a forceful refutation of the polygenist anthropologists Agassiz, Morton, Nott, and Gliddon delivered in Belleville in 1860, he stated that the purpose of revelation was "moral and religious." The Bible, he warned, "was not given to gratify an idle curiosity, or even to unveil the mysteries of science, but to reveal to us the way of life, and make us know the path of duty." Thus he argued that "all scriptural allusions, to matters pertaining merely to any branch of physical science, may be couched in language accordant with the prevalent ideas of the age, however incorrect, scientifically, these ideas may be."[56] The admission that *some* parts of the Bible might express the language and thought of their time implicitly recognized a role for biblical criticism in separating "essential" doctrines from the "incidental" accretions to revelation. MacLaren also suggested that "plenary inspiration" was fully compatible with a notion of progressive revelation. In a sermon preached in 1903 he described the Bible as a "ripening plan," a "revelation gradually unfolded, as the education of the race advances, and men are able to bear it, and when it is finally completed in the New Testament, the world has seen nothing like it."[57]

Far from being an uncompromising opponent of evolution or historical criticism, MacLaren drew a clear distinction between Christian and non-Christian forms of these modern approaches. Speaking at Knox College at the opening of the 1886 session, he noted that the majority of evolutionists, including Charles Darwin, presupposed that some higher power had created the universe. Such a theory, he believed, "admits the absolute creation of matter, life and man by God," while attempting to "trace more successfully the order of God's working." Thus, like other prominent Princeton theologians, he was willing to accept an idea of evolution compatible with the notion of design[58] and founded on the sound procedure of careful induction. This he contrasted with the "modernist" New Theology espoused by Theodore Munger, who rashly attempted to restate fundamental doctrines like plenary inspiration, the atonement, the trinity, and future probation according to the assumptions of scientific naturalism. Despite his sarcastic denunciations of the "modernists," MacLaren's views clearly did not rule out the possibility of an accommodation between Baconianism and evolution. Rather, his careful attempt to define the limits of the doctrine of plenary inspiration was designed to reduce the possibilities for conflict between critical thought and the traditions of evangelicalism.

Unlike McLaren, some Canadian Free Churchmen found that it was no longer possible to assume that the books of the Bible presented a literally accurate account of the divine will operating in human conscience and history. Had not even Scottish "reverent critics" A.B. Davidson and Robertson Smith accepted the German position that the Bible must be viewed historically? There appeared to be little common ground between those loyal to the Baconian belief in an inerrant and fully inspired Scripture and younger men, Andrew Browning Baird and R.Y. Thomson, for example, who in the late 1870s had experienced at first-hand the Scottish "biblical revolution." In 1881 Knox College faced a student revolt over the teachings of MacLaren and William Gregg, who according to one dissatisfied student were unable to deal with philosophical subjects and disliked students who had the courage to ask questions.[59] Even within the usually placid classrooms of the colonial colleges there was pressure for a freer play of criticism in relation to the biblical text, and considerable admiration for the Scottish critic Robertson Smith, who in the late 1870s was subjected to a lengthy heresy trial for allegedly accepting the main points of Wellhausen's "documentary hypothesis." In 1880 R.Y. Thomson wrote to Andrew Baird praising him for "placing on record your own estimate of Robertson Smith, at the risk of departing from what seems to have become in

Canada, the routine orthodox way of regarding him, where even the credit of sincerity seems to be only very grudgingly – if at all – accorded to him."[60]

The avoidance of an open rift within Canadian Presbyterianism over the question of higher criticism in the 1880s was a testament to the efforts of three prominent clergymen. William Caven (the principal of Knox College), Donald Harvey MacVicar, and John Mark King dominated the life of the colleges between 1870 and 1900, and successfully harmonized the rival Baconian and critical tempers. When Thomson and Baird returned from their exposure to "reverent criticism" and "historical theology" in Scotland in the mid-1880s, they encountered what would seem to have been a remarkably similar current of ideas at their *alma mater*, Knox College. There Caven had already charted a course that would mediate the preacher's need for inductive certainty in interpreting the Bible to the congregation, and the excitement of younger spirits who urged accommodation of evangelical theology with higher criticism and the idea of development.

Having served Canadian Presbyterianism as both professor and preacher, Caven, who took over the reins of Knox College in 1870, was ideally suited to the task of reconciling these tensions. He was born in Scotland in 1830, and his family moved to Canada in 1847. In 1852 he entered upon a fifty-year career in the Presbyterian ministry. After attending the United Presbyterian seminary in London, Ontario, he was called to the pastorate of St Mary's Church. After the union of the United Presbyterians with the numerically larger Free Church in 1861, Caven rapidly assumed a leading role in the intellectual life of the new church. By 1866 he had been elected to the chair of exegesis and biblical criticism at Knox College and four years later rose to the the principalship, a position he held until his death in 1903.[61]

Speaking at the opening of Knox College in 1877, Caven introduced to his students the new alliance of historical criticism and theology honed in Scotland. "The very nature of the case," he declared, "requires that Theology should be a progressive science." He defined progress in very specific terms, reminding his audience that "theology is the same now that it has been in every age of the Christian era, so far as its great central truths are concerned, but continually changing by the growth of new truths, which an increasing knowledge of the Bible has furnished."[62] This aptly expressed the Presbyterian attempt to harmonize two central tensions present in the minds of late nineteenth-century clergymen. Caven's insistence on the unchanging nature of the "great central truths" articulated the evangelical creed's demand for certain, immutable religious truth, while the metaphor of "growth" and "increasing knowledge" reflected the church's contact with the new biblical criticism and historical scholarship then revising the old theology of history.

Caven's definition of theology in relation to critical thought illustrated the continued power of the evangelical creed in shaping and defining the intellectual life of college and congregation. He and his colleagues did not introduce a mere "mirror image" of Scottish thought,[63] but adapted "historical theology" to accommodate the powerful Baconian imperatives of the colonial evangelical creed and the biblical literalism of the Princeton theology. Although forged in the church colleges, this body of beliefs, usually termed "biblical theology," expressed the adherence of clergymen-professors to the popular theology of evangelicalism, and bridged the world of scholarship and the culture of the pulpit and the Sunday sermon. Despite concessions to newer forms of biblical criticism and evolutionary thought, Caven and his staff not only preserved the traditional theological curriculum at Knox College, but also continued to affirm the centrality of the Bible as the sole reliable guide to faith and inquiry. From the moment of his inaugural address in 1866, Caven dwelt on the practical nature of this biblically-based education. Its purpose, he declared, was "qualifying candidates for the ministry," and the important disciplines of theology, church history, and the interpretation of Scripture were specially intended to teach the student how to preach.[64]

Caven's subtle reworking of the Scottish "historical theology" in the Canadian setting was consciously designed to promote the pre-eminence of preaching in the intellectual life of the church. To this end, he insisted upon biblical "fact" as the authoritative source of a sound theology. He advocated the use of the new historical scholarship in Baconian terms by urging upon professors and preachers the practice of biblical criticism or "exegesis" as the essential precondition for the formulation of doctrine.[65] He hoped that the new historical approach would maintain the close union between biblical study, theology, and preaching, the triad that sustained the vital connection between college and congregation. But how to ensure that history and the critical method would respect the priorities of the evangelical creed?

During his long career, Caven reminded successive generations of young Presbyterian ministers that "the study of theology be prosecuted in a spirit in which scientific fidelity is properly blended with devotion." If such harmony could be attained, he apprehended little danger in "harmonizing the old and the new; of the earlier centuries with the present; the conservative and the progressive will so happily combine that each shall but supplement and regulate the other."[66] This ideal involved the continued assertion of a hierarchy of faith and knowledge familiar to men like McCulloch and the earlier exponents of the evangelical creed. Although historical scholarship was held essential to the "scientific" character of theology, the historical method itself was held in constant subordination to the "facts" revealed in the biblical text and to the Christian experience of the preacher or interpreter. "It is quite conceivable," concluded Caven's most characteristic refrain, "that Biblical criticism and exegesis ... should be carried to great perfection, and yet very essential prerequisites to theological science be wanting." The maintenance of sound doctrine involved the existence of "spiritual life," the cultivation of "humility and reverence," and the realization that "none but the Spirit of God can interpret for us the things which are of God."[67]

Though committed to fostering the alliance of evangelicalism and the new critical approach to the Bible, Caven remained firmly committed to the Baconian foundations of evangelical education. He went so far as to assert that the historical method could never be of itself the criterion of theological research or scholarship. True theology, he stated in an 1879 lecture, "will still keep close to Scripture; it will steadfastly remain biblical. It will be increasingly felt that the faith of the Church can only embrace what is either expressly set down in Scripture or may be deduced from it by good and necessary inference. And scrupulous care will be exercised not to incorporate into our system anything which does not clearly rest upon inspired authority." Although the new biblical criticism was a valuable ally in reinforcing theology's claim to scientific status in the face of assaults by evolutionary naturalists, it could neither alter nor determine the substance of Christian faith. Caven believed that the central doctrines of the faith had been divinely revealed. While progress in theology was possible, it could only be achieved within certain limits.[68]

He left no doubt in the minds of his students about what those limits were. The Presbyterian church would not use the new knowledge to alter her course or to cast aside the old theology. Rather, new insights would be incorporated in harmony with the old. He urged his students to be confident in the face of challenges from modern thought, proclaiming that when criticism had completed its work, "we shall simply be where the early Christians were, and the great passages of Scripture which yield important doctrinal results are generally so clear that interpretation can do little more for them."[69]

When kept under the pious control of men such as Caven, the higher criticism and evolutionary theory were thoroughly tamed by the evangelical imperative. The historical method, far from undermining theology, could be enlisted as a useful servant of the church. By directing attention to the biblical text, the new scholarship renewed the bond between professor and preacher. More importantly, it linked the Canadian church colleges to the wider world of inquiry by insisting on the compatibility of faith and critical research in a culture where this belief had been eroded by the impact of mechanistic views of evolution. Best of all, it did not encourage uncertainty on the subject of the essential doctrines. The "reverent" criticism of the Bible testified to the total historical accuracy and doctrinal validity of the text of Scripture, and thus confirmed the unity of theology and history central to the evangelical task.

This reworking of the balance of piety and critical thought was designed to shore up the pillars of the evangelical creed by ensuring that issues raised by the new biblical scholarship would not divide college and church. Caven's position as the chief mediator in a struggle that could have ruptured Presbyterianism was equally important in the shaping of the Protestant response to evolutionary thought in Canada. During the crucial years between 1860 and 1880 he elaborated his ideas against a background of intense negotiations between the Free Church and Church of Scotland Presbyterians in Canada. Caven's synthesis of evangelicalism and evolution could be said to have served as the intellectual basis of the eventual rapprochement that resulted in the reunification of the two churches in 1875. His insistence on reverence, humility, and the supremacy of the Bible in his accommodation of piety and critical thought won over to the side of "biblical theology" leading Free Church clergymen MacVicar, then principal of Montreal College, and King, then principal of Manitoba College, who might otherwise have greeted historical criticism with hostility. On the other hand, Caven's insistence on the application of criticism in theological study reassured the clergymen of the numerically smaller Church of Scotland who looked to Queen's University and to the intellectual leadership of William Snodgrass and George Monro Grant. The protean nature of "biblical theology," and its apparent power to reconcile immutable certainty with the progress of human knowledge and culture, eased the tensions that, in the American churches, had divided "conservatives" and "liberals."

As the direct heirs of the evangelical revolt against the eighteenth century, professors and preachers in the Canadian branch of the Free Church insisted on maintaining the supreme authority of biblical revelation as the basis for their religious outlook. But Caven, MacVicar, and King devised a way of making the higher criticism palatable to the traditions of the evangelical creed, by incorporating critical thought within a Baconian structure of truth and finding a middle way between higher criticism and the traditional lower criticism, while firmly denying the claim of historical criticism to alter or revise the "facts" of Scripture or their divine inspiration.

King clearly described the spirit underlying the merging of higher criticism and the Baconian outlook in his important address, "The Spirit in Which Theological Enquiry Should be Prosecuted." His attitude was a significant indicator of opinion within the Presbyterian church for, unlike Caven, King was a professor of theology. Born in Scotland in 1829, he was educated at Edinburgh University, receiving an M.A. in 1856. In that year he arrived in Canada and, after serving as pastor of Gould St Church, Toronto, was called to the principal's chair at Manitoba College, Winnipeg in 1883.[70] Though his opinions had been formed in an earlier age of theological discussion, King had an open mind on the newer questions. He even invited eminent Scottish biblical critics such as George Adam Smith to lecture to the summer school.

King's admonitions on the subject of higher criticism rested on two premises. First, inquiry into religious matters must proceed with an unprejudiced spirit, but at all costs the student should endeavour to avoid "premature generalizations, hasty and unwarranted inferences, mistaken views of fundamental doctrines," as these could lead to "the loss of faith for large numbers" and could cripple the energies of the church. Second, and more importantly, because the integrity and inspiration of the biblical text was the basis of theology, King insisted that the proper spirit of inquiry presupposed the existence of God and "the facts of a divine revelation." Doctrines such as the divinity of Christ, the redemptive character of His death, and the supernatural character of the believer's life were fundamental, and lay "beyond impeachment within the church."[71] While retreating from a position of total acceptance of biblical "inerrancy," King stood firm on biblical inspiration and authority. Although critics might explode the books of the Bible into fragments of tradition, he was no less certain than McCulloch or Burns that these writings contained a miraculous, divine power that could speak to human consciences. If King and his colleagues conceded that there was a human element in the Scripture, they were no less adamant that the

Bible contained certain historical and doctrinal truths on which they could base a "living scriptural orthodoxy – a firm and honest belief in doctrines settled by a diligent, comprehensive, inductive study of the whole Word of God."[72]

The forceful presence of these men and their students in the councils of the church between 1870 and 1900 established a delicate balance. Caven, King, and MacVicar ensured that the "progressive" and "critical" tendencies within the Scottish "biblical revolution" would not override the older evangelical emphasis on reverence and induction. But a more practical difficulty remained. How to ensure that the work of the biblical scholar in the college would continue to assist and support the preacher? Could the new historical approach to the Bible be reconciled with "doctrinal preaching,"[73] the expository preaching of the Presbyterian tradition based on the integrity and factual accuracy of the biblical text?

The insistence that biblical critics respect the central doctrines of Christianity and popular views concerning Scripture was a conscious attempt by college leaders to draw a distinction between the proper use of criticism and the German separation of biblical scholarship from theology and the life of the church. Moreover, the preservation of a Baconian approach depended on their ability to limit the application of evolutionary explanations to religious truth. Thus their efforts were directed to keeping the historical study of the Bible separate from the all-encompassing evolutionary naturalism that would have denied the conscious, miraculous purpose of God in revelation and human history.

In an address delivered in 1884 to the students of Presbyterian College, Montreal, the Rev. John Scrimger, professor of exegesis at the college, conceded that much of the Bible was indeed a human product, and not equally inspired in all its parts. But, he hastened to add, it was "composed under such a divine superintendence as to render it inspired and authoritative, and so placed on a somewhat higher level than ordinary history, even when strictly accurate. In so far as it is inspired it might be regarded as a revelation ... because even the simplest narrative must exhibit something of God's character or will." Scripture witnessed a process of development, but this was different from an evolution by naturalistic mechanisms or social "laws."[74] This important statement by a practicing biblical scholar expressed the emerging consensus within the Presbyterian colleges on the relationship of the Bible and historical criticism. In 1893 Caven introduced the position elaborated in the colleges to the wider church in an address to the General Assembly of the Presbyterian Church at Brantford. He offered a dual explanation of Scripture: first, it was the word of God; but second, it was "written by the hand of man." This balance of the divine and human elements enabled Caven to view the Bible as a process of progressive revelation, a development of the religious consciousness under divine guidance, not natural law.[75]

The position adopted by Caven and Scrimger might be regarded as a misguided attempt to reconcile two incompatible elements – the Baconian certainty anchoring the evangelical creed and the higher criticism founded on the evolutionary insights afforded by historical study – or dismissed as an eclectic attempt to extract from German influences what suited them best.[76] In the Presbyterian colleges, however, historical criticism was clearly designed to affirm the supremacy of the Bible as the ruler of faith and theology, and the place accorded higher criticism in evangelical education reflected the continued power of the older theology of history that had dominated colonial preaching in the early nineteenth-century revival. Recognition of the affinity between theology and history formed the substance of an address to the students of Presbyterian College, Montreal by the Rev. John Campbell, the professor of church history. Both disciplines, he declared, dealt with "fact," and not with theories or speculations. History promised to scrupulously observe and judge all the "facts," especially those of a moral nature. Few professors, clergymen, or students would have quarreled with Campbell's conclusion that the Bible was "a history, first and foremost, and as a history it takes its place to be judged by history."[77] Because historical study preserved the supremacy of the biblical text as the source of evidence concerning God's activity in the world, Campbell and his colleagues considered it the perfect ally in theology's struggle for relevance.

"The Bible," Campbell concluded after two decades of historical study at Montreal College, "still proves itself the true and faithful Word, the great standard of historic fact as well as of spiritual truth and life."[78] This statement indicates the conviction in college circles that professors had successfully incorporated the new history into the evangelical creed, despite the concessions to higher criticism. In the process they had created a new field of study in which theology was inductively based on insights provided by history and philology. The name of the new discipline, "biblical theology," implied that these prominent Presbyterians had not transformed biblical study in their colleges into a "research ideal" aimed at independent investigation of religious questions and the training of an academic elite.[79] The whole tenor of the Presbyterian college was directed to ensuring the cautious presentation of critical results in the interests of reverent faith and sound preaching. The resolution of questions such as the authorship and dating of the various books of the Old Testament followed not the "documentary hypothesis" of Wellhausen, but the familiar outlines of the traditional canon. For Scrimger, the biblical scholar was the servant of the church, and should be content to "abide by the opinions that have been most generally held by the Church." He clearly intended to warn his students to avoid "startling novelties" in interpretation. Faith, not mere critical knowledge, was the measure of a sound biblical scholar.[80]

That such Bible scholars and historians found it possible to accommodate the supremacy of faith and theology to the "biblical revolution" by accepting a form of "reverent criticism" points to the success of leading Presbyterians in resolving a highly sensitive issue: the definition of the proper application of higher criticism in relation to the biblical text and the traditions of evangelical education. The coming of higher criticism between 1875 and 1890 has been said to mark the decline of the traditional theology in evangelical circles, and the triumph of a religious "liberalism" or "modernism" stressing practical good works over Bible and creed.[81] But the success achieved by the numerically dominant colonial Free Church tradition in confining and constraining the higher criticism compels revision of standard definitions of "liberal" and "modernist" as applied to the Canadian Protestant experience.

According to one prominent American historian, religious "liberalism" was generally humanistic, and posited a universal religious experience behind the churches, Scriptures, and creeds of Christianity. It valued good works over professions and confessions of faith. By the late 1890s some "liberals" had moved further, toward a "conscious, intended adaptation of religious ideas to modern culture."[82] To apply such labels to Caven, MacVicar, and King, or even to younger professors such as Baird or Scrimger would be to ignore the evangelical character of their thought. None of these clergymen would have accepted that a universal religious experience stood before or above the biblical revelation of the "facts" of Christianity, and none would have exalted good works over sound doctrine. All would have resisted the claim of historical criticism to final of authority in the life of the church, and all would have adamantly opposed the adaptation of Christian belief to modern culture. They would have retorted that "biblical theology" enabled them to adapt evolution and the higher criticism to the fundamental tenets of the evangelical creed. This, in their eyes, confirmed the vitality of their religion, as well as their belief that their theology would not be imprisoned by modern culture, but would stand above and transform individual and society.

G.M. GRANT AND THE "QUEEN'S TRADITION": THE ORIGINS OF LIBERAL PROTESTANTISM?

Writing to Nelles in 1881, Principal Grant of Queen's University summarized his views on the proper relationship between religion and critical thought. Castigating the "weakness, the unbelief of mere traditionalism," he urged a positive encounter with the new insights provided by historical and scientific study. "Just because I have faith in the great spiritual truths of Revelation & in the supernatural facts on which Christianity is based," he declared, "I demand freedom to investigate & to think, for myself & for others." This freedom of investigation implied that clergymen-professors should strive to scrape away "from the fair face of truth the dust & grime of centuries, that all may behold & be entranced by the surpassing beauty of her countenance."[83]

Grant's impatience with "traditionalism" could be seen as a Canadian expression of the "liberal" tendencies sweeping the world of transatlantic Protestantism in the 1880s. After all, Queen's University, which Grant dominated between 1877 and 1902, was also the home of John Watson, a student of Edward Caird and an internationally renowned idealist philosopher. By 1890, several generations of Queen's students had been exposed to Watson's Hegelian message that no opposition existed between religion and science, and that the essence of Christianity was less bound up with Bible, creeds, and doctrines – the stuff of traditional faith – than with the practical application of Christian social ideals to secular society.[84] The forceful idealist presence at Queen's has led to the characterization of Grant as a "modernist," an advocate of the new fashions in higher criticism who was so profoundly influenced by the new philosophy that he was more interested in practical social service than in theological matters.[85]

Grant's contemporaries, however, held a different view. John Watson, for example, despairingly described the principal's views as "traditional and antiquated," closer to the evangelical assertion of dogma than to the spirit of critical inquiry the philosopher wished to promote at Queen's.[86] Grant's letter to Nelles also revealed an outlook that placed him and other prominent clergymen of the Church of Scotland in Canada in an intellectual climate removed from the lofty debates of the philosophical idealists. His insistence on "spiritual truths" and "supernatural facts" appealed to the legacy of the evangelical creed and its theology of history. He assumed that although these truths or doctrines needed the purifying influence of historical investigation and critical thought to maintain their influence in Christian life and culture, they were immutable and enduring.

The foundations of Grant's religious outlook can be traced, not to the impact of Hegelian ideas at Queen's, but to the same revolution in Scottish culture that gave rise to the "biblical theology" of the Canadian Free Church. Born in 1835 at Albion Mines, Nova Scotia, Grant attended the Pictou Academy before going to Glasgow in 1853 to train for the Church of Scotland ministry. While full of admiration for the zeal and self-sacrifice of the Free Church, he was deeply offended by its intolerance and what he considered its tendency to "priestcraft." Grant preferred the "broad sanity" displayed by John Tulloch, principal of St Andrew's University, John Caird, a powerful preacher and later the chief promoter of the Hegelian philosophy in Scotland, and, in particular, by the most "practical" and evangelical of the Church of Scotland leaders, Norman McLeod, minister of Barony Church, Glasgow, whom he regarded as the greatest man he ever knew.[87]

This remarkable trio decisively reoriented the theology and preaching of the Church of Scotland in the years after the Disruption. They were united by a common approach: the desire to mediate between traditionalism and rationalism by insisting upon a living, practical theology. Their outlook was best stated by Tulloch in his 1854 inaugural address at St Andrew's University. Truth, he declared, could not be held unquestioningly in any outward formula, for it was the product of revelation and free inquiry. Insistence on rigid creeds or confessions of faith destroyed the conditions for a living theology.[88] A similar emphasis on practical activity characterized the preaching of John Caird and McLeod. Forms and doctrines, they declared, were not ends in themselves. Religion consisted "not so much in doing spiritual or sacred acts as in doing secular acts from a spiritual or sacred motive." For McLeod, whose Glasgow parish Grant attended, the church was a great social system ordained for the well-being of humanity, and specially charged with the work of social and educational improvement in an industrial society.[89]

The recurring theme among these Church of Scotland clergymen was "broad" or "catholic," words implying the equation of religion with the experiences of life. This outlook encouraged ministers to view doctrine not as an inflexible set of axioms recorded in confessions of faith, but rather as something progressive, modified by the historical tendencies of the different periods of church history. Such ideas left a twofold and lasting impression on George Grant. First, his encounter with this variant of "historical theology" enabled him to reconcile the traditions of the evangelical creed with the historical criticism of the Bible then penetrating the Scottish university faculties. Second, the preaching of MacLeod encouraged a distrust of speculation, and an awareness of the possibility of conflict between the critical inquiry promoted by idealist philosophers like the Cairds, and the "facts" of the Christian revelation.

This potential for conflict conditioned the response of Grant's younger countrymen Daniel Miner Gordon and Daniel James Macdonnell in the early 1860s. Both men attended Glasgow University where John Caird had just assumed the principalship and the professorship of divinity. While impressed with Caird's personality, they had reservations about his attempt to recast theology according to Hegelian categories. Like their older colleague, they held that the "facts" of Scripture and Christian life were more important than philosophical speculation. Macdonnell's biographer noted that "the same temper of mind which led him to crave with such intense earnestness indubitable authority for all the dogmatic statements of our faith, forced him also to drop any theme or idea of speculative theology which had not to do with the vital spiritual interests of men."[90] The idea of religion bound by the inexorable scientific law of evolution was unacceptable to these young preachers because it threatened to open the certainty of theology to the relativism of critical philosophy. Though Grant, Macdonnell, and Gordon certainly admired the social ethic of idealism, they were acutely conscious of the fact that the Cairds treated doctrines as mere ideas, not based on the biblical realities so close to the heart of Presbyterian congregations.

Thus between 1870 and 1890 the interlocking triad of theology, preaching, and education in the smaller Church of Scotland in Canada resembled that which prevailed among the Free Church clergy. Though anxious to address questions raised by evolution and the higher criticism, Grant and his colleagues sought an accommodation anchored on the Baconian definition of the relationship between revelation and reason. For all his abhorrence of rigid creeds and his plea for a fearless scientific criticism of the Bible[91], first broached in 1862, in an address to Nova Scotian Presbyterians entitled "The Young Man's Life," Grant remained a firm champion of the older evangelicalism in his insistence on the unity of theology and history.

The continuing power of the evangelical creed over Grant's religious outlook was displayed during a moment of controversy in 1875. When the critic William Dawson LeSueur, writing under the pseudonym "Laon," audaciously proclaimed the irreconcilable opposition between evangelical religion and scientific thought, Grant's riposte was swift, charging that Laon had caricatured and misrepresented Christianity. More importantly, Grant's defence of Christianity in the face of the new critical thought revealed his reliance on the affinities between the new historical theology and the older Baconian emphasis. "We believe," he declared,

that scientific truth is God's truth, and we accept it reverently ... We believe that theologians have erred in their interpretations of Scripture, that scientists have erred in their theories or interpretations of phenomena, and that the critics modern culture glories in most, have erred in their criticism; that, in one word, to err is human, and that therefore modesty becomes the true scholar. We believe that history is the record of Providence, and we believe that history truly read shows the miracles recorded in Jewish history in "a different light from those recorded in Roman, Grecian, or Indian history."[92]

Far from advocating a religious "modernism" in response to critical thought, Grant was stating a position acceptable to previous generations of colonial clergymen-professors, and to his Free Church counterparts Caven, MacVicar, and King. The Bible was a special revelation that should be treated with humility and reverence, a sacred history revealing the miraculous reality of a divine providence guiding human hearts and society.

The views of Grant, Macdonnell, Gordon, and Snodgrass on the relationship between theology and history so closely resembled the reconciliation of evangelical doctrine and biblical criticism advanced by the clergymen-professors of the Free Church that "historical theology" served as the intellectual cement of the Presbyterian union of 1875, in which the numerically smaller Church of Scotland joined the Free Church. A year later, however, the Presbyterian Church was sorely tested by a sermon preached at St Andrew's Church in Toronto. Macdonnell, Grant's close associate, expressed doubts about whether the doctrine of eternal punishment set forth in the Presbyterian creed, the Westminster Confession of Faith, was consistent with certain passages of Scripture.[93] Although Macdonnell's sermon involved neither evolution nor higher criticism, it worried those clergymen-professors preoccupied with the search for a balance between the evangelical creed and the critical temper.

Grant himself was privately critical of Macdonnell, calling his sermon "injudicious," but he was more concerned with the conduct of the leaders of the Free Church party. In a letter to Snodgrass, then serving his last year as principal of Queen's, Grant denounced the "keen, relentless, inquisitorial attitude" of the Knox professors,

Caven and MacLaren.[94] Though Macdonnell was acquitted of any charge of heresy, the entire episode of the "trial" revealed the persistence of subtle differences within the new Presbyterian body over the meaning of "historical theology." While Grant, Macdonnell, and their Free Church counterparts would have agreed on the Baconian insistence on the supremacy of faith and the biblical revelation in theological inquiry, the Church of Scotland party at Queen's were more prepared to use the new accommodation of theology and historical knowledge to revise doctrines they regarded as non-essential.

This spirit was the guiding force behind Grant's educational enterprise at Queen's University. The goal of the principal and his supporters, expressed in the annual Queen's Theological Alumni Conferences held in the years after 1893, was the "enlargement" of Christianity through the reconciliation of theology with other disciplines. For Grant, the Christian religion was "true philosophy," for it sought the truth in every department of life.[95] This statement should not be taken, however, as an affirmation of a commitment on Grant's part to replace evangelical theology with Watson's idealist philosophy or with forms of social service popular among "liberal" Protestants.

From the very beginning of his tenure as principal and professor of divinity, Grant intended, like Caven at Knox College, to establish the primacy and independence of theology in modern culture. He urged upon his students the "historical theology" elaborated at Edinburgh in the 1870s by his friend Robert Flint, a contemporary at Glasgow University. In his inaugural address in 1877 he praised the inductive outlook promoted by the new discipline, saying that to "collect all the facts and rightly interpret them" was a pious activity that would prove "subversive to all anti-Christian theories."[96] Although he conceived of theology as a progressive science, he clearly regarded it as the central discipline of the college. "All subjects," he declared in a Convocation Day speech, "lead up to Theology. Very few of you intend to study the special science of Theology, but every thinking man must be a Theologian. He must have a theory with regard to the great questions that lie at the root of all thought."[97]

For Grant, a true theology was progressive, based upon close study of the books of the Bible placed in their historical setting. But it also looked to the past, to the inductive certainty of the "facts" as revealed in Scripture. These were the twin emphases of biblical study at Queen's. Grant and his associates took great pains to separate biblical criticism from an ironclad evolutionism, by stressing that the Bible contained a special divine element, and that faith, not critical acumen, was the essential criterion of biblical scholarship.[98] This continued loyalty to the Baconian emphasis of the evangelical creed most clearly distinguished Grant from the philosopher John Watson. Given the centrality of the Incarnation in his theology, Grant was reluctant to interpret the Christian faith as the product of the logical evolution of eternal principles. He refused to abandon the idea of a miraculous providence intervening at critical moments in human history. While Caird and Watson idealized the figure of Christ as the epitome of ethical qualities inherent in the human spirit, Grant dwelt upon His uniqueness and finality, proclaiming that "He is a cosmical and historical miracle or something new in Humanity."[99]

Far from surrendering the central tenets of his creed to the critical scrutiny of the philosophers, Grant shared the traditional hostility of evangelical preachers to "speculation," and would have emphatically agreed with the forceful criticisms of idealism advanced by King at Manitoba College.[100] If the standard picture of late Victorian Protestantism is correct, and "liberalism" in the form of idealism, higher criticism, or social service was the dominant current within the Presbyterian Church, then Grant, who is usually regarded as standing at the confluence of these currents, was a man clearly out of sympathy with the spirit of the age. But if the period between 1870 and 1890 is viewed in a new light, as a time when clergymen-professors were able to strike a delicate balance between their creed and elements of critical thought, then the attitudes of Grant and his colleagues become more comprehensible. Neither "liberal" nor "conservative," their theology, elaborated in a continuous conversation between evangelicalism and evolutionary thought, colonial college and metropolitan university, lecture hall and pulpit, aptly expressed the continuing vitality of a religious outlook that traced its origins to the age of the revival.

SAMUEL NELLES AND VICTORIA COLLEGE:
THE METHODIST TRADITION, CRITICAL
THOUGHT, AND THE FRAMING OF AN
"INDUCTIVE THEOLOGY"

The encounter between tradition and evolutionary thought in the Presbyterian Church between 1860 and 1890 was mediated by the legacy of the evangelical Awakening and by the continuing influence of the Scottish metropolis in the crucial spheres of education and biblical study. Though the Methodist clergy had similar links to the intellectual world of the revival, they lacked the direct connection to overseas centres of learning that served to moderate the impact of the higher criticism on their Presbyterian counterparts. Yet by

1890 Methodists had found a resolution to the tension between the evangelical creed and evolution remarkably similar to the "biblical theology" of Caven and Grant. With a minimum of turmoil, influential preachers and clergymen-professors combined higher criticism with the Methodist traditions of learning that had governed the relationship of faith and reason in college and congregation between 1820 and 1860.

The Rev. Samuel Nelles was the key figure in guiding the Methodist encounter with evolutionary thought. First president and later chancellor of Victoria College, he dominated its intellectual life from 1850 until his death in 1887. As a young man he had absorbed Ryerson's Baconian tenets and the theology of Richard Watson, with their inflexible insistence on the supremacy of the Bible, and on a theology based on the inductive certainty of biblical facts and Christian experience as the only means of organizing scientific, historical, and philosophical knowledge. But Nelles had been exposed to conflicting influences. Before entering Victoria College, he had attended the Genesee Wesleyan Seminary in Lima, New York, and, in 1846–47, he had transferred to the Wesleyan University of Middletown, Connecticut, to complete his undergraduate training.[101]

For a young Methodist, a stay in the "burned-over district" of western New York State in the 1840s was a source of great religious excitement. The area contained a welter of competing revivalist, utopian, and millenarian sects: Shakers, Millerites, and Mormons, as well as the main-line evangelical denominations.[102] All rested their expectations on biblical prophecy, on the belief in the coincidence of revelation and universal history. Such religious pluralism, however, subverted any notion that Nelles might have held concerning Methodism's monopoly of religious truth. These influences were later reinforced at the Methodist university in New England, Wesleyan University, where he would have encountered the beginnings of the assault on Common Sense philosophy led by Horace Bushnell, the Transcendentalists, and other American partisans of romanticism and idealism.

The experience of the American religious scene at this critical juncture in Nelles's life left a lasting impression on his theological outlook. Not only did his journals and notebooks make frequent references to American authors and theological issues throughout the late 1840s and 1850s,[103] but also they recorded the agonizings of a mind profoundly dissatisfied and ill at ease with prevailing opinions in the Methodist Church regarding the relationship between Scripture, intellect, and experience. Nelles often engaged in a private world of romantic fantasies in which he took the shape of a "monstrous Heresiarch," flirting with what he considered unorthodox religious opinions, and confidently "erect[ing] my own Reason as umpire in the great trial"[104] between the old creeds and modern culture.

Whatever these private musings might reveal about his psychological state, they placed Nelles at a point of transition in the intellectual life of Canadian Methodism. They signalled a clear breach with the world of Watson and Ryerson. By the time of his appointment to the chair of moral philosophy at Victoria College in 1850, Nelles had worked out a new balance of faith and reason decisively at variance with the older evangelical theology based on biblical literalism. "I persist," he wrote in 1848, "in regarding the Bible as only a part of *Revelation* or ... *as one mode* of revelation." While adhering to the older evangelical belief that all truth was contained in Scripture, he drew an important distinction, claiming that the books of the Bible did not present "the *letter*" of divine authority. Scriptural truth, he believed, required the illustration of "*Reason and Nature*" to appeal to the mind and the heart. Moreover, he claimed the right to seek assistance from grammatical analysis, history, archaeology, and geography, the human sciences that the German critics so effectively deployed in their own biblical researches.[105]

When he assumed the presidency of the struggling Methodist college in 1854 at the age of thirty-one, Nelles was poised to introduce his private views to a wider audience of students and clergymen. While his lectures and addresses to the college community actively urged the harmony of piety and intellect as the goal of a college-trained ministry, he used his position to proclaim his discomfort with certain crucial features of the popular theology of Methodism. In particular, Nelles had long been troubled by what he considered the predominance of "feeling" in the preaching and life of the Methodist church. While admitting that emotion constituted an important element of religion, he argued that "feeling is not to be constantly thrust forward on the thought as the great essential *directly* to be sought after, but rather to follow as in the train of reason and practical endeavor. If we take care of other things feeling will take care of itself."[106]

His criticism of the older world of the Methodist revival, whose theology, Nelles believed, was founded on the twin pillars of biblical literalism and feeling, made him the most prominent representative of a current that by 1860 was beginning to transform Canadian Methodism. His appointment as principal of Victoria College coincided with a gradual decline in the importance of revivalism as a means of grace within the church itself. Nelles was among the first to grasp the need for new religious practices and institutions in a society that had moved beyond the pioneer stage. In such a society, he believed that the strength of Methodism would lie not in the power of feeling or in the old popular faith in biblical inerrancy, but in the appeal of an educated ministry to the conscience of the people. He quickly realized the crucial importance of the college to the life of the church, and he used his experience of the American religious scene in the 1840s to transform Victoria College from an institution dominated by the spirit of the revival to an institution promoting "Christian nurture,"[107] the gradual growth of religion in mind and heart through training and education, rather than through the turmoil and cataclysm of the revival meeting.

Nelles's support of a greater role for reason in the interpretation of the Bible, buttressed by the idea of "Christian nurture," contributed directly to the formulation of a new view of Christian theology. In the late 1840s Nelles was already advancing the view that "Christianity is progressive – theoretically as well as practically ... The human mind is progressive. Christianity is adapted to the human mind, therefore it is progressive too." Again, Nelles's experience of the American religious climate dominated by millennialism and notions of optimistic perfectionism was the key to his views on the progressive nature of religious truth. Though based on an unchanging divine will, theology drew fresh insights from philosophy, history, and science in its attempt to discern the will of God in both individual and society. Clearly expressing the new spirit at Victoria College, Nelles proclaimed:

Now in many cases new views will continually break in upon the Church and as they do – Christianity will grow better, will unfold a new leaf of the yet rising plant. We have only to cling to the Bible. It is all unfolded there. And from the above considerations how important a science does Biblical Interpretation become. As science advances – as society advances – the Bible will become clearer and clearer. As we come to know more of human nature and more of the material universe we will learn more of the divine will – more of the *Spirit of Christianity* – and growing more will *practice* more. Scripture will become more and more harmonious – sects more united ... Whosoever advances society advances Christianity and still more does he who advances Christianity advances society.[108]

Like the individual and society, theology was an organic product susceptible to growth and progress. Millennial belief dictated that a progressive theology could not be separated from practical life, from human conduct and morality. Only by acknowledging a wider role for reason in relation to the Bible, Nelles maintained, could such a theology be an active force in shaping the perfect society that he saw unfolding in North America.

Nelles's early acceptance of a progressive interpretation of the nature of theology was of crucial significance for Canadian Methodism. His views on the relationship of the Bible, theology, and reason were framed without the influence of Darwinism or the higher criticism, the catalysts usually associated with the rise of such beliefs within the Protestant churches. His formulation of the idea of "progressive revelation" long before the appearance of Darwin or German thought on the Canadian scene raises certain questions. How did Nelles acquire these beliefs, and from what intellectual traditions did he develop such heady views on the progressive nature of religious truth? And can Nelles's own estimate of his revolt against Methodism be accepted at face value?

It would be easy to accept that, at a stroke, he had demolished the intellectual world of Watson and Ryerson in the name of an ethical, humanistic "liberalism." But a closer look at Nelles's religious opinions places him in a world still defined by the evangelical creed and by the Methodist quadrilateral of Scripture, reason, experience, and tradition. Despite his impatience with certain practices of the Methodist Church, Nelles firmly believed that the church contained within its own theology the seeds of the new outlook on the relationship between faith and learning. He admired the flexible spirit of John Wesley's rules, which required only repentance and desire for salvation as conditions of church membership, with each individual forming his own creed from personal study of the Bible with the assistance of Christian teachers. This flexibility was balanced by the firmness of his own personal creed, flowing from a vital religious experience, the gift of faith "such as I never had before. I am enabled now to cast myself wholly upon the arms of my Saviour."[109] The assurance conferred by this experience guided his theological investigations and college teaching for over forty years, reinforcing his belief in the ultimate harmony of piety and learning. Writing in his journal in 1848, Nelles summarized his beliefs, which he based upon the unity of God, the divinity and redemptive mediation of Jesus Christ, and the reality and awfulness of sin. In the spirit of the evangelical tradition, he urged Christians to "stand more on the Bible and less on formularies, more on great, common principles less on distinctive, trifling badges."[110]

Though critical of the biblical literalism of Ryerson and Watson, Nelles was unwilling to exalt reason over faith. Even more than his predecessors, he was conscious of living in an age of philosophical turmoil, and of witnessing the breakdown of the comforting harmony between Christianity and Common Sense. His lectures to the students of Victoria College in praise of the unity of piety and intellect always had a darker side, and were punctuated with intimations of open warfare between religion and critical thought, warnings that "Parnassus has repudiated the lore of Calvary."[111] For this reason, he valued the Bible and his creed over any particular philosophical opinions. One of his most characteristic utterances was in praise of eclecticism in philosophy,[112] a luxury afforded to him only by a firm faith in the articles of his own creed and in the revelation of Christianity in the Bible.

For Nelles, the term "reason" assumed a meaning far more consonant with the traditions of Methodist theology than with its use by German critics to alter the historical, doctrinal, and moral content of the biblical text. Reason was practical and experimental, rather than speculative. The proper exercise of reason, he insisted, required a perspective that accepted "a considerable balance of probability in favor of Christianity." Through the exercise of faith, the "surrender of the heart," the student would discover "more evidence – of an internal kind – and more satisfactory and logical than the other." As at Ryerson's Victoria College, the method of research involved an inductive quest for religious certainty far removed from the cool, logical subtleties of the Scottish philosophers or the biblical institutes of Germany, a process marked by "patient search, and candor, and *believing trial*."[113] Nelles's unity of creed and college education reflected the sober, practical piety of evangelicalism, and appealed to the conscience and the moral sense in the discovery of religious truth. Though more willing than his mentor Ryerson to advocate freedom of inquiry in relation to the Bible, Nelles still hedged the exercise of reason with the powerful sanctions of piety. The crucial factor, Nelles believed, lay not with the critical acumen or learning of the scholar, but with the vital religion of experience: prayer, Scripture reading, repentance, and faith were more important to the spirit of inquiry than critical and linguistic skills.

Although Nelles accorded a higher place to reason and inquiry in the lecture halls of Victoria College than Ryerson had conceded, the insistence on Baconian induction remained paramount in the intellectual life of the college. While the new president placed a high value on the language of practice and experiment, he did not intend to subordinate the Bible and theology to either the natural or the human sciences. The most obvious clue to Nelles's approach was his use of Butler's eighteenth-century texts in his moral philosophy class until well into the 1860s. Nelles used Butler not to reinforce a rigid biblical literalism, but to underline the close relationship of religion, morality, and science.[114] To realize the intricate connections of evidence was to discourage views of Scripture and doctrine founded on speculation, rather than on the certainty of careful induction. "The use of our reason in Scripture," Nelles declared, "is first to decide what is Scripture and secondly to get the true idea of Scripture. When we are once satisfied that God has spoken so and so, all enquiry ends, we have nothing to do but obey."[115] Behind the pursuit of knowledge lay the yearning for certainty, the hope that in a world of increasing moral and scientific turmoil, the Christian believer could find a secure anchorage.

For a decade the search for a viable balance between reason and faith, criticism and certainty, stability and progress preoccupied Nelles as both professor and preacher. The result could best be termed "inductive theology," a discipline receptive to inquiry and to the idea of the progress of religious truth, but as insistent as the earlier theology of Methodist preachers on the integrity of the Gospel as the universal law of life and character.[116] By 1860 Nelles had used "inductive theology" to subtly shift the popular theology of the revival in the direction of "Christian nurture" and away from a literal view of Scripture, not by introducing higher criticism, evolutionary forms of inquiry, or speculative philosophy, but by introducing the Methodist theology and the Baconian heritage of the late eighteenth century to the tenets of millennial optimism. Far from encouraging an unbridled critical spirit, Victoria College under President Nelles remained the servant of the church, an institution devoted to the elaboration of the evangelical creed and the Christianizing of human knowledge.

"INDUCTIVE THEOLOGY" AND REVERENT CRITICISM: VICTORIA COLLEGE AND THE EVOLUTIONARY CHALLENGE, 1860–1890

In an unpublished memoir of his life as a Methodist preacher and professor, the Rev. Nathanael Burwash recalled a painful test of his faith that had occurred while he was a young minister at Belleville in the early 1860s. A young man who had fallen away from the church lent him a copy of Bishop Colenso's critical work on the Pentateuch and, despite feeling well-equipped against the assaults of scepticism from his study of the great classics of Christian evidences, Paley, Butler, Watson, and Horne, the encounter proved deeply troubling. The work of the English biblical critic compelled Burwash to realize that "here was a new field and a new method which challenged you on the fundamental basis of philosophy and on the ground of the historical statements of scripture itself. I read the books and sometimes seemed to feel all certain ground sinking from under my feet."[117]

This meeting of higher criticism and the theology of Methodism did not, however, lead to loss of faith or to "doubt," that intellectual bogeyman of mid-Victorian Protestant Christians. Four years after this troubling encounter, Nathanael Burwash was appointed to the faculty of Victoria College as professor of natural science,and in 1871 to the new chair of theology. By 1880, he was dean of the faculty of theology, and in 1887 succeeded Nelles as president and chancellor of the college, a position he occupied until his retirement in 1913.[118] As the most prominent intellectual figure in late-Victorian Methodism, Burwash was responsible for the training and spiritual welfare of a generation of preachers, a position scarcely compatible with any lingering doubts about the authority of the Bible and the central tenets of the evangelical creed. How to explain Burwash's resolution of the challenge of higher criticism to his faith and his decision to continue as a minister of the Methodist Church? Did his course of action reflect a wider pattern of response to the challenge of evolution and critical thought within Canadian Methodism?

Burwash's ability to preserve the substance of his theology in the face of the evolutionary challenge reflected his exposure to the reworking of the balance between faith and reason undertaken by Nelles in the 1850s. As a student at the college between 1854 and 1859, Burwash was exposed to the intellectual challenges to doctrinal certainty represented by the collapse of Common Sense and natural theology. He absorbed the reconciliation of the old Baconian empiricism and elements of critical thought characteristic of the emerging "inductive theology." In the three decades after the appearance of Darwin, Nelles's theology proved so accommodating and flexible that, with minor adjustments, its main outlines were more firmly ensconced in the life of college and congregation by 1890.

With its roots in the experimental theology of the Methodist revival, "inductive theology" subordinated notions of authority, doctrine, and the newer criticism to an ideal of practical Christian living. Nelles's insistence that the student undertake an earnest, inductive quest for truth also offered an effective counterpoise to "doubt." He regarded the temper of the doubter as compatible with that of the Christian seeker. In an important address, Nelles told the professors and students of the college that

doubt so far from being sinful in itself is the very dawn of a purer light.

Doubting can never be sinful when it arises from any appearance of error in what we have held or may be proposed for our belief, and some appearance of truth lying in the contrary supposition. The mind must be determined by the evidence; if the evidence fail any dogma it would be wrong not to doubt; it is necessary to abandon such dogma.

And yet it is hard to abandon dogmas that we received as sacred in the days of childhood. Such notions become so thoroughly imbedded in the soul that we cannot easily eradicate them: often in attempting to do so we uproot also the most valuable truths along with what we have found to be pernicious errors. None but a very strong and patient understanding can safely undertake this work. [119]

Nelles believed that aspiring preachers and students of the Bible should balance freedom of investigation and a careful collection and sifting of the evidence with a cautious regard for tradition, and an awareness that these beliefs could not be uprooted without grave danger to religious faith.

This blending of reverence with a willingness to incorporate insights provided by new forms of knowledge dictated Nelles's response to the intellectual crises of the 1860s. During these years, he sensed a universal movement throughout Christendom portending a period of transition and drift in religious thought. He read widely in philosophy and history, noting particularly the work of Immanuel Kant in his search for a more adequate Christian apologetic than that offered by Butler. [120] The debate, he recognized, had shifted from arguments over proofs of Christianity and the vexed question of the relationship of revelation and nature to the problem of the essence of Christianity itself. Nelles recognized that historical study of the Bible could contribute greatly to the uncovering of the essential elements of the faith. In an 1869 address to a group of Methodist clergymen, he urged an attitude of tolerance toward the efforts of biblical critics, even though some of these scholars might be tainted with "heterodoxy." "The old heretics called themselves Christians; so do modern unbelievers. To some this may seem no improvement. May we not hope otherwise? It is concession, it is coming to terms: it is substituting inquiry for assault." [121]

Since the mid-1860s Nelles had introduced some of the questions raised by the higher criticism to his students. Relying on the New Testament commentaries of the "Liberal Anglican" scholar B.F. Westcott, he attempted to chart a course between the evangelical popular theology of plenary and verbal inspiration and the extreme critical view of the Bible as a collection of Hebrew legends constructed out of "man's poetic faculty." Agreeing with the English critic that the literal and the subjective might be harmoniously combined, Nelles accepted the transcendental character of revelation while assigning to it a substantial human element. There was, he indicated, no trace of designed connection between the separate books of the Bible, as they were written at different times, by different authors, and with different styles and designs. The formation of the Bible was thus a product of development. "Truth itself," he reminded the assembled students at a Sunday lecture in 1865, "does not change. Human conceptions change. This arises from [the] nature of the soul & from nature of religious truth." Man's development as recorded in the Bible and in universal history bore witness to the workings of divine providence, and progress in religious consciousness was firmly under the miraculous guidance of the divine presence.[122]

Nelles's new preoccupation with the question of the historical character and setting of the Christian religion, and his confident assertion of the progressive character of divine revelation were not confined to Victoria College. The close connection between Bible study and preaching meant that any concession to a greater role for reason in the interpretation of the Bible carried wider implications, both for Methodist theology and for the relationship between college and congregation. The first effects were felt, however, in the intellectual content of "inductive theology" itself. In the 1850s Nelles, influenced by Butler and the prestige of the sciences, dwelt extensively on the intricate and seamless connection between revelation, morality, and nature. His reading of German philosophy and biblical criticism in the 1860s, however, compelled him to abandon the attempt to find an analogy between theology and the natural sciences. Nelles readily relinquished this endeavour and eagerly turned to the task of subtly balancing faith in revelation and the study of history as a means of elucidating the "laws" of human character and conduct.

In this respect, Nelles's journey paralleled that of the proponents of the Scottish "historical theology," who developed a new intellectual structure from the elements supplied by the eighteenth-century traditions of Common Sense philosophy and natural theology. Although late twentieth-century historians assert that the years between 1860 and 1890 were a time of growing opposition between historical science and biblical revelation, the initial impact of the new historical knowledge revealed not the futility of the evangelical creed, but its intellectual vitality. It may be argued that the movement toward the "historical" did not mark a substantial break with the Butlerian-Baconian inheritance of the evangelicals. In the Methodist colleges, Victoria and Mount Allison, the works that Nelles, Burwash, and Charles Stewart used to introduce the new historical method to students – the Rev. A. S. Farrar's *A Critical History of Free Thought in Reference to the Christian Religion* (1862), George P. Fisher's *Essays on the Supernatural Origins of Christianity* (1877), and the Rev. F. W. Farrar's *History of Interpretation* (1886) – all praised Butler's notion of moral government, and insisted that the process of history itself bore witness to his dictum of the supremacy of supernatural purpose over natural processes.[123] The movement of the question of history to the centre of transatlantic religious debate enabled Nelles and his colleagues to reaffirm one of the central emphases of their religious heritage. His own preaching and reflections in the 1840s and 1850s had centred far more on the connections between the Bible, history, redemption, and prophecy, long recognized by the evangelical creed in the British North American colonies as the meeting place of the divine will and human conscience and character.

The new mood, the subtle shift from science to history was captured by Nelles's former student Burwash, Victoria College's new professor of natural science. At his inaugural address in 1867 he broke with tradition, refusing to construct a grand harmony of revelation and nature. Rather, in the new spirit fostered by Nelles, he humbly confessed his own ignorance, admitting that while both the Bible and nature were true, he could not "harmonize science in all its teachings with the general interpretation of Scripture."[124] By this time, younger clergymen-professors were thorough converts to "inductive theology" and its emphasis on the union of creed, character, and historical study. They believed that this discipline would bridge any gap between religion and intellect. More importantly, the historical character of Nelles's theology would preserve the independence of religious thought by placing the Bible firmly upon a foundation of a modern knowledge that respected the data of faith and revelation in the face of assaults by speculative philosophy and Darwinian science.

But before "inductive theology" could integrate divine revelation and human knowledge, it must be accommodated to the traditions of preaching and popular theology that characterized the life of Methodist congregations. Nelles's lectures on the new higher criticism were delivered in an environment where preachers such as Henry Flesher Bland relied on the traditional apologetic of Paley and Butler to insist on the plenary inspiration of the Bible regarding historical fact, miracle, and doctrine. Furthermore, Baconian induction continued to shape the theology of many Methodist preachers even after 1870. For the Rev. Albert Carman, professor of mathematics at the Belleville Seminary of the Methodist Episcopal Church, and after 1884 general superintendent of the Methodist Church of Canada, true knowledge remained grounded in the immutable standard of Scripture. The Bible, he declared in a sermon delivered in the 1860s, "is infallible and like the principles of science, suitable to all climes. It goes at the delivery of truth aright, beginning with the axioms and primitive truths of morals, thus surpassing the Philosophy which so long stumbled on vague theories ignoring axioms." Carman's views on religious development diametrically opposed those of Nelles. Revelation was a matter of fixed truths, inflexible laws, and rules deriving their authority from the immutable facts in the Bible.[125]

Nelles and his circle at Victoria College faced a serious problem. Was even a limited accommodation between the popular theology of Methodism and the evolutionary outlook of the higher critic possible? Here the flexibility of "inductive theology" encountered its most severe test. A "reverent" form of the higher criticism could be accommodated to the "inductive theology" that Nelles had been elaborating since the late 1840s. Loyal to the foundations of Methodist tradition and to the prevalent spirit of Baconian inquiry, the main assumption of this outlook involved a subtle but nonetheless important devaluing of the intellect. "Inductive theology" was premised upon the existence of a gap between theory and experience, or what the Henry Bland termed "the knowledge of the intellect and that of the heart." In other words, a preacher or even a professor like Nelles or Burwash, trained in the tenets of "inductive theology," recognized doctrine, the product of the intellect, as only one element in religion, and subordinated the intellectual activity of the college classroom to the practical task of Christian living and the building of Christian character. Thus, clergymen-professors could reassure students and preachers that the impact of criticism on doctrine would not affect the essential character of theology or seriously impair the traditional meaning of the biblical text. As Bland recognized in a sermon delivered in 1890, the Methodist stress on Christian experience was far from being a retreat into anti-intellectualism. Rather, it was a source of religious stability in an age when the authority of the Bible was apparently dissolving under the assaults of evolutionary thought. Despite their differences on the role of reason in interpreting the Bible, both Bland the preacher and Nelles the professor could agree on the most vital issue. What Bland termed the "experience of the heart," the inductive verification of the Bible not by critical or historical methods but by the personal experience of conversion, belief, and Christian living,[126] provided the ultimate certitude.

The "inductive theology" forged at Victoria College was an attempt to maintain a balance between Methodist tradition, the Baconian outlook, and the advances in biblical criticism. Between 1870 and 1890, it served as the main intellectual force in Canadian Methodism, guiding a transformation of both education and the role of theological training in the church colleges. Prior to 1860 the Methodist Church did not insist on a college-educated ministry, preferring to rely on preachers with Christian experience, who were trained by a personal course of reading. Nelles's efforts to centre the educational endeavour in the colleges, thus promoting a learned piety, finally bore fruit in 1871 when a faculty of theology was established at Victoria College. By the late 1880s the church had set a compulsory two-year attendance at college for all aspiring ministers, and in 1900 Victoria, Montreal's Wesleyan College, Mount Allison University, and Winnipeg's Wesley College supplied nearly half of the candidates for the Methodist ministry.[127] Such a physical expansion of church colleges, to say nothing of the reorientation in the intellectual life of the clergy occasioned by the new emphasis on a formal theological education, could not have been accommodated to the traditions of preaching and the life of the congregation without the influence of "inductive theology," which reduced the possibility of tension between the college and the wider Methodist community by subordinating criticism to the heritage of the revival.

The affinities between Nelles's reconciliation of faith and the new historical scholarship and key tenets of the Baconian outlook won for both "inductive theology" and the new theological faculty the crucial support of Edward Hartley Dewart, the influential editor of *The Christian Guardian*, and William Withrow, editor of *The Canadian Methodist Magazine*. Unlike Nelles and Burwash, both these clergymen were close to popular preaching and evangelical tradition in their views on biblical authority, inspiration, and the role of reason in theological inquiry. They sensed, however, the weakness of the old Butlerian apologetic in the face of historical criticism, and therefore they heartily endorsed the ideal of an educated ministry. Old sermons on Christian evidence, argued Dewart in 1870, were useless against modern science, as "scholarly infidels," through their mastery of the tools of textual criticism, had stolen a march on "orthodoxy." The effective remedy lay in the improvement of theological education, with stress on the critical study of the Bible necessary to meet infidelity with its own weapons.[128]

The public insistence on the Baconian character of the college theological education and its use in the battle against infidelity served to recommend "inductive theology" to preachers loyal to older versions of the evangelical creed. Nelles's synthesis of theology and history permitted some clergymen to reconcile the certainty of plenary inspiration and the authority of a historically and doctrinally accurate Bible with the idea of evolution. "Inductive theology," with its exclusive reliance on the interaction of providence and human history, divine will and human character, accomplished easily what for many Protestant Christians was a source of religious and moral distress in the decades after Darwin: it rendered the separation of natural science and Christian theology not only necessary, but also intellectually respectable.

In 1877 the Rev. J.B. Clarkson wrote that the provinces of theology and the sciences should be carefully demarcated. "Different principles of interpretation," he stated, "are demanded in the two departments. The grand aim of science is, by an induction of facts, to discover the laws through which Deity operates in the created universe. On the other hand, the exclusive object of religion is moral character."[129] Far from signalling the retreat of theology into irrelevance, the inductive basis of theology in historical fact and moral character testified to its independence and its superiority to all other branches of inquiry. According to the Rev. W.S. Blackstock human history was the special field of divine providence, revealing "a divine plan, and every separate part of it is, though in a way that transcends our comprehension, contributing its share toward the accomplishment of the divine purpose."[130]

Blackstock's reference to history as something mysterious and miraculous indicated the authoritative status still enjoyed by the Bible in Methodist education and preaching in the three decades after 1860. Nelles and other prominent advocates of the new theological education believed that, far from displacing theology from its dominant position, higher criticism had allowed it to remain the "queen of all the sciences." In an important article written in 1878, Nelles described theology as "by no means infallible in its human side, always capable of receiving new lights and better adjustments." But he as forcefully stated the claim of certainty, defending the necessity of sound doctrine for any true religion.[131] The meaning was clear – the new historical science was not an end, but a means. Critical study must always be guided by theological considerations and the wider life of the church.

While this might be regarded as a view that Nelles had advocated for nearly thirty years, the formulation of theology in progressive terms was significant because a similar balancing of the traditional and the critical had been struck by Dewart and Carman, men generally regarded by historians as "conservative" in their response to evolution and higher criticism. Addressing the Theological Union of Victoria College in 1879, Dewart spoke for the advocates of tradition when he declared that "truth is unchangeable, but human conceptions of truth are not." A true biblical theology, he maintained, should attempt to explain all attested facts of matter and mind.[132] Such statements, made before 1880, reflected a confidence that the evangelical inheritance of the revival had successfully tamed the historical criticism of the Bible, placing evolution itself under the guidance of the tenets of faith. For men such as Carman and Dewart "inductive theology" not only secured the independence and intellectual authority of the biblical revelation, but reduced the issue of criticism to one of method. This method, if properly guided as it had been by Nelles and Burwash, would elucidate but never challenge the central tenets of the evangelical creed.

FIXING THE LIMITS OF INDUCTIVE THEOLOGY: NATHANAEL BURWASH, VICTORIA COLLEGE, AND THE WORKMAN AFFAIR, 1880–1892

In a lecture delivered in 1872 to candidates for the Methodist ministry, Nelles listed the qualifications he considered necessary in aspiring servants of the church. First, he declared, these men must possess a sound conviction of personal religion and the call of the Holy Spirit. Almost last on the list came "educational attainments."[133] Such was the hierarchy of faith and learning that prevailed in the lecture halls of Victoria College in the decades after Darwin. In charting a course designed to reconcile the theology of the Methodist revival with the new critical thought, clergymen-professors reminded their students that reverence was the proper attitude in investigating religious questions. Humility and willingness to engage in an inductive quest for religious certainty were more important than a display of intellect or critical skill.

The maintenance of this balance was the crucial issue confronting Methodist educators in the years after 1880. It rested on two related assumptions. First, although the evolutionary idea of a progressive revelation explained the method of divine intervention in human affairs, it most emphatically did not affect the miraculous activity of God in the human conscience, society, and history, or impair the authority of the Bible and the central doctrines of evangelical faith. But could these injunctions be sustained in the face of the increasing prestige enjoyed by the new human sciences? Second, this limitation of the application of evolutionary metaphysics to Christian revelation was paralleled by a conscious attempt to preserve the church college as an institution of cultivated piety. Like its Presbyterian counterpart, "biblical theology," the Methodist "inductive theology" did not encourage independent, critical research of the Bible. Rather, it was closely linked to the life of the preacher and the congregation and the need for religious certainty in an age of intellectual transformation.

The task of fostering this balance fell to Burwash, who became first professor of theology in 1871, then dean of the faculty of theology, and finally successor to Nelles as president and chancellor of Victoria College. Having attended Victoria College in the early years of Nelles's leadership, Burwash was already versed in the tenets of "inductive theology." The main premises of this approach were reinforced during his stay at the Sheffield School of Science, which was affiliated with Yale University. In the late 1860s this leading Congregationalist university was already well-known as an institution whose professors had succeeded in enlisting German historical and philological methods in the traditional evangelical pursuit of the divine truth in the visible world.

Although taking courses in the scientific department, Burwash would have certainly been aware of the rejection of static views of man and society and the criticisms of the Common Sense philosophy undertaken by the Yale circle. In the years before Darwin, Yale theological scholarship had developed a historical cast. Later, its leading figures firmly believed that Darwin had not created an abyss between faith and critical thought. They told their students that the new progressive, organic explanations of the universe and society would affirm divine reality. Burwash would doubtless have approved of the similarities between "inductive theology" and the ideas of these American professors. In their hands history, far from adopting the secularizing tendencies of evolutionary naturalism, emphasized knowledge of a world ruled by divine providence, and stressed the uniqueness of the individual and free will. [134]

For Burwash, the years spent at Yale confered the legitimacy of a great centre of learning on the lessons already learned under Nelles. They reaffirmed the possibility of an alliance between evangelical theology and a reverent use of the new historical scholarship. Burwash's greatest contribution as head of the faculty of theology was the construction of a curriculum largely based on "biblical theology," a careful grammatical study of the Scriptures in their historical setting. In 1892 the examination in divinity at Victoria College reflected this blending of tradition and criticism. Theological students were examined on Wesley's sermons, biblical history, exegesis of the Old and New Testaments, church history, and the Greek language. Reflecting the suspicion of speculation and philosophy encouraged by "inductive theology," metaphysics, systematic theology, and apologetics occupied a lesser place in the curriculum. [135]

Burwash's greatest contribution to the intellectual life of Victoria College lay in shaping, on a day-to-day basis, a rationale for the new advances in biblical criticism compatible with Methodist traditions of education and scholarship. He believed that history served Methodist theology's demands on human reason more acceptably than either idealist philosophy or natural science. A sermon preached in the early 1890s defined precisely the nature and scope of the function of reason. The reasoning faculty, Burwash declared, served two purposes – verification and variation – and could "of itself furnish us with no new ideas. It can but combine and compare those already at hand." [136] Unlike philosophy, which proceeded by the method of speculation, or natural science, which increasingly discounted moral "facts", history paid scrupulous regard to the content of the Bible – the data of faith – and to the experiences and feelings of the divine communion between the spirit of God and the human soul. [137]

History, therefore, was the ideal medium of theological study, for only it assured the continuation of the all-important link to the traditions of Baconian induction that could defend the accuracy and authority of the biblical text against the assaults of evolutionary naturalism. As the record of fact and experience, history retained the certainty of biblical revelation, and provided theology with independence and relevance in relation to science and philosophy. Victoria College's orientation toward liberal culture and the training of preachers firmly indicated the desire of clergymen-professors to preserve close links with the wider life of the congregation. This, in turn, ensured the cautious presentation of the results of biblical criticism.

Burwash's procedure in the classroom reflected the influence of several powerful currents in the intellectual life of Canadian Methodism. His own training at Victoria College and Yale ensured his insistence on both the scientific nature of historical study and the reverent implications of the new biblical criticism. This balance enabled him to combine the notions of progress and providence. In 1880 he declared that there was "a progressive order in the revelation of religious truth to the human race and also to the chosen people." [138] These views were, however, modified by other considerations. The strength of men such as Dewart, Withrow, and, after the union of 1884, Carman in the church councils reinforced the Baconian cast of Burwash's own thought. Though devoted to biblical criticism, the reverent tenets of his outlook led him to refute the conclusions of Wellhausen and other German critics, and to deny the connection between revelation and natural "laws" of mind and society when these violated the integrity of biblical text or doctrine. The Bible, Burwash argued, contained words and "facts" not subject to ordinary grammatical analysis. Furthermore, the divine presence in Scripture was consistent and miraculous. "We believe," he reminded students and preachers, "that the supernatural is involved in, or perhaps we should say links itself to, the very laws of our spiritual being; that it is not a magical interference operating from without, but a divine power working from within. So we believe revelation itself has its laws of development, in which, as in nature, God hath unfolded his plan."[139]

"Biblical theology," as shaped by Burwash between 1870 and 1890, involved the conscious rejection of evolutionary naturalism. Premised on the belief in the active purpose of God in human history, it explicitly adhered to the evangelical belief in the superiority of revelation to all natural and social processes. Even among the increasing number of Victoria College graduates who went to Germany for postgraduate training, the power of the evangelical creed continued to limit the application of higher criticism to Scripture and theology. One of these young graduates was Francis Huston Wallace, professor of New Testament and successor to Burwash as dean of the faculty of theology. In the 1880s he spent a year at the University of Leipzig, and later wrote that the German university system "produces great scholars; perhaps its weakness is that it encourages the love of novelty quite as much as the love of truth." He detected what he termed a "ruthlessness" of speculation in German theology, a sure sign of divorce between professors and preachers. Wallace's own approach as a professor stressed accurate and minute exegesis, rather than "premature attempts at original research."[140]

The strictures of "inductive theology" constrained speculation, novelty, and the German approach to higher criticism. They shaped the study of the Bible in the college, and united college and pulpit, preventing the relationship between faith and critical thought from becoming the focal point of tension between theological parties within the church. Throughout the 1880s even traditionalists like Withrow and Dewart exhibited a tolerant attitude toward the new knowledge. In an important comment written on the Robertson Smith heresy trial, Dewart stated:

There are two distinct modes of historical study ... The one, the old way, is the careful collation of testimony, and the building of our historical structure mainly from recorded data. This method concedes the general truth-fulness of traditional testimony, and of contemporaneous and other ancient record; and recognizes that the *living picture* of those who lived in the midst of passing events is more truthful than that we can hope to form now. The other method suspects all testimony, and submits it to a process of subjective analysis called historical criticism; and out of the solution it precipitates, by the aid of a preconceived theory, a restatement of the facts of the case such as it presupposed to be the very truth.[141]

Dewart's editorial was the first clear statement of the potential for conflict between the old theology of history founded upon the authority of the Bible as a reliable account of the past, and historical criticism, which held that reason could determine the validity of "facts" and thus of the doctrines. Men like Dewart accepted the presence of the new studies in the college classrooms only because Burwash separated the critical method from the tenets of evolutionary naturalism and carefully adhered to the integrity and traditional meaning of the biblical text.

But what would occur if the balance was disturbed, if the college professor sought the right to investigate the biblical text and apply critical methods without reference to evangelical doctrine or the popular theology of Methodism? The Workman Affair challenged the status of "inductive theology" and raised the prospect of a divorce between college and pulpit at the very moment when Burwash had apparently succeeded in imposing the Methodist consensus on a second generation of theological professors. The Rev. George Coulson Workman, the focus of the controversy, had spent many years of study in Germany before assuming the chair of Old Testament exegesis at Victoria College. Workman's doctoral thesis, *The Text of Jeremiah*, was written under the direction of Franz Delitzsch, of the University of Leipzig. Delitzsch was considered "conservative" in his belief that the Pentateuch was authored by Moses, and in his refusal to admit the validity of the "documentary hypothesis" arrived at by Wellhausen in the 1870s. Because of his respect for the traditional picture of the origins of Judaism and Christianity, he was considered "safe" by Canadian Methodists. Shortly before Workman returned to Canada, his mentor announced his conversion to Wellhausen's evolutionary naturalism,[142] which apparently denied the historical accuracy of much of the Old Testament.

When Workman assumed the Old Testament chair at Victoria College in 1890 the tenets of "inductive theology" were already threatened. In 1887 the college had federated with the University of Toronto, and although the institution did not move from Cobourg to the city until 1892, this shift brought the college ideal of learned piety and the subordination of research to faith into conflict with an emerging modern university "research ideal" that accorded a wider sphere to the new evolutionary forms of critical thought.[143] Although the Workman controversy has usually been treated in isolation as a simple case of antagonism between supporters and opponents of higher criticism, or as an incident in the emergence of a Canadian tradition of academic freedom,[144] the affair revealed other concerns of greater importance to the intellectual life of Canadian Methodism. The controversy was defused with ease, indicating that the important issue was the role of reason and historical criticism in relation to faith, experience, and preaching in the formulation of a science of theology, not the division between "conservatives" and "liberals" over higher criticism.

Shortly after his arrival at Victoria College Workman delivered a lecture entitled "Messianic Prophecy," advancing conclusions at variance with the old evangelical triad of revelation, history, and prophecy, a unity explicitly defended by "inductive theology." In a clear departure from Burwash's approach, which was premised on respect for the integrity of the biblical text and for traditional beliefs, Workman attacked the ancient popular belief that the Old Testament prophecies concerning the Messiah had been fulfilled in the New Testament, claiming that this could no longer be sustained in the light of the new historical knowledge provided by Old Testament critics.[145] From the standpoint of the preacher, Workman's separation of history and prophecy threatened to deprive the pulpit of a source of intellectual authority. Worse, Workman implicitly claimed the right of the scholarly critic to dictate the content of belief, thus exalting reason as the arbiter of religion, faith, and practice.

This was no simple case of higher critics versus the advocates of biblical literalism. Dewart's rebuttal, *Jesus the Messiah in Prophecy and Fulfilment*, was a predictable restatement of the traditional evangelical position. But it was surprising that Workman found no supporters, even among younger clergymen-professors like Francis Huston Wallace and John Fletcher McLaughlin. The consensus even among those most sympathetic to critical thought was that Workman had gone too far in subjecting the Bible to novelty and speculation. Wallace called Workman a man of "considerable ability," able to master a subject and present it clearly and forcefully, but possessing "no subtlety of thought, richness of imagination, or grace of style, a wooden man, and withal very opinionative and dogmatic." More to the point, Wallace suspected Workman of Unitarianism, a doctrinal position incompatible with his rank of professor in a Methodist

College. It was on this question that Workman's colleague defended his position, that of being "with Dewart, though not quite for Dewart's reasons."[146] Burwash and the college council agreed with the traditionalists that Workman was unfit to teach in the theological faculty, and he was shifted to the chair of English Bible in the arts faculty, his place in Old Testament taken by McLaughlin, a professor pledged to respect the balance of piety and critical thought struck by Nelles and Burwash.

The resolution of the Workman affair forcefully demonstrated the limits of critical thought in the face of the intellectual traditions of the evangelical creed. From their encounter with evolution and higher criticism both Presbyterians and Methodists had, by 1890, developed the intellectual structures necessary to reconcile the culture of the revival, founded on the authority and certainty of the Bible and the personal experience of conversion, with the equally insistent claims of the culture of inquiry whose quest for certainty was now founded on the outlook of evolutionary science. In forging this accommodation, Canadian clergymen-professors relied on their relationship to the two older transatlantic societies, incorporating into their education and preaching the balance between progressive views of history and evangelical theology developed in Scottish universities and in some of the American denominational colleges.

In the Canadian colleges, however, Caven, Grant, Nelles and Burwash adapted these progressive views to the distinctive heritage of the revival in British North America. The Baconian outlook that served in the United States as the matrix of militant opposition to evolutionary thought acted, in Canada, as the means of harmonizing critical thought and the evangelical creed. The persistence of the Baconian outlook in the new disciplines of "biblical theology" and "inductive theology" was crucial to the definition of the intellectual world of Presbyterians and Methodists between 1860 and 1890. It weakened the disturbing implications of Darwinian thought, while enlisting the prestige of historical criticism in support of the main tenets of evangelicalism. More importantly from the perspective of late Victorian culture, the alliance of Baconianism and historical scholarship served evangelicals as a means to transform the wider Canadian community.

5 History, Prophecy, and the Kingdom of God: Toward a Theology of Reform

"The wise will disregard theorists and study the past to estimate what the future is to be," Grant advised in a sermon outlining his hopes for Canada's destiny, and underlining the conflict between the tenets of the evangelical creed and the assumptions of late Victorian social thinkers and idealist philosophers. Confident that the application of evolutionary naturalism to the study of humanity provided scientific certainty regarding human origins and the progress of mind, morality, and society, many of these secular thinkers had by 1890 rejected the intellectual claims of Christian tradition as antiquated, unscientific, and immoral. Faced with such a challenge, Grant and his colleagues recognized that knowledge of the past was the crucial issue between evangelicalism and the "human sciences." The interpretation of history, he declared, was a difficult task, "but only as we interpret it aright are we able to cast the true horoscope of a nation, & however difficult, it is a duty incumbent on us."[1]

Grant's phraseology may seem quaint to late twentieth-century historians. The phrases "true horoscope" and "interpret it aright" imply a belief in theological and moral certainty foreign to a generation of scholars attuned to the relativist implications of their researches into the human past. Although it would be tempting to identify Grant as a transitional figure in the transformation of Protestant theology into secular thought, and to dismiss his historical outlook as a quirk drawn from an outmoded "orthodox" theology in full retreat before the triumphant advance of evolutionary thought, his views on the nature of the human past were by no means odd or isolated. In 1897 Burwash informed his students in 1897 that "prediction of the future is the highest test of historical science."[2]

In the intellectual climate of the Protestant churches in late Victorian English Canada, Grant and Burwash used the terms "horoscope" and "prediction" to express their abiding commitment to the fundamental assumptions of the evangelical creed, not to display an interest in mysticism or the spirit world. These words expressed the confidence of prominent evangelicals that by assimilating historical criticism into their traditions of preaching and education they had successfully resolved the tensions implicit in the encounter of their theology with evolution. Historical study of the Bible, they believed, not only reinforced the "scientific" status of theology, but also testified to eternally valid religious and moral principles. Grant and Burwash accepted, as firmly as McCulloch and Ryerson had, the authority of the Bible in history, doctrine, and morality. They maintained that, because the biblical record disclosed a theology of human history as well as the "facts," Christian believers possessed through faith the power of prophecy, the ability to predict the future of both church and nation.

The evangelical triad of theology, history, and prophecy to which Grant and Burwash appealed did not merely bind the generation of post-Darwinian clergymen to the traditions of the past. Their sermons and lectures between 1890 and 1905 recognized that Canada had entered a prolonged period of rapid social, economic, and cultural transformation. Like many of their contemporaries, Presbyterian and Methodist clergymen were aware of a profound shift in values occasioned by urbanization, immigration, and industrialization. While in 1880 the moral verities of individualism held sway in social, economic, and political life, the early years of the twentieth century witnessed a growing consensus among university figures, politicians, journalists, social thinkers, and historians that the creation of a harmonious industrial society required a variety of reforms. Reform, in turn, meant at least some concessions to collectivism, an outlook whose proponents sought to use the state to balance or mitigate unrestrained individualism in the name of the welfare of the community.[3]

To what extent did this far-reaching cultural transformation affect the thought and action of Canada's Protestant churches? The prominence of Presbyterian and Methodist clergymen in various movements devoted to the Christianization of national life and the active commitment on the part of segments of the Protestant churches to the collectivist social vision between 1890 and 1920 has intrigued students of English-Canadian intellectual and cultural history. It has challenged them to locate precise links between evangelical theology and the new consciousness of industrial and urban problems that emerged during these crucial decades.

The publication of Richard Allen's study *The Social Passion: Religion and Social Reform in Canada 1914–1928* in 1973 sparked a vigorous and continuing debate on the question of the intellectual roots and significance of the "social gospel," the commitment of the Protestant churches to actively seek the Christianization of Canadian society. While unanimously accepting that the preaching of a social message was the distinctive and dominant characteristic of the late Victorian Presbyterian and Methodist Churches,[4] historians have disagreed over whether social activism indicated a rise or a decline in their influence. Between 1890 and 1920, Allen has argued, an unresolved tension between the ideas of individual regeneration and social action characterized the theology of Canadian Methodists and Presbyterians. He contends that the "social gospel," though in some ways a half-way house between religious and secular outlooks, succeeded in making theology relevant to the wider English-Canadian culture by holding in check the individualistic, "otherworldly" tendencies of the evangelical religion characteristic of the age of revival. Furthermore, the involvement of the churches and the representative clergymen Salem Bland and James S. Woodsworth in "radical" social reform both created and legitimated a home-grown tradition of democratic socialism that continues to influence the cultural climate of the late twentieth century.[5]

Critics of this assessment of the social gospel have pointed to the tension recognized by Allen between the "transcendent" and "immanent" elements in the Christian message, and the ultimate incompatibility of evangelism, with its emphasis on the individual soul, and the involvement of the churches in the salvation of society. Though the social gospel may have succeeded in conferring a religious meaning on movements of social and political reform, they contend that it crippled evangelicalism, subtly but effectively stripping it of any miraculous content by resolving the "sacred" into the "secular." These historians have argued that social activism grew up in churches whose theology was already assailed by Darwinian evolution and biblical criticism. As a response to the growing intellectual climate of doubt and to the magnitude of the nation's social problems, Presbyterian and Methodist clergymen sought to revitalize religion by concocting a social vision out of an unstable melange of philosophical idealism, evolutionary naturalism, higher criticism, and sentimental humanism, all of which subverted traditional views of God, man, sin, and redemption. By 1920, they have concluded, the "social gospel" had weakened Protestant religion by inducing clergymen to discard any distinctively Christian message, or theology, from the preaching and life of the churches, in favour of "sociology," which emphasized not the salvation of the individual soul, but the "regeneration" of society.[6]

Both the secularization thesis and the appropriation of the "social gospel" legacy by custodians of democratic socialism rest upon a flawed understanding of religion in English Canada at the turn of the century. Both are based on a stimulus-and-response model of intellectual change, whereby Protestant clergymen made the momentous shift from an "orthodox" theology of individualism to one emphasizing the social nature of Christianity out of a desire to solve the "social problem." Such a procedure implicitly denies coherence and substance to the intellectual resources of the evangelical churches prior to 1890. Furthermore, each set of arguments is based upon a reading back of desirable or undesirable characteristics of late twentieth-century Canadian society into the thought and experience of clergymen active in the decades between 1890 and 1920. This approach to the study of religion involves an implicit failure to examine precisely the relationship between evangelical theology and the climate of social reform.[7] In their search for the religious roots of present-day currents of secular thought or democratic socialism, historians have not paused to question whether late Victorian clergymen felt as keenly as late twentieth-century academics the dichotomy between "transcendent" and "immanent" forms of religion, revivalist religion and social Christianity, or whether the traditional content and message of evangelical theology and preaching actually succumbed to the collectivist outlook and the prestige of the rising social sciences, both of which appropriated the canons of evolutionary naturalism.

Despite their obvious links to the early nineteenth-century world in which the authority of the Bible stood supreme, the sermons of Grant, Burwash, and other prominent college clergymen and preachers on the application of theology, prophecy, and history to Canadian life were as much a part of Protestant religion in the age of reform as were the "radical" political efforts of Salem Bland and the Winnipeg settlement house of J.S. Woodsworth. The views of these Presbyterian and Methodist clergymen testify, to the resilience and vitality of the alliance of Baconianism and historical criticism of the Bible forged between 1860 and 1890, not to the intellectual weakness or incoherence of the evangelical creed in the face of the "social problem." More importantly, the interest that men such as Grant and Burwash took in religious and social reform was sustained by their "biblical theology." A blending of doctrine, preaching, and history, it formed the vital bond linking college and pulpit – the principal body of ideas they drew upon in articulating their vision of the place of the church in Canadian society. It may be argued that this theology, which claimed the prophetic power to interpret both past and future, rather than acquaintance with idealist philosophy or "social science," was central to the relationship between religion and social reform in Canada at the dawn of the twentieth century.

THE "NEW" OLD TESTAMENT: THE
PROPHETS OF ISRAEL AND THE
PREACHING OF HISTORY

Writing in 1900, Grant recalled his student days in Glasgow fifty years earlier. "The complaint I had with the Scottish pulpit forty or fifty years ago," he declared, "was radical." According to Grant, an earlier generation of Scottish preachers identified religion exclusively with "soundness of creed" and were fearful of departures from the literal text of the Bible. Both the style and the substance of the pulpit were "timid and dull, though the timidity and dulness were often hidden behind loud oratory and vehement gesticulation." But were Grant's complaints as radical as he implied? He praised modern preaching not for having abandoned doctrine in favour of social ethics, but for having overcome earlier defects through a historical understanding of the Bible. He defined the preaching of the late nineteenth century as "practical rather than doctrinal. Doctrine is of course implied, but it is presented to the people in its relation to life and not as the contents of a museum."[8]

Grant's writing and preaching during the 1890s focused on the contrast between sterile "doctrine" and "practice" or "life." Critical of beliefs founded on what he considered an unreal distinction between "the Sacred and the Secular," he repeatedly urged his theological students to avoid abstractions and to deal with the "facts." Their preaching, he declared, must be founded on an awareness that religion "deals not only with the individual but with society." Only thus could the preacher inspire his congregation to action, and aim to "establish the Kingdom of God on earth," the perfect society.[9] Was this the critical watershed for Canadian Protestantism, the moment of creation for a new religious outlook? Grant's apparent rejection of the heritage of the revival, with its stress on a miraculous providence and an individualistic, other-worldly evangelism, in favour of social action applied to worldly problems, has led historians to place Grant in the pantheon of the founders of English-Canadian secular thought.[10] His emphasis on the salvation of society and the building of the Kingdom of God on earth, they contend, points away from the traditions of the evangelical creed and towards the "social gospel" founded on an evolutionary vision of spiritual and material progress.

But Grant and his contemporaries recognized no final dichotomy between the tenets of the evangelical creed and the Christianization of society, despite their recognition of the tension between elements of the older theology and the problems confronting industrial Canada. A close study of the writings and sermons of leading Methodist and Presbyterian clergymen-professors around the turn of the century indicates not an unconscious discarding of theology in favour of "sociology," but the confident application of the traditional union of theology, history, and preaching, all based on the authority of the Bible, to the problems of a rapidly industrializing society.

Even Grant's great address, "Practical Preaching," in which he charted a course for Canadian Presbyterianism in the midst of the social turmoil of the 1890s, did not simply dispense with traditional doctrines and identify the Christian message with social science or reform. Grant believed that the inspiration for social reconstruction lay in a revival of religion, not in the application of the human sciences to the problems of industrialization and urbanization. He implied that only by preaching the reality of the Bible, the "mirror of Eternal law and universal history," could clergymen enlist their congregations in the task of buiding a righteous, Christian nation. Grant's aversion to theorizing and metaphysics dictated this approach, which based "practical" methods and "reality" on "biblical" truth. Such expressions did not foreshadow an accommodation between evangelicalism and the new human sciences but appealed to the Baconianism that had been part of the evangelical legacy since the great revivals of the late eighteenth century. Grant cautioned his students against preaching on social problems "until the eternal verities possess your own soul, & until your congregation has learned to trust you as a man of God."[11] This statement demonstrates that Grant's theology and concept of the ministry was shaped more by evangelical tradition than by the inroads of idealist philosophy and "sociology." He explicitly subordinated social action to the preaching of biblical doctrine,[12] and he believed that a theology firmly anchored on the tenets of the evangelical creed was the precondition for social reform.

Significantly, Grant's address did not contain the references to idealist philosophy or social thought that might be expected from so obvious a transitional figure. On the contrary, his thoughts on "practical preaching" were illustrated by examples drawn from Scripture. "Every great Preacher," he declared, "has a passionate enthusiasm for the establishment of the Kingdom of God upon earth." He explicitly encouraged his students to emulate the Old Testament prophets, whom he characterized as men directed by true feeling, divine grace, a large view of life, common sense, and a clear understanding of revelation. Understanding of the divine purpose was accessible through faith and the study of Scripture, which recorded a "historic movement, with men of God announcing from time to time according to the need the eternal principles by which nations alone can live."[13]

The prominent mention of the prophets of Israel in connection with the preaching and social concerns of the 1890s involved far more than a frantic attempt to shore up the historical relevance of the Christian message in the face of cultural crisis. It reflected the interaction between the critical study of the Bible and the persistent popular belief, central to evangelicalism, that the Biblical narratives and prophecies had historical as well as theological and moral value. For late Victorian clergymen, however, the historical importance of the Bible lay in more than the light it shed on the origins of the human race and God's dealings with humans. Their acceptance of certain insights of the new historical criticism had not seriously impaired either their belief in the factual accuracy and integrity of Scripture or their conviction that its books contained the key to universal history. Even after the "biblical revolution," Presbyterian and Methodist preaching rested on the assumption that the relationship between God and humanity recorded in the Bible could explain the rise and decline of all human societies, past, present, and future. This knowledge conferred cultural authority on the evangelical clergyman. Through the power, bestowed by faith, to preach to the wider community the all-important equation of theology and history they hoped to direct the destiny of their nation on a foundation of eternal and immutable moral law miraculously revealed.

A sermon preached by Burwash in 1884 testified to the crucial role of the college in reconciling the new critical study of the Old Testament and the traditions of the Methodist pulpit. Applying Victoria College's "inductive theology" to the task of preaching history, he drew an analogy between the national life of ancient Israel and that of late nineteenth-century Canada. "Of old," he declared, "the church was not only dependent on the state but the state was nourished by the church. The vigour and perpetuity of its political life was dependent on the strength derived from the infusion of a moral principle and religious power into the state itself." Referring to the prophet Isaiah, Burwash said that "the permanent state of the future will more and more depend upon this foundation of moral strength," the union of the moral and the intellectual infused into national life by "the spiritual life of the living and universal church of Jehovah." [14]

Burwash's references to Old Testament prophecy, like those of his Presbyterian counterpart Grant, drew upon the blending of higher criticism and the traditional theology of history accomplished in the evangelical colleges between 1870 and 1890. The thinking of Canadian clergymen-professors drew heavily from the ideas of Scottish biblical critics such as A.B. Davidson. This eminent Edinburgh scholar was instrumental in elaborating both the practice of "reverent criticism" and the continued equation of theology, history, and prophecy characteristic of the new "biblical theology." According to Davidson, the Old Testament stood as a sacred history. For him, the key to understanding the religious development of Israel and, by implication, the origins of Christianity was not the theorizing of social evolutionists but the interaction between two theological principles, the one dynamic, the other static. These he defined as "Promise," the hope of the coming of the Saviour, and "Law," the moral code that God revealed to Moses. [15]

Here, Scottish biblical critics believed, lay the historical and theological significance of the prophets of Israel. In their writings, the prophets stood at the focal point of Israel's history, as the mediators of Promise and Law who interpreted the divine message in light of Hebrew law and history. The prophets, Davidson and Robertson Smith contended, were the ancient preachers of the church and the direct precursors of Christian teaching. The Scottish proponents of "historical theology" observed that the prophetic preaching was directed to moral ends and arose out of the exigencies and events of national life. Though their inspiration was spiritual, the prophets were concerned with the application of the divine moral law to the community, and thus assumed the mantle of national statesmen calling the people to righteousness. [16]

The emphasis on the central place of the prophets in the origins of Christianity served a second but equally important function for the Scottish "reverent critics" of the Bible. The "historical theology" that gained prominence in the Scottish universities after 1870 was itself an accommodation between the new historical criticism and the evangelical equation of theology, prophecy, and history. The

Scottish critics' view of the relationship between God and these prominent Hebrew religious figures as the creative force in Old Testament history offered a powerful alternative to Wellhausen's mechanism of social evolution as an explanation for religious development. Davidson's remark that "the history of Israel is a history of prophecy"[17] preserved the idea of the Old Testament as a sacred history in an era when many scholars applied the logic of criticism to treat its narratives as merely another repository of philological or anthropological curiosity. The stress on the role of the prophets in Israel's history also linked the new "historical theology" to older Christian ideas of a creative interaction between history and prophecy. Davidson actually exalted prophecy over philosophy of history. As the agent and interpreter of a special divine influence in the course of events, the prophet could "foresee, too, whither the history was moving, and was able with certainty to forecast."[18]

The importance of the prophets was, however, not simply a function of their creative role in the history of Israel and the Christian church. Because evangelicals held as a central article of their creed that the Bible contained the principles governing universal history, the preaching of the prophets on the right relationship between God and humanity, individual and community could be applied to all human experience. According to Davidson, the prophets were the first men to envision a perfect society, a faith confirmed by their realization that their God was the "God of history." History was seen as a "moral process," with "a goal which is also moral, and which will at last realise perfectly its principles, seen to be imperfectly realised now." He argued that the message of these ancient Hebrews was not simply restricted to the destiny of their own people – their sense of history enabled them to foresee the Christian millennium, the salvation of all people and their inclusion in the "universal kingdom which will be a perfect kingdom of God upon the earth."[19]

By the late 1870s some prominent Canadian Methodists and Presbyterians were eagerly appropriating the Scottish exaltation of the prophets. This new emphasis on the prophetic teaching admirably bridged the gap between the evangelical need for a providential history ruled by revelation and the new historical criticism's insistence on human factors in religious development. As mediators of the divine and human elements in history, the Old Testament prophets conferred the sanction of religious authority on the practice of biblical study in the late nineteenth-century Methodist and Presbyterian colleges. In an 1877 lecture Burwash reminded his students of the "moral independence" of the prophets, and later pointed to the prophetic books as recording the communion of the divine element and a "prominent human instrument." Because of this special quality, he declared, the prophetic books afforded the perfect field for the biblical critic.[20] For clergymen-professors who believed in the intersection of divine will and human freedom as the guiding force of history, the activities of the prophets not only furnished the inspiration for college biblical study, but also guaranteed the sacredness and authority, and thus the cultural prestige, of their theology of history.

The blending of divine and human, creed and criticism represented by the prophets was most forcefully articulated in evangelical circles by James Frederick McCurdy, who had been appointed professor of oriental studies at University College, Toronto, in 1886. McCurdy was educated at the University of New Brunswick, but instead of taking his theological training in Scotland he attended Princeton University, where he experienced the stimulating attempts of leading scholars James McCosh, A.A. Hodge, Benjamin Warfield, and William Henry Green to reconcile the rigorous systematic theology of Calvinism with evolutionary thought.[21] McCurdy then spent several years of postgraduate study at Leipzig with the German scholar Franz Delitzsch, who until the late 1880s stood firmly opposed to Wellhausen's "documentary hypothesis" in interpreting the Old Testament.

By the 1890s, however, McCurdy had followed his German mentor into the camp of the evolutionary higher critics. His study of ancient Israel, *History, Prophecy, and the Monuments*, was published in three volumes between 1895 and 1901. His position outside the confines of the Presbyterian church colleges no doubt eased his acceptance of Wellhausen's critical theories,[22] but his great work owed far more to the evangelical sense of interaction between revelation, history, and prophecy than to German critical theory. McCurdy forcefully argued, as had several generations of his predecessors, that the study of history involved far more than "mere entertainment or hero-worship." The events recorded in both the Bible and the history of man, he declared, pointed "with equal directness to an extra-human Providence that prepares, controls, and combines the factors of history, and makes all things converge to and subserve the dominion of the truth that uplifts and serves humanity."[23]

Proof of this providential vision of history, McCurdy believed, lay in the prophetic books of the Old Testament. The teachings of these great religious figures completed and sanctified the national history of Israel. Furthermore, their example inspired people in all nations in their struggle for righteousness and justice. Prophecy was the true philosophy of history, for it bridged "over the certitude of faith the interval between the present struggle and doubt and the future assured triumph" by showing that human history was directed by the divine impulses of truth and freedom.[24] History, for McCurdy, as for his predecessors McCulloch and Burns, was the interaction between a stable, eternal divine revelation – "truth" – and the unfolding human experience – "freedom." This interpretation of the Old Testament narratives by a biblical critic outside the church colleges was significant testimony to the continued intellectual power of the evangelical creed. Despite concessions to the critical method, McCurdy preserved intact, in an age supposedly dominated by evolutionary ideas of man and society, the intimate connection between revelation, prophecy, and history that had sustained the preaching and aspirations of the evangelical clergy during the age of revival.

THE PROPHETIC TEACHING: CHURCH, NATION, AND THE VISION OF RIGHTEOUSNESS

The discovery of the historical significance of the prophets by some influential Presbyterian and Methodist clergymen in the two decades after 1870 would seem merely curious were it not for the persistence in the Canadian colleges of the structure of history that had informed evangelical preaching in the early nineteenth century. Although, clergymen-professors continued to insist on the correlation between history and prophecy and the close relationship between biblical revelation and the record of the human past, their quest for authority involved drawing even more precise links between past and present. Postmillennialism, an outlook inherited from the age of McCulloch and Ryerson, involved a reading of events of biblical and human history directed by a vision of the future. This mixture of prophecy, history, Protestantism, and messianic nationalism continued to influence their reading of the Bible and the history of the church, as well as their aspirations for Canadian society.

This interpretation of history, preached to their students and congregations, viewed human destiny as a gradual, upward spiral.[25] Progress was neither inevitable nor universal. The history of the Christian church oscillated between the decline and the revival of "true" religion, between creative periods of "fruitfulness" and ages of "barrenness" and "heathenism." This pattern and the conviction that the same principles of divine providence and human freedom determined the course of history in all ages held implications for the waning years of the nineteenth century. Late Victorian Canadian clergymen believed that the present and future were tending in a "better" direction, that the moral and social progress of their own age was due to a "purified" form of Protestantism introduced by the alliance of evangelicalism and newer forms of critical thought. They held, as an article of faith, that their own century was replicating, more intensely and enduringly, the great creative periods in biblical and human history, the age of the Hebrew prophets and the first century of the Christian church.

"History," McCurdy wrote in the concluding volume of *History, Prophecy, and the Monuments*, "is the fulfilment of prophecy as the finished statue or painting is the fulfilment of the artist's dream." The great Hebrew prophets, he declared, were the first to discern the workings of God's purpose in human society, the slow but certain transformation of the "ideal" into the "actual." McCurdy's study of the prophetic age was, however, not intended simply to satisfy historical curiosity. The preaching of the prophets held a clear message for modern times. "It is their visions and none other that are being fulfilled in the moral progress of our race. Prophecy is thus not merely the interpreter and forerunner of history, but also its guide and goal."[26]

At this point the "historical theology" of college and congregation intersected with the social and intellectual climate of late Victorian Canada. McCurdy's study of ancient Israel was written at a time when, historians claim, the churches were becoming increasingly aware of the evils and perils of urban industrial civilization. Like many other Presbyterian and Methodist clergymen, he observed with trepidation the collapse of social harmony in the strife between organized labour and monopoly capital, the weakening of the old rural community through depopulation and the rapid growth of cities, and the increasing evidence of urban vice and misery – drunkenness, prostitution, and poverty.[27] But far from despairing of modern culture, McCurdy confidently turned to the evangelical creed, to the creative interaction of prophecy and history, for a remedy. "The prophetic ideal," he declared, "is a living force which assures its own fulfilment." What the Hebrew prophets saw was the realization of a "universal brotherhood redeemed by Jehovah's grace and the redemptive ministry of Jehovah's suffering servant." McCurdy contended that the realization of the power of these principles in individual and social action would enable late nineteenth-century Christians to eradicate "tribalism surviving in militarism, and injustice materialized in cruel greed," the enemies of human society. Through the new historical study of the Bible, clergymen could apply the message of the Old Testament prophets to the solution of modern problems.[28]

It is not surprising that McCurdy sought to apply the lessons of biblical history to the problems of his own time. Despite the rise of evolutionary and critical thought, and the supposed destruction by the higher critics of the historical certainty of biblical "facts," clergymen-professors such as McCurdy and his Methodist counterpart John Fletcher McLaughlin continued to believe that the age of the prophets contained a definite message for modern times. As McLaughlin told the students of Victoria College, higher criticism had identified as "legendary" many portions of Scripture once regarded as historical, making it more difficult for preachers to use the Old Testament. Nonetheless, he claimed, a rational basis for authoritatively relating past and present could be found if the Old Testament was regarded as "a unique historical discipline," the preparation of the Hebrew people for a great destiny. McLaughlin believed that the Israelite prophets themselves had understood this aspect of history. Since the same revealed principles of providence and expanding liberty ruled past, present, and future, the teaching of the prophets, he maintained, addressed Canadian society with particular force.[29]

Such statements testified to the persistent role of the evangelical creed in shaping the response of prominent clergymen to urban and industrial realities. Clergymen-professors had always stressed the "practical" nature of biblical study and history, and the close link between the intellectual life of the college and the concerns of the congregation and the wider community. Between 1890 and 1905, by applying the new historical view of the prophets to their vision of social reform enlisted the new historical criticism of the Bible in the pursuit of a traditional objective – the continued elaboration of a popular theology bridging lecture room and pulpit. Evangelical leaders such as Grant, Burwash, and the Rev. Samuel Dwight Chown believed that, through the preaching of "historical theology" and its application to the problems of the present, the cultural authority of the study of history could be used to entrench the doctrines of Protestant Christianity in the moral and social life of the individual and the nation.

For Canadian clergymen-professors, the prophets' importance in biblical and universal history assured the continued intellectual power of the equation of history and prophecy. Furthermore, the teachings of the Hebrew prophets offered a powerful model for late Victorian clergymen. According to the Rev. John Scrimger of Presbyterian College, Montreal, the prophets were not narrowly concerned with individual piety, but acted as magistrates, judges, educators, and teachers, in dealing with broad questions of morality and spirituality. The prophets, Scrimger declared, appealed to the intellect, imagination, patriotism, and conscience of their hearers, their mission being largely a political one, although governed by a special supernatural revelation.[30] Between 1885 and 1900 Scrimger and many others presented the Israelite seers as models for evangelical clergymen struggling to Christianize national life. Writing in 1894 the Rev. Septimus Jones described the prophets as national poets, historians, preachers of patriotism, and exponents of the law, who predicted future events. Canada's need, he urged, was for "prophets and preachers with patriotic hearts. We need prophets more than we do fashioners of theological systems. Prophets who shall bring out the inner and spiritual side of truth and duty, in its applications to all relations of life – domestic, social and national. We need Christian prophets."[31]

The attempt by clergymen both inside and outside the colleges to link themselves through "historical theology" with the preaching and activities of the Hebrew prophets coincided with and largely shaped the intellectual response of the Protestant churches to social questions in the 1890s. In 1896 McCurdy drew a direct analogy between the perils facing contemporary society and the moral and social evils denounced by the prophets of Israel in the seventh century, B.C. "The problems which preoccupied the Old Testament lawmakers and prophets," he stated,

are those which still press most urgently upon serious men. Deceit, selfishness, lust, with the innumerable forms of treachery, cruelty, and dishonour, which are their perennial offspring, are still active everywhere, openly as savage brutality, or disguised as hypocritical *finesse*. These issues have never been dealt with again in any literature or national history as they were dealt with in the Old Testament and in the personal life of the ancient Hebrews. Hence the Old Testament cannot be dispensed with, in our own time at least, either as a work of classical literature or as a manual of moral and sociological principles.[32]

Echoing a myriad sermons preached at the time, this statement clearly shows the direction of evangelical thought at the turn of the century. Despite the challenges of higher criticism to the authority of the Bible and the evangelical creed, McCurdy and his colleagues held as an article of faith that the Old Testament possessed authoritative meaning as theology and history. Because its narratives revealed the interaction of providence and human freedom, for

clergymen and their congregations its intellectual and cultural legitimacy surpassed that of the rising human sciences, which relied
on scientific method and evolutionary metaphysics.

Historical analogies between the times described in the Old Testament and the late nineteenth century abounded in the sermons
and writings of Methodist and Presbyterian ministers in the fifteen
years after 1890. In an article written in 1897 the Rev. C.B. Ross, a
Presbyterian, described the social and religious conditions of the
Kingdom of Israel in the eighth century b.c. Despite great commercial activity, he declared, grinding oppression, greed, and social
unrest prevailed and the people were reduced to a deplorable moral
condition, sunk in idolatry and witchcraft. "We are confronted," he
warned, "by similar problems to-day. We are told that the poor to-
day are robbed by trusts and combines, that the poor man cannot
obtain justice, and that fraudulent contracts abound."[33] The lesson
was clear. Many evangelical clergymen feared that the new industrial
civilization would bring not social harmony and material prosperity,
but a recurrence of the same vices of infidelity, greed, and cruelty.
Forsaking the dictates of providence could, according to their tenacious theology of history, lead only to degeneracy and national
ruin.

It might be argued that clergymen-professors and preachers
sought the biblical images and metaphors of the Hebrew prophets
only to legitimate their own urgent sense of mission as social critics.
By so forcefully warning their contemporaries of imminent national
ruin, Methodist and Presbyterian clergymen apparently placed
themselves in the camp of "conservative" university professors and
social critics such as Andrew Macphail and James Cappon, who in
numerous jeremiads published in literary journals lamented the decline of a "moral ideal" in the face of industrial civilization and the
new mass culture.[34] Their perception of the content and application
of the prophetic legacy was, however, conditioned not by a pessimistic desire to escape engagement with the social and cultural transformation, but by a theology of history in which providence and
prophecy inspired an optimism concerning the future.

In an address aptly entitled "The Prophets as Preachers to their
Own Times," Chown, then a rising star of Canadian Methodism,
declared that Canada had "a purpose and destiny as definite as that
which the prophets saw in ancient Israel." As general secretary of
the Methodist Church's Department of Temperance and Moral Reform Chown was directly involved in the formulation of the church's
strategy for the Christianization and reform of Canadian society. His
mention of the Hebrew prophets was significant, not only because

he forcefully restated the historical premises of the evangelical creed, but because he presented the prophetic teachings as optimistic, rather than pessimistic. Despite disappointments, and even defeats and capture by heathen nations, the prophets had continued to preach the reality of the coming Kingdom of God on earth. "May we not," he argued,

through the study of the prophets, have a similar faith begotten in us concerning Canada. The prophet of Israel, standing upon the hilltops of Judea, saw but a few thousand acres. We stand in the midst of millions of square miles of more fertile soil and with vaster resources, and should have a vision incomparably larger, more thrilling, and sublime than his. Canada is God Almighty's last opportunity upon this planet of planting a Christian nation on virgin soil. Let us lay every foundation in the cement of right-eousness. Let every drop of our blood burst with patriotism and every energy of our being be consecrated to the christianizing of this glorious land.[35]

The postmillennial legacy made possible an optimistic rendering of both biblical and national history. Chown and his contemporaries, who saw themselves as part of the prophetic succession, maintained that, like their Hebrew predecessors, late nineteenth-century Canadians must heed the authority of the biblical message in its injunctions to righteousness in the life of both individual and community.

Chown's use of the Old Testament to advocate the Christianization of Canadian society raises an important question concerning the nature of the link between "historical theology" and reform sentiment within the Protestant churches. According to the standard account, this prominent Methodist leader was part of the "idealist tradition," an "unadulterated" theological liberal and a central figure in the momentous transformation of evangelical theology into a form of "sociology."[36] His appeal to the historical evidence of the Old Testament indicated, however, a deeper commitment to the centrality of the biblical explanation of the origin and progress of human societies. Though active in promoting moral and social reform, Chown revealed in his sermons a positive reluctance to abandon the intellectual supremacy of the evangelical creed despite the evolutionary human sciences and the "social problem." Preachers and clergymen-professors, by linking the Old Testament to their own society, revealed their idea of the proper relationship between evangelism directed at saving the individual and a religion directed to the Christianization of Canadian society, and between theology and social science.

Was the message of the prophets, and thus implicitly of evangelical "historical theology" itself, weighted to the older emphasis on the redemption of the individual, or did it direct clergymen to place a primary emphasis on collectivism, to insist on the salvation of society as a precondition of saving the individual? This question lies at the heart of the problem of secularization of English-Canadian thought and culture. In his book, *Prophetic Ideas and Ideals*, written in 1902, the Rev. William George Jordan, professor of Old Testament at Queen's University, described the prophets' message as "largely a national or social one; individual piety is implied and the problems of the personal life begin to emerge, but in the main their address was to the community." He maintained that the preacher who studied prophetic teaching would be well prepared for dealing with social questions, able to "combine boldness with wisdom, and to express in powerful, appropriate forms the passion for righteousness."[37]

For Jordan, however, the social preaching of the Hebrew prophets drew its power from an element deeper than simple observation of social conditions or acquaintance with prevailing forms of thought and culture. He was convinced that for modern believers "the essential principles" at the heart of the prophets' national message provided the most important lesson. The ability to recognize and reform social evils was founded, he believed, on an immutable, eternal principle, the firm and prior possession of an *individual* sense of communion with God.[38] This assessment of the primacy of individual regeneration drew on the work of the Scottish biblical critics Davidson and Robertson Smith, and was echoed by most of Jordan's colleagues in the Methodist and Presbyterian theological colleges. According to McCurdy, the great achievement of prophetic teaching was not the rebuking of public sin, but the clarification of the true relation of the individual soul to God.[39]

An individualist explanation of the relationship between humanity and God thus lay at the heart of the social teachings of the Hebrew prophets. The grounding of collectivist social action in the theological principles of a personal sense of sin and Christ's saving grace, though read back into the biblical past, reflected a persistence of the tenets of the evangelical creed in the colleges and pulpits of the Protestant churches between 1890 and 1905. Among Presbyterian and Methodist clergymen-professors, the result was a careful but firm resolution of the tension between evangelism and social reform in favour of the old creed's emphasis on sin, the soul's encounter with God, conversion, and preaching.

Even Grant, perhaps the foremost advocate within the colleges of the role of the Christian religion in the community, adhered to the evangelical balance of individual and social concerns. Speaking to the students of Queen's University in the early 1890s, he encouraged young clergymen to consider "man as a member of the organism of humanity, which mediates its life through the manifold agencies and activities of the family, the city, the nation, the Church, and our industry or calling, instead of with man as an independent unit." It was time, he stated, for the churches to realize that religion dealt "not only with the individual but with society, because it deals with man, and only in society does the individual find self-realization."[40] Grant's ideas might be taken as but a restatement of the thought of the British philosopher T.H. Green, and therefore a full-fledged endorsement of collectivism, and a directive to downplay the traditional message of evangelism in favour of social reform. Closer examination of his thought reveals, however, that Grant drew not on idealist philosophy, but on his contact in the 1850s with the Glasgow preaching of his mentor, McLeod, who addressed the question of the role of the church in society. The social ethic of both clergymen was dominated by the persistence of a strong individualist bias. Grant held as an article of faith that Protestantism had "discovered the individual and gave him his rightful place in the Church and society ... they taught that man as man entered into union with God in a spiritual act, and that every man who did so was a being, a priest, and a prophet." Thus Grant believed that the social organism's inherent rationale was the preservation and fulfillment of the moral and spiritual life of the individual.[41]

In accepting the interlocking relationship of individual and society, preachers and clergymen-professors looked to the workings of God's grace in the human soul rather than to the evolutionary metaphysics of the social sciences to effect the uplifting of their society. The continued primacy of the evangelical creed was particularly evident when Methodist and Presbyterian ministers advanced remedies for the specific ills they believed were afflicting their nation. Commenting on Edward Bellamy's influential *Looking Backward* in 1889, J.A. Macdonald, a student of Caven at Knox College, and later a prominent Presbyterian publicist and advocate of Christian social reform, argued that the survival of the church depended on the willingness of Christians to adapt to "present-day human needs." Adaptation, however, did not mean that the Bible should be discarded in favour of sociology or ideologies of social and political reconstruction. Rather, clergymen should "turn again to their textbook – the Bible," where, Macdonald claimed, they would find "the true principles of political economy enunciated more clearly by Moses and by Christ than by Malthus, or Spencer or Mill, or Rogers, or Cairnes, or Ashley."[42]

Macdonald's description of the Bible as a "textbook" of political economy has been taken by one prominent Canadian historian as proof of the secularization and adaptation of the biblical message in the face of urgent social problems and the popularity of explanations provided by the new sciences of human behaviour.[43] Another explanation is, however, possible. Rather than marking the resolution of evangelical theology into social ethics, Macdonald's promptings indicated his confident faith in the ability of the Christian revelation to solve the nation's social problems. For clergymen of this stamp, the Old and New Testaments contained the immutable moral principles of individual and social life. Macdonald's answer to the evils of industrial civilization was not stated, but implied. It lay, not in formulating precise schemes of social reconstruction, but in the province of faith, in the willingness of believers to live their religion, to apply the doctrines of the Bible to modern life.

Most of Macdonald's Presbyterian and Methodist colleagues who took an active interest in the question of reform shared this view. In contrast to certain of their late Victorian contemporaries, their sermons and addresses contained few references to widely read political or social treatises. Even Chown, the most prominent evangelical advocate of social reform, offered the readers of the *Christian Guardian* in 1904 no more than the "politics of the kingdom of God," a vision of a "well-governed Christian state," where "altruism will have free play, and the law of the Cross will be written upon the laws and institutions of the land."[44] The difficulty of determining the intellectual currents that shaped Chown's reformist outlook is lessened, however, when the continued evangelical, biblical, and individualist foundations of "historical theology" are taken into account.

Chown's preaching, like that of many of his colleagues both inside and outside the church colleges, relied extensively on the use of ideas and images drawn from the prophets of the Old Testament. "We shall establish the Kingdom of God," he declared, through "the development and application of prophetic principles." He defined the meaning of prophecy as "*a keen intuition of righteousness in human relations and an over-mastering determination to make it vital and dominant in the life of the nation.*"[45] His view of the Hebrew prophets and, by implication, of the Christian minister, was derived from the portrait of the Old Testament supplied by Scottish biblical critics. According to Robertson Smith, whose influential *The Prophets of Israel and their Place in History to the Close of the Eighth Century, B.C.* secured a wide audience in the 1880s, the prophets were reformers, but not innovators. "True reformers," Smith explained, "do not claim to be heard on the ground of the new things they proclaim, but rather because they alone give due weight to old truths which the mass of their contemporaries cannot formally deny, but practically ignore."[46] The prophets' place in history was not due to their elaboration of new religious doctrines, political structures, or forms of social organization. These Hebrew leaders, he believed, had used their preaching to reawaken a dormant religious consciousness, inspiring the entire nation to righteousness.

The evangelical interpretation of history established the direction and precise limits of the Presbyterian and Methodist churches' involvement in social reform in the decades around the turn of the century. For most clergymen-professors and many preachers, "applied Christianity," which has often been identified as the thin edge of the wedge of secularization, involved nothing more than a biblical injunction to the congregation to imitate the prophets in their equation of "piety" and "patriotism." According to Grant, this did not mean the advocacy of collectivist solutions, or the taking of sides in labour strife. Rather, it meant the willingness to "mediate and to assist righteous principles with authority."[47] When clergymen mentioned a specific solution, it always involved the application of an explicitly Christian ethic drawn from the Bible and weighted to the faith and morality of individual believers. For example, many evangelicals identified "political partyism" as the chief obstacle to the realization of the Christian state. Although both Grant and Burwash denounced this evil, neither pressed for institutional reforms. The remedy, they believed, lay within the conscience of the individual voter and in the "consecration" of the politician's vocation.[48]

Although the phrases "practical" preaching and "applied Christianity" have often been interpreted as marking the mid-point in the journey of "orthodoxy" to "secular thought," they held a different meaning in the intellectual and cultural context of the late Victorian Protestant churches. Grant, Chown and other clergymen-professors and preachers used them to reveal the persistence and vitality of the evangelical creed and its sense of historical interaction between past and present. More precisely, these ideas were proof of a desire to relate the individual and society, evangelism and reform harmoniously in a seamless pattern dictated by the doctrines of a personal sense of sin and encounter with God, not by the theories of collectivist social thought.

The individualist bias of Canada's Protestant clergymen was not a mere anachronism in a universal, transatlantic current of collectivist thought. Although the years between 1890 and 1905 marked a fundamental reorientation of social thought, most British, American, and Canadian political economists, historians, social critics, and philosophers, while directly relying on an evolutionary outlook, struggled to interpret collectivism in terms compatible with the continued freedom of the individual.[49] According to one recent treatment of social science in Canada, until about 1905, academics and university graduates continued to believe that reform was an internal, rather than an external matter, dependent on an individual act of will.[50] By linking the biblical era prophetically to the late nineteenth century, the "historical theology" taught in the church colleges and preached in numerous pulpits not only justified the application of the evangelical creed to the concerns of the nation, but also established an intellectually respectable theological alternative to the evolutionary human sciences.

TRANSCENDENCE VS IMMANENCE: THE PERSON OF CHRIST AND THE KINGDOM OF GOD

In a sermon preached in 1899 Burwash, the advocate of a cautious "inductive" theology, declared that he sensed "a real culmination of world forces" as the nineteenth century came to a close. "All things," he declared, "seemed to be coming to a head the work of the past seems to be coming to a fruitage and a new age and a new life of the world seem about to dawn."[51] Such expressions of confidence at the beginning of a new century might be taken as merely ritual invocations of hope, but they expressed a mood prevalent in Methodist and Presbyterian colleges and pulpits. Burwash and his colleagues believed that the nineteenth century had witnessed not only great political, social, and material transformations, but also the revival of religion spearheaded by the evangelical churches.

According to the view of history sustaining Burwash's creed, the "progress" of society was not an automatic mechanism. It depended on the conscious infusion of spiritual principles – the tenets of Protestant Christianity – into the lives of individuals and communities. The more clergymen preached and applied their theology to man and society, the closer the churches would come to ushering in Christ's Kingdom, variously described as the "millennium" or "the ideal social state." Burwash and his colleagues believed that they had, by the late nineteenth century, entrenched the vital principles of their creed in the life of their society and that they were, in the words of Grant, "living in millennial days, or at least ... on their threshold."[52]

The churches' post-millennial expectations were intimately related to the impact of "historical theology" on the evangelical creed. Clergymen-professors maintained that their accommodation of historical criticism to the Methodist and Presbyterian traditions of preaching and education enabled them to use the study of history to identify, refurbish, and preach the original "true" principles of Christianity held by the earliest Christian communities. Robert Falconer, Francis Huston Wallace, and other scholars of the New Testament impressed upon their students that history could purify, though not alter, the basic teachings of the church. Their view of the historical process as a gradually ascending spiral led them to believe that recovery of the Christian past enabled their churches not only to understand the thought and experience of an earlier age, but also to recapitulate it – the application of "historical theology" to the New Testament documents and the records of the early church would enable Methodists and Presbyterians to appropriate the enthusiasm, energy, and inner vitality of primitive Christianity. A "living" theology would in turn stimulate the spiritual and moral life of the individual believer and the Christian community, thus accelerating the achievement of the millennium.

Two central ideas dominated the evangelical search for a vital Christian theology – the "Person of Christ" and the "Kingdom of God." These themes permeated the writing and preaching in the church colleges between 1890 and 1905. But did the interpretation of Christ prevailing in lecture hall and pulpit at the turn of the century reflect the persistence of the old creed's insistence on a personal sense of sin, the personal encounter with Christ, and the salvation of the individual as the precondition for social redemption, or was it merely a variant of a pervasive "liberalism" then shaping transatlantic religious circles? Did Methodists and Presbyterians preserve a sense of Christ as a divine, miraculous presence, the transcendent redeemer of both the sinful soul and human culture, or did they accept a portrait of Jesus as but an idealized human being, the culmination of evolutionary processes immanent in their society? Had these late Victorian clergymen capitulated to secular thought, abandoning a static body of "orthodox" theology and accepting that Christ was simply an ethical humanist "Social Reformer,"[53] or did their view of Jesus and the Kingdom of God reflect a more complicated attempt to balance two dynamic elements in their culture – the heritage of the revival and the findings of historical criticism and the rising human sciences?

In his 1893 inaugural address as professor of New Testament exegesis at Presbyterian College, Halifax, Falconer firmly indicated what he believed constituted the bedrock of religion and theology in an age of criticism. "*Theology and religion,*" he declared, "*have one ultimate source and standard*. What is this? Everything revolves around the *Person of Christ*."[54] Although he used phrases reminiscent of the Baconian foundations of the old creed, such as "ultimate source" and "standard," his statement could be interpreted as but another reflection of a growing emphasis on the "humanity" of Christ, rather than on His divine, miraculous attributes. Falconer's address could be said to testify to the transition from an earlier "orthodoxy" dominated by a sense of transcendence to an evolutionary, "liberal" religion emphasizing an immanent, humanized Jesus and a purely ethical Christian teaching.

Historians who have assessed the transatlantic roots of this momentous intellectual transition in the evangelical churches have traced the picture of "liberal" theology's "humanized" Jesus to the influence of two German scholars, the theologian Albrecht Ritschl and his disciple, the church historian Adolf von Harnack.[55] As leading figures in the revolt against the Hegelian philosophy that occurred after 1870, both men sought to establish the independence and uniqueness of Christianity in the face of dogmatic or speculative "hypotheses" by exalting the "facts" of feeling and Christian experience. More boldly than his mentor, Harnack removed the doctrinal element from the Gospels, contending that these documents offered no support for the traditional dogmas of the Christian church. Jesus, he argued, had not intended to found a religious community based on notions of His own divinity. Rather, the "essence" of His message was ethical and social, consisting of the preaching of the moral and spiritual Kingdom of God, the infinite value of the human soul, and the commandment of love. Harnack denied the physical resurrection of Jesus, dismissing the miraculous and the mystical as an evasion of the moral kernel of the Gospel. He regarded the dogmas of the church as petrified relics of the imposition, after the the second century A.D., of speculative Greek philosophy on a warm and vibrant Christian faith oriented to the primacy of the moral and the ethical.[56]

A superficial view of evangelical thought in late Victorian Canada would indicate the presence, as in Britain and America, of the "liberal" Ritschlian theology in the theology and social consciousness of the Presbyterian and Methodist churches. Certainly Falconer, Francis Huston Wallace, and other younger scholars had studied in German universities in the 1890s, and had attended Harnack's stimulating lectures on the history of the early church delivered at the University of Berlin. Wallace, the professor of New Testament exegesis at Victoria College, recalled that contact with Ritschlian ideas had "broadened and humanized and, I think, Christianized my theology."[57] Both he and Falconer praised Harnack's emphasis on the personal experience of Jesus as the historical "essence" of Christian faith. For these young men, who grew to maturity in the Darwinian age when "science" and "religion" appeared diametrically opposed, Ritschl and Harnack offered an exciting prospect. They gave the sanction of historical reality to an irreducible "minimum" of belief, a reality that lay in human feeling and experience, beyond the corrosive speculations of philosophy and the criticisms of evolutionary science.

Just two years after Falconer delivered his address on the centrality of the "Person of Christ," the Rev. John Currie spoke to the students and faculty of Presbyterian College, Halifax, on "The Theology of Ritschl." Although he initially struck an admiring note, Currie warned that instead of merely interpreting Christianity, Ritschl and Harnack had created a new religion. He called their search for the revelation of God in the experience of the soul subjectivism, an insufficient basis for a Christian faith achieved at the price of ignoring the objective, revealed "facts" of the miracles, resurrection, and divine nature of Christ.[58]

These forceful criticisms indicated that the Ritschlian "theology," despite its appeal, had run afoul of several of the central tenets of the evangelical creed. For men like Currie, the portrait of church history and the low estimate of theology advanced by the German scholars raised two dilemmas. First, because Harnack claimed that the "true" or "historical" Jesus of the Gospels was a very different being from the "Christ" proclaimed by the doctrines of the church, his history divorced theology and religion, regarding the former as a non-essential aspect of Christianity. This assailed the intellectual foundation of evangelicalism, the equation between historical "fact" and Protestant doctrine. Second, if doctrine was not grounded in historical reality, did this not reduce evangelical religion to the realm of vague feelings, experiences, and impressions divorced from reason, thus undermining its position in the thought and culture of the late Victorian era?

Despite its seminal influence on American Protestantism, Ritschlianism occupied a very different place in the Canadian evangelical churches. Like its contemporary, British philosophical idealism, it played a limited role in stimulating, among clergymen like the Methodist preacher Salem Bland, the urge to study and apply the social and ethical implications of the Gospel message.[59] But clergymen-professors, the principal guardians of evangelicalism, treated the ideas of Ritschl and Harnack as dangerous threats to their creed. The consensus was perhaps best stated by Burwash. In a review of Harnack's *History of Dogma* in 1896 he said that while the German scholar's work was superb philosophy, it was severly flawed as historical narrative.[60]

The Methodist leader's choice of words was revealing. In evangelical circles, where the practical and the factual were valued over the speculative or the metaphysical, to characterize something as "philosophy" was *ipso facto* to challenge its intellectual validity. Not only had the *History of Dogma* offended against the Baconian rules of study that sustained the evangelical creed, but, claimed Burwash, it also ignored the "facts" of a supernatural character. Harnack had failed to account for the most important factor in the history of the church – the operation of the Holy Spirit. Because he believed that doctrine was founded in historical fact and therefore inscrutable, Burwash rejected the German historian's central contention. The doctrines of Christianity, he believed, originated in divine revelation, in the writings of the New Testament – they were not the outcome of some dialectic between the Gospels and Hellenistic philosophy.[61]

In their encounter with Ritschlianism, evangelical scholars strove to preserve the identity between the "Jesus of History" and the "Christ of the Church" and, in a broader sense, the connection between doctrine and historical fact. This alone, they believed, could assure the continued supremacy of theology as the cornerstone of college education and pulpit preaching. But in rejecting the history of Christianity according to Harnack, Burwash and his Presbyterian counterparts were compelled to offer an intellectually viable alternative. From the perspective of an age devoted to the notion that the study of history established a structure of intellectual certainty, a view shared by most Canadian evangelicals, it was difficult to refute the claims of the Ritschlian scholars. Harnack was confident that through historical criticism of the New Testament he had recaptured the "essence" of the personality and teaching of Jesus, thus rescuing Christianity from the assaults of evolutionary naturalism.

The construction of an alternative view of the New Testament and the Christian past in the Canadian colleges was assisted by the continuing contact, throughout the 1890s, between Methodist and Presbyterian clergymen-professors and the current of "historical theology" then dominant in Scotland and England. In the 1870s, the impact of American revivalist Dwight Moody's preaching in the British Isles spawned a widespread "Back to Christ" sentiment conducive to a growing emphasis on righteousness, service, and philanthropy. Strongly influenced by Moody, the Scottish university professors Alexander Balmain Bruce and Henry Drummond declared that the sole essential element in religion was Christ, who harmonized differences among Christians through the ethical power of His personality.[62]

It fell to Andrew Martin Fairbairn, a Congregationalist and principal of Mansfield College, Oxford, to systematize the concerns of the "Back to Christ" movement and to incorporate them into the structure of "historical theology." His two key works, *The Place of Christ in Modern Theology*(1893) and *The Philosophy of the Christian Religion*(1902), had a transatlantic influence, inspiring a generation of evangelical clergymen. Like Harnack, Fairbairn argued that through the study of history it was possible to know Christ as He actually was. On two key issues, however, he diverged from the views of the famous German scholar, and aligned himself with Moody and Bruce. The "historical" Jesus, he declared, was not merely a teacher of ethics who proclaimed the coming of the Kingdom of God. Jesus had founded the Church and acted throughout its history as its creative organism. Though lacking elaborate dogmas or structures, the primitive Christian community anchored its unity on two essential doctrines – the Fatherhood of God and the belief in the Son's divinity. Christ and the Gospels, not Greek philosophy, Fairbairn concluded, were the well-springs of doctrine.[63]

"Historical theology" as interpreted by Fairbairn averted the divorce between doctrine and history proposed by Harnack and the Ritschlians. It preserved doctrine and the great traditions of the Christian intellect as vital components of religion, and rejected the dichotomy between the "Jesus of History" and the "Christ of the Church." Neither aspect, he declared, could exist without the other, for they were bound together in a dialectical process.[64] History could remain the ally of theology, for it testified not only to an "essential" Jesus, but also to "essential" doctrines that guided the life of the Christian church. From an evangelical perspective, Fairbairn's ideas indicated that even in an age of doubt theology need not capitulate to historical criticism, but could absorb and direct the historical temper, thus retaining its vital and independent position as "queen of all the sciences."

Between 1890 and 1905 this continued insistence on the primacy of theology as an intellectual discipline informed the teaching of even those clergymen-professors most sympathetic to Ritschlian ideas. Despite his admiration for Harnack's genius, Falconer took his stand within the precincts of "historical theology" when he declared in his inaugural address at Presbyterian College, Halifax, that

the second main result of Christianity having a personal centre is that *doctrines are an essential part of it*. This is denied by some, and they have raised a great hue and cry to rid religion and theology of metaphysics ... But doctrines cannot be removed from our religion, for the very reason that it is based on a living Christ. If religion were a mere sentiment, nothing but a feeling of dependence, or even if it were a code of morals, there might be some plausibility in attempting to remove what is regarded as an encumbrance. But since the Christian religion is a union of the whole person, mind, heart, and spirit, and intellect, will and affections with the entire consecration of every faculty to the Christ of God, we can never have a doctrineless religion.[65]

Here was one of the younger generation of clergymen-professors, educated at the University of Berlin and exposed to most of the "liberal" religious currents of the day, forcefully proclaiming his distance from the main tenets of theological "liberalism." Falconer's address reflected the continued power of the evangelical creed's insistence on the unity of revealed theology, religious experience, and human knowledge. It was not simply a cultural legacy from an earlier age, but a living intellectual tradition that could stand respectably amid the competing alternatives provided by the evolutionary human sciences, idealist philosophy, and the Ritschlian "liberal" Christianity of ethics and feelings.

This need for a theology to act as arbiter of human intellectual and cultural endeavour was the common theme that united Presbyterians and Methodists, professors and preachers between 1890 and 1905. In 1900 Professor Samuel McComb, professor of church history at Queen's University, directly assaulted the Ritschlian position. There is, he said, "an impulse in the mind which urges it to reflect upon its perceptions, emotions, and purposes, to seek in them law and order, source and cause." McComb warned against relying on "religious impressions merely – we must ask: Do they point to a spiritual reality as their origin and goal?" This reality, he declared, directed the believer unmistakably to the historical importance of "dogma," not, as Harnack claimed, as a barrier to faith, but as a factor creatively shaping both the past and present life of the church.[66]

McComb's reflections on the church's continuing need for the intellectual discipline of a sound theology found an echo among the Methodists at Victoria College. Because the Methodists lacked the long intellectual traditions of their Presbyterian counterparts, they were in some respects more vulnerable to Ritschlian "liberalism." Both held to a practical view and insisted on the primacy of experiencing Christ in awakening the believer's faith. In opposition to the German scholars, however, Burwash reminded his students that he would tolerate no opposition between reason and faith. "Such unity," he declared, "is essential to the highest perfection of each, and of the man who in himself included both."[67] Significantly, Burwash's scholarly *magnum opus* was not a work of historical criticism but a theological treatise in which he reiterated the impeccably evangelical belief that the great "facts" or doctrines of the faith were embodied in the Gospels and in the entire traditon and life of the church.[68] Doctrine, the product of reflection on the "facts" of revelation, was, he held, a requirement for a truly Christian experience.

For Burwash, McComb, Falconer, and their colleagues, theology was not a static, formalized system of metaphysical truths. They championed a "living" theology, a practical discipline that paid due attention to all the "facts": divine revelation, the experience of the believer, and the historical record and tradition of the Christian community. According to Falconer, "theology must be orthodox, that is, in its main outlines be in agreement with the expression of belief held by the communion of saints which we call the Church. Deviation to any large extent from the creed of the Church must be due either to defective experience, or to defective intellectual training."[69] Though based on the immutable and certain "facts" of divine revelation, theology, these evangelicals believed, was a progressive discipline. It could be "purified" or improved without weakening or discarding the fundamental tenets of the divinity of Christ, individual responsibility for sinful acts, personal encounter between the believer and Christ, and the saving grace of God manifested in the lives of individuals and communities in past and present.

Between 1890 and 1905 professors and preachers in the Methodist and Presbyterian churches were fired by the belief that they had entered a new creative period of Christian thought, an era analogous to the Apostolic Age or to the Reformation. The researches of biblical scholars and church historians into the meaning of the Gospels and the early records of the Christian church, they believed, had confirmed the reliability and apostolic authorship of the central documents of the faith. Such scrutiny had validated the divine nature of Christ, and removed Jesus from the prison of the evolutionary dynamic, where both Harnack and the idealist philosophers had placed Him. Furthermore, the historical studies of Falconer and Wallace contained a message for their own generation. Their portrait of the primitive Church revealed a united, spiritually vital community, with a creed rooted in the historical "facts" of Christ's divinity, atoning sacrifice, and resurrection, and with a practical ethic of cooperation and communion in work, worship, and study.[70]

In an editorial written in 1901 J.A. Macdonald declared that the convergence of historical criticism and the "Back to Christ" movement had "made necessary a new apologetic, and a new exegesis has already provided the materials for a re-statement of theology." Theological certainty, he asserted, depended on giving the "Fact of

Christ" a pre-eminent place in the "thought and life and creed of the Church."[71] Falconer claimed that "Christianity can be traced back year by year, century by century to a Person who once lived on earth, of whose sayings and deeds we have a definite record, a record now acknowledged to be trustworthy,"[72] indicating that these clergymen believed they had successfully forged a powerful alliance between historical criticism and the traditions of theology inspired by the late eighteenth-century religious revival. Far from being reduced to irrelevance by the advance of evolutionary thought, theology, for these evangelicals, remained rooted in the tangible, historical reality of divine revelation and human action.

This belief led Chown to exclaim early in the twentieth century that the "child of the Sunday school today has possession of a more perfect system of theology than the early saints in the Church."[73] His confidence flowed from a realization that the evangelical creed could encompass both the stability of tradition and the dynamic of improvement. His theology, he felt, had withstood the challenge of Darwinism and the "higher criticism" by developing the intellectual strategy of "historical theology," and thus apparently preserving the dominant place of theology in education and culture.

Burwash attributed this "purified" character of evangelical theology to the achievements of his own generation, claiming that the experience of the "Person of Christ" as a living reality in both history and their own lives encouraged believers to affirm their evangelical convictions, and also compelled them to look outward to the wider community. Though based on the individuality of God and humanity, evangelical religion, he believed, must have a strong ethical orientation.[74] A similar insistence on the triad of personality, morality, and ethical activity marked the theological writings of leading figures in the Presbyterian colleges. The Rev. Daniel Miner Gordon, who succeeded Grant as principal of Queen's in 1903, sought to apply to the traditions of Calvinist theology the notion of the personal bond between God and the believer, usually described by the late Victorian generation in terms of the familial tie between a father and his child. Any opposition between the old doctrine and the new, Gordon declared, involved a misunderstanding, for the idea of fatherhood included the Calvinist notion of divine sovereignty.[75] The meaning was clear. For clergymen living under the long shadow of Darwin, the alliance of history and evangelical doctrine promised to revitalize theology, reaffirming the central tenets of the evangelical creed and making it a living force in the personal and social life of Christian believers, while acting as an antidote to lax and sentimental religious views.

The "historical theology" of both lecture hall and pulpit at the turn of the century preserved, against the alternatives offered by Ritschlian "liberals" and evolutionary naturalism, the biblical basis of the Christian faith and the divinity of Christ as a personal saviour. A revealing barometer of the persistence of the traditional creed was the question of sin. According to prevailing historical views, Burwash, Grant, Falconer, Chown, and other late Victorian clergymen were influenced by a pervasive climate of ethical humanism that arose in the wake of Darwin. In response, it is claimed, they diluted the evangelical doctrine of individual responsibility for sin and man's need for divine redemption, either by regarding sinful acts as the consequences of social ills that could only be eradicated by collectivist reforms, or by defining sin in evolutionary terms, as but a temporary stage that could be eradicated through moral, social, and material progress.[76]

Writing in 1897 Chown bluntly reminded his readers of one of the most important tasks of the evangelical preacher. "The pulpit needs to speak emphatically to-day upon the horrors from which men are saved, as well as the beauties of the life to which they are saved."[77] Coming from a clergyman generally regarded as the leader of the "liberal" social gospel tendency within the Methodist Church, this forceful insistence on the reality of sin seems to belie the prevailing interpretation of a great theological and religious decline in late Victorian English Canada. But Chown's views are consistent with the dominance of "historical theology" in the preaching and education of the Presbyterian and Methodist churches.

After several years on the preaching circuit, Chown attended Victoria College in the 1880s, where he absorbed the "inductive theology" of Nelles and Burwash. In his *Manual of Christian Theology*, a distillation of the lectures he delivered to candidates for the ministry, Burwash had forcefully advanced the contention that there could be no compromise between evangelical theology and the sentimental views of the human condition promoted by optimistic currents of evolutionary thought. Humanity stood in need of divine forgiveness. "Sin," he declared, "is ... very far from being a mere negation, a failure to reach a good. It is not the mere absence of right relation, it is a positive wrong relation. It is thus a reality, and as such a new thing as well as a wrong, a thing not made by God but our own doing – we have done the positive wrong." Burwash believed that sin originated in the abuse of the moral constitution, for which humanity stood individually and collectively responsible.[78] This assessment was not only in keeping with the traditional theological teachings inherited from Wesley, Ryerson, and Nelles, but was also echoed by Falconer, the newly-appointed principal of Presbyterian College, Halifax, a man who might have been expected to be more attuned to the "liberal" spirit of the age. In a 1907 article Falconer defended the biblical doctrine of sin as the only correct one, and praised Scripture as "a salutary tonic against all those easy-going theories which are so often untrue, either to man's own conscience or to the awful facts of the world."[79]

Individual regeneration, for these prominent clergymen, implied not the evolutionary achievement of some cultural ideal, but the moral encounter between a sinner and a personal redeemer. Their theology dictated, however, that the believer apply Christian faith to the the wider sphere of social life. It was precisely at this point, historians have argued, that late Victorian clergymen broke most decisively with evangelical "orthodoxy," discarding its certainties in favour of a purely ethical and social message that emphasized the realization of the Kingdom of God, not through a transcendent, miraculous providence, but as the logical result of natural processes inherent in the evolution of the human mind and society.

Speaking in 1905, the Rev. Salem Bland, who had recently been appointed to the chair of New Testament exegesis at the Methodist Church's Wesley College in Winnipeg, advanced the notion that Christianity was an entirely social religion. Salvation, in his view, involved less the encounter of the sinner with Christ than the application of social ethics to the problems of politics, industry, and urban life in the Canadian community.[80] As the son of the prominent Methodist preacher Henry Flesher Bland, Salem Bland's intellectual odyssey began within the confines of the evangelical traditions of preaching and education. After attending McGill University and Victoria College, he spent many years in the 1880s and 1890s as assistant to his father in Eastern Ontario. During this time he was influenced by the spirit introduced to Queen's University by Grant, and participated in the annual Theological Alumni Conferences at that institution. By the turn of the century, though still loyal to the doctrine of a "transcendent" Kingdom realized through individual regeneration, Bland had been exposed to popular evolutionist, Ritschlian, and philosophical idealist literature, which directly influenced his later proclamation of an "immanent" gospel of social salvation.[81]

But was Bland's journey from evangelical creed to "social gospel," from a religion of transcendence to one of immanence, typical of the experience of a majority of Canadian Protestant clergymen between 1890 and 1905? At first sight, the rising interest in social questions in the churches around the turn of the century would suggest that it was. Closer examination reveals, however, not a simple dichotomy, but a more complex pattern of response in both college and pulpit.

For example, Chown, who became the general superintendent of the entire church in 1910, described the Christian believer as one who "has sympathies as wide as the world and as deep as the most degraded member of the human race." The disciples of Christ, he declared, combined the role of "missionary" and "Christian political economist" so perfectly that their "views of sociology are shot through with ... the keener lightning of the Sermon on the Mount and the Lord's Prayer."[82] Though Chown's use of the term "sociology" seemed to imply a thoroughgoing commitment to the "social gospel" and a consequent dilution of evangelical theology, he believed that the regenerated society, or Kingdom of God, was not a purely earthly, immanent ideal, and was firmly convinced that Canadian life could not be reformed on a purely secular basis. The Kingdom would be established only through the influence of regenerated individuals.[83] This indicated a continued adherence to a belief in a transcendent Christ accomplishing the salvation of society through the prior redemption of individual sinners.

The contrasting views of Bland and Chown on the reform of Canadian society revealed the presence of two divergent currents within late nineteenth-century evangelicalism. While Bland derived his "social gospel" from strands of theological "liberalism" present in Britain and America, Chown's blending of evangelism and ethics, the personal and the social, with the accent on individual redemption, indicated the presence of a neglected, but more powerful current of ideas at work within the Methodist and Presbyterian churches. His insistence on the primacy of individual salvation echoed the views of Caven and Burwash, both of whom constantly and forcefully reminded their students that Christianity was above all the encounter of the individual with a personal saviour. "Man's relations to God," declared Caven, "must first be set right and the Kingdom of God established within him."[84]

For Burwash, Caven, and Chown, the harmony of the personal and the social had its roots in their theology of history and their understanding of the Bible, not in evolutionary social science. The sources of their outlook were a prophetic, post-millennial interpretation of history dominated by a miraculous providence, and their churches' traditions of preaching and education. Their social ethic was drawn neither from evolutionary thought nor from sentimental humanism, but from an equally powerful transatlantic intellectual current, "historical" or "inductive" theology – the biblical, Baconian alternative to the evolutionary challenge.

In 1889, Alexander Balmain Bruce, professor of New Testament at the University of Glasgow, and a leading promoter of "historical theology," wrote that the core of Christ's doctrine lay in the preaching of the Kingdom of God. Bruce was one of many Scottish religious figures who found no difficulty in reconciling the revivalist evangelism of Moody with the "reverent" historical criticism of Scripture. His critical examination of Christ's preaching concerning the Kingdom placed the achievement of this ideal in the inward, spiritual life of the believer. Individual salvation, he said, imposed wider responsibilities. Jesus had never intended the Kingdom to be purely otherworldly. It was also concerned with the condition of men in the "here and now," for it was destined to become "a society on earth."[85]

Assured by historical study that the Kingdom of God had a dual yet harmonious nature that led to the convergence of evangelism and social reform, Canadian clergymen-professors and preachers saw no need to discard their creed in favour of "sociology." They were convinced that their creed encompassed not only the salvation of the sinner in Christ, but also the creative element in the process of social regeneration. In 1894 the Methodist student W.G. Watson stated the consensus when he declared that the Kingdom of God was essentially ethical and spiritual in nature, ushered in by persuasion and preaching, not by secular means. "The power of righteousness," he concluded, "advances slowly but steadily, just in proportion as men's hearts are quickened by redeeming grace."[86]

These views echoed those of his theological mentors and expressed the thrust of preaching and teaching in Canada since the days of McCulloch and Ryerson. For the evangelical, personal religion and social life could not be separated, for both were founded on the simplified but nonetheless tenacious doctrines of the evangelical creed. To the agonizing of late twentieth-century historians over the perceived dichotomy between transcendence and immanence, theology and social action, Burwash, Chown, Grant, Falconer, and Caven would have retorted that their religion, even after Darwin, tolerated no such divisions. Because Scripture and Christian experience taught that God was present in the soul and life of the believer, the divine element was immanent in history and in human society. But, equally important, the biblical doctrine of God was one of transcendence. Their God had consciously entered history at certain well-defined, creative moments, most obviously at the Incarnation of Christ. The divine will, not the natural laws of mind and society, remained the determining factors in human progress. Though they held sacred and secular, divine and human in balance, the regeneration of their community, they believed, clearly lay with a providence superior to human reason and action.

HISTORY, THEOLOGY, AND THE "SOCIAL SCIENCES": A THIRD GREAT AWAKENING?

"I venture to think," wrote Principal Donald Harvey MacVicar of Presbyterian College, Montreal, in 1898, openly challenging the popular views of the British social thinker Herbert Spencer, and implicitly, those of all other late Victorian practitioners of the "human sciences," "that the true solution of the fundamental problems of Sociology will ultimately be found in the teachings of Christianity." MacVicar contended that Spencer's treatment of the subject "from the fathomless abyss of the past" as well as his all-encompassing standpoint of evolution offered only "shadowy conjecture" to address the pressing problems of the individuals relationship to society. MacVicar urged his students not to rely on evolutionary naturalism, but to begin from the sure revelation of the nature and character of God and humanity contained in the Bible. Through a certain historical revelation, Scripture taught that "sociology" would find its completion in the development of Christ's Kingdom.[87]

MacVicar's reflections offer two keys to the interpretation of the religious climate in late Victorian English Canada. First, they indicate that even after forty years of supposed assault on the doctrines of Christianity by evolutionary thought, clergymen-professors had not capitulated to the evolutionary dynamic. They firmly believed that their biblical theology was an independent and self-sufficient foundation of religious belief, culture, and intellectual activity. Second, they demonstrate the position of Canadian evangelicals within the transatlantic framework of religious and cultural change in the late nineteenth century.

The American historian William McLoughlin has argued that for American Protestants, the period between 1890 and 1920 marked a "Third Great Awakening." Despite the division of the Protestant churches into "liberal," "conservative," and even "fundamentalist" theological parties, the encounter of Protestant Christianity with "reform Darwinism" was a creative moment, not only for the churches, but for the wider American culture. McLoughlin claims that because the churches absorbed some of the tenets of Darwinist social thought, they participated in a broader movement of social reform that "revitalized" the entire culture. "Liberal" and "social gospel" Protestant clergymen applied the logic of evolutionary social theory to Christian theology, stressing the importance of "intellect" and "culture" in human development and, in common with a powerful group of university academics and secular reformers led by John Dewey, William James, G. Stanley Hall, and Richard T. Ely, promoted new forms of social welfare and control, and a more positive, collectivist role for the state in American society.[88]

By contrast, the thought and preaching of a majority of Canadian clergymen remained dominated by biblical language and themes. Even in 1905, few of MacVicar's colleagues referred to the evolutionary human sciences and, when they did so, it was always to disparage them, and to proclaim the superiority of biblical explanations of the behaviour of the individual and the rise, progress, and decline of societies. Despite the attempt by Canadian historians to argue that Canada followed the American pattern, where the content of theology was informed and altered by the methods and outlook of the social sciences, and where "conservative," "progressive," and "radical" wings grew up within the churches in response to the "social problem," the experience of some prominent and articulate late Victorian clergymen-professors and preachers active in movements of social reform indicates quite otherwise. Despite the presence of men such as Salem Bland, who were strongly influenced by the international climate of "reform Darwinism,"[89] the thought and actions of the dominant group of clergymen-professors shaping the evangelical mind suggest a firm resistance to the anchoring of theology and social action in the evolutionary paradigm. In the Canadian context, theology and evolutionary social thought remained separate entities, wary competitors in a struggle for intellectual supremacy that had been going on since the early nineteenth-century revival had established an uneasy relationship between Awakening and Enlightenment.

It might be countered that Methodists and Presbyterians had thoroughly assimilated the "historical revolution," and that history is a "social science." True, "historical theology" was a response to the Darwinian challenge, but it was a solution largely premised on the pre-Darwinian tenets of evangelical culture: the Baconian structure of certain biblical "facts"; the "prophetic" relationship between Scriptural narrative and human history; and the pre-eminent role of theology in explaining changes in the human world. Although Grant, Burwash, and Chown regarded history as a source of authority, they by no means considered it independent of theology. Only as far as the historical scholarship of their time testified to the activity of God and to the doctrines of human free-will and moral responsibility could it be considered the ally of theology. These clergymen remained tied to the view of history held in Britain and America in the 1830s and 1840s. When in the late nineteenth century historical criticism began to become a "social science," by seeking origins and causes in a process of evolution independent of revelation,[90] Canadian clergymen did not adapt their views, regarding their theology of history as superior to any secular interpretation.

Unlike their American counterparts, who adapted their theology to evolutionary social thought and, in the process, contributed to a cultural awakening, Canadian clergymen remained moored by their theology of history to the early nineteenth-century world of the Second Great Awakening. Their affinities lay, not with the evolutionary, social Christianity of Washington Gladden or Walter Rauschenbusch, or even with that of Salem Bland, but with the forceful evangelism of Chalmers, Charles Grandison Finney, and Lyman Beecher. Although active in various causes of social reform, their involvement was couched in the millennialist, prophetic, biblical terms coined during the pre-Darwinian era, and was not the consequence of any creative dialogue with evolutionary social thought. Even the effort to relate the "individual" and the "community," which Canadian historians have identified as a new factor in the late nineteenth-century churches, was but the continuation of attempts by the earlier revivalism to usher in the millennium, or "godly commonwealth," by perfecting the individual.[91] The central paradox, some would say the tragic flaw, of late nineteenth-century evangelicalism in Canada was its inability to engage in a creative conversation with the new "human sciences" of psychology, sociology, and economics. It is a strange irony that churches that had in the early part of the century anchored themselves within the province of the human, the moral, and the historical more emphatically than their American and British counterparts were unable to assimilate the social-science paradigm, and to use it to construct a new relationship between God, the individual, and society. The explanation for this failure lies in the powerful, sustained institutional presence of the evangelical creed in college and congregation. Far from unconsciously promoting "social science" and "secular thought," this theology posed an active obstacle to their assimilation by Canadian thought and culture.

Prominent Canadian clergymen saw no reason to worry about the absence of a dialogue between their theology and the human sciences. On the contrary, they believed that it testified to their cultural and intellectual triumph. They had avoided the debilitating struggles over evolutionary science and higher criticism, and averted the division of their churches into militant "liberal" and "conservative" wings. Their theology, based on immutable certainty and an explanation for moral and social progress, possessed, they believed, both historical and scientific legitimacy and the authority of practical success as a popular creed. In 1905 the superiority of the evangelical creed over its evolutionary competitors was unquestioned within Canada's Protestant churches. A mere five years later, this optimistic resolution appeared to have succumbed to uncertainty and crisis.

6 The Paradox of History: College and Creed in Crisis

With a plaintive note of uncertainty, Nathanael Burwash, recently retired as Chancellor of Victoria College, reflected in 1914 on the changes that had taken place in Canadian Methodism over the past four decades. In an address delivered to the Nova Scotia Conference on the eve of World War I, he observed that while he had witnessed a vast growth of the church in numbers, wealth, and activity, a "worldly spirit" had crept into Methodism, displacing the deeper spiritual life. Burwash warned his colleagues that the church had lost the "revival spirit and power of conversion & with it individual responsibility and zeal for the salvation of souls."[1] For Burwash's audience this was a serious matter. The questions of revival, conversion, and individual salvation lay at the heart of the evangelical creed. Any waning of the "revival spirit" meant a loss of preaching power and, ultimately, of cultural authority for the Protestant churches in their efforts to Christianize Canadian life.

Burwash was not merely articulating the concerns and frustrations of an older generation of evangelicals at odds with modern society. His achievements marked him as one of the leading architects of the Baconian accommodation with the new historical criticism in the crucial decades after 1860. Nor was he alone in fearing for the survival of the evangelical creed. The glowing confidence that prevailed in college and pulpit in 1900 had been replaced, only ten years later, by an atmosphere of crisis, gloom, and uncertainty. Even Chown, who so eloquently championed an "applied Christianity" directed at the social problems of an industrializing and urbanizing society, admitted that "the truths of Scripture," once so vital in arousing the consciences of Christian believers, "are now dull, and their thrust ineffectual."[2]

It would be well within the standard framework of historical interpretation to explain the pessimism of Burwash, Chown, and other leading clergymen as the logical outcome of a process that began around 1860, when men such as Caven, Grant, and Nelles surrendered the integrity of the "old-time evangelism," with its emphasis on revivals and individual conversion, in exchange for what twentieth-century historians have regarded as an intellectually dubious accommodation with Darwinian evolution, higher criticism, and social activism. Seen from this perspective, the "crisis" of the evangelical churches was nothing more than the pre-ordained retreat of Christianity in the face of the inexorable secularizing imperatives of modern civilization. According to this view, the plaintive response of evangelical leaders in both college and pulpit between 1905 and 1914 was a belated awakening to the sobering facts, a realization of their unwitting complicity in the de-Christianization of Canadian society.[3]

Such a view casts early twentieth-century Protestants as passive prisoners of a one-dimensional and almost ironclad historical logic. But neither passivity nor acceptance of inevitability in the face of external challenges to the authority of the Bible or to the intellectual and cultural supremacy of its creed had characterized the evangelical mind between the nineteenth-century revival and the dawn of the present century. In the four decades after 1860 most Canadian clergymen had preserved, through active debate, the integrity and coherence of their theology in the face of challenges from Darwinism, higher criticism, and the evolutionary "human sciences," while delicately balancing and adjusting their traditions of preaching and education in the light of scientific and historical discoveries.

Two conflicting alternatives are open to the historian seeking to reconstruct the thought and experience of Canadian Protestant clergymen in the decade prior to World War I. The secularization thesis acknowledges that the external impact of Darwinism, higher criticism, and the "social problem" on a body of thought termed "evangelical orthodoxy" provides an intellectually satisfying point of origin for the crisis that overtook many clergymen-professors and church leaders between 1905 and 1914. Such an approach, however, strips the early twentieth century of its historical distinctiveness, and casts Methodist and Presbyterian clergymen either as reactionary defenders of a tradition unchanged since the 1850s, or as the unwitting promoters of a secular outlook, reducing them to shadowy, ineffectual figures doomed to fight a battle in which defeat was ordained by the inflexible logic of a historical process.

Despite the outwardly compelling arguments of the secularization thesis, nagging questions remain. Was the dialectic of secular thought as victor and religious "orthodoxy" as victim, constructed by late twentieth-century historians, actually at work in the Protestant churches between 1905 and 1914? And if during those years evangelicals came to a belated realization of the havoc wrought by Darwin and higher criticism, why then, and not in 1880 or 1890? Why would Burwash, who was clearly aware of the secularizing implications of Darwinism and the higher criticism, voice his fears for the future of the evangelical creed only in 1914, and not in the 1870s or 1880s? Why would Carman, usually cast as the uncompromising foe of the new knowledge and academic freedom, wait until 1909 to launch a public campaign of harassment against "higher critics" in the colleges? Why is there no earlier expression of his supposed militant hostility?

The failure of the secularization thesis to account for either the timing or the intensity of the mood of crisis that overtook the evangelical churches compels the historian to seek sources other than the supposed perpetual dichotomy between evangelicalism and evolution and the rise of theological "liberalism" after 1880. The fears of men such as Burwash and Chown must be set against a transatlantic background. Historians who have studied both British and American religious environments generally agree that between 1900 and 1914 an internal "crisis of confidence" arose in evangelical and nonconformist churches.[4] British scholars contend that the problem was social, rather than intellectual. Tied to an ideology that equated progress with growth, British church leaders viewed with alarm the problem of declining membership, which recent scholarship has traced to the failure of nonconformist churches to recruit and train the children of their adherents.[5] George Marsden, however, has placed greater weight on intellectual factors, arguing that the years between 1910 and 1914 witnessed a hardening of lines between "liberals" and "conservatives," heralding "the end of an era for the American evangelical establishment." Marsden holds that the rupture of the fragile evangelical consensus between 1917 and 1925 occurred over the question of the relationship of Christianity to American culture.[6]

Although both Marsden and the British scholars have moved the debate away from the impact of external factors on Christianity, preferring to focus on an internal crisis of confidence, it is difficult to apply all of their insights to the Canadian Methodist and Presbyterian churches. The extreme statements of Burwash and Chown suggest far more than a response to a perceived social crisis of numbers. Both men emphasized a loss of authority, or preaching power, in the face of the "worldly spirit," indicating that before World War I Canadian clergymen recognized far more crucial changes in the cultural environment and in the substance of the evangelical creed itself. Thus Marsden's insistence on the importance of the intellectual factor, the tension in the minds of clergymen between Christianity and civilization, emerges as the significant factor in understanding the difficulties faced by the evangelical churches in the early twentieth century.

Between 1905 and 1914 Burwash and Chown were more pessimistic than any of their predecessors had been concerning the problem of the relationship between their creed and the wider Canadian culture. Their gloom did not stem from any belated concern over Darwin's impact, but expressed the dilemma of evangelicals confronted with a cataclysmic revolution in ideas far more profound and unsettling than that faced by Caven, Grant, and Nelles. In the ten years before World War I, clergymen-professors and preachers felt the corrosive force of currents of thought that had been at work in Europe and America since the 1890s. Usually lumped together under the term "relativism," these new developments in history, philosophy, psychology, and the social sciences rejected the search for moral, metaphysical, scientific, or doctrinal absolutes, preferring to view human experience and the universe as uncertain and open-ended, not governed by fixed, unchanging laws.[7] Unlike Darwinism and the higher criticism, the "relativist revolution" struck at the central pillar of evangelical thought, the belief that historical study, whether it be of the Bible or of human societies, provided some assurance of certainty or predictability in understanding and influencing the behaviour of individuals and communities.

It would be claiming too much to assert that the impact of "relativism" in history, philosophy, and social thought dramatically transformed the basic beliefs of the evangelical churches. Only a small elite of clergymen-professors and some influential preachers such as Chown were aware of these developments in Europe and the United States. Yet because of the place and function of the church college these new currents of thought rippled through the Presbyterian and Methodist churches. Evangelicalism was at once a tradition of academic study and a popular culture of preaching. The authority of the clergyman rested upon his ability to offer his congregation an accessible and intelligible interpretation of the products of the human intellect, and particularly historical experience, in light of the tenets of the evangelical creed.

The encounter between evangelicalism and "relativism" affected the relationship between theology and history, causing a rift that neither evolution nor historical criticism had effected between 1860 and 1890. After 1905 a mood of doubt concerning the historical validity of the biblical narratives and, by implication, the place of revelation in human culture, fostered an internal crisis of confidence that sapped the energies of many Canadian Methodist and Presbyterian clergymen. By 1914 the strategy adopted by clergymen-professors, traditionally the frontline of defence for the evangelical creed, had opened a serious rift between college and pulpit. This, in turn, called into question the validity of evangelicalism as an academic tradition, and the cultural authority of the creed itself. The disruption of harmonious relations between the worlds of professor and preacher, though less noisy and visible than the struggle between "conservatives" and "liberals" in the American churches, marked the end of an era for evangelicalism in Canada.

HISTORY AND THE BIBLE: THE RECESSION OF CERTAINTY

"The windows of our being," declared the Rev. Daniel Miner Gordon in 1903 at his inauguration as Grant's successor to the principalship of Queen's University, "look out upon the things unseen and eternal as well as upon those that are seen and temporal." Gordon's address restated the principles that had governed education in the evangelical colleges in Canada for nearly a century. Like his predecessor he believed that mind and conscience acquired knowledge of God's will through faith. Faith, in turn, was founded on the assurance that the Bible contained a certain, objectively verifiable record of God's dealings with individuals and nations. "If we would build our morality upon a sure foundation," he said, "it must be based on religion, and the Bible is, without question the most potent and religious literature in the world." Gordon concluded that there was no conflict between the demands of evangelical faith and the intellectual requirements of the twentieth-century college, for "the spiritual ideal of the University will, I trust, continue to be in the future as it has been in the past, framed by that Word which endureth forever."[8]

The confident attitude of Gordon and his colleagues at the dawn of the new century rested on the belief that the theological and historical validity of the Bible, the central foundation of the evangelical creed, remained unimpaired in education and preaching despite the encounter with evolution and the higher criticism. The work of Wellhausen and other German critics that, by the ruthless application of evolutionary naturalism to the Scriptures, had done so much to question and erode the historical basis of the Old Testament was, even in the late 1890s, deemed unacceptable by the majority of Presbyterian and Methodist clergymen-professors, who refused to abandon their belief in the authoritative nature, supernatural character, and factual accuracy of the Old Testament. Even among those for whom a literal reading of Scripture was no longer possible, the consensus was that the Old Testament, and particularly the Pentateuch, contained inspired and therefore trustworthy historical documents written by contemporaries of the events described, and not by others centuries later, as the German critics claimed.[9]

Firmly constrained by the traditions of education and preaching established in the church colleges between 1820 and 1850, historical criticism, for these professors and their students, was a source of certainty rather than of anxiety. History preserved the sense of God's miraculous activity in the world and the authority of the Bible, and elevated theology to the status of a science. The evangelical alliance of theology and history, far from being a relic of the late eighteenth-century revival, expressed Christian belief in terms culturally acceptable to the late nineteenth century. In Britain, the United States, and English Canada in the 1870s and 1880s,[10] even writers with a more secular outlook viewed the study of history as an abiding source of moral principles governing individual and social conduct.

Canadian clergymen-professors and their students at the turn of the century differed, however, from secular academics and educators who sought to use the cultural prestige of history to infuse morality into the fabric of their societies.[11] They were constrained to draw illustrations and applications of moral ideas explicitly from the biblical narratives, which they regarded as a superior, divinely revealed history, a standard beyond the human mind and experience. The historical process was not simply permeated with an immanent, divine spirit, as the German scholar Leopold von Ranke and many European, American, and British historians believed. For these clergymen-professors and preachers, God actively entered history at certain specific moments, miraculously altering the course of human thought and action. This sense was captured by the Rev. John Edgar McFadyen, professor of Old Testament criticism at Knox College, when he declared in 1903 that "there is a mystery about all facts, and most of all about Biblical facts."[12] Historical criticism in the church colleges was thus limited and hedged with restrictions, particularly against any challenge to "the moral and spiritual sovereignty of the Bible."[13]

After 1905, however, this view of the relationship between the Bible and human history as well as the conviction that the standard of individual and social conduct remained fixed in a transcendent realm beyond the control of human reason were confronted by a transatlantic intellectual crisis. Though less well-known than the "Darwinian revolution," the transformation of European, American, and British social thought that began around 1890 offered a more profound challenge to religion and culture. It involved nothing less than a reorientation of the study of the individual and society, and affected, not humanity's place in relation to physical nature, but the nature of consciousness and the character of truth and meaning.

This revolution in social thought was also a profoundly disquieting revolution in values. The philosophical debate in continental Europe, Britain, and the United States centred on the nature and role of history as a standard of human behaviour. From about 1820 until the 1880s, both Canadian clergymen-professors and their transatlantic competitors in the secular human sciences had, for all their differences, been united by a belief that history was ultimately "metaphysical," postulating a divine, or at least a moral, reality beyond the historical world, a reality that endowed human life with rationality and ethical purpose. Truth and morality might be elucidated historically, but this by no means implied that it was relative. It was the hallmark of Victorian religion and social thought to distinguish between "true" and "false" religion, "higher" and "lower" races, "civilized" and "savage" nations.[14] Although the pervasive influence of the natural sciences, particularly after 1860, had accelerated the rise of a more naturalistic outlook that viewed the divine presence in history as increasingly tenuous, both religious believers and scientific materialists remained committed to an ideal of truth that emphasized certainty and fixity. Though on opposite sides of the debate, they retained this common point of reference.

By the 1890s philosophers, historians, and social thinkers in Germany and Italy transcended the debate between religion and science, idealism and materialism that was really a conflict over the character of immutable truth, not over its existence. They denied, in the name of experience and consciousness, the fixed and certain nature of truth, and interpreted the whole of reality, even supposedly absolute and unchanging human moral values, in historically relative, subjective terms. They pushed to its limits the logic of "historicism," the outlook shaped in Germany between 1780 and 1850, and studied each institution, each idea, each ideal as a one-time event linked to a specific historical and cultural setting.[15]

By positing that human values were time-specific and culture-specific, they rejected the sanctions that so effectively sustained Victorian thought. Their unflinching acceptance of "historicism" prepared the way for the relativization of all values. They undermined the premise that had seemed so secure to the transatlantic intellectual community of the 1860s – that the past could be objectively known and thus could serve as a guide to human conduct in the present and the future. By the turn of the century intellectuals were floundering in a quicksand of shifting opinions. The German scholars Wilhelm Dilthey, Max Weber, and Ernst Troeltsch, the Italian philosopher and historian Benedetto Croce and the Americans William James, John Dewey, Charles Beard, and Carl Becker all stressed the subjective nature of historical writing and the impermanence of any conclusion reached.[16]

In the Methodist and Presbyterian church colleges, the period between 1890 and 1905 marked the apogee of confidence in the ability of evangelical theology to redeem and transform Canadian society. Caven, Grant, Burwash, and Chown were convinced that their "historical theology" conferred immutable certainty on the Bible and its doctrines, and established the intellectual and cultural supremacy of theology over the logic of evolutionary naturalism. By 1905, however, professors in the theological colleges, perhaps even earlier than their rivals in philosophy and the "human sciences," were increasingly aware of the implications of the "revolution" in human values and the nature of history for the central tenets of their creed.

Canadian Methodist and Presbyterian professors and preachers felt the cutting edge of this transformation most keenly in the area of biblical studies. Although traditionally hostile to German practices of biblical criticism, evangelical scholars often pursued postgraduate study in German universities[17] where, by 1900, they encountered increasing scepticism concerning the validity of historical study as a basis for theology. In the field of Old Testament study, for example, both evangelicals and naturalistic critics such as Wellhausen had, for all their differences over the dating, authorship, and "sacred" character of the narratives, at least accepted that the earliest part of the Old Testament, the Book of Genesis, contained a kernel of historical "fact" out of which a "true" history of the origins of the Hebrew religion might be constructed. Indeed, the common ground of debate enabled clergymen-professors faithful to the inductive method of criticism to develop defences against evolutionary naturalism that used the critical method to assure, almost intact, the historicity and inspired character of the Old Testament books.

Developments in the German universities after the turn of the century, however, altered this congenial climate of attack and defence. Hermann Gunkel, perhaps the most important name in Old Testament criticism, advanced a method known as "form-criticism," which sought, through analysis of component units of oral tradition, to penetrate behind the literary narratives. There were, he contended, orderly processes in the development of oral tradition, determined by "the laws of folk-psychology."[18] In *The Legends of Genesis*, first published in 1901, Gunkel argued that the accounts of the early history of Israel were not historical. Rather, they grouped two types of legendary material, both mythical in nature, and drawn, in part, from "heathen" Babylonian sources. Both evangelical "reverent" critics and Wellhausen's evolutionary naturalist disciples found their positions undercut. What historical detail the Book of Genesis contained, Gunkel asserted, was enshrouded with the mist of legend, and could not be precisely identified or dated by methods of historical or literary criticism. He concluded that the religious significance of these narratives did not rest on their historical validity, but on the moral ideas expressed in the myths.[19]

Though the "Comparative Religion" school of German biblical scholars, which grouped figures such as Gunkel, the New Testament scholars Johannes Weiss and Wilhelm Bousset, and the church historian and philosopher Ernst Troeltsch, pursued a different line of investigation, it was allied with the "form-critical" approach through one central assumption. According to Troeltsch, their chief theorist and publicist, the "Comparative Religion" school simply recognized that "human religion exists only in manifold specific religious cults which develop in very complex relations of mutual contact and influence, and that in this religious development it is impossible to make the older dogmatic distinction between a natural and supernatural revelation."[20]

Troeltsch here proclaimed a radical disengagement of theology and history. Far from offering a basis of certain "fact" on which scholars could construct a viable, "scientific" theology, the study of history led faith to an impasse. Although emotionally committed to the supremacy of the "prophetic-Christian" faith, Troeltsch and his colleagues rejected the notion that history conferred scientific validity upon theology, and concluded that history, far from proving the absolute truth of Christianity, could not even draw a precise distinction between natural and supernatural religion. Thus theology was not a "science" resting on some immutable "essence" or body of principles, it was a confession of faith. Christianity, like other religions, was in a constant state of flux. Troeltsch's *Social Teachings of the Christian Churches* presented Christianity as merely one historical religion belonging to the West, and identified it as a part of the total culture of the age. Like the biblical message, Christian social ethics were only relative. Theology thus assumed the status of mere ideology in a culture increasingly characterized by competing value systems, and offered no absolute standard by which to guide human behaviour.[21]

Troeltsch's scepticism concerning the viability of historical study as the means to anchor Christian doctrine reflected a religious environment that had lost the most basic sense of a meaningful encounter with Jesus and the origins of Christianity. Both evangelicals and Ritschlians such as Adolf von Harnack were in agreement on one key issue: Jesus was a historical person who preached a message both spiritual and ethical, individual and social. Though they disagreed on the role of theology in the study of history, both assumed that the application of historical study to the New Testament and to the history of the church would enable believers to identify some permanent "essence" of Christianity, some fundamental dogmatic expression, whether it be the "Jesus of History" or the "Fact of Christ," that would link Christian communities in the present with the Age of the Apostles.

Published in 1892, *Jesus' Proclamation of the Kingdom of God*, a short work by Johannes Weiss, Ritschl's son-in-law, called these assumptions into serious question. Weiss demonstrated that Jesus neither considered the Kingdom a religious experience nor equated it with the achievement of some supreme ethical ideal, whether individual or social. The Kingdom was, rather, the visible messianic rule foretold in obscure books of late Jewish apocalyptic writing. Both evangelicals and Ritschlians were troubled by the implication that Jesus did not transcend the thinking of his contemporaries to found a new religion, but shared their beliefs in the imminent end of the world through the arbitrary action of an imperious God. Even worse, from an evangelical standpoint, Weiss argued that Jesus did not see his death in terms of redemption for sin, but as a desperate attempt to usher in a cataclysmic, earthly Kingdom of God with Himself as Messiah.[22]

An enigmatic Jesus now confronted the Protestant world. The most advanced critical scholarship revealed a saviour whose person and message apparently could not be disentangled from their roots in Jewish tradition and the pagan religions of redemption. Was this a message with any abiding meaning beyond its historical and cultural setting? Or did the historical enterprise, as Albert Schweitzer's *The Quest of the Historical Jesus* implied, only lead religious believers to a pessimistic relativism, to the impasse of a Jesus utterly incomprehensible to the modern mind?[23]

Far more than evolutionary science or social thought, the historical study promoted in German theological faculties after 1900 was deeply subversive of the evangelical alliance of theology and history. Troeltsch and his colleagues were less outright opponents of the evangelical creed than inhabitants of a completely different intellectual universe, where certainty, either scientific or religious, was no longer possible. The evangelical accommodation of the decades between 1860 and 1890, it may be argued, was founded on the belief that both the Baconian induction that anchored the tenets of the late eighteenth-century religious revival and the historical criticism honed between 1830 and 1860 could establish religious certainty. Through "historical theology," Presbyterian leaders such as Grant, Gordon, Caven, Gandier, and Falconer and their Methodist counterparts Nelles, Burwash, and Chown preserved the substance of the intellectual world of Wesley and Chalmers. Their training and basic assumptions concerning the nature of religious knowledge did not, however, prepare them or their disciples for a world in which, in the space of a single decade, the divorce between faith and history would shatter the carefully-laid foundations of preaching and education in their churches.

INTIMATIONS OF TROUBLE: THE DEFECTION OF THE GUARDIANS

In the early twentieth-century evangelical colleges, where a rising generation of preachers were being trained, the historian can detect scarcely a ripple of conflict over educational goals or over the balance between faith and reason, theology and historical criticism. Both Presbyterian and Methodist colleges remained devoted to the aims of their founders, and emphasized not intellectual discipline or critical erudition but the practical application of faith and preaching to the problems of the missions and of individual souls. In 1902 a Presbyterian observer, demonstrating this allegiance to tradition, declared that the role of the college was to "train men for service in the Church who shall not only be scholars and theologians but preachers in the best sense of the word."[24]

Nor was there an obvious breach with the evangelical belief in the inspired nature of the Bible and its authority as both theology and history. A cursory glance at the writings of clergymen-professors in 1914 would reveal the almost monolithic persistence of the evangelical creed and the culture it sustained. Methodist and Presbyterian scholars maintained their prejudice against German "speculation," much preferring the sober, inductive accumulation of "facts" that preserved the integrity of the biblical narratives as a text that the preacher could confidently proclaim as the Word of God. This continuing need for authority induced the young Methodist scholar A.P. Misener to state in a letter to his mentor Burwash that although German theology showed a "steady perseverance in the mastering of the detail of their work," the attention to detail "seems to me in certain areas to starve out of them certain other qualities, such as the imaginative."[25]

Between 1905 and 1914, however, clergymen-professors and their students engaged in a quiet but intense struggle with the relativistic implications of "form-criticism" and the methodology of "Comparative Religion," a debate that subtly, but nonetheless palpably, altered the balance between theology and history, preaching and scholarship. Signs of this transformation were not immediately evident, for the colleges used a number of strategies to minimize the impact of the new learning on biblical study and theology. As with higher criticism in the 1860s and 1870s, evangelical leaders treated any theology emanating from German universities with considerable caution. In 1906 an anonymous Presbyterian observed that the central contention of "Comparative Religion" rested on the premise that early in its development Christianity came into contact with the Syncretic, "heathen" religions of the Greco-Roman world, and derived its notions of resurrection and redemption from this source. This, he declared, meant the dispersion of the "pure" apostolic faith into a welter of mystery-religions and, from the point of view of evangelical theology, a loss of confidence in the central doctrines of the Resurrection and the Christology of the early church.[26] And while Professor J.M. Shaw of Presbyterian College, Halifax, recognized that the new German criticism separated the historical Jesus from the Christ of the Church, he repudiated this distinction. Such theories, he wrote, rested not on historical method but on philosophical presuppositions.[27]

The response of these early twentieth-century evangelical scholars to the challenge of historical relativism was, however, more complex than mere negation. Since the early nineteenth century, when a rising evangelicalism had confronted the philosophical and historical legacy of the Enlightenment, Methodist and Presbyterian clergymen, encouraged by the breadth and flexibility of their creed, had not simply erected barriers between their faith and various forms of reason. Whether the challenge was Scottish Common Sense philosophy, Darwinian evolution, or higher criticism, their first impulse had always been to engage critically, to "capture," or to "tame" what to the modern mind might seem a serious threat to their theology. They appropriated the method while discarding or at least neutralizing the underlying assumptions, replacing them with a firm insistence on biblical inspiration and authority and on the intellectual supremacy of theology over other forms of thought.

They believed that their impregnable and expansive structure of theology, history, and preaching, empowered them to actively select and accommodate, and thus "Christianize" and control, the scientific, historical, and philosophical currents in Victorian culture. Thus their creed functioned not so much as a barrier, but as a screen, filtering new ideas before they influenced pulpit and congregation. This mood indicated a more widespread optimism among evangelical clergymen, founded on the conviction that, through conversion and application of the teachings of the Bible to human problems, they were progressively accomplishing the redemption of an entire culture.

This belief in the power of the evangelical creed marked William George Jordan's synthetic work *Biblical Criticism and Modern Thought*, published in 1909. As professor of Old Testament at Queen's University since 1898, Jordan felt compelled to introduce his students and a wider readership in the Presbyterian Church to some of the new developments in the theory and practice of biblical study. Following the lines laid down by his predecessors in the 1870s and 1880s, he evinced all the tolerance and breadth of the Scottish "historical theology," and urged acceptance of Hermann Gunkel's "form-criticism," which was justified, he argued, because the German method approximated that of the traditional inductive criticism. Jordan rejected, however, the extreme versions of the "Babylonian theory" proposed by Gunkel and other German scholars, believing that it imperilled the life and integrity of the Old Testament. "However much Israel might be dependent on Babylon in matters of history and science," he declared, "religiously she was free and independent – that is, her prophets and leaders had a clear, strong message of their own."[28]

While Jordan's attempt to tame the "form-critical" method in the name of evangelical scholarship was to be expected, his equation of this product of historical relativism with Baconian induction was surprising. Jordan and his colleagues seemed to have made a crucial error at just this point. They assumed that "form criticism," like the earlier higher criticism, was merely another form of evolutionary naturalism, which, after carefully separating method and assumptions, they might employ to serve their goal of theological and moral certainty. Jordan appeared not to understand that Gunkel and his associates, unlike Wellhausen, were no longer even involved in the old debate over the inspired or "sacred" character of the Old Testament history. They denied that *any* of the biblical narratives were historical records, and contended that the Bible was the final, literary form of oral tradition, much of which was legendary. Any attempt to accommodate "form-criticism" to the evangelical creed implied a renunciation of the Baconian premises of the reigning "historical theology," which assumed the presence of at least enough contemporary historical material to offer certainty about the starting point of the progressive revelation that culminated in Christianity.

The perils of attempting to assimilate this corrosive form of historical relativism to evangelical traditions of biblical scholarship were illustrated by the work of the Rev. Alexander Reid Gordon, who occupied the Old Testament chair at Presbyterian College, Montreal. Gordon was a typical product of the transatlantic "historical theology," a Scotsman educated at Glasgow, where George Adam Smith, one of the leading Old Testament "reverent" critics, held evangelical and critical tendencies in balance during the 1890s. Gordon had, however, pursued postgraduate studies with Hermann Gunkel at the University of Berlin, and his work, *The Early Traditions of Genesis*, published in 1907,[29] marked an attempt to find a middle way between two rapidly diverging approaches to the role of theological assumptions in the historical study of religion.

Gordon's lengthy work of criticism was informed throughout by the need to adapt Gunkel's insights to the tastes of an evangelical audience. While admitting the existence of Babylonian traditions of creation and deluge parallel to the Book of Genesis, he minimized the influence of "heathen" elements in the formation of the biblical narratives. The Bible writers, Gordon asserted, "do not simply reproduce the materials they receive. They touch and recast them in their own spirit." This, he concluded, meant that the Hebrew and Babylonian cycles were totally different.[30] Gordon's work was not simply a rehashing of his Berlin studies, for at several points he tried to shift the balance back towards the historical, rather than the legendary character of the Book of Genesis. "We cannot," he declared, "dismiss national legends as mere empty fables. As the deposits of national tradition, arrayed in the fair garb of fresh and spontaneous poetry, they always embody a substantial basis of historical fact underneath the imaginative dress. And this basis is probably greater than the Western educated mind is prepared to allow ... Students of anthropology are often surprised by the correspondence of tribal traditions to discovered facts."[31] Theological students and clergymen reading this assessment could rest comforted by Gordon's main argument, that the historical integrity, and thus, the religious meaning of Genesis was not impaired, even by the scrutiny of "form-criticism."

On another level, however, *The Early Traditions of Genesis* broke quietly, but nonetheless decisively, with the Baconian foundations of "historical theology." For all his attempts to recover the historical origins of the Israelite religion, Gordon was constrained to agree with Gunkel's main contention that Genesis was "legendary." Having done so, he was faced with the problem of trying to minimize the damage. From the standpoint of a preacher or a member of a congregation, however, these subtle distinctions were mere hairsplitting. The evangelical creed had always drawn an explicit line between "true" and "false" religion, Christianity and "heathenism." The former was based on historical fact, the latter on myth or legend. To those educated in a Baconian culture of certainty, where historical events and theological realities were clear and were forcefully articulated, Gordon's admissions came close to equating the Bible with "heathen" legend, and thus to denying its value as the standard for belief and conduct. Gordon's Old Testament researches could only cast doubt on the conviction that historical scholarship anchored the validity of theology on the objective "facts" of God's progressive revelation.

The new "relativist" temper in Europe and America indicated that historians wished to pursue their discipline independently of theological and moral imperatives. If, as Troeltsch, Weber, Croce, and the Americans Becker and Beard proclaimed, theology and history were no longer compatible, could evangelicals rest assured that history would somehow ultimately validate, rather than undermine, the essential doctrines of Christianity? Even in the sensitive area of biblical study, it now appeared less certain that historical criticism would reach a consensus over exactly which "facts" could serve as a reliable basis of belief. This, in turn, raised a serious problem for professors and preachers raised in a climate where the certainties of history and theology were taken for granted. Would the "historical theology" that had sustained the Protestant churches in the face of evolutionary naturalism become more historical than theological?

Writing in 1909, James Denney, professor of New Testament language and literature at Glasgow, illustrated the growing disjunction between historical criticism and traditional faith. Outwardly, at least, his *Jesus and the Gospel* preserved the unity between the "historical Jesus" and the "Christ of the Church." His conclusions, however, reduced doctrine to a vague "Christian attitude," which he held to be "all that is vital to Christianity … it is not bound up, as it is often supposed to be, with this or that intellectual construction of it." The church "must bind its members to the Christian attitude to Christ, but it has no right to bind them to anything else." History, he contended, could justify, only a vague "broad churchism," not doctrine.[32]

In its continued attempt to appropriate developments in historical study and biblical criticism, "historical theology" emerged, not as a structure of certainty, but as, at best, a halfway position. Although Jordan and Gordon might have claimed to be engaged in an impeccably evangelical activity, they could be said to have conceded too much to the relativist temper, to have lost sight of their primary aim, the training of clergymen for preaching and conversion, in the interests of addressing an international community of biblical scholars.

The relationship between the Bible and criticism in the theological colleges in 1910 compared to that in 1890 was marked by a discussion increasingly technical, esoteric, and inaccessible to the ordinary Christian believer in both subject-matter and tone. For example, between 1910 and 1914, Ernest F. Scott, professor of New Testament at Queen's University, published two books, *The Kingdom and the Messiah* and *The Beginnings of the Church*, addressing the problems raised by the new "apocalyptic" message discovered by the German "Comparative Religion" school. Like his Old Testament colleagues, he attempted to negotiate a middle way. He argued that recent criticism had exaggerated the significance of "apocalypticism" in the Gospels. Nevertheless, he admitted that although Weiss and Schweitzer had gone too far in separating the "historical Jesus" from the teaching of the Church, such eschatological, messianic elements derived from Judaism were present, and did provide a "framework" for Jesus's preaching.[33]

Although Scott's books were intended to refute the main arguments of Schweitzer and other "radical" German critics, from the standpoint of students and preachers raised in a culture of certainty, there was only a fine line between admitting the presence of an apocalyptic "framework" in the New Testament and full agreeing with the central hypotheses of the advanced German school. Clergymen and believers outside the college who were unfamiliar with the day-to-day practice of criticism might well have asked whether the historic Jesus was a divine redeemer with a transcendent yet accessible and intelligible message, or whether He was simply a man whose thought was inseparable from the messianic concepts of His own age. To even consider the latter idea implied that Harnack and other church historians may have been correct. If the doctrines of Christ's divinity and redeeming power had no basis in the Gospels, but were constructions imposed centuries later on the Church, then theology was not validated by the historical experience.

When compared with the relative seamlessness of the "historical theology" of the generation of Nelles, Burwash, Grant, and Caven, the disjunction between the practice of history as an academic discipline and the requirements of an authoritative theology was all the more striking. Those clergymen-professors who experienced the impact of Darwin between 1860 and 1890 were certain of the difference between "reverent" criticism and higher criticism, and were aware of the need to maintain the dominance of theology and the integrity of the biblical narratives over historical scholarship. Scott and some of his colleagues were devoted to the intellectual supremacy of theology and to the same ideal of bridging the worlds of scholarship and preaching. But, in assessing the historical value of parts of the New Testament in the light of the challenge posed by Schweitzer and the advocates of "Comparative Religion," they subtly, but unmistakably, accentuated the "historical" side of the evangelical equation.

Influenced by the writings of Scott, Jordan, and Gordon, some clergymen-professors crossed a crucial intellectual and cultural watershed. Though committed to the supremacy of the evangelical creed in thought and culture, they had ceased, by the time of World War I, to address the wider concerns of the evangelical congregation, and were imprisoned in the narrow confines of the professional scholar's study. They directed their message not to the pulpit, but to an international community of biblical scholars speaking an arcane, professional language comprehensible only to those with sophisticated linguistic and historical training.

The Methodist and Presbyterian theological faculties were not the only group to pursue the goal of professionalism early in the twentieth century. University academics, affected by the "social crisis," also began to separate the professional "experts" from other members of the community.[34] Unlike their secular counterparts in the rising social sciences, however, the clergymen-professors, in their pursuit of the professional ideal, lost their influence in the wider community.

From the founding of the colleges during the Second Great Awakening, the authority of these prominent evangelicals had rested not simply on their scholarship, but also on the delicate balance of the relationship they formed with their congregation through preaching. For the evangelical, sound preaching was directed at the transformation, or conversion, of the individual listener and thus to the Christianization of the community. According to the historian Donald Scott, who has studied the momentous transformation in the perception of the clergyman's role that occurred between 1790 and 1850, the notion that clergymen were members of a "profession" rather than holders of "office" meant that their claims to power and prestige in the wider culture were judged by "results" – visible success in converting sinners and effectiveness in movements of moral reform such as temperance and abolitionism. This led, he maintains, not to increased social and cultural authority, but to a waning influence in the community.[35]

The changed cultural position of the clergyman-professor in the first decade of the twentieth century was, to a certain extent, analogous to this earlier loss of authority. Yet in many respects it was a response to a more acute problem. The process described by Scott took place within the framework of a society that still accepted the intellectual and cultural supremacy of explicitly Christian tenets concerning the individual and society. By 1910 college clergymen shared their intellectual authority with historians, philosophers, and social thinkers, whose adherence to theological explanations of the human world was, at best, vestigial. In the wider society, the clergyman now competed with the mass-market magazine, the spearhead of an ethos of consumption at odds with the tenets of the evangelical creed. By 1920 consumerism, promoted by advertisers, social scientists, the media, business, and even many clergymen in an effort to counteract what one historian has described as the "weightlessness" and uncertainty of late nineteenth-century life, had decisively reoriented North American culture away from a system of values defined by self-sacrifice and production, to one shaped by a desire for personal fulfillment and pleasure.[36] It might be argued that by increasingly turning toward the scholarly aspects of their task, clergymen-professors were themselves contributing to this process. Although they sought to take firm hold of a precise body of knowledge that might counteract the loss of certainty associated with this cultural transformation, their scholarly preoccupations weakened evangelicism's crucial bond between college and pulpit.

To avoid the growing difficulties of maintaining theological certainty in a climate of historical relativism, college teaching among both Methodists and Presbyterians increasingly accentuated the moral rather than the historical value of the biblical narratives. In 1913 the Wesley College student James Wilkins argued that while the Old Testament contained no infallible record of facts, it was a "typical record of the growth and development of Religion" and thus constituted an indispensable illustration of the evolution of religion in the individual from its simplest to its most complex forms.[37] The religious value of the biblical history had become subjective, a matter of personal experience, and not the objective "scientific" pursuit insisted upon by an earlier generation of professors and preachers. Richard P. Bowles, who in 1913 succeeded Burwash as chancellor of Victoria College, in an article addressing the problem of biblical revelation, declared that Scripture could not be identified with objective truth – record and revelation were two different matters. Bowles dismissed the idea of plenary inspiration that had guided evangelicals since the age of McCulloch and Ryerson. He argued that the Bible consisted of "certain great experiences out of which came the written word of Holy Scripture." It held meaning for twentieth-century Christians because "what I experience tells me of the experience out of which came the book that moves me."[38]

Bowles's position was indeed precarious, for it raised the possibility that neither Scripture nor theology provided any objective standard. By resolving faith into competing individual experiences, it came close to overtly challenging the Methodist "quadrilateral" that had guided the teaching of theology at Victoria College since the 1840s. Although evangelicals had always held that individual experience of God was one of the elements of faith, they had been equally insistent that experience was also subject to the test of the biblical "facts" and doctrines, the certain foundations of belief and preaching.

If the meaning of biblical "facts" became increasingly uncertain under the impact of "form-criticism," "Comparative Religion," and historical relativism, historical study, to early twentieth-century clergymen-professors, demonstrated that theology was but a transitory, human construction, dependent on the experience of time and place, rather than on divine revelation. It was difficult to escape the implication, although evangelicals had, with considerable success, attempted to do so, that theology had less in common with actual revealed "truth" than with theories or ideologies of politics or philosophy. And, as a rising generation of pragmatic philosophers, social thinkers, and historians argued, all these changed with the flux of experience. Was theology the sovereign, independent "science" as the Baconian method claimed, or was it at best a philosophy of history acting as a prudent guide to human conduct?

Two clergymen-professors, the Rev. E.F. Scott and John Dall, both from Queen's University, sought, in the five years before World War I, to resolve the increasingly disturbed relationship between theology and history. In his inaugural address in 1909, Scott attempted to define the relationship of theology to the specialized modern knowledge that had apparently usurped its traditional place in the university. Although theology could never reassert its old position as "queen of all the sciences," this did not mean that it should exist on sufferance, as a mere vassal of modern science, he insisted. "Theology ... illuminates and completes the work of the other sciences. It interprets to them the higher truth to which they are reaching forward, and on which they depend for their whole progress and aim."[39]

While advocating a continued adherence to "historical theology," Scott begged the question of theology's status. It might be argued that in relation to the rival disciplines of history, philosophy, and the "social sciences," which since 1880 had used notions of biological evolution to explain the development of the human mind and society, theology lacked a distinctive method independent of history and, some would claim, even a reliable source of data. The recession of certainty in the historical validity of the biblical narratives robbed theology of its status as a precise "scientific" body of truths known to all believers, by which human actions and culture might be judged and transformed. Constrained by the requirements of the historical method to deny the binding nature of Scriptural authority and the historic creeds of the church in the name of religious experience, the "historical theology" practiced by Scott and his associates reduced evangelical theology to one among many ideologies, its usefulness no longer the consequence of its basis in a divine revelation, but solely dependent on its ability to promote Christian character and holy living, and the realization of the Kingdom of God in society.[40]

The weakening of the sense of a divine presence in the historical process was a corollary of this dilution of theology in the evangelical colleges. Though adopting some of the insights of higher criticism, the generation of Grant, Nelles, Burwash, Caven, and King had always preached that history was a sacred process, given meaning by specific interventions in time by a divine providence. Though immanent in history, God was also a transcendent, conscious being, not to be simply equated with life, growth, or progress, the catchwords of the late Victorian age. This conviction enabled Presbyterians and Methodists to link history, theology, and prophecy in their educational institutions and preaching.

A comparison of the fundamental beliefs of the nineteenth-century evangelicals with the views expressed in 1912 by Dall after his appointment to the chair of church history at Queen's University demonstrates the sense of disorientation felt by this first generation of clergymen to confront the problem of historical relativism. Like Scott, Dall was trained in the Scottish "historical theology," and, outwardly at least, his address sounded all the traditional evangelical themes. In opposition to social thinkers Troeltsch, Croce, and

Becker, he argued that a "science of history" was possible. "Science" he defined simply as "the results of observation systematically classified." Empirical study and precise induction, he said could bring order to the seeming chaos of historical events without impairing human free will and moral responsibility, the keystones of Christian belief.[41]

Up to this point, Dall's address was impeccably Baconian and avoided the pitfalls of historical relativism. But when it came to firmly postulating either a method or a role for a "science of history" that would confer some permanence or rationality on its "facts" or conclusions, or on the central tenets of the evangelical creed, he was on less firm ground. Like Troeltsch, he was reduced to stating his sense of history as a confession of faith, not as a firm declaration of "scientific" principle. "If we deny the possibility of a science of history," he declared, "we reduce history to a mere chaotic chronicle, incapable of rational explanation of any kind."[42]

Dall was voicing the paradox that confronted clergymen-professors in the decade before World War I. Their training and their evangelical traditions of preaching and education taught them that, through historical study, it was possible to discover some bedrock of "scientific" and moral certainty on which to ground faith and theology. The irony of Canadian evangelicalism was, however, that the more historical criticism was applied to the Bible and to the history of the church, the less certain the fundamental doctrines seemed to the human mind. For Dall, very little of the sense of history as a process infused by the divine presence remained, other than a belief in progress, a belief that "though individuals may suffer, when we take stock of a century at its end, we shall find that the world is better and happier than it was at the beginning … Lift up your hearts; for the world is moving onwards. Its chariot wheels may crush for the moment, but it does not move to evil. It is guided from above, and guided, we may be sure, with wisdom and goodness which cannot fail. This is the comfort which in the blackest darkness must afford light."[43] Unlike the preaching of an earlier generation of college clergymen, this peroration lacked the confidence of firm belief. Rather, it seemed a ritual invocation in the face of a troubling loss of certainty in both the biblical record and the divine presence in human history.

"Historical theology," once the bulwark of the evangelical creed against the challenge of Darwinism and the "human sciences," increasingly fettered Canadian clergymen in the inflexible logic of the historical method, which no longer could affirm the validity of theology as a category of knowledge. The internal contradictions of historical criticism, as understood in the early twentieth century, and a theology still heavily infused with an eighteenth-century, Baconian spirit crippled the evangelicals' efforts to "tame" or "Christianize" human culture and intellect. Contemporaries of Scott and Dall, though reluctant to abandon their theological heritage, looked less and less to the intervention of divine providence, and increasingly to "progress," as the explanation for the moral and social process of history in the human world. In 1910 the editor of *The Presbyterian* observed that "the outlook is as good and reassuring as the world has seen, and religion is central to all that is best." Such a view was founded upon the conviction that "progress" was both a divine and a human process, in which "the divine spirit and the human spirit have been acting together, with the results of growth and continuity of thought."[44]

Thus the theology of the early nineteenth-century revival no longer served to interpret and shape history, and in the years between 1905 and 1914 became increasingly irrelevant for biblical scholarship and other branches of historical study. Deprived of the conviction of the absolute certainty of the Bible, and confronted with the massive industrialization and urbanization of the early twentieth century, the claims to authority advanced by the "social sciences," and the emergence of the ethos of 'consumption',[45] the clergymen-professors, the chief guardians of the evangelical creed, could no longer effectively govern, synthesize, and validate the insights of the "human" sciences. As a "ritual of consensus,"[46] the evangelical creed would survive in the cultural life and literature of twentieth-century English Canada. As an academic tradition integrating the thought and culture of the transatlantic English-speaking world into a body of religious beliefs, however, its encounter with the revolution in human consciousness had, by severing it irrevocably from the historical ideas that had nourished it for over a century, ended its quest for supremacy over the natural and "human" sciences.

THE LOSS OF CERTAINTY: THE CLASH OF COLLEGE AND PULPIT, 1909–1912

"The scientific spirit," declared the American Presbyterian scholar J. Gresham Machen in a 1913 address, "seems to be incompatible with the old spirit of simple faith."[47] Machen's reflections on what he perceived as the growing disjunction between "Christianity" and "culture" stemmed from the recognition that evangelical Protestantism faced a serious intellectual crisis. "If we are thoughtful," he wrote, "we must see that the desire to know and the desire to be saved are widely different," and nowhere was this more evident than in the growing gulf between the scholar and the congregation. The university scholar, he added, "must apparently assume the attitude of an impartial observer – an attitude which seems absolutely impossible to the pious Christian laying hold upon Jesus as the only Saviour from the load of sin."[48]

Although delivered in response to what Marsden has described as a mood of conflict and tension that presaged the public rupture of the American evangelical establishment in the Fundamentalist controversies of the 1920s, Machen's views were a particularly apposite comment on the situation within the Canadian Methodist and Presbyterian churches. Machen taught and preached a view of history similar to that held by most Canadian evangelicals prior to 1905. He accepted the influence of supernatural forces in human history and explicitly adhered to the Baconian notion of eternally valid "facts." Thus "truth" was clearly definable, rational, and objective, accessible not to an inner circle of scholarly initiates, but also to the unaided faith and intelligence of the wider Christian congregation.[49]

This notion of truth, so fundamental to the transatlantic evangelical creed, had been undermined by the strategy pursued by Canadian clergymen-professors when confronted with the relativistic implications of the new biblical study. Between 1905 and 1914 Baconian "historical theology" was quietly, but systematically emptied of explicitly doctrinal content, and became powerless to "tame" the manifestations of the wideranging revolution in human consciousness. Unlike some American churches, where the fragmentation of evangelicalism into "liberal" and "conservative" wings dated back to the 1870s, Methodists and Presbyterians between 1905 and 1914 sought to avoid any public divisions over the futility of "historical theology." Probably most clergymen hoped that a new consensus would emerge if the churches stepped up their missionary energies and devoted more effort to the "applied Christianity" of moral and social reform.

The impasse of "historical theology," however, drove a permanent wedge between the college and the congregation. By 1912 biblical criticism was no longer a matter for open discussion, as it had been since the founding of the colleges. Since 1909 clergymen-professors had faced a reaction from a growing number of preachers and believers outside the college who, for the first time, argued that the practice of biblical study in the lecture rooms had robbed the ordinary evangelical Christian of the authority of an inspired Bible. Rather than addressing the problem, the college authorities, in the name of internal peace, responded by effectively divorcing biblical criticism from popular preaching. After 1905 professors and preachers, who had shared, even under the impact of Darwin and the higher criticism in the 1870s and 1880s, a common outlook on questions of Scriptural authority and inspiration, lost the intellectual unity that had been sustained by the language of induction and historical certainty for more than a century.

The tensions spawned by the intellectual ineffectiveness of "historical theology" were most evident in the Methodist Church in the years immediately prior to World War I. In Methodist circles, the ideal of a college-educated ministry had only been established in the 1870s, through the efforts of Nelles and Burwash. Even in 1900, only about half of the active ministers had attended college, leaving fertile ground for the seeds of division between scholars and preachers, a split noted by James Mills in *The Christian Guardian* as early as 1898. Lamenting the lack of strong, commanding preachers in the church, Mills blamed the college curriculum for "not making good preachers, not training the young men as they should in the art of sermonizing and public speaking; instructing them in Old and New Testament exegesis, but not showing them how to use the Scriptures in preaching."[50]

This indictment of Burwash's "inductive theology" swelled to a loud chorus between 1909 and 1912. The controversy of 1909, involving Carman, the general superintendent of the Methodist Church, and Jackson, professor of English Bible at Victoria College, not only exposed a split between college and congregation over the nature and authority of the Bible, but also revealed that "inductive theology," which for four decades had provided the intellectual tools of scholars and preachers, no longer functioned as the vital bridge between lecture hall and pulpit. While some historians have interpreted the Carman-Jackson controversy as a moment in a long history of tensions between "liberals" and "conservatives" over the question of higher criticism,[51] closer examination links this dispute not only to the theological issues of the 1870s and 1880s, but also to the specific problems raised by the failure of Baconianism to deal with the crisis of religious authority in the years after 1905.

Carman, the central figure in the controversy, was in many respects an unlikely leader of a "conservative" assault on the higher criticism. True, he had constantly championed the Baconian structure of truth derived from the methods of Paley and Butler, and he believed that the Bible was an infallible book, a revelation from God. Like Machen, he held that knowledge rested upon self-evident axioms and accepted "facts"; only thus could believers maintain the absolute authority of the Bible.[52] But Carman had largely supported the efforts of Nelles and Burwash to promote an "inductive theology" at Victoria College, and had shown moderation over the issue of Workman's ill-fated lecture on messianic prophecy. Nor was he an uncompromising opponent of the idea of evolution, for his sermons and addresses in the 1870s and 1880s made frequent and approving references to the dynamic language of process and growth.

Carman first openly expressed hostility toward higher criticism in response to an address delivered in 1909 to the Toronto Young Men's Christian Association by the Rev. George Jackson, a visiting English Methodist scholar who had been appointed to the chair of English Bible at Victoria College. Jackson stated his conviction that the church's future hinged upon abandoning a literal reading of the Book of Genesis. Educated men, he claimed, were driven to surrender their faith because it conflicted with modern thought. To resolve the difficulties, Jackson recommended to his audience a frank admission of the legendary and mythological nature of the early chapters of Genesis.[53]

Such views brought Jackson into conflict not only with the literalist position defended by Carman, but also with the "inductive theology" taught by Burwash and his disciples, which defended the basic historical reliability of the books of Scripture. This open challenge to what he believed was the evangelical consensus that led Carman to lash out at Jackson's brand of criticism:

It settles nothing but fills the air with cloud and dust, the Church with suspicion, confusion, and strife. When a man affirms that the opening chapters of the Bible are mythical, legendary, I am inclined to ask, What does the man mean? Does he mean that the solid positions and sublime acts solemnly recorded are mythical and legendary, or does he mean that the literary garb is mythical, legendary, or that the rhetoric is more exuberant than his historic sense would justify? The record of sure and certain facts is not a myth, a fancy, a legend, no matter how gorgeous or how simple the rhetoric. Surely it cannot be that we are to teach truth from a book filled with vain chimeras, misconceptions, and lies.[54]

This was precisely the point at issue between the Baconian universe of Carman and the world of the early twentieth-century "form-critics" – the difference between a world in which theology and history were reliable and certain, and one in which faith apparently lacked a foundation grounded in the "facts" of divine revelation.

Yet this alone does not explain the violence of Carman's language or his persistent attempts to secure Jackson's removal from Victoria College. In his unpublished autobiography, Burwash claimed that

Jackson had broken an unwritten rule by engaging in public discussions of biblical questions that had hitherto been confined to college and intellectual circles. Burwash's quest for an educated ministry had been premised upon his belief that Methodism had a dual mission, one "to the rich among her people" and one "to the intellectual, for both were the children of the mental and moral quickening inherent in Methodism itself and both ... were faced by the problems of a materialistic philosophy or of a destructive criticism." In practice, however, Burwash recognized that a dual message was required, one for the educated, and one for "the poor and the backward" for whom "the old message would suffice."[55] Burwash and the Victoria College faculty had built their careers on the belief that "inductive theology" was comprehensive enough to provide such a dual emphasis: the harnessing of historical criticism to the fervour of the traditions of revivalistic evangelism.

Burwash, however, did not really believe that the future of Methodism depended on the avoidance of public discussion. Between 1860 and 1900 there had been frequent "public" discussions of biblical criticism in church newspapers and college classrooms, in forums such as *The Canadian Methodist Magazine*, and at college alumni conferences. Burwash himself had taken a prominent role in these discussions, promoting his "inductive theology," a synthesis of Methodist tradition and historical scholarship, as an alternative to the critical outlook prevalent in Germany. What he meant by avoiding "public" discussion was silencing men such as Workman,[56] who promoted critical views at variance with both the Baconian tenets of "inductive theology" and the popular beliefs concerning the inspiration and authority of Scripture.

In one respect, however, Burwash was correct. Something had been broken, but not by Jackson. It involved an issue of far greater consequence than the public discussion of biblical criticism. When placed within a context of growing tensions between the questioning of the Baconian outlook in the college by men such as Jackson at Victoria and Workman at Wesleyan Theological College, Montreal, and the increasingly vocal persistence of a form of biblical literalism among a group of clergymen and laypeople represented by Carman, the Carman-Jackson controversy was but the noisiest of a series of events that between 1905 and 1912, ruptured any existing consensus within the church over the authority of the Bible and the delicate relationship between faith and knowledge, classroom and pulpit.

In the three years preceding Jackson's appointment to the Victoria College faculty, many Methodists outside the college circles sensed a disjunction between the practice of historical criticism and the traditions of Methodist theology. In the winter of 1905 a number of Methodist Conferences in Ontario sponsored "District Institutes for the Extension of University Teaching in Biblical Literature and Church History." Difficulties arose over the work of the London Institute, which comprised the Rev. Eber Crummy, A.E. Lavell, and A.J. Irwin, who taught, respectively, Old Testament literature and history, church history, and New Testament literature and history. The aim of the Institute, as stated by Lavell, was to foster a "sane, scientific, clear, sympathetic knowledge of the Scriptures by the people, not merely the ministry." Such knowledge, its members believed, was "essential for a true revival in the Church".[57]

This aim of promoting greater harmony between the university and the ordinary believer was impeccably evangelical in tone. The books used in the course were not the radical interpretations advanced by German critics, but the eminently "reverent" and respectable histories of A.B. Davidson and George Adam Smith, the leading representatives of "historical theology." Yet by 1906 complaints were reaching the office of the general superintendent that Crummy, Lavell, and Irwin were advancing ideas of biblical authority at variance with popular beliefs. One correspondent angrily charged that Crummy had refused to accept the Bible as an absolute standard of truth.[58]

The most troubling element in this situation was a growing belief among preachers and people that the college and Burwash's "inductive theology" no longer stood as the guardian of Methodist traditions regarding the authority of the Bible. This attitude was eloquently illustrated by Morley Pettit, a Methodist probationer in the Hamilton Conference. Writing in 1908 to Burwash to inform of his decision to leave the ministry, Pettit condemned the "teaching and tendencies of some of the prescribed text books, of many of the editorial articles of our church organ, and of many of the leading men in our conference," alleging that "first, the Old Testament text book denies the personal revelation and leading of God to man. Second, the text book on the Gospels denies the Atonement."[59] Several of Carman's correspondents personally attacked Burwash and the college, alleging that Victoria had become a hot-bed of higher criticism and Unitarianism.[60] Carman and his numerous supporters were left with the impression that the colleges, ostensibly designed to train ministers and teach Christian truth, were alien institutions where the canons of the historical method were held in higher esteem than theology.

Because Burwash and his associates tolerated the presence of Workman and Jackson in the college classrooms, many rural preachers and laypeople feared for the continued validity of the biblical narratives as history and theology. In a 1909 letter to Burwash, C.A. Jones claimed that he spoke for those who adhered to a traditional position on questions of the authority and inspiration of the Bible while accepting the modified views of biblical literalism promoted by "inductive theology." "I do not believe," Jones declared, "that necessarily every sentence and date or detail ... in the Bible ... is inspired or infallible, but I do believe that every narrative in the Bible is true." According to this Methodist, faith and theology were completely dependent on the maintenance of the integrity of Scripture, "to believe the Bible as a whole, Old and New, or reject both together. If those narratives [the Pentateuch] are not history, neither is the story of the Incarnation and the resurrection of Jesus Christ."[61]

Significantly, such opinions were openly expressed after by Canadian Methodists only 1905, not in the 1880s or 1890s. The controversies over the inspiration of the Bible and the frustration experienced by many preachers when they found that the college authorities, ostensibly devoted to the harmony of education and preaching, would not respond to their concerns and would not dismiss Jackson led some observers to directly link the presence of higher criticism in the colleges with what they termed a decline in the evangelistic spirit in the Methodist Church. In *The Christian Guardian* in 1905 William Hincks wrote that he detected a "declining belief in the supernatural, as it was understood thirty years ago," which he traced to the higher criticism, the impact of the theory of evolution, and the emphasis placed by the church on social righteousness, all of which, he believed, had steadily undermined "the public belief in the Bible on its supernatural side."[62]

The relationship between classroom and pulpit was further troubled by Salem Bland, who held the chair of New Testament and church history at Wesley College, Winnipeg. Already prominent as one of the few advocates in Canada of the recasting of evangelical theology through the application of the evolutionary naturalist insights of "reform Darwinism," between 1906 and 1914 Bland spoke to his Wesley College students of a radical departure from the central tenets of the evangelical creed. In response to the problems faced by the "inductive theology" of Victoria College, Bland pursued the logic of subjectivism, and sought the validation of the Christian message through its identification with the highest products of human culture. He posited what he believed was a new and vital religion in alliance with modern science, and boldly declared that "biological Christianity" was the completion of all things.[63]

Bland's radicalism extended to a denial of the "inductive theology" that since the 1850s had formed the matrix of much of Methodist scholarship. He criticized "reverent" critics who secured the historical character of the biblical books "only by sophistry." His reading of the German critics of the "Comparative Religion" school led him to a denial of the historicity of much of the New Testament revelation, and specifically of the Gospel of St. John.[64] But his breach with the evangelical creed was signalled at Wesley College in 1914 by his open denial of the Bible as the ultimate standard of authority for Protestants. The Bible, he told his students,

cannot be the religion of Protestants. It is far too comprehensive. "This is the book" it was said long ago, "where each his doctrine seeks; this is the book where each his doctrine finds." There is no fantastic or monstrous system of thought which does not contrive to find support in the Bible. The irrational and tyranny-gendering dogma of transubstantiation, the priestly pretensions and arrogance of a sacerdotalized clergy, the intolerant and unloving exclusiveness of some Christian sects, the persecuting efforts of all state churches in turn, the hysterical and abnormal phenomena that have so frequently disfigured revivalism ... all find some den or hiding place in the luxuriant growths of the Bible.[65]

Bland's emphatic separation from the intellectual legacy of Baconianism represented only a minority position within the Methodist Church. But the fact that he could articulate his views with impunity in the classroom only reinforced the growing gulf between professor and preacher.[66]

The presence of theological "radicals" such as Bland, the perceived failure of "inductive theology" to rally college and church around an acceptable standard of biblical authority, and the noisy overtones of controversy between professors and church authorities all suggest that what Machen diagnosed as the breakdown of the evangelical mind in America was already underway in Canada by the time of World War I. "The situation before the churches is quite serious," declared the Rev. C.T. Scott in a letter to Carman. Scott discerned "an inevitable cleavage between so called 'liberal' and 'conservative' elements which may issue in a new alignment of christian forces."[67] Significantly, this marked the first time that the expressions "liberal" and "conservative" had been used by a Canadian clergyman to define the existence of theological "parties."

Scott's warning testified to the failure of "inductive theology" to balance the "historical" requirements of reason and scholarship and the demands of "theology" that such scholarship must reinforce and affirm the literal truth of Scripture. The result of five years of controversy on the subject of biblical authority was a statement of compromise, drafted by Burwash and John Fletcher McLaughlin, that required professors to subscribe to a "personal" vital relation to Christ and the Bible – an ambiguous resolution that left open the question of whether scholarship would be governed by the doctrines and disciplines of the church. Such a course meant that in future biblical criticism would be separated from the practical work of the church, as ministers urged silence on disputed theological points in the interests of teaching "applied Christianity."[68]

To clergymen such as Carman and the Rev. A.K. Birks, this was tantamount to evasion. In a comment written in the summer of 1909 Birks argued that no theological school could take itself seriously if it preserved a discreet silence on "the modern interpretation of the Bible." He urged that historical criticism should be vigorously combatted "wherever such interpretation contravenes our standards."[69] For this Methodist, Burwash's road of silence contributed to the further isolation of the college professor from the world of popular religion. It reflected the impasse of the evangelical creed in the face of the crisis of historical knowledge.

Although the tensions between college and pulpit were most visible among Canadian Methodists, similar stresses marked the Presbyterian Church in the five years before World War I. Despite their older tradition of an educated ministry, which linked the tasks of professor and preacher, Presbyterian ministers and believers from outside the college, like their Methodist counterparts, displayed similar doubts and uncertainty concerning the ability of "historical theology" to safeguard the authority and supremacy of the Bible.

To add to these intellectual troubles, college and church faced an internal crisis of leadership caused by the deaths, between 1902 and 1904, of the key figures in the articulation of "historical theology," the leader of the theological colleges. Grant, Caven, King, and MacVicar had shaped Presbyterian education and preaching during the critical decades after 1860, and their deaths left the colleges without a stabilizing influence just as the relativist challenge became most acute. Potential successors, men such as Falconer, who was appointed principal of Presbyterian College, Halifax, in 1904, Walter Murray, a Halifax colleague of Falconer's, and J.A. Macdonald, editor of The Westminster, were able representatives of the rising generation, but they left the active ministry to pursue secular callings, Falconer as President of the University of Toronto, Murray as the founder of the University of Saskatchewan, and Macdonald as editor of The Globe. While Alfred Gandier, William George Jordan, and John Scrimger were adequate replacements, they lacked their predecessors' authoritative presence and access to the wider culture, and were unable to define a constructive new relationship between scholar and preacher.

In 1896 the Presbyterian minister W.D. Armstrong wrote that, as a matter of "mental and moral self-respect," preachers must have a sound knowledge of the modern points of biblical controversy and convey that knowledge to their congregations.[70] Armstrong's views reflected the conviction in both college and church that "historical theology" offered an adequate synthesis of the traditions of the evangelical creed and the post-Darwinian evolutionary science and historical criticism. But the growing complexity of biblical study and the decision of clergymen-professors to narrow their cultural horizons and adopt the outlook of a scholarly elite rendered this balance increasingly difficult to maintain. A clergyman from outside the college, the Rev. J.N. Maclean, discerned the central flaw in the Scottish "historical theology," and the growing gulf between faith and scholarship that was paralyzing the evangelical mind. "The constructiveness of the Scotch criticism," he remarked in a letter to Professor Andrew Browning Baird of Manitoba College,

is not all it boasts to be. It seems to me to consist in *stopping* before the Majestic Figure of Christ and refusing to yield up faith in Him – a faith for which the old fashioned view of the Bible is largely responsible. In other words the constructiveness consists in a refusal to be a party to the demolition of every thing Divine in the Bible. *Logic scarcely warrants this refusal.* Only Christian experience does. That is practically the only authoritative asset the preacher does claim. It may all be true; I fear not if it is true. But it should be *assumed* and *taught* with awful caution.[71]

Maclean caught the tension at the heart of the "historical theology." Like some of their Methodist counterparts, certain leading Presbyterian college professors had assumed that historical scholarship would provide a precise basis for a "science" of theology. When, after 1905, the opposition between the Baconian outlook and the study of history bred uncertainty concerning the nature of biblical authority, elements in the church added a corollary. Implicit in Maclean's letter was the contention that there was really nothing to distinguish the practitioner of "reverent criticism" from his German counterpart, who abandoned any theological presuppositions to follow the logic of the historical method.

At the turn of the century, a large group in the Presbyterian Church led by William MacLaren, who succeeded Caven as principal of Knox College in 1903, was still devoted to the idea of biblical literalism and to the Princeton theology of Charles Hodge. Though not necessarily hostile to the idea of evolution,[72] this group viewed the disjuncture between Baconianism and history with alarm. At the opening of Knox College in 1907 MacLaren issued a warning against the tendency to apply the idea of evolution to spiritual and moral phenomena: "When Christian men accept evolution as the correct account of the history of the universe they can scarcely avoid reconstructing their views of the Bible to suit their hypothesis."[73]

MacLaren's views appealed to many evangelicals outside the college. They were increasingly troubled by the failure of "historical theology" to posit a firm and factual basis of biblical authority, and believed that the college clergy had sacrificed so much to prevailing historical opinion that there was very little of the old biblical message left to preach. Matters of individual and moral responsibility were neglected, complained Mrs J.W. Van Norman, as preachers insisted on education and "socialism," a term she contemptuously equated with what she believed was a growing tendency to address social questions, rather than spiritual rebirth.[74] These opinions were confirmed by overseas missionaries such as D.D. Macleod, who remarked when discussing the Presbyterian mission in Formosa in 1908 that "the Gospel has a sacred mystery about it which captivates the heart of the darkest heathen. I am fully convinced that there must be absolute confidence in the unfailing integrity of the Word of God. Higher Criticism so called may be very fascinating in the Scholastic workshop, but it demoralizes the energies of the soul in the presence of such dire need as is to be seen in the heathen world."[75]

These attitudes indicated a growing belief among some Presbyterians that the practice of historical scholarship, once vaunted as the bedrock of harmony in the Canadian churches, was driving apart professors and preachers. Those faithful to an inerrant Bible and an inductive view of truth were often disposed, after 1905, to equate even "reverent" criticism with infidelity, and to blame higher criticism for the weakening of the "old gospel" and the decline in candidates for the ministry.[76] In the 1880s and 1890s the church press had played a vital part in introducing its readers to scholarly discussions concerning inspiration, authority, and biblical criticism, but by 1910 clergymen-professors increasingly wrote for a professional audience that read either British theological journals or college publications such as *Queen's Quarterly*.

In part, this change reflected the growing complexity and technical nature of criticism, but the widespread questioning of "historical theology" within the church imposed silence in the interests of harmony. According to the Rev. T.B. Kilpatrick, professor of New Testament exegesis at Manitoba College, no benefit came from public discussion of disputed points of biblical scholarship, and he pressed the need for an applied Christianity.[77] As in the Methodist Church, the policy of silence indicated a false harmony that masked an intellectual evasion of the conflict between the new historical scholarship and the evangelical creed. Clergymen-professors such as J.E. McFadyen of Knox College found it easier to separate the offices of professor and preacher than to address the tension afflicting the church. Such a division, he argued, was essential given the time required to master the processes of criticism. "The preacher," he concluded, was bound "to ignore those processes in his public work." The pulpit "does not exist for the exhibition of critical method."[78] Though he based his arguments on the evangelical tradition of "practical preaching," he advocated a course that neither Caven nor Grant would have condoned.

Canadian Presbyterianism, however, had no one like Carman to give shape or voice to the protest against the subordination of the evangelical creed to the logic of the historical method. So the opposition was diffused, turning away from the ever-present problem of biblical authority and focusing on the more immediate issues of church union, the structure of theological education, and the secularization of Queen's University.[79] It was no coincidence that these difficulties arose between 1904 and 1912, the years of the great divorce between the intellectual world of Baconianism and the twentieth-century world of historical and doctrinal relativism. All three involved a polarization of theological opinion, although not along the expected "liberal" and "conservative" lines.[80] They were symptoms of a creed in disarray, of a theology that had ceased to function as an instrument of intellectual and cultural solidarity.

THE IMPASSE OF EVANGELICALISM: THE AGONY OF SAMUEL DWIGHT CHOWN

In an address delivered in January 1912 Chown, elected in 1910 as Carman's associate in the office of general superintendent of the Methodist Church, reflected on the decline of the Baconian outlook and the rising popularity of subjectivist and relativist modes of thought in evangelical circles. "To me," he declared, "there seems to be much assumption in the expression 'the authority of the Christian consciousness'." A long evangelical tradition beginning with Wesley and extending to Ryerson, Nelles, and Burwash, he reminded his audience, rejected the belief that consciousness was "uncaused or unconditioned." Rather, it rested "upon the foundation of the scriptures," and was "dependent upon the Bible and if true to itself must carry the limitations of its birth in criticizing the word."[81]

From his prominent position within the church, Chown had witnessed a decade of intellectual difficulties for the two central elements of the evangelical creed: the plenary inspiration of the Bible as the foundation of theology and culture, and the equally important theology of history, by which clergymen sought to "tame" and Christianize the products of human knowledge. These had been weakened, he believed, by the increasing subservience of college education and biblical scholarship to the historical method, rather than to evangelical faith and theology. The growing abyss between evangelicalism and the historical writing and "human sciences" practised in the early twentieth century had raised a host of problems in the churches, among them the loss of solidarity between college and pulpit. It was time, he said, to restore the lost balance, to limit the potentially subjectivist insistence on conscience and experience by the objective authority and certain standard of the word of God.[82]

Chown's was not an isolated voice in the Methodist and Presbyterian churches in the years immediately preceding World War I. At the induction of Professor William Morgan in 1912, Principal Gordon of Queen's University declared that the work of creating a spiritual atmosphere must be based on the "great truths" of Christian revelation. He identified the word of God, the Bible, as the constant, authoritative element informing all attempts to relate Christianity to the world.[83] This search for balance in Canadian evangelical circles, though unsystematic and unfocused, paralleled the emergence of a critique of "liberal" theology in both Germany and America in the years prior to 1914. Operating within the framework of "liberal" assumptions, several theologians censured the prevailing religious outlook in those countries for its lack of realism concerning human sin, its sentimental optimism, and its overdependence on the "historical Jesus" as the bedrock of certainty.[84]

But how to recover the intellectual and cultural prestige of the evangelical creed, and how to state the authority and supremacy of the Bible and the "scientific" nature of theology in terms comprehensible to a society whose university elites after 1905 looked more to the explanations and solutions provided by the evolutionary social sciences than to a faith and theology forged in the late eighteenth century? This was the most urgent problem confronting Chown and many of his Methodist and Presbyterian colleagues between 1912 and 1914. The survival of the evangelical theology as a force in the wider Canadian culture hinged upon its resolution.

Chown's search for a new equilibrium between faith and knowledge envisaged a return to some of the doctrinal verities of the great age of the revival. Like certain more traditionally inclined Methodist clergymen trained in the prophetic, postmillennial cast of the evangelical theology of history, who posited an intimate connection between preaching, revivals, and the growth of the perfect society, Christ's Kingdom[85], he was preoccupied with the inability of preaching to stimulate a "religious revival." To remedy this situation, and to ensure that the preacher would continue to possess an authoritative message, Chown urged restraint upon the theological colleges. While he believed that evangelical religion stood for liberty of thought, he reaffirmed the traditional cautions against biblical criticism functioning outside its limited sphere. The church, he declared, should promote in its colleges a common-sense approach to biblical study, and resist certain conclusions that might damage faith.[86]

Chown and many of his contemporaries did not realize, however, that it was too late to restore any semblance of balance to the "historical theology" taught by Grant, Caven, Nelles, and Burwash. The accommodation between Baconianism and "reverent" historical criticism that had sustained the evangelical creed was, by 1910, seriously compromised by the scrutiny of the Bible by subjectivists and relativists. Chown's inability to offer an alternative to the traditional foundations of education and preaching testified to this impasse of the evangelical mind. Although he yearned to construct an intelligible faith, he could not separate evangelicalism from the logic of a historical criticism that invalidated all "facts" and moral certainties in the face of human experience and consciousness.

Unlike his colleague Carman, he refused to take the lead in a movement of reaction, where a Baconian theology of certainty, buttressed by biblical literalism, would reassert its dominance over history, philosophy, and criticism. On the contrary, many of his addresses were paeans of praise for critical thought. In 1912 Chown even commended the pragmatic philosophy of William James for "giving us a flood of thought, asserting the primacy of the spiritual over the material and of the freedom of the will over ... Determinedism[sic]." Pragmatism won his high praise, for it indicated that "beneath all our frivolity and ineptness of philosophic thought a new craving for the world of spirit and freedom is awakening. Men are getting ready for the appeal of a new and greater evangelism. Let us gladly spread our sails to the new breath of the Spirit of God."[87] Tied to the "inductive theology" of Victoria College, Chown believed that new developments in the sphere of human reason, no matter how subversive of the inductive cast of the evangelical creed, could not but identify a more certain, and therefore more rational, basis for religion.

Chown's inability to recognize the moral and theological relativism inherent in any system of thought constructed upon historical scholarship led him to assume that although some minor adjustments might be necessary, there was nothing fundamentally wrong with the evangelical creed. While greater personal spirituality might be desirable, the remedy for the crisis of intellectual and cultural authority, he thought, lay in the more efficient application of evangelical theology to the Christianization of Canadian life. Between 1910 and 1914 Chown tried to promote the study of "sociology" among clergymen, urging the construction of a new theological curriculum to put ministers in touch with modern social needs.[88] "Sociology," which he defined as "the science of the conditions of human welfare," had definite ethical biases and implications, specifically calling for formation of the type of character required by the Sermon on the Mount.[89]

The study of "sociology" advocated by Chown was, however, anything but a systematic intellectual response to the crisis of college and creed. Rather, his "social science" further revealed the inability of the evangelical mind to transcend the hopeless dichotomy of a theology of certainty dependent upon a relativistic method that stripped it of authority. According to one Canadian historian, Chown's lectures on "sociology" were "excellent illustrations of a certain stage in the transmutation of Christian moral philosophy of the nineteenth-century variety into a moralistic, yet essentially secular, study of social relationships."[90] Closer scrutiny of the aims and assumptions underlying Chown's advocacy of "sociology" reveals, however, a persistent failure to address either the outlook or the methods of the social sciences. His "sociology" was not an independent discipline, but another name for "historical theology," and marked an attempt to recover the energies of the evangelical creed. For him, personal regeneration and the supremacy of doctrine and ethics, not the study of society or social problems, was the motive power for social reform.[91]

Significantly, Chown's addresses cited no works by the American sociologists who had by 1914 forged an independent position for their discipline in a number of major American universities, and who claimed the authority of a value-free, scientific sociology, rather than an alliance with Christian ethics or theology. His exhortations for a wider social outlook in religion were drawn from the appeals for national righteousness of the Old Testament prophets and the teachings of Jesus. The postmillennial assumptions that still governed the Methodist outlook were fully in evidence when Chown declared that the practice of the "sociology of the Prophets, the Lawgivers, and the great Master," the "perfect sociology," would realize the Kingdom of God on earth.[92]

"Perfect sociology," with its pervasive links to the theology of history that had dominated college and pulpit since the revival, was but another name for a refurbished and more effective evangelical creed. In this important respect, Chown was not a transitional figure in Canadian thought, a man wavering between clergyman and social scientist.[93] He was very much a clergyman who belonged to the Baconian universe of McCulloch and Ryerson. He did not look to the "human" and "social" sciences to recast and restate theology, but assumed the intellectual adequacy of his religious heritage. He sought the supremacy of evangelical theology, not its modification, in what he viewed as the continuing contest with the legacy of the Enlightenment.

Chown's dilemma sprang from his battle to maintain the traditional certainties of evangelical belief while preserving an openness to new currents of thought. This battle explains why he yearned for the power of the revival while praising the apparently subversive doctrines of William James. It was also symptomatic of a creed at a moment of acute cultural tension. Was "perfect sociology" an adequate medium to address the intellectual difficulties faced by clergymen-professors in their attempt to address historical relativism, and the broader issue of the fate of the evangelical creed in a North American society turning to consumerism for its values and cultural legitimacy? Viewed in this light, Chown's quest for a "perfect sociology" was less a concession to theological "liberalism" than an attempt to restore the harmony between the academic tradition and the popular preaching of the evangelical creed.

7 The Passing of the Evangelical Creed: War, the College, and the Problem of Religious Certainty

"The old evangelism," wrote Chown from retirement in 1930, "consisted of the public proclamation of the gospel of salvation from sin through Jesus Christ, and a call for the complete dedication of life to the service of God and the people." This preaching aimed to produce the experience of "conversion," an "immediate and vividly conscious personal transaction between the Divine Being and the individual soul."[1] In the half-century since his entry into the Methodist ministry, Chown argued, he had witnessed the dilution of the core of the evangelistic message – the conviction of the immediacy and horror of sin, and the sense of redemption and entry into newfound spiritual freedom. Significantly, he did not regard the period after World War I as any less religious than the days of his youth. However, he discerned a decided "metamorphosis" in "the mental atmosphere in which the pastor does his thinking."[2]

Chown blamed "the wisdomizing tendency as applied to theology" for this transformation. When he embarked on his long and successful career as a preacher, moral reformer, and church administrator, evangelical theology offered something direct and accessible to the hearts and minds of the congregation. Based on the authority of Scripture, this theology, Chown declared, was "an experimental science" intimately related to the life of the believer. By 1930, however, theology had become for many, a scholarly discipline governed by "nebulous philosophical concepts." Moreover, it no longer acknowledged the supremacy of the evangelical message as the arbiter of the realms of intellect, culture, and society.[3]

Late twentieth-century historians have interpreted Chown's lament as a symptom of Protestant Christianity in full retreat before a flood-tide of secularism in English-Canadian culture. The years between the World War I and the Great Depression, they have claimed, witnessed the rapid decline of the social, intellectual, and cultural prestige of both clergymen and the churches themselves, despite many Methodist and Presbyterian clergymen's confidence that their theology had achieved considerable success during World War I. The struggle lent impetus to their aim of "Christianizing" the state through a series of reforms aimed at uplifting private and public morality and implanting the ideal of "service" into political life. For prominent clergymen such as Chown, the war held out the hope of harmonious social relations in a purified society, an end to regional tensions and the strife between labour and capital. The war also accelerated the movement toward the union of the Methodist, Congregational, and Presbyterian Churches, which clergymen hoped would further the effective Christianization of individual and national life. After lengthy negotiations, Church Union was accomplished by 1925.[4]

To the historical mind of the late twentieth century, however, these achievements were at best Pyrrhic victories, which could not arrest the long-term decline of churches that had capitulated to a secular outlook five decades earlier. This interpretation originated with the work of Richard Allen in 1973. He argued that the source of the churches' difficulties, epitomized by the Progressive Party, various forms of "radical" Christianity, and the failure of the temperance movement, lay in their inability to resolve the dichotomy between individual regeneration and a commitment to social action. The post-1914 history of the Protestant churches in Canada, according to this interpretation, is a footnote to the long secularization that began with Darwin in 1860. The failure doomed the United Church, it has been argued, to a perpetual and sterile oscillation between the theologically reactionary "old" evangelism of individual conversion and moral reform and the "social gospel" informed by the evolutionary, secularizing insights of the social sciences.[5]

A closer examination of Chown's longing for the spiritual power of the "old evangelism" indicates, however, the presence of currents within the Protestant churches that are not fully explained by the bipolar model of opposition posited by the secularization thesis. For Chown, the adversary of the "old evangelism" was not the "social gospel" but "the wisdomizing tendency." His career had been premised on the harmony of the individual and social emphases within the evangelical creed, and even the experience of the World War I and the 1920s did not induce him to abandon this outlook. Yet his message, written in the first year of the Great Depression, clearly reflected the frustration and disorientation felt by many Canadian clergymen. The issue involved something more fundamental than the dichotomy between individual regeneration and social action. For Chown and many of his colleagues, it involved the theological foundation of social action in the the churches: the nature of religious authority itself.

"My own confession of faith," Chown wrote, "is that in the revolt from the supernatural the pendulum of thought has been permitted to swing to the naturalistic natural, when it should have halted at the divine natural."[6] This statement might well be read as a belated and ineffectual realization of the absolute opposition between the theology of "orthodox" Protestantism and the evolutionary, critical, and historical thought that the Darwinian movement had spawned. Another interpretation is, however, possible. Chown's expression "the divine natural" clearly eschewed any outright opposition to evolutionary thought. His persistent refusal to recognize a divorce between the evangelical creed and evolutionary science is crucial in understanding the mind of the evangelical churches between World War I and the Great Depression. His main concern, more immediate than the impact of evolution on his theology, was not the failure of evangelicalism itself, but the inability of his generation, despite so many successes, to find some foundation for the reconstruction of the harmony between intellect and preaching, college and pulpit, which had been weakened by the cultural impact of the "revolution" in the human sciences in the decade before 1914.

Many clergymen, both inside and outside the colleges, were preoccupied throughout the 1920s by the need to find some substitute for the Baconian language of inductive certainty that, from the end of the eighteenth century until the first decade of the twentieth century, had addressed the mind of the believer most directly through the study and preaching of history. Under the impact of relativism, however, the "historical theology" practised in Presbyterian and Methodist theological faculties systematically stripped theology of any distinctive substance or method, and ceased to provide a matrix of certainty acceptable to preachers and their congregations, many of whom demanded a firmer and more literal adherence to the authority of the Bible.

Between 1914 and 1930, the intellectual life of the Presbyterian and Methodist Churches was far from being the sterile oscillation portrayed by late twentieth-century historians. Both professors and a large number of preachers engaged in a stimulating, transatlantic discussion that aimed to rejuvenate the evangelical creed, to posit some acceptable restatement of the relationship of theology to the currents of philosophy and natural and social science then being debated in Europe, Britain, and the United States. They maintained that the recasting of their tradition was imperative for several reasons. First, experiences of the war had confronted and challenged many clergymen's most cherished assumptions, and affected their understanding of central Christian doctrines. Second, the Baconian outlook, while still acceptable to large groups of Christian believers, could not address the problems of knowledge and cultural authority raised by history and the "social sciences" after 1905. Third, many Methodist and Presbyterian clergymen, traditionally preoccupied with the relationship of individuals to God and the wider community, were determined that they and their congregations should have access to the insights provided by these disciplines. They hoped thus to reaffirm the alliance between faith and knowledge that had been weakened by the impact of the "human sciences" and to re-establish evangelicalism as the cornerstone of cultural unity and intellectual endeavour in English Canada.

A MODERNIST WAR: THEOLOGY AND THE EXPERIENCE OF THE TRENCHES

"In the spiral movement of history," declared the Rev. Alexander Reid Gordon of Presbyterian College, Montreal, in 1917, "we have reverted to another age of social interest and aspiration. The modern prophet must therefore aim at giving clarity and purpose to the people's striving for a higher national life."[7] This appeal to the historical example of the Old Testament prophets was written in the blackest year of World War I. Revolution in Russia, mutinies among the French army, the German submarine blockade of the British Isles, and the internal divisions over conscription and the formation of the Union Government impelled Gordon, trained in the postmillennial tenets of Canadian Presbyterian "historical theology," to attempt to discern a meaning for these alarming events. His direct reference to the evangelical theology of history, that triad of biblical revelation, universal history, and prophecy, indicated a desire to find, amidst the calamities afflicting the Allied powers in their struggle with German militarism, some evidence of redemptive divine purpose in historical phenomena, which alone could give moral sanction to the struggle, and elevate human history from the chaos of events. For many clergymen-professors, preachers, students, and congregations, a belief in the conscious presence of God in human history, a conviction given authority by the revealed history of Scripture, still offered the possibility of predicting with certainty the optimistic resolution of calamity, and the progressive emergence of a perfected, "Christianized" society.

Despite the cracks in the intellectual structure of evangelicalism that appeared in the years before World War I, Gordon's proclamation of the links between biblical and contemporary history illustrated that the "historical theology" of the evangelical creed remained for some the foundation of wartime teaching and preaching. The conviction, based upon the historical reading of the Bible, that the trials of war would usher in a "higher national life" inspired Chown to proclaim that God was using the war to accomplish His purpose. Canada, he declared, was in the process of transformation from a nation of "mammon-worshippers" to one infused with the "higher Christian manhood," conscious of its destiny in a wider union with the British Empire.[8]

The emphasis of Chown and numerous other clergymen on "nation," "Christian ethics," "higher life," and the moral purification of Canadian society has led historians to assert that the experience of World War I shifted the balance in the Protestant churches from evangelism to social action, from a primary emphasis on the conversion of the individual to the social organism as the principal focus of religious energy. Richard Allen has argued that the years between 1914 and 1918 marked the "crest" of the "social gospel" in Canada,[9] since by 1919 both Methodist and Presbyterian Churches were committed to a complete reconstruction of the social order. But these events must be considered in their historical context. With the possible exceptions of men such as Salem Bland, who in 1917 was dismissed from his New Testament professorship at Wesley College, and J.S. Woodsworth, whose pacifist opposition to the war forced his withdrawal from the Methodist ministry, most of the clergymen who formulated these reform proposals had absorbed through their education and preaching the tenets of the pre-war "historical theology." Despite the focus on the social teachings of the prophets and Christ's preaching of the "Kingdom," the post-Darwinian evangelical creed had preserved a balance of evangelism and social reform weighted towards the individual, and based on the traditions of personal experience and conversion as the dynamic forces in any process of social change.

Even under the stresses and strains of war and post-war unrest, most clergymen adhered to the individualist orientation of their theology. Far from ushering in the triumph of an unadulterated "social gospel" in the churches, as both Richard Allen and Michael

Bliss have claimed, the war marked the apogee of the theology of reform proclaimed in the Methodist and Presbyterian colleges and pulpits between 1890 and 1905. In 1920 Chown, usually identified as a leading advocate of the "social gospel," declared that there was a great difference between Christian ideals and Christian character. He defined the task of evangelism as the development of Christian character, while social service must inspire men with the altruistic ideals of Christianity. But, he cautioned, only evangelism supplied the necessary power for post-war reconstruction. From the Presbyterian Church, the Rev. Samuel Dyde, principal of Robertson College and later principal of Queen's Theological College, echoed Chown's belief in the primacy of individual regeneration, insisting that the spiritual sphere was the foremost area of church activity.[10]

In their attempts to postulate a dichotomy between the "old evangelism" and the "social gospel," some historians have neglected more profound religious issues that confronted the Canadian churches. The war raised intellectual difficulties for the generation of preachers and professors represented by Chown, Dyde, and Gordon. As the struggle in the trenches dragged on without end or meaning, some clergymen began to question the very assumptions that, until 1914, had sustained their educational institutions and preaching. If, as Gordon and others maintained, history was ultimately a benign process providentially guided by God, with the perfect Christian society realized in the gradual "Christianization" of individuals and communities, the slaughter of the war represented a grotesque, inexplicable discontinuity. How could "historical theology," the intellectual prop of the evangelical theology of reform, premised on an optimistic, post-millennial theology, explain what was widely perceived as the reversion to "barbarism" of the most "Christian" nations?

Like the "revolution" in the understanding of human history and consciousness, though more directly and shockingly, the experience of World War I struck at the cultural and intellectual assumptions underlying "historical theology." Though historians have usually linked this to a wartime re-examination of the problems and prospects of Canadian society,[11] some clergymen drew on more immediate and profound sources of experience – the battlefront itself, the peculiar conditions of "trenchland," and the attitudes and convictions of the front-line soldier.

In a 1916 sermon Edmund Henry Oliver, principal of Presbyterian College, Saskatoon, and a military chaplain serving overseas proclaimed: "Civilization comes through fire, redemption comes through a cross, life through death. We are learning to-day what sacrifice means, for the human race is marching to its Calvary."[12] Such preaching, which linked the sacrifice of the younger generation in the trenches to the redeeming death of Christ, offered to Canadian soldiers a more adequate explanation of the conflict than appeals to civilized values, to history as a divine and ultimately benign process, or to the traditional patriotism of the evangelical churches. In 1918 Professor E.F. Scott of Queen's explicitly linked Christ's sacrificial death to the wartime slaughter. "We sometimes speak of the Cross," he declared, "as if it marked the end of sacrifice." Deeper reflection on the meaning of the Cross, however, led to the conclusion that it "was not the end, but the beginning of true sacrifice ... And He meant that by example of His Cross we also should be inspired to give our own selves, as our living sacrifice."[13]

Oliver and other military chaplains addressed the soldier's insistent demand for realism in his confrontation with the impersonal life in the trenches, and his need for patient endurance in the face of suffering. The recurrence of the words "sacrifice" or "service" were symbols of revolt, forceful indicators of an impatience with and rejection of convention common to soldiers of all nationalities. As one historian of the cultural experience of World War I has argued, the battlefront was "a school in what was essential and what was not; and even those who hated it insisted that it left a lasting mark on them by changing their system of priorities and putting their pre-war cultural attitudes to the test of facts."[14]

The brutality and monotony of trench life called into question many of the old categories of religious thought and experience for both the soldiers and their chaplains. What, for example, did concepts of personal sin mean to men in constant and imminent danger? What did the idea of redemption as a gradual, historical process mean to soldiers confronted with the meaningless waste of human life? And what of the idea of a conscious, active divine presence guiding human history in an upward, unfolding spiral? Was "trenchland" part of God's plan of salvation?

Recent attempts to probe the meaning of these questions for the thought of the Canadian Protestant churches have neglected certain important facets of the wartime experience. D.B. Marshall has argued that the war was merely part of the perpetual oscillation between "otherworldly evangelical orthodoxy" and a worldly, secularizing search for relevance characteristic of the Canadian Protestant churches. The conflict, he contends, created a situation in which some clergymen and soldiers simply abandoned their faith and left the church, while others searched for the nostalgia of the old-time evangelical religion.[15] Based on the need to force the religious experience into radically opposed categories, this approach ignores the meaning of the preaching of Oliver and others, who neither left the church nor sought to discard the intellectual legacy of "historical theology." These men sensed that the impact of war was profoundly religious, and sought to use it creatively to influence the spiritual and intellectual life of their churches. The cataclysm, they believed, stripped away inadequate concepts of Christianity and permitted the construction of a new scale of theological priorities.

In 1918 E.A. Corbett observed that for the soldier, the old categories of religious experience simply did not apply. The war, he declared, had not drawn the fighting men to the church, but he spoke for many chaplains when he emphatically affirmed that the spirit of Christianity was not lacking at the front.[16] As the Methodist C. Wellesley Whittaker explained, while the religion of "trenchland" was far removed from the familiar evangelical pieties, it was simple yet impressive, without platitudes, formality, or doctrinal differences.[17] The experience of suffering and sacrifice gave many soldiers a new point of contact with Christ, the Rev. John Kelman declared in 1917. This new consciousness of Christ was based not on theology, but on experience: "Now they are going through, so far as we can, suffering such as Christ bore for the sins of man. In their experience of sacrifice to-day comes the great Christ of the Cross, and these men who once lived in self-indulgence realize suddenly that Christ is their brother."[18] Such religious experiences were at odds with the pre-war evangelical message anchored on "historical theology." While few pre-war clergymen succumbed to "liberalism" by denying divine transcendence and the miraculous nature of the God's presence in the world, the cultural and intellectual prestige of historical study and its conjunction with theology in curriculum and preaching had encouraged professors and their students to look for meaning and certainty within what they believed was a gradually progressive tendency of the historical process itself.

"Historical theology" offered an inadequate gospel for those who functioned in a brutal universe of shells and bombs, and were daily confronted with the triviality of human life and human ethics, and the meaningless chaos of human experience that even "prophetic" history could not interpret. The soldiers sought the meaning of their lives and deaths above all things. Many found it in the mystery of the Cross. As one historian has noted, the experience of the World War I battlefront generated a psychic climate conducive to a new appreciation of the miraculous and transcendent elements of Christianity. Pastoral fantasies, dominated by the archetype of the shepherd, persisted in the trenches, as well as a reversion to "prerational" forms of explanation for human events, with rumours of divine intervention often circulating among the frontline troops.[19] Even if the most extreme forms of these manifestations are discounted, there is ample evidence that in the years between 1914 and 1918 renewed emphasis was placed on personal redemption, divine transcendence, and experiential religion, elements that emerged as the central themes of the post-war evangelical mind.

By the later stages of the war, the force of these impulses was beginning to be felt in the theological colleges. According to some clergymen-professors, the war had revealed humanity's helplessness in the face of evil, despite the intellectual and cultural "progress" of the nineteenth century. A 1918 sermon preached by the Rev. Robert Law, professor of New Testament at Knox College, manifested the new interest in questions of life, redemption, and immortality. "The tragic events of the times in which we live", he declared, "are compelling us so to think and to-day the Hope of the Gospel is nearer and dearer to multitudes than ever before ... We feel the tragic incompleteness of all human life, feel that it cannot be a circle closing us in, it must be a path leading elsewhere. It is so manifestly a fragment, a beginning, a sowing-time of which the full harvest must be hereafter."[20] This new mood of pessimism marked a further crack in the edifice of "historical theology." The traditional equation of prophecy and history was premised on a belief that the historical process, though divinely ruled, was ultimately rational and thus subject to human understanding and control. The recurrence of the word "tragic" revealed an awareness that the catastrophic reality of human sin implied that the process might not be an upward spiral, in which biblical events could indicate the direction of universal history. It was a powerful reminder that the meaning of history lay not with human actions, but with a God who was often inscrutable and unpredictable.

If the war cast doubt on the evangelical equation of theology, prophecy, and history, it also inspired some clergymen to attempt a revaluation of the place of Jesus in evangelical theology, not through the recovery of a lost belief in the divinity of Christ, but through the reinterpretation of that faith in the light of the suffering in the trenches. Although some late twentieth-century historians believe that pre-war "liberalism" reduced Christ to a merely human "social reformer,"[21] few clergymen even in 1914 would have denied that Jesus was a transcendent, miraculous figure, the redeemer of humanity both individually and collectively.

The challenge faced by chaplains and clergymen-professors, whose chief task was to make some sense of the wartime catastrophe, was to relate the doctrine of redemption preached by the evangelical churches to a world where both life and death seemed largely mean-ingless. Principal Clarence Mackinnon of Presbyterian College, Hal-ifax, and other clergymen who had witnessed the conditions of "trenchland" accented those elements in the New Testament that dwelt upon Christ's confrontation with the realities of evil and suf-fering. Mackinnon went so far as to describe Jesus as the "Great White Comrade of the Trenches" in his attempt to state a traditional doctrine in language that soldiers might understand.[22] Similar views were advanced by E.A. Corbett, a member of the Student Christian Movement. Implicitly identifying Jesus with the soldiers, Corbett termed Him "the majestic man who faces a man's problems, meets a man's temptations and is compelled to make the decisions and choices of a man."[23] Here was a fully human Jesus, yet one who, through suffering and sacrifice, had disclosed His divinity and tran-scended the ordinary categories of life. By analogy, the front-line soldiers, who had undergone a similar experience, were closer than their compatriots who remained at home to realizing the union of the divine and the human represented by Christ.

The new mental climate that emerged from the trenches, though a powerful catalyst of theological ferment, did not precipitate a de-bilitating divorce between personal religion and social action. The role of the church in society was not the central preoccupation of those who sought to interpret the experience of the trenches. The realization that many soldiers looked to the transcendent, mysteri-ous elements of Christianity was balanced by the knowledge that the battlefield also stimulated an awareness of concrete reality, and thus the need for a religion that would meet the tests of life. The Methodist chaplain, the Rev. A.E. Lavell, explained that this dictated a religion shorn of obsolete conventions and creedal statements, and based upon "Faith in God, as set forth by Jesus. The practical unity of religion and 'the square deal all round.' Religion as right character, right thinking and willing, and human service. The complete rea-sonableness of real religion."[24]

Lavell's "real" religion did not imply the return of a revivalist evangelism that preached a message directed exclusively to the in-dividual. Among many preachers, the war did direct preaching to-ward emphasis on the transcendent power of God, the reality of sin, and the necessity of prayer and repentance.[25] This emphasis on what might be viewed as the restatement of traditional doctrines should, however, be viewed in its proper context. It was balanced by the realization that the conditions of life at the battlefront bred an awareness of humans not only as individuals in need of conver-sion and redemption, but also as members of a brotherhood or a society. Most recent histories of the front-line experience have stressed the importance of the idea of "comradeship," the fraternal bond that united all combatants.[26]

In one sense, this balancing of transcendent "reality" and concrete "reality," individual repentance and "comradeship" might be interpreted as an attempt to encompass the new world of the trenches within the theology of history and reform characteristic of pre-war evangelicalism. For many clergymen, both inside and outside the theological colleges, this was undoubtedly the desired goal. Their education and preaching had been shaped by the "historical" or "inductive" theologies introduced by Grant, Caven, Nelles, and Burwash, and although appalled by the catastrophe of war, they could not readily revise a coherent theology that had endured for over a century. For some, it was perhaps easier to assimilate and "tame" the wartime experience, much as an earlier generation had shaped and directed the impact of Darwin. The existence of ineradicable evil and meaningless suffering, the chaos of experience, and the ideal of "comradeship" that many clergymen had encountered during the war were, however, not themes that could be easily incorporated into the intellectual legacy of the evangelical creed. The 1920s in Canada witnessed pronounced shifts in the intellectual life of the evangelical churches, as professors and preachers strove to come to terms with the cultural legacy of World War I, through a series of discussions and debates that by 1930 had largely severed the evangelical creed from its intellectual foundations in eighteenth-century notions of biblical authority and historical certainty.

BETWEEN TRADITIONALISM AND MODERNISM: CLERGYMEN CONFRONT THE 1920S

In a lecture delivered at Emmanuel College, Toronto, in 1927, the Rev. Richard Roberts, pastor of Sherbourne St United Church, Toronto, outlined his provisional definition of the task and goals of theology. "I propose," he declared, "to be both a traditionalist and a modernist, in the belief that a frank dualism is a healthier state of mind than a premature and muddled synthesis." Roberts's religious outlook was both transcendent and immanent, organized around the doctrines familiar to several generations of evangelical clergymen and professors: revelation, incarnation, redemption, inspiration, and grace. He stressed that this was not a nostalgic yearning for a lost age of pre-Darwinian evangelicalism, and affirmed his belief in "the main thesis of an Immanence theology, – the inborn and indwelling Christ, the 'new man', the Kingdom of God as the 'purpose and goal of the evolutionary process', Jesus as the ultrahuman 'emergent' in the course of biological development."[27]

Roberts recognized that the attempt to combine transcendence and immanence, the doctrines of evangelicalism and the tenets of evolutionary science would involve him in "inconsistencies and in paradoxes." Many late twentieth-century historians have seized upon these contradictions as evidence of the confusion, perplexity, and decline supposedly afflicting the United Church in the decade after World War I. This analysis accents the failure of the church on two fronts. It had fallen short in its attempt to effect a complete reconstruction of Canadian society, a defeat underscored by the retreat from Prohibition and the tribulations of the Progressive Party in federal politics. This, in turn, created a mood of disillusionment, and led to irreconcilable tensions between what Allen has termed the "conservative," "progressive," and "radical" wings of the "social gospel" front. Allen contends that although this movement had displayed remarkable unity between 1914 and 1921, the experience of the 1920s fragmented the impulse to social action and led to a collapse by 1930.[28]

What Allen has termed the "disenchantment of social service" has convinced others that the churches confronted a far more intractable problem in the 1920s. The failure of the churches to reform Canadian politics and society indicated the rise of a secular temper that, according to the Rev. George Campbell Pidgeon of Bloor St United Church, Toronto, had abandoned any feeling of dependence on God, and stood in uncompromising opposition to Christianity.[29] The intellectual challenge to theology, posed by secularism according to one recent study, had by 1930 sapped even the most central foundation of evangelicalism – the ability of clergymen to preach and stimulate a religious revival. This was a serious issue for church leaders who believed that only through a revival could faith transform and redeem thought and culture.[30]

Yet Roberts's definition of theology was not an expression of gloom in the face of the intellectual problems posed by the secularizing tendencies of the history, philosophy, and science of the 1920s. Destined to head the church as moderator between 1934 and 1936,[31] he was confident that the theology of the new United Church could master the perplexing, but ultimately creative tension between transcendence and immanence, evangelicalism and evolution, Christian faith and modern thought. In this respect, Roberts stood within the main current of the Methodist and Presbyterian legacy, a tradition so forcefully represented by a succession of professors and preachers who since the 1860s had attempted to anchor the cultural and intellectual authority of their creed on the discussion and assimilation, not the simple negation, of elements of evolutionary science and the higher criticism of the Bible.

But where Grant, Nelles, Caven, Burwash, and even Chown believed that the interaction of faith and thought would produce some absolute certainty by which human thought and activity could be firmly directed, Roberts's emphasis that Christian believers lived "in a world of relative knowledge"[32] testified to the drastic change in the religious climate in the decade since World War I. The frank recognition of "relativity" meant that many clergymen, particularly those associated with the theological colleges, now moved in an intellectual universe where evangelical religion had lost the protective carapace of Baconianism, and consequently sought a new relationship with the human intellect.

The success of Roberts and his colleagues in promoting a new theological outlook is all the more remarkable when contrasted with the theological climate of Europe and America in the 1920s. European religious circles reacted to the grotesque discontinuity and irrationality of war by repudiating what many thinkers considered the relativism of historical time. Generally covered by the rubric "modernism," this movement encompassed currents of literature, philosophy, art, and theology. Despite the apparent divergence of approaches, all were united, in the words of the American historian Carl Schorske, by the attempt "to distinguish our perception of our lives and times from all that has gone before, from history as a whole as such." "The modern mind," Schorske contended, "has been growing indifferent to history because history, conceived as a continuous nourishing tradition, has become useless to it."[33]

In the sphere of religious thought, this revulsion against history was most evident in the work of the German theologian Karl Barth, and in the writings of the "neo-orthodox" scholars Rudolf Bultmann and Emil Brunner. Before World War I, these men had been associated with the work of the relativist "Comparative Religion" school so subversive of the belief in historical certainty. What they perceived as the failure of the churches during the war led them to seek a "disengagement" of theology and history. Barth, the leader of the movement, appeared to deny the validity of human reason in the interpretation of religion, and posited an acute contradiction between revelation, which he termed "super-history," and human history. Barth and his followers proclaimed the irrelevance of historical research, and even of the historical personality of Jesus, to the faith of the believer.[34]

These distinctive tenets of the emerging "theology of crisis"[35] were characterized by a "modernist," some might say existential, sense of absolute contradiction between the uncertain, constantly changing record of human civilization, and the eternal, unchanging, incomprehensible revelation of God. With its rejection of the relationship between revelation, history, and theology, the term "neo-orthodoxy" was perhaps a misnomer. To draw a comparison, even the supposed "pure" revivalistic evangelism of the years before the Darwinian "revolution" held, through the ideas associated with millennialist thought, an acute sense of the intimate connections, prophetic foreshadowings, and parallels between the Bible and human history. In their attempt to divorce revelation from history in the search for a certain theology, Barth and his followers were "modernists" who, rather than returning to the sources of evangelical tradition, broke decisively with its theology of history.

If the prevailing climate of theological discussion in Europe broke with nineteenth-century evangelicalism by dictating a "modernist" separation of biblical revelation and the understanding of history, the American religious scene offered even less comfort to those like Roberts who attempted to bridge the theological dualities of transcendence and immanence, "traditionalism" and "modernism." The early 1920s witnessed the sustained attempt by militant "conservatives" in some American denominations, Presbyterians and Baptists in particular, to drive their "liberal" co-religionists from the churches. According to American historian George Marsden, this theological polarization flourished in the atmosphere of crisis gripping the churches immediately after World War I. Fearing for the future of Christian civilization, these fundamentalists, an alliance of denominational conservatives, premillennialists, and adherents of "holiness" movements, launched a vigorous and popular anti-evolution crusade. Denouncing "liberalism" as an "anti-Christian" philosophy, prominent religious leaders such as Augustus Strong and J. Gresham Machen sought to redress the balance in favour of the biblical literalism and Baconian concepts of knowledge and history that they believed had been undermined by evolutionary naturalism.[36]

Although the Canadian Presbyterian and Methodist Churches, and the United Church after 1925, remained free of the more extreme "liberal" and "fundamentalist" public controversies that bedevilled American Baptists and Presbyterians, many Canadian clergymen were troubled by the religious turmoil in America. The pre-war theological climate of evangelical preaching and education had rested on a carefully constructed balance between Baconianism and higher criticism. The same cultural and intellectual stresses plagued both American and Canadian religious circles, and in both societies, professors and preachers were aware of the incompatibility of Baconianism and the philosophies of the human mind, history, and society that had emerged after 1890. Furthermore, between 1905 and 1914 both preachers and congregations had become increasingly attuned to the difficulties posed by higher criticism for the theological traditions of evangelicalism.

How to account for a different response to a similar set of cultural and intellectual circumstances? Closer examination of Canadian Methodism and Presbyterianism in the 1920s reveals the presence of three factors that, in combination, account for the difference. Canadian churches were not free of theological conflict, but it was centred on issues other than the authority of the Bible and the question of evolution. Between 1919 and 1926, the Presbyterian Church was bitterly split over the question of church union, with one-third of the group eventually voting against union with the Methodists. N.K. Clifford, who has made a detailed study of the argument over church union, posed the question of fundamentalist influence on the anti-unionists. He determined that although many of the anti-unionists might be described as denominational "conservatives," their views on biblical inspiration and authority were not radically different from those of their unionist opponents.[37]

The second issue involved the problem of leadership. American Presbyterians could look J. Gresham Machen, Clarence Macartney, and, from outside the ministry, William Jennings Bryan to openly denounce "liberal" theology and to uphold the literalist, Baconian alternative. Because of the union controversy, Canadian Presbyterianism had no comparable leader in the early 1920s, although the theological outlook of men such as the Rev. George Campbell Pidgeon might well have qualified them to head a group of militant "conservatives" within the church. A minister of Bloor St Presbyterian Church, Toronto, Pidgeon became the first moderator of the United Church in 1925. He had studied with MacVicar at Presbyterian College, Montreal, in the 1890s and had preserved his mentor's emphasis on the centrality of the Bible and evangelical doctrine.[38] The foundation of his preaching was far more "literalist" than the interpretations of the Bible advanced in some Canadian theological colleges by the 1920s.

Although he decried the impact of secularism on Christianity, and sought to move the United Church toward the traditional emphasis on revivalism and personal conversion,[39] Pidgeon refused to categorically oppose the interaction of theology and "modern" knowledge. His role was similar to that played by Grant, Caven, and

MacVicar between 1870 and 1890. His public statements, though insistent on the traditions of evangelicalism, sounded a note of moderation and reconciliation. He reminded his congregation that the fundamentalist controversy involved the "nonessentials" of the faith, and publicly criticized the methods adopted by American fundamentalist leaders, saying that they had erred in forgetting the inclusive nature of Christianity.[40]

Pidgeon's rebuke to fundamentalism indicated that most United Church clergymen wanted to perpetuate the religious outlook of the nineteenth century by avoiding doctrinal and biblical disputes. This attitude was reinforced by the continued influence of the British – more specifically the Scottish – intellectual climate on the Canadian theological colleges. Between 1926 and 1929 Emmanuel College, the new institution grouping Knox and Victoria professors who supported church union, received an infusion of new faculty members from Scottish universities. Principal Gandier recruited the Rev. John Dow for the sensitive area of New Testament criticism, while the Rev. John Baillie was appointed to the chair of systematic theology.[41]

Although the distinctive Scottish blending of evangelical theology and evolutionary higher criticism had, by about 1910, ceased to serve as the focal point of cultural unity between college and congregation in English Canada, its imperatives in theological education persisted. Throughout the 1920s the practice of theology in the Scottish universities offered significant intellectual sustenance to those clergymen who, like Roberts, sought to preserve a vital connection between evangelical theology and historical scholarship. Strongly represented in Canadian theological colleges, the Scottish approach avoided the extremes of a Barthian "modernism" founded on despair concerning the historical process and the aggressive Baconianism of the American fundamentalists, which verged on an outright denial of the knowledge of the Bible provided by historical criticism since 1860.[42]

As a result of the Scottish presence, harmony prevailed within the United Church colleges on the crucial issues of the nature of the Bible and the place of theology in relation to other branches of knowledge. As in the 1860s, the peculiar position of the English-Canadian churches within the world of transatlantic Protestantism permitted, to a far greater extent than in the United States, the existence of the theological dualisms of evangelicalism and evolution, transcendence and immanence, "traditionalism" and "modernism" that trouble late twentieth-century historians. A decisive illustration of the continued power of the mediating religious currents emanating from Britain was the curious reception of Barth's "neo-orthodoxy" by the United Church. By the end of the decade some clergymen were mildly interested in Barth's harsh opposition of revelation and human reason, but those who wrote on the subject were by no means approving of such "modernism,"[43] often observing that, in attempting to preserve the absolute authority of the Christian revelation, the German scholar had sacrificed most of the links between Christianity and culture, something they were not prepared to do – by inclination or by training. Thus "neo-orthodoxy" had no widespread currency within the church until the 1930s brought a fresh mood of crisis to colleges and pulpits.

HISTORY, REALISM, AND THE BACONIAN PROBLEM: TOWARD A PHILOSOPHICAL THEOLOGY

In 1915 S.H. Hooke, Professor of Oriental Studies at Victoria College, described the interaction of the main intellectual currents of the age with the mood of wartime Canada. Like Chown and other evangelical preachers, he regarded the war as an essential process of purification for religious ideas and values. But in contrast to the more traditional approach of many of his colleagues, who attempted to define the war in terms of their tradition of "historical theology," Hooke singled out for particular praise currents of thought that might at first sight seem at odds with the tenets of evangelicalism. These he grouped under three categories: "Vitalism" in philosophy and psychology; "Expressionism" in art; and "Collectivism" in politics and economics. These movements, he said, were not the opponents of Christianity, but profoundly religious forces in civilization, marked by a common yearning for reality, the same spirit that moved the soldiers and chaplains at the battlefront.[44]

Such a statement might be dismissed as part of the wartime excitement that seized the Methodist and Presbyterian Churches. Vitalism, Expressionism, and Collectivism marked so radical a departure from the Bible-centred theology, Baconianism, and individualism characteristic of the evangelical mind in Canada that Hooke's presence at Victoria College could be regarded as simply an aberration. Yet when linked to post-war developments within the church colleges, his ideas afford a clue to the most troubling intellectual and cultural problem confronting the evangelical churches. Hooke's three categories were an intellectual shorthand describing the direction taken by history and the "human sciences" after 1890. In the decade before World War I, the Canadian church colleges had felt the first impact of the "revolution" in the interpretation of human experience and consciousness launched in Europe and America.

Despite the efforts of Chown and other church leaders, the problem of the relationship between evangelical theology and historical study in an intellectual climate increasingly hostile to doctrines, philosophies, and theories founded on the assumption of absolute certainty had by no means been settled by 1914. The violence of the world conflict intensified, rather than resolved, the difficulty of maintaining a culture founded on a coherent religious faith and a theology informed by an alliance of Baconianism and history. The chaos of time, experience, and history unleashed at the battlefront intersected with the pre-war intellectual currents defined in Hooke's article. The post-war theological discussion among Methodists and Presbyterians was characterized neither by the impact of Barthian "modernism" nor by the fundamentalist assault, both of which, from widely divergent perspectives, attacked the relationship between evangelical theology and the study of history as practiced in the late nineteenth century. Rather, an attempt to define the scope, role, and content of theology in relation to history and the "human sciences" informed the intellectual life of the church colleges.

Theology in the evangelical colleges between World War I and the Great Depression was shaped in response to questions raised by the philosophies of vitalism and pragmatism. Represented by the dominant figures of the French thinker, Henri Bergson, and the American philosopher and psychologist William James,[45] these currents of thought sought to address the uncertainty that had overtaken history, social science, and psychology after 1890. Both Bergson and James denied the absolute sanction of the dogmas of either religion or science. Faith, for these philosophical radicals, was based not on the immutable certainty of doctrine or on appeals to historical "facts," but on consciousness and experience, and thus its substance was in constant flux. From the point of view of Protestant clergymen, was the changing character of experience a sufficient basis of authority for the maintenance and sustenance of Christian faith in a world that demanded that belief be rational and comprehensible?

Although one influential account of the intellectual life of the Canadian universities between 1900 and 1914 has argued for the dominance of forms of Hegelian or absolute idealism,[46] ideas that might loosely be described as "pragmatism" entered the Canadian church colleges in the years immediately prior to World War I. In his popular and influential work, *The Varieties of Religious Experience*, published in 1902, William James assigned priority to experience, rather than to intellect, metaphysics, or dogma, in assessing the validity of diverse forms of religious expression. This approach accorded well with certain emphases of the evangelical creed and spoke, in a way that the abstract idealist philosophy of John Watson could not, to professors and preachers concerned, above all, with the practical task of influencing and transforming the spiritual life of the individual.

Despite these affinities, "pragmatism" contributed in no small measure to the pervasive mood of uncertainty concerning the ability of "historical theology" to posit a ground of certainty for the central tenets of Christian belief. In 1912 an article by A.B. Macallum published in *Acta Victoriana*, the college journal of Victoria College, aptly expressed the meaning of pragmatism to the pre-war generation. The standard of religious doctrine, Macallum declared, was clearly function or usefulness, rather than any inherent property of truth. "It follows that the long discussions of the past on the nature of truth have been but vain dallyings with illusory ideas. There is no absolute truth knowable to the human mind." All creeds, he concluded, whether they be doctrines of religion, politics, or morals, were shifting and temporary constructions that in future would be relegated to the category of superstition by newer and more adequate expressions of belief.[47]

The implications of this article were clear. Both Presbyterians and Methodists had long insisted that their creed be related in an "experimental" or practical sense to the life of the believer, and that their theology was absolutely true, drawn as it was from the inspired and immutable body of divine revelation in the Bible. This theology, in turn, provided the principles of morality that sustained intellectual endeavour and preserved the explicitly Christian characteristics of culture. Neither Ryerson nor Nelles, nor even their successor Burwash would have claimed that experience or function was the sole determinant of religious truth. Under the influence of William James, however, Macallum preserved the emphasis on practicality, or usefulness, while denying that the evangelical creed could convey anything more than a "relative" or temporary truth.

The publication of such an article in the journal of Canada's largest Methodist college was a significant measure of the penetration of pragmatism and associated ideas into evangelical circles. Methodists were particularly susceptible to the new currents, because their structure of education and preaching had always accorded experience an important role in the achievement of faith and in the definition of theology. At Victoria College, the course of study throughout the 1890s and the early twentieth century stressed not the Hegelian idealist works of Edward Caird or John Watson, but

The Philosophy of Theism, written in the 1870s by the American philosopher Borden Parker Bowne. Bowne foreshadowed James's pragmatism and prepared the way for a favourable reception of James in Canada by his orientation toward the functional aspects of religion, his insistence on "coherent probability" rather than absolute rational proof for the Christian faith, and his appeal to the practical reason for the right to believe what life required.[48]

It was not surprising that Chown's sermons made frequent and by no means hostile references to William James and the pragmatic philosophy.[49] This philosophy was so popular among both Methodist and Presbyterian clergymen that Professor John Watson of Queen's University, a leading representative of Edward Caird's absolute idealism, engaged in open warfare against pragmatism and its representatives in a series of articles and books published just before World War I. Sensing that his lifelong attempt to reconcile religion and science through the medium of Hegel was being undermined, Watson sought to counter what he described as the insidious influence of "personal idealism" and "new realism," represented by James and Bergson, in America and Europe, and in colleges and pulpits closer to home.[50]

The problems of experience, history, and certainty raised by the currents of pragmatism were intensified by the intellectual and religious legacy of the World War I. Although few soldiers and chaplains read William James, the chaos of the trenches posed questions similar to those asked by European and American social thinkers. Could any certainty of meaning, theological or moral, be found in a human world that appeared to be in ceaseless, confusing flux? And how could the apparent discontinuities and suffering in the historical process be realistically interpreted in the light of evangelical beliefs on the relationship between the Bible and the human mind? Was individual experience the sole criterion of religious value, or was there some external standard of authority, outside the historical process, that could sanction the tenets of theology and morality? For many professors and preachers active in the decade after the World War I, these questions could only be answered by redefining theology's relation to culture.

Hooke and J. Davidson Ketchum, leading figures in the Student Christian Movement and frequent contributors to *The Canadian Forum* on religious questions, raised the questions most pointedly. Prior to the 1920s, a small, and sometimes vocal fringe of writers and publicists in late Victorian Canada, such as William Dawson LeSueur and the avowed agnostics and secularists so ably portrayed by Ramsay Cook, openly challenged the cultural authority of the evangelical creed.[51] In the wider culture of English Canada, the intellectual difficulties of the evangelical accommodation of theology and history in the 1920s were intimately linked to the decline, not of Christianity itself, but of what one historian has termed the "culture of Victorianism," the belief in a world of expanding knowledge and material progress sustained by immutable principles of theological and moral certainty.[52] Seen in this light, the ideas of Hooke and Ketchum concerning God, science, and the role of experience could not simply be ignored by those clergymen who wished to preserve the intellectual hierarchy in which theology governed and disciplined history and the other "human" and natural sciences.

In an article published in 1923 Ketchum declared that real faith in the personal God presented by the Christian churches had become quite impossible for the modern mind. He claimed that a new idea of religion was taking hold, in which modern biology, psychology, and sociology would supply a "new God" with a definite relationship to human life and endeavour. Science would emerge, Ketchum concluded, as "His Prophet and His Priest."[53] Hooke asserted that the modern mind acknowledged no principle of authority, be it that of Church council, or of Christ himself, that could not be tested in the realm of experience. Yet he recognized that experience provided but a tenuous basis of authority, providing a standard only for the individual who actually had the experience.[54]

How then to arrive at a principle of religious certainty that would relate revelation, Christian traditions, and the modern experience of reality? For a small minority, particularly those associated with the Student Christian Movement and *The Canadian Forum*, the only solution was to follow the advice of James and Bergson, to dive into the flux of experience, and to surrender any principles of dogmatic or historical certainty in the interests of a fuller personal life.[55] This approach was at odds with pre-war evangelical theology, which, despite its use of history, was always careful to establish the limits of evolution, and to preserve the sense of a divine will and activity independent of mind, nature, and society. Hooke, Ketchum, and their associates claimed, however, that transcendence was incomprehensible to the modern mind, which had accepted the world-picture of evolutionary science. For the "modernist" Christian, the only answer was to place God within the natural and cultural processes of the world – to see, not a being of unchanging will and immutable character, but an entity itself subject to evolutionary law.

Most disturbing to evangelicals, this group asserted that historical study, the traditional, if increasingly vulnerable, intellectual foundation of evangelical culture before 1914, could not validate Christianity's doctrinal claims. Hooke's *Christ and the Kingdom of God*, published in 1919, was the first book published by a Canadian church college that accepted, rather than refuted, the insights of the Swiss scholar Albert Schweitzer. Like Schweitzer, Hooke dismissed the "historical" Jesus and by implication the "Christ" of the Christian creeds as a figure incompatible with the messianic Jesus of the Synoptic Gospels.[56] By 1927, under the influence of this "apocalyptic" interpretation, Hooke's views had hardened. Christianity, he declared, contained no timeless essence or permanently valid body of doctrine. The biblical narratives, even those of the New Testament, presented no absolute religion, but a stage in the evolution of humanity. Historical scholarship proved, at best, but a testimony to a "creative force."[57] "Historical theology," that late nineteenth-century amalgam of Baconian induction, higher criticism, and a limited application of evolutionary theory, was to Hooke a contradiction in terms. History pointed to no intellectually respectable principle of religious or moral authority, but dissipated Christian doctrine in a chaos of relativism.

What alternatives existed for professors, clergymen, and believers assailed by the open criticisms of "historical theology" and the Baconian ideal? The presence of men like Hooke within the colleges themselves illustrated that the old consensus on the relationship of history, biblical criticism, and theology had been undermined. According to Allen, the religious views of Hooke and his pragmatist followers "obviously contributed much to the birth of the secularism which attended the decline of social service."[58] However, another interpretation is possible. The tension between a "historical theology" in decline and the "modernism" represented by Hooke, Ketchum, and their followers did not, according to some dialectical process, stimulate a secular temper in the church colleges. Rather, it led directly to the revival of theological discussion and contributed to a search by a number of influential clergymen for a new and dynamic relationship between Christianity and culture.

This new mood was demonstrated by the foundation in 1924 of the *Canadian Journal of Religious Thought*, the culmination of several years of prompting by clergymen-professors who urged the reinterpretation and restatement of the essential doctrines in the light of wartime experience and the impact of pragmatic and vitalistic philosophies. The opening editorial aptly expressed the commitment to redefining the content and method of theology:

A few years ago, at the close of the war, many were saying that in the future the Church would pay less attention to doctrine and more to practical living and ... social reconstruction ... The very insistence of the practical problems have led men to endeavor to get a deeper understanding of the Christian faith ... The dominant interest in many religious quarters to-day is the search for reality ... Consequently men are seeking the content of their faith: and doctrine, in no narrow sense of the term, is coming back into its own again. It is not something external to religion, but is the attempt to express in terms of reason the true inwardness of the Christian faith.[59]

This confident outlook within Presbyterian and Methodist church colleges, and the insistence on the importance of theology in relation to social activism raises a serious difficulty for those historians who interpret the post-war decade as a period of religious decline caused by the inability to resolve the paradox between personal evangelism and social service, "old-time" revivalism and religious "modernism." Any attempt to define the 1920s as a time of religious retreat and decline must first come to terms with this exciting intellectual renewal and experimentation within the Protestant churches.[60]

The most crucial intellectual problem facing the church colleges in the 1920s was once again the delicate issue of the proper relationship between theology, history, and the "human sciences." Clergymen-professors were acutely aware that fundamentalism, Barthian "neo-orthodoxy," and the "modernism" of the *Canadian Forum* radicals denied, from divergent perspectives, the main premises of the traditional "historical theology." As taught to several generations of students and preachers, "historical theology," based upon the evangelical doctrines of sin, redemption, and divine activity, was an alternative to evolutionary naturalism and to progressive concepts of society originating in the Enlightenment.

Few professors or preachers in English Canada subscribed to an unqualified belief in the inevitability of progress. Nonetheless, their prophetic sense of the relationship between past, present, and future, and of the complex relationship of the biblical record and human history had been based firmly on Protestant, post-millennialist convictions that the tendency in the human world, at least since the time of the Reformation and the expansion of Europe, was toward the conjunction of material and moral improvement. In the wake of the wartime experience, however, such beliefs became more difficult to sustain. In 1918 the Rev. Robert Law declared that the war had "given a severe blow to an optimism" he defined as "evolutionary, materialistic, humanitarian. Its presupposition was a necessary and almost automatic evolution of human affairs in the right direction. The god of our idolatry was progress (spelled with a capital P)."[61]

Perhaps these reactions did not do justice to the pre-war theology of history, but the scepticism concerning the idea of progress clearly expressed the growing feeling that the Christian believer could no longer hold with any certainty the belief that the historical process ultimately testified to theological verities. Chastened by the harsh realities of the wartime experience and the loss of certainty in the wider culture, the religious writings of the 1920s lacked both the note of millennial optimism and the note of conviction in the conjunction of history, prophecy, and theology.

In 1928 an editorial in *The Canadian Journal of Religious Thought* criticized the historical method of study, identifying the central difficulty as the attitude involved in the practice of history. By attempting an "objective" and value-free examination of the past, the historian stood "too often outside the periphery of the movement or person [studied] ... these may be understood as the product of their age, or their primitive religious experience comprehended as a part of the general religious experience."[62] This was the rock on which "historical theology" foundered, the question of whether the attitude of the historian or that of the theologian should dominate the equation. Such attitudes were not symptoms of disillusionment, or of an attempt to separate faith and culture. Recent historical treatments of the 1920s have emphasized that disillusionment was not the dominant characteristic of the post-war years, as the vast majority of social thinkers and literary figures in both Europe and America looked to the post-war world as a time of reconstruction, a "new era" that could open wider social and cultural possibilities.[63] Sustained by this climate of hope, clergymen-professors refused to follow either the "crisis theologians" or the fundamentalists in severing revelation and human history, religion, and reason. "For an unintelligent Protestantism," declared the Toronto preacher R. Edis Fairbairn in 1927, "there can be no future."[64]

Fairbairn's challenge was eagerly addressed by Canadian church college professors who sought a continuing rationale for the interaction of Christianity and culture, theology and history. Gandier and Baillie sought to transcend the pre-war intellectual crisis of "historical theology" without transforming the discipline into a species of "modernist" pragmatism, or retreating into the Baconian, literalistic assertions of the fundamentalists. Beginning from the premise that divine revelation and human discovery were complementary, Baillie deplored the tendency to separate "divine" from "ordinary" history. "There is," he concluded, "no 'ordinary' history and no 'common' order of nature, because neither history nor nature is ever wholly uninvaded by the express presence of that same God who was manifest in Christ."[65]

By affirming the relationship between Christianity, history, and nature, Baillie and Gandier ran squarely into the troublesome question of the authority of faith and theology in a world apparently dominated by the uncertainties of physical, natural, and "human" science. To what extent could doctrine, inherently absolute and immutable, be reconciled with a culture whose heroes William James, Albert Einstein, Alfred North Whitehead, and John Dewey, to name only the most prominent, proclaimed that spiritual and human realities could only be understood in terms of "relativity," "flux," and "process"? To accept fully the logic of "modernism," as stated by Hooke and his colleagues associated with *Canadian Forum*, meant the final dissolution of doctrinal and moral certainty, and by implication the evangelical creed itself, into a morass of pragmatic relativism. On the other hand, continued allegiance to the Baconian traditions of "historical theology," in the name of objective historical research, rendered theology intellectually and culturally irrelevant.

Between 1925 and 1930 clergymen-professors in the United Church colleges engaged in a sustained attempt to address this dilemma. The most significant work to emerge from this reassertion of theology was Baillie's *The Interpretation of Religion: An Introductory Study of Theological Principles*, published in 1928. Baillie's first concern was to address the thorny question of the status and relevance of theology in relation to the historical method that had arisen since the 1890s. He forcefully asserted that the subjection of religion to the canons of "historicism" had rested, from the very beginning, on false premises. Historians such as Troeltsch, he claimed, by striving to formulate a "natural science" of religion, mistakenly treated the faiths of mankind as so much dead matter.[66]

A more significant gauge of the evangelical mind of the 1920s was Baillie's direct assault on the intellectual legacy of Francis Bacon, which since the late eighteenth century had served as the matrix of education and preaching in the Canadian Presbyterian and Methodist Churches. Baillie linked the rise of historical relativism after the 1890s to the "error" perpetrated by Bacon, who assumed that there was an absolute distinction between "facts" and "values," with only the former having truly "scientific" status. Baillie charged that this reduced history to a mere chaos of facts, and subordinated both history and theology to an agenda and methodology established not by reference to the world of human culture or the spirit, but to natural science.[67]

At a stroke, Baillie renounced his allegiance to the Baconian universe where "facts" and "doctrines" were regarded as one and the same, and where preachers, professors, and students sought in the biblical record some definite, authoritative record of theological and moral certainty. His attack on the Baconian tradition marked the moment of cultural transformation in which the evangelical theology, forged in the debate between the Awakening and the Enlightenment, burst the chains imposed by induction and the prophetic, millennialist vision of the past, and acquired a vocabulary and methods that would enable it to engage the philosophies and "human sciences" of the twentieth century in a discussion at once critical and creative.

Baillie's own outlook was powerfully shaped by the impact of neo-Kantian idealism, a philosophy popular in both Germany and the United States in the years after 1860. In the 1920s, neo-Kantianism was enjoying a revival and reorientation at the hands of the British philosopher Alfred North Whitehead, whose 1926 Lowell Lectures, published as *Religion in the Making*, were read and discussed by a number of Canadian Protestant clergymen.[68] Significantly for the tone and substance of United Church theology, neo-Kantianism offered an intellectually respectable alternative to "crisis theology," fundamentalism, and the pragmatic relativism of Hooke and the *Canadian Forum* circle. All these argued that "historical theology" was useless, because historical study could unearth no incontrovertible, authoritative "facts" at the root of the principal documents of the Christian religion. Neo-Kantians countered by claiming that history fulfilled an important function in relation to theology. Although it could not establish the equation of "fact" and "doctrine," it testified to the existence of universal values, derived from individual moral experience, or conviction, but ultimately sanctioned by a universal and transcendent moral ideal.[69]

At this point this powerful current of philosophy converged with the equally forceful religious experience of World War I. Neo-Kantians such as Whitehead identified the central theme of religion as "individuality in community,"[70] echoing the insistence of Protestant chaplains on the affirmation of the human personality in the midst of a dehumanizing slaughter. Principals Oliver and Mackinnon had emphasized not so much the *doctrines* of the "old-time evangelism," but the *values* of suffering, sacrifice, and comradeship, based on the Cross of Christ. In much of the theological writing of the 1920s these values assumed the position of the central religious experience, epitomizing God's redemptive activity. John Baillie of Emmanuel College, William Morgan of Queen's Theological College, and William Creighton Graham of United College, Winnipeg, argued that master values which alone conferred meaning and relevance upon human history stemmed from this experience.[71]

These leading clergymen-professors subtly shifted the Baconian equation of "fact" and "doctrine" that had sustained the "historical theology" dominant in pre-war colleges and pulpits. Values in history, not the absolute truth of facts, were of primary importance to them, and the founding of faith in the consciousness of values afforded a standpoint from which to reassess the relation of theology to history, the conundrum that pre-war evangelicals had been unable to resolve. Basing his contentions on the neo-Kantian separation of "natural" and "cultural" sciences,[72] Baillie declared that theology was in no way a mere client of historical study. It was a science "of the spirit," concerned with the empirical investigation of reality, not with metaphysics.[73] This bold assertion enabled him to circumvent the issue that had plagued the colleges since the turn of the century: the inability of theology to acquire a methodology or set of concerns independent of the logic of "scientific" history.

In separating their discipline from the inflexible relativism of historical inquiry, however, clergymen such as Baillie were not engaging in a "revolt" against history such as that conducted by Barth and the American fundamentalists. Rather, they sought a close and faithful collaboration based on a division of labour. The resolution lay, Baillie believed, in a frank recognition of the subjective nature of historical study, a course the Baconian "historical theology" was unable to countenance. Shorn of its claims to absolute and all-encompassing certainty, history might be guided by the principles of Christian faith, based on perceptions of value. Following the insights of the great Italian scholar Benedetto Croce, Baillie stated:

But religious judgments being what they are, and making claim to objective truth as they undoubtedly do, it is psychologically an impossible feat, as well as logically a self-contradictory desire, *not* to make one's own fundamental religious convictions the criterion of religious truth. If we believe them to be true (as we must do, if they are really convictions), then we are, *ipso facto*, making them the criterion. And, once again, what other criterion is at all conceivable? Moreover, if one does not set aside one's conscience in seeking to surprise the secret of beauty, why then should one have to lay aside one's faith in seeking for "religious truth"?

It was thus the duty of theology "to provide the historical study of religion with a proper point of view, proper presuppositions, and a succession of proper questions ... It is from a sound outlook that the historiography of religion must take its cue."[74]

Baillie's final statement on the relationship of theology to history was written on the eve of a worldwide depression. At first reading, it might seem but a late echo of the hierarchy of knowledge that flourished in the Methodist and Presbyterian colleges under

McCulloch, Ryerson, Nelles, Caven, Grant, and Burwash. But closer examination places Baillie in a different intellectual world. The "sound outlook" emphasized in his lectures was not based on the supposition that "facts" and "doctrines" were one and the same, or that inductive certainty anchored theology, history, prophecy, and preaching. Rather, Baillie appealed to the notion of "values," a philosophical category at once less explicit and more subjective than the central tenets of the old evangelical creed.

In transcending the legacy of Baconianism in the 1920s, Baillie and his colleagues supplied a language and concepts that enabled the theological outlook of the United Church to move, in the space of a single decade, from the intellectual world of the late eighteenth-century Awakening to a twentieth-century cultural climate dominated by relativity, process, and uncertainty in both morals and science. The "new" theology remedied the critical deficiency of the creed as represented by a succession of clergymen from McCulloch to Chown: the inability to incorporate into the nature of man and society the insights of the "human sciences," those competitors of the evangelical creed that had arisen in the backwash of the Enlightenment.

Despite their intellectual achievements, the clergymen-professors who wrote between World War I and the Great Depression did not acquire the cultural authority held by the pre-war leaders of evangelicalism. Although the theological overture to the "human sciences" seemed to augur an age of cooperation, the disciplines of political economy, history, psychology, and sociology had by 1930 secured an independent place within English-Canadian universities, and men such as Harold Innis and George Sidney Brett,[75] to name only two leading practitioners, carried out their inquiries with little reference to theology. It might be claimed that the attempt to establish a proper division of labour merely placed theology in the position of one other discipline jockeying for prestige within the academic milieu.

At the same time, the recasting of the evangelical creed in the language of neo-Kantianism brought a final resolution to a process that had begun with the internal crisis of the historical discipline in the 1890s. The increasingly formalized discussion, seemingly exclusively addressed to philosophers and social scientists, isolated clergymen-professors from their traditional constituency, the clergymen and congregations who demanded a message of doctrinal and moral certainty as the basis for human action. The "wisdomizing tendency" described by Chown in 1930 had overtaken the church colleges. The insistence on "values," and the frank recognition that history was a subjective discipline, could scarcely convey the old assurance that the march of events was providentially guided, and thus both comprehensible and predictable to the Christian believer. Nor could the new forms of biblical criticism that flourished in the wake of the "revolution" in the colleges provide the certainty of Baconian induction. The discarding of Baconianism and the prophetic history broke the cultural unity that had once marked the relationship between the evangelical churches and English-Canadian life. The once open and comprehensive theological spectrum that had accommodated both Carman and Grant became the centre of a conflict, embittered by the Great Depression, that polarized the traditions of individual regeneration and the insistent claims of social action.

The Evangelical Mind and the Persistence of the Eighteenth Century

For over a century the Baconian method of biblical study and its equation of theology, prophecy, and history gave shape and coherence to education and preaching in the Methodist and Presbyterian church colleges of English Canada. This evangelical creed attempted to harmonize the tensions between a rising tide of revivalism and the eighteenth-century balance of reason and authority represented by a late manifestation of the Scottish Enlightenment. The revival stressed belief as the fruit of experience, rather than of mere assent to confessions of faith or participation in a common ritual. Faith was the outcome of a personal encounter between the sinner and Christ. For men such as McCulloch and Ryerson, "experience" involved the union of the intellect, the will, and the emotions. Their theology was eminently practical, oriented not to the solution of metaphysical problems, but to the conversion of the individual and the entrenching of Christian belief and ethics in the social life of fledgling communities.

Baconian induction and the prophetic-millennial vision of past, present, and future answered the need of professors and preachers for a practical and experimental theology, that spoke with authority to the human mind. By claiming to be a "science," Baconianism acknowledged a role for the intellect in interpreting the Bible, yet effectively barred it from the exercise of any form of criticism or speculation that would cast doubt on the Bible's accuracy in matters either of fact or of doctrine. The alliance of Baconianism and the centuries-old popular belief in the literal truth of Scripture established biblical study and theology as the dominant disciplines in the hierarchy of knowledge in the colonial evangelical colleges. Furthermore, the equation of theology, history, and prophecy built on this structure of certainty, reassuring preachers and their congregations that the actions of individuals and the fate of entire societies were ruled by a conscious divine providence that ensured the gradual but certain triumph of the "Protestant nations" and the achievement of the millennial Kingdom of Christ through the missionary and reforming efforts of the evangelical churches.

The persistence of the evangelical creed as an intellectually coherent and popular theological tradition in both college and congregation until the early twentieth century that constitutes the principal stumbling block for the dominant approach to English-Canadian intellectual history. Premised on the concept that Canadian society has been undergoing a process of secularization since 1860, most studies argue that the social sciences emerged in the universities after 1880 because religious "orthodoxy" was weakened by the Darwinian "revolution." The unstated implication is that although "evolution" and evangelical "orthodoxy" were fundamentally incompatible, the social sciences themselves were but secularized forms of the evangelical theology they displaced. Where the pre-Darwinian Methodist or Presbyterian clergyman's goal was the "redemption" or "regeneration" of the individual soul of the unconverted sinner, the social scientist of the early twentieth century evinced a similar desire to regenerate or redeem society.[1]

This study advances the argument that the evangelical creed must be studied in relation to the intellectual and cultural context of the years between the Second Great Awakening and the Great Depression rather than to the supposed "triumph" of secular thought in the late twentieth century. It challenges both the explanation and the historical periodization used by adherents of the secularization thesis to account for the transition from a society supposedly dominated by theology to one ruled by the secular outlook of the social sciences, by redrawing the traditional map of English-Canadian intellectual history between 1820 and 1930, and by offering an alternative view of the task and methods of the intellectual historian in assessing the presence and role of religious ideas in culture.

Stemming from a flawed assessment of the nature and function of Presbyterian and Methodist theology and colleges in English Canada, the late twentieth-century historian's view that the evangelical creed was coterminous with the philosophical tradition of Scottish Common Sense has precluded a proper understanding of its intellectual strength and cultural role. For McCulloch, Ryerson, and the

Free Church Presbyterians of the age of the great revival, theology was not an inaccessible, esoteric body of speculative or epistemological concepts. Rather, it acted as both an academic discipline and a means of communicating to a wider audience through preaching. The task of the college was thus both scholarly and popular, and the ideas taught by clergymen-professors were closely related to the world of popular belief.

Furthermore, English-Canadian intellectual historians have assumed that the currents of thought that influenced the United States affected their society with equal intensity, posing another obstacle to the understanding of the evangelical creed and its relation to early nineteenth-century culture. While the rising Methodist and Presbyterian Churches in the British North American provinces held Baconianism and the aggressive theology of history in common with many of their British and American counterparts, at this early stage the evangelical creed in the English-Canadian colleges diverged significantly from the intellectual legacy of its transatlantic parents. Lacking the impress of pre-Enlightenment theological traditions and the extensive exposure to the philosophical legacy of Scottish Common Sense that powerfully influenced some Protestant churches in the United States, the evangelical mind in British North America developed in relation to the early Victorian discovery of history, without reference to the natural sciences.

The early nineteenth-century study of history, which claimed to understand, through the exercise of reason, the well-springs of human action and the constant moral principles underlying the behaviour of individuals and societies, was in many respects a rival of the evangelical creed, which advanced a similar claim based on faith and theology. So powerful was the cultural prestige of the study of history, and so firm the commitment of the evangelical clergyman to understanding and transforming human actions, that theology in alliance with history, and not philosophy or natural theology, emerged as the indispensable discipline in the colonial colleges in the three decades before 1860. History, far more than the increasingly esoteric and metaphysical Scottish philosophy or the troubling discoveries of geologists and natural philosophers, directly addressed the minds of the congregation and offered a realm of religious and moral certainty. So firm was the grip of history on the evangelical mind that the most direct and serious challenges to the colonial theology were those raised by the "improper" exercise of historical reason, particularly in the sensitive area of biblical criticism.

The linking of theology to a cultural climate infused by the study of history, rather than to one dominated by philosophy or the natural sciences, ensured the survival, unity, and coherence of the English-Canadian evangelical creed in the face of the challenges posed by evolutionary science and the higher criticism between 1860 and 1890. The generation of college leaders most ably represented by Grant, Caven, Nelles, and Burwash felt no need to adopt the evolutionary metaphor or to substantially revise their creed. They used their colonial position and the authority and prestige of history creatively to construct a powerful intellectual alternative to evolutionary naturalism. Variously termed "historical," "biblical," or "inductive" theology, its themes were the preservation of the Bible as an authoritative body of "facts" and doctrines to which both professors and preachers could confidently appeal, and the overriding prophetic belief in the links between the biblical record and the unfolding history of their own age.

Their position on the periphery of a Scottish Common Sense philosophy in decline, and their relative lack of interest in the relationship of religion and the natural sciences, as opposed to the more vital encounter of religion and the sciences of the human mind and society, left Methodist and Presbyterian leaders without the intellectual and institutional structures that enabled American and British clergymen both to assimilate and to resist Darwin. They encountered evolutionary naturalism in the sphere of history, in the application of ideas of social evolution to the Bible and to the record of human societies. In facing this problem, however, the Baconian and historical tenets of the evangelical creed forged in the late eighteenth century provided a strategy of defence as well as a means of incorporating some of the insights derived from historical criticism into the evangelical structure.

It makes little sense to speak of a Darwinian "watershed" in the 1860s and 1870s, the traditional line that historians have fixed between "orthodoxy" and "secularism," when considering English-Canadian Presbyterian and Methodist clergymen at that time. In a recent study of British and American scientists and clergymen, the British historian James R. Moore challenged the view that Darwinism could be regarded as "revolutionary" in either the scientific or religious sense.[2] Ironically, Moore's comment applies particularly to the one group of transatlantic Protestants his seminal study did not consider. The years between 1860 and 1900 were a flourishing period for the evangelical creed in the wider cultural life of English Canada rather than a time of troubles for the evangelical churches or the prelude to the triumph of secular forms of thought.

The continued Baconian character of "historical theology" also directs the student of the late nineteenth century toward a reassessment of the place of English-Canadian evangelicalism within the

North-American context. Between 1860 and 1890 the attempt by some American church leaders to recast their theology according to evolutionary assumptions caused considerable division in the Protestant churches. Marsden has argued forcefully that the "Baconianism" derived from the philosophy and theology of the eighteenth century was incompatible with views of human beings, society, and history constructed according to the evolutionary paradigm. Much of the intellectual basis of fundamentalism, he claims, lay in the disjunction.[3]

Yet in English Canada, Methodist and Presbyterian clergymen-professors managed not only to construct a limited accommodation of Baconianism and higher criticism, but also to apply it to both college curricula and preaching as a source of unity, not discord. The encounter between the Baconian evangelical creed and the evolutionary outlook in English Canada generated a spectrum of opinion differing in emphasis but united by shared assumptions, rather than overt theological "parties" divided over the question of biblical inspiration and authority. The Baconian tradition in the Methodist and Presbyterian Churches and colleges, it may be argued, precluded the emergence of twentieth-century fundamentalism, rather than providing its foundation. The radically different consequences of the Baconian legacy in English Canada and the United States suggests a revision of Marsden's paradigm, giving less emphasis to Baconianism, and far more to the persistence of Calvinism and of traditions of Paleyite natural theology and philosophical theology in the older society.

The secularization thesis is critically flawed by the lack of evidence for its central argument that between 1880 and 1900 evangelical theology was resolved into a system of social ethics, the prelude to the emergence of the "modern" social sciences. This study posits that the "historical theology" dominating the Methodist and Presbyterian church colleges in the late nineteenth century preserved the earlier Baconian and prophetic ideas forged in the encounter between the evangelical revival and the Enlightenment, and was not greatly affected by the impact of evolutionary social and historical ideas.

"Historical theology" prevented rather than aided the resolution of theology into social ethics . English-Canadian intellectual history between 1880 and 1920 can best be explained by recognizing that theology and the social sciences functioned in separate spheres. The social sciences' approach to social analysis was developed independently, with reference to earlier traditions of evolutionary social thought, not by "secularizing" or appropriating the redemptive language of evangelical theology. The separation between the rival tenets of theology and the social sciences can best be illustrated by the persistent belief in Methodist and Presbyterian colleges and congregations until the early twentieth century that historical study testified not to the presence of natural or social laws governing mind and society, but to the intellectual and cultural authority of both the Bible and their theology, which preserved the supremacy of the individual experience of God's presence while directing the believer to an active role in society.

Clergymen-professors and many preachers diverged most sharply from their competitors in the social sciences over the issue of God's active presence in history and human society. By 1890, it may be argued, most philosophers, historians, political economists, and social thinkers had accepted some form of evolution, whether moral or material, as the explanation for intellectual and social developments. Many viewed society as a conscious, living organism, and not simply as the sum of its individual parts. "Historical theology," the dominant discipline in the Methodist and Presbyterian church colleges, constituted an almost insuperable barrier to conversation between theology and the social sciences. It had been specifically formulated as a rival to social evolutionary assumptions, and continued to insist that the principles of social development rested not with the operation of natural laws, but with the miraculous actions of providence. Furthermore, the legacy of the early nineteenth-century revival enshrined in "historical theology" encouraged preachers to view religious "experience" in terms of individual conversion, repentance, and holy living. Although their creed by no means precluded social action, and indeed encouraged it, men such as Chown and Grant continued to insist upon the individual, rather than upon "society," as the primary focus of their energies.

As an alternative to the traditional polarization of English-Canadian intellectual history around the central discontinuity of Darwin's impact, this study suggests that the historian seek the deeper continuities characterizing the religious and cultural history of the nineteenth century. The evangelical creed in English Canada was marked at the outset by a discontinuity between the worlds of Revival and Enlightenment, and between those of the colony and the parent societies, Britain and America. This discontinuity enabled clergymen-professors in the smaller transatlantic society to largely sidestep the impact of Darwin and, with minor adjustments, to preserve the main tenets of their creed. The continuity of the evangelical structure was, however, challenged between 1905 and World War I. The central issue was the problem of historical certainty as the foundation of the authority of the Bible, not the relationship between theology and the natural or social sciences.

While it would be too much to claim that the impact of historical "relativism" caused a loss of faith in college and congregation, it subtly weakened the important connection between the professor and the preacher. The cultural authority of evangelical thought rested on the dual commitment and role of the clergyman-professors, whose task was to integrate the currents of thought in the transatlantic world into the evangelical creed, while bearing in mind the need of the preacher for a message of theological and moral certainty. The particular accomplishment of the generation represented by Grant, Nelles, Caven, and Burwash was their "taming" of historical criticism in such a way that the theological imperatives of their creed were preserved almost intact.

The intellectual, social, and cultural currents present in the years immediately prior to 1914 were, however, not easily amenable to such a discipline. For professors and preachers, the most troubling of these included the developments in biblical scholarship associated with historical relativism, the impact of the social sciences on the educated, and the less tangible but ultimately insurmountable difficulties faced in adjusting a structure of theological and moral certainty to the needs of a culture increasingly attracted by an ideal of self-absorption and self-fulfillment. It might be argued that the American-style theological "parties" that began to emerge in the controversies afflicting the Methodist and Presbyterian Churches after 1905 marked the end of the accommodating spirit of Canadian evangelicalism, which until this time had distinguished it from its more polarized American counterpart. The rifts in Canada were a symptom of the difficulties faced by a culture undergoing "Americanization."

These controversies and the more general climate of theological uncertainty in the Canadian colleges between 1905 and 1930 launched a movement that irrevocably altered the position of the clergyman-professor and, more importantly, the nature and function of theology. In a remarkable development intensified by the experience of wartime, clergymen-professors questioned the Baconian formulations that had sustained their theology for over a century, and in the process, transformed their theology of history. By 1929 theology, as an intellectual discipline, stood on a more adequate footing in relation to history and the social sciences. The transformation of evangelical theology involved, however, the sacrifice of much of the old creed, particularly its ability to make the world of the college and, most importantly, the key discipline of biblical scholarship, accessible and intelligible to a wider audience.

The continuity underlying the intellectual life of the evangelical churches in English Canada between 1800 and 1905 dictates a reconsideration of the intellectual historian's task, particularly in the explanation of the dynamic interaction between religion, thought, and culture. Since the emergence of a specialized intellectual history in the 1960s, most historians of religion have imitated the political historian, orienting the history of ideas and culture around great events and great men, with the emphasis on sharp breaks such as the Darwinian "revolution" or World War I, which marked the "death" of one set of ideas and the "birth" of new forms of thought and culture.

The procedure of the political historian, however, should not be applied to a religious and cultural phenomenon such as the evangelical creed. With its emphasis on pivotal events, watersheds, and the central role of dominant personalities as factors in historical change, such an intellectual history is unable to explain the continuity of cultural traditions. In the case of religious ideas, the tendency is to look for some event or individual that will serve as the catalyst or precursor of "secularization" or "modernization," allowing the historian to ignore the troubling presence of powerful currents of religious belief and quickly reach the safer and more familiar terrain of the late twentieth century. Such a practice denies the historical legitimacy of a vast range of cultural and intellectual experience.

The persistent strength of the late eighteenth-century Baconianism and its related theology of history, however, suggests the need of a history less oriented to the meaning of particular events and more informed by the vision of the "longue durée"[4] advanced by the French historian Fernand Braudel. Although Braudel's argument was specifically concerned with the continuity of relatively unchanging structures underlying the economic and social life of human communities, it can be applied to religious, intellectual, and cultural phenomena, to mental "structures" or bodies of belief such as the evangelical creed, which retained, even in an age of rapid social and intellectual transformation, much of their integrity and institutional power. The existence and character of such strands of tradition in English Canada has, until very recently, gone generally unnoticed.[5] Yet their existence calls for the intellectual historian, in the interests of understanding the past, to step outside the comfortable confines of the late twentieth century, and to reassess, in terms of the beliefs and values of an earlier age, the validity of catch-all, universal categories such as "secularization" and "modernization." Only thus will the religious experience of English Canada become a legitimate and fruitful field of inquiry.

Notes

ABBREVIATIONS

AV Acta Victoriana

BAP The British American Presbyterian

CCE&PR The Canada Christian Examiner and Presbyterian Review

CMM The Canadian Methodist Magazine

CMQ The Canadian Methodist Quarterly

CMR The Canadian Methodist Review

CMNR The Canadian Monthly and National Review

CP The Canadian Presbyterian

ChG The Christian Guardian

E&MR The Ecclesiastical and Missionary Record

E&MR The Ecclesiastical and Missionary Record of The Free Church
(N.S.) of Nova Scotia

H&FR The Home and Foreign Record

KCM Knox College Monthly

MCJ Manitoba College Journal

MM&R The Methodist Magazine and Review

MR The Monthly Record of the Church of Scotland in Nova Scotia
and Adjoining Provinces

P&W The Presbyterian and Westminster

NAC National Archives of Canada

PANS Public Archives of Nova Scotia

PCJ Presbyterian College Journal

PR The Presbyterian Review

PW The Presbyterian Witness
QJ Queen's Journal
QQ Queen's Quarterly
Theol. The Theologue
UCCA United Church of Canada Central Archives
VW Vox Wesleyana

INTRODUCTION

1 Smith, *Guesses at the Riddle of Existence*, vi, 3, 96. This work comprised a number of articles written between 1895 and 1896. The most complete biography of this important figure is Wallace's *Goldwin Smith: Victorian Liberal*. Smith's agnosticism and religious views have been explored more recently in Cook's *The Regenerators: Social Criticism in Late Victorian Canada*, chapter 3.
2 Bland, "Christianity's Millstone," *Queen's Quarterly* 3, no. 4 (April 1896): 271–8.
3 Chadwick, *The Secularization of the European Mind in the Nineteenth Century*, 17. Other key studies include McIntyre, *Secularization and Moral Change* and, more recently, Cox, *The English Churches in a Secular Society*. Both stress the importance of social rather than intellectual factors in explaining the rise and impact of secularization.
4 Readers may require some explanation of my terminology. I have tried to keep the theological language in this study to a minimum. Some may be surprised at the infrequent appearance of words such as "liberal," "conservative," "orthodox," "modernist," "radical," and "progressive." When they are used, it is always with quotation marks. There is ample reason for this approach. As descriptions of theological "parties" or tendencies within particular churches, they fall short in depicting the character of English-Canadian religious thought. These words originate from American religious debates, and particularly from the acute phase of conflict between evolutionism and fundamentalism. The language of conflict is of doubtful validity in analyzing the religious experience of societies whose theological traditions do not predate the evangelical revival. To use these traditional pigeon-holes to categorize Canadian Protestant clergymen is to depreciate the richly-nuanced religious life of Victorian Canada. On the perils of using the language of conflict in describing nineteenth-century religion, see Moore, *The Post-Darwinian Controversies*, 19–122.
5 This interpretation of intellectual change originated in Canada with Allen's *The Social Passion* a study of the rise of the "social gospel" in the Protestant churches after 1890. It has been most forcefully expressed by McKillop who, in *A Disciplined Intelligence* and most recently in a volume of essays entitled *Contours of Canadian Thought*,

explores the roots of academic philosophy and the social sciences in English-Canadian universities, paying particular attention to the conflict of scientific and religious world-views in these institutions. Cook's provocative study, *The Regenerators*, more forcefully raises the question of the secularization of the wider culture outside the churches. Marshall's recently completed doctoral thesis, "The Clerical Response to Secularization," concentrates specifically on clergymen and their attempts to adapt their churches to the secularization of thought and culture.

6 The "optimistic" interpretation has been advanced by Allen's *The Social Passion* and McKillop's *A Disciplined Intelligence*. Both contend that the inspiration for social reform and progressive politics lay in the activist theological "liberalism" of the 1880s.

7 This view has been most powerfully advanced by Cook, whose *The Regenerators* offers a telling critique of the still-dominant "optimistic" view. Marshall's "The Clerical Response to Secularization" echoes Cook's views.

8 See Moore, *The Post-Darwinian Controversies*, for an interpretation of this most significant intellectual phenomenon.

9 See the seminal article by French, "The Evangelical Creed in Canada," in Morton, ed., *The Shield of Achilles*. Although it was published nearly twenty years ago, no historian has taken up French's challenge to address and analyze the inner components of evangelical belief and culture.

10 King, *The Theology of Christ's Teaching*, xvii-xviii.

11 There is no modern study of the culture of Anglican evangelicals – a significant and surprising gap in the historiography of English Canadian religion, given the rich literature available for the British scene. Canadian Baptists have been more fortunate. Two recent studies, Rawlyk's *Ravished By the Spirit*, and Rawlyk, ed., *Canadian Baptists and Christian Higher Education*, address issues fundamental to the present study, particularly concerning the continued cultural influence of the revivalist tradition.

12 See the comprehensive treatment by Masters, *Protestant Church Colleges in Canada*.

13 On Wesley College, see Bedford, *The University of Winnipeg*. The strong links between Wesley College and the "social gospel" have been amply explored in Allen, *The Social Passion*. For the role of Salem Bland's views in the crisis of the evangelical creed, see chapter 6.

14 Masters, *Protestant Church Colleges in Canada*; McKillop, *A Disciplined Intelligence*, chapter 1.

15 The best example of this type of intellectual history in Canada is McKillop's *A Disciplined Intelligence*, which argues for a direct importation of Scottish philosophy and natural theology into the Anglo-Cana-

dian colleges in the early nineteenth century. McKillop also contends that the controversies over evolutionary science and biblical criticism, and their resolution in philosophical idealism, theological "liberalism," and the "social gospel," all influenced the Canadian cultural scene after 1870. This model, derived from the work of the American historian V.L. Parrington in the 1930s, has recently been subjected to severe criticism from the intellectual historian Henry F. May. See his *Ideas, Faiths, and Feelings*.

16 In the United States, the tradition of "philosophical" or systematic theology, stretching back to Puritan New England, has been the subject of much historical study. The pioneering work was Miller's *The New England Mind*. For a more recent assessment of the concerns of Puritan theologians see Norman S. Fiering, "Will and Intellect in the New England Mind," *William and Mary Quarterly* (1972): 515–58. General studies of philosophical theology in other historical contexts include: Marsden, *The Evangelical Mind and the New School Presbyterian Experience*; and Kuklick, *Churchmen and Philosophers*. These two studies explore the New England theological tradition in the eighteenth and nineteenth centuries. For a competing strand of speculative theology, powerful among Presbyterians in the American South, see Bozeman, *Protestants in an Age of Science*. Developments on the European scene, particularly the impact of Immanuel Kant's philosophy on theological discussion, are treated in Welch, *Protestant Thought in the Nineteenth Century*, vol. 1, 1799–1870. The British relationship between philosophy and theology is analyzed in Reardon, *Coleridge to Gore*. The development of biblical scholarship is ably surveyed in the recent work by Rogerson, *Old Testament Criticism in the Nineteenth Century*.

17 Marsden's brilliant study, *Fundamentalism and American Culture*, has received little attention from English-Canadian cultural historians. For an application of some of Marsden's questions to Canadian religion, see Gauvreau, "Baconianism, Darwinism, Fundamentalism."

CHAPTER ONE

1 Details concerning the Pictou Academy are drawn from the following sources: McCulloch, *Life of Thomas McCulloch*, D.D. Public Archives of Nova Scotia [PANS], Records of the Pictou Academy, reel 1, "Memorial on Behalf of the Literary and Philosophical Institution at Pictou, Nova Scotia," ca 1824; PANS, Thomas McCulloch Papers, MG 1, vol. 553, no. 15, McCulloch to "Dear Brother," n.d.; ibid., McCulloch Papers, vol. 551, no. 13, *Second Report of the Glasgow Society for promoting the Interests of Religion and Education among the Settlers in the North American Provinces* (Glasgow, 1830). For a more recent study of McCulloch, see

Hamilton, "Education, Politics, and Reform in Nova Scotia, 1800–1848." See also the studies by Wood, "Thomas McCulloch's Use of Science in Promoting a Liberal Education," 56–73, and McMullin, "In Search of the Liberal Mind," 68–85.

2 An account of McCulloch's early life can be found in McCulloch, *Life of Thomas McCulloch*, 7–10.

3 The Scottish educational background during the eighteenth century, particularly its philosophical tone, has been treated by Davie in the *The Democratic Intellect*.

4 McCulloch, *The Nature and Uses of a Liberal Education Illustrated* 3, 19. This was also the theme of McCulloch's address to the theological class in 1820. See *Life of Thomas McCulloch*, appendix A, "A Lecture delivered at the Opening of the First Theological Class in the Pictou Academy," 197–215.

5 There is little published Canadian historical literature on the relationship between religion and culture. Older interpretive articles include Wise, "Sermon Literature and Canadian Intellectual History," in Bumsted, ed., *Canadian History before Confederation*, 254–69, and French, "The Evangelical Creed in Canada." More recently, Westfall has tried to connect Protestant religion to the wider culture of Upper Canada. See "The Dominion of the Lord," 47–70 and "Order and Experience." The one larger monograph, McKillop's *A Disciplined Intelligence*, 9–10, mentions in passing the role of religion, but avoids entirely an issue of great concern to early nineteenth-century Protestants, the connection of Christian doctrine and culture. McKillop prefers a sociological definition, contending that a "moral imperative," he equates with the Christian religion, undergirded the life of the mind.

6 Frye, "Conclusion," in Klinck et al., eds, *Literary History of Canada*, vol. 2, 338–49; McKillop, *A Disciplined Intelligence*, chapters 2, 3, and 4.

7 This has been most forcefully noted by Hilton, in *The Age of Atonement*. Hilton argues that Anglican and Presbyterian evangelicals owed much to the rationalistic and mechanistic assumptions of eighteenth-century thought.

8 The intellectual concerns and the transmission of the Enlightenment can only be understood in the light of its "urban" nature. See the seminal article by Nicholas Phillipson, "Culture and Society in the 18th Century Province," in Stone, ed., *The University in Society*, 407–48. For an understanding of the Enlightenment as a city culture in the United States, see Bender, *New York Intellect*.

9 There is a vast British and American literature on the religion and culture of the great early nineteenth-century religious revival. It is difficult to escape the conclusion that much of transatlantic culture was shaped by the Second Great Awakening. See, for example, Standish

Meacham, "The Evangelical Inheritance," *Journal of British Studies* 3, no. 1 (Nov. 1963): 88-104; Rosman, *Evangelicals and Culture*; Semmel, *The Methodist Revolution*; Hilton, *The Age of Atonement*. For general interpretations of the American scene, see Smith, *Revivalism and Social Reform*, and Miller, *The Life of the Mind in America*. For a more synthetic and thought-provoking analysis, see McLoughlin, *Revivals, Awakenings, and Reform*. Specific studies of the evangelical mind include Marsden, *The Evangelical Mind and the New School Presbyterian Experience*; and for the American South, Holifield, *The Gentlemen Theologians*. Studies of the social dimensions of American revivalism include Marty, *Righteous Empire*; Boyer, *Urban Masses and Moral Order*; and Paul E. Johnson, *A Shopkeeper's Millennium*. For a critical review of the literature of evangelicalism, see Sweet, "The Evangelical Tradition in America," in Sweet, ed., *The Evangelical Tradition in America*.

10 See the stimulating article by Noll, "Common Sense Traditions and American Evangelical Thought," 216–38.

11 Cragg, *Reason and Authority in the Eighteenth Century*, chapter 4.

12 United Church of Canada Central Archives [UCCA], Samuel Sobieski Nelles Papers, "Religion and Learning," college address, 1857. See also Nelles Papers, "Educational Preparation," address delivered Nov. 1851. When consulted, this collection was in the process of reorganization. Thus many citations lack box and file numbers.

13 My interpretation of this point has been influenced by Rosman's *Evangelicals and Culture*, a study of British evangelicals that rejects the old dichotomy of "Evangelical" and "Enlightenment," arguing for areas of substantial affinity between the two.

14 The notion of "phases" of the American Enlightenment is discussed by May in *The Enlightenment in America*. For application of this concept to the influential Scottish Enlightenment, see Hoeveler, Jr., *James McCosh*. The more recent work by Sher, *Church and University in the Scottish Enlightenment* has also posited the notion that the "Enlightenment" in Scotland went through several phases.

15 The foundation dates for these colleges are provided in Masters, *Protestant Church Colleges in Canada*. Pictou was chartered in 1816, followed by Queen's University in 1841, Knox College in 1844, and Presbyterian College, Halifax, in 1848. While there is no comprehensive history of the early Presbyterian colleges, see, for Queen's University, Neatby, *Queen's University*. For the Maritime colleges, see Falconer and Watson, *A Brief History of Pine Hill Divinity Hall*, and for the early history of Knox College, see Nicholson, "Michael Willis," 113–114. Masters argues that the aim of these Presbyterian colleges was the training of a professional class, the clergy.

16 PANS, Records of the Pictou Academy, reel 1, "Memorial on Behalf of the Literary and Philosophical Institution at Pictou, Nova Scotia"; McCulloch Papers, McCulloch to "Dear Brother."

17 Thomas McCulloch Papers, *Calvinism: The Doctrine of the Scriptures, or A Scriptural Account of the Ruin and Recovery of Fallen Man and a Review of the Principal Objections which have been Advanced Against the Calvinistic System*. This work was actually written between 1820 and 1830. McCulloch's papers contain an unpublished manuscript. See McCulloch Papers, MG 1, vol. 555, no. 2, "Preface to a Work on Calvinism and the Fallen Man," n.d. See also McCulloch Papers, MG 1, vol. 552, no. 118, "Man's Natural Condition," n.d. For his teaching of theology at Pictou, see *Life of Thomas McCulloch*, 70.

18 On the intellectual inheritance of Calvinism in America, the starting-point is provided by Miller's *The New England Mind*. See also Norman S. Fiering, "Will and Intellect in the New England Mind," *William and Mary Quarterly* (1972): 515–58. For a more recent interpretation, see Kuklick, *Churchmen and Philosophers*, 14. Kuklick argues that the New England Divinity tradition continued until the 1880s.

19 For the dialectic of Calvinism and the Enlightenment, see May, *The Enlightenment in America*. The opposition of Calvinism and revivalism in the early nineteenth century is treated in McLouglin, *Revivals, Awakenings, and Reform*, and, in more interpretive fashion, by Douglas in *The Feminization of American Culture*, and by Marsden, *The Evangelical Mind and the New School Presbyterian Experience*. For a more recent assessment of the Calvinist intellectual tradition, see the stimulating article by Mark A. Noll, "Common Sense Traditions and American Evangelical Thought," *American Quarterly* 37, no. 2, (summer 1985).

20 See Smith, *Revivalism and Social Reform in Mid-Nineteenth-Century America*; McLoughlin, *Revivals, Awakenings, and Reform*; and Brown, *Thomas Chalmers*.

21 McCulloch Papers, MG 1, vol. 555, no. 1, "The Prosperity of the Church in Troublous Times," sermon preached at Pictou, Friday, 25 February 1814.

22 *Life of Thomas McCulloch*, 8. For the Scottish background of the Secessionists and the career of John Brown, see Mackenzie, *John Brown of Haddington*. John Brown of Haddington wrote an extensive *Dictionary of the Bible* in 1771 and was widely read in church history. His lifelong ambition was to write a History of Redemption. See also Drummond and Bulloch, *The Scottish Church, 1688–1843*, 30, 111.

23 McCulloch Papers, MG 1, vol. 550, no. 73, "The Seven Apocalyptic Churches," *The Acadian* (4 April 1828): 1; Thomas McCulloch, *Popery Condemned by Scripture and the Fathers*; *Life of Thomas McCulloch*, 7–9.

For his literary ambitions, see McCulloch Papers, vol. 553, no. 27, McCulloch to James Mitchell, 16 January 1828; ibid., McCulloch to James Mitchell, 24 June 1828. See also Susan Buggey and Gwendolyn Davies, "Thomas McCulloch," *Dictionary of Canadian Biography*, vol. 7 (Toronto, 1988) 538–90. For the growing popularity of antiquarianism and the historical novel in early nineteenth-century Scottish culture, see Sher, *Church and University in The Scottish Enlightenment*, 316–17.

24 McCulloch Papers, *William, and Melville*. A similar emphasis is adopted in his *Calvinism*, 74–82. For the idea of God as "moral governor," see *Calvinism*, 68–9; McCulloch Papers, "Man's Natural Condition." For the "New School" compromise between Calvinist doctrine and evangelical piety, see Marsden, *The Evangelical Mind*, and for the outlook of British evangelicals, Rosman, *Evangelicals and Culture*, 10.

25 For the rise of millenarian movements in both Britain and the United States, see Harrison, *The Second Coming*, which focuses on the movement led by Joanna Southcott, which flourished in Britain during the first decade of the nineteenth century. For the American scene, see the older work by Whitney Cross, *The Burned-Over District*. Closer to home, McCulloch was troubled by the presence of what historian George Rawlyk has described as a highly successful New Light Baptist counter-offensive in Nova Scotia in the early nineteenth century. According to Rawlyk, the New Light preachers stressed "the central importance of the conversion experience, intense piety, ecstatic worship forms, Biblical literalism and the pure church ideal." See Rawlyk, *Ravished by the Spirit*, 92–3.

26 McCulloch, *Calvinism*, 202–3. There is an extensive literature on the conflict of Calvinism and revivalism, and the culture of the Enlightenment in America between 1790 and 1820. See, for example, the final chapter in May, *The Enlightenment in America*. More generally, the cultural problem has been traced to the tension between feeling and intellect. For a general statement of the problem, see McLoughlin, *Revivals, Awakenings, and Reform*, 119–20 for the new theological orientation. Marsden's *The Evangelical Mind*, 6, 58 traces the impact of the revival on Presbyterian groups in the United States. In recent years, interpretations of the Second Great Awakening have adopted a very r egative view of the culture and theology of this critical period. Douglas, in *The Feminization of American Culture*, has argued that evangelical theology in this period softened the demands of God, and euphemized the Calvinist theology. The result was a religion devoid of intellectual content. More recently, the historian James Turner has suggested that the evangelical's concern with morality brought God into the processes of the world, and thus paved the way for the culture of unbelief that arose after 1870. See *Without God, Without Creed*.

For a critique of this interpretation, and a more positive revision of the achievements of evangelicals during the Awakening, see Terry D. Bilhartz, *Urban Religion and the Second Great Awakening: Church and Society in Early National Baltimore* (Rutherford, 1986).

27 McCulloch, "A Lecture delivered at the Opening of the First Theological Class in the Pictou Academy," 204. The Presbyterian tradition of theological learning stressed, in the early nineteenth century, the completion of a four-year arts degree at a university, and a further three-year program of study to qualify as a minister. See Drummond and Bulloch, *The Church in Victorian Scotland,,* 243–5.

28 McCulloch, *The Nature and Uses of a Liberal Education,* 6–7, 12–13; McCulloch, "A Lecture," 204. For the evangelical insistence on utility, see Meacham, "The Evangelical Inheritance."

29 McCulloch, "A Lecture delivered at the Opening of the First Theological Class," 200.

30 On this point, see Davie, *The Democratic Intellect,* 11. For the impact of Common Sense in Canada, see McKillop, *A Disciplined Intelligence,* 24–6.

31 For the intellectual life of the Scottish universities in the eighteenth century, see the splendid account by Richard Sher, *Church and University in the Scottish Enlightenment.* Sher's principal argument revolves around the notion of "phases" of the Scottish Enlightenment. What he considers the major tendency in the Enlightenment was in fact a "Whig-Presbyterian Conservatism" represented by William Robertson, Hugh Blair, and Adam Ferguson. Although these men were "moderates," they were not deists or sceptics, and preserved the theological basis of moral philosophy. Sher argues that the "Common Sense Enlightenment" began about 1785, and saw moral philosophy emerge as a form of study less oriented to preaching and more heavily influenced by metaphysics, Newtonian science, and epistemology. See also the older account by Davie, *The Democratic Intellect.* The classic account of the succession of Common Sense philosophers was written by one of its last great practitioners – see James McCosh, *The Scottish Philosophy.* For a modern treatment of Scottish historical and social thought, see Burrow, *Evolution and Society.*

32 According to the recent study by Sher, the theological differences between the "moderate" party and the "popular" party in the period 1740–1780 have been generally overstated. The issues dividing them were church patronage and the role of polite learning in the preaching and life of the Scottish church. See *Church and University in the Scottish Enlightenment,* 57–9. However, theological and political differences became far more pronounced in the early nineteenth century.

33 For a discussion of the "moderate" theology, see Drummond and Bulloch, *The Scottish Church, 1688–1843,* 104-7.

34 McCulloch Papers, "The Prosperity of the Church in Troublous Times." For the "anti-moderate" position of Presbyterian missionaries in Canada, see Moir, *Enduring Witness*.

35 For the relationship of Chalmers to the Enlightenment, see the modern biography by Brown, *Thomas Chalmers*, 48, 165–6. A discussion of McCosh's views on the tensions between evangelicalism and earlier phases of eighteenth-century culture is presented in Hoeveler, *James McCosh*, 31. Chalmers's theological outlook is explored more fully in Rice, "An Attempt at Systematic Reconstruction in the Theology of Thomas Chalmers."

36 According to American commentators, Common Sense Realism had been transplanted into the American college setting as early as 1760. See, for example, Sloan, *The Scottish Enlightenment and the American College Ideal*; Sydney Ahlstrom, "The Scottish Philosophy and American Theology," *Church History* 24 (1955).

37 McKillop, *A Disciplined Intelligence*, 24–6.

38 Biographical details on Chalmers can be obtained from Brown, *Thomas Chalmers*, which accents his activities in social reform and missions, rather than his theology. See, for the theological implications, Rice, "An Attempt at Systematic Reconstruction," 176. The cultural battle involving evangelicals and Common Sense philosophers is assessed in Davie, *The Democratic Intellect*, 268–9, 286–7, 330.

39 Hoeveler, *James McCosh*, 53, 68. For the life of John Cairns, intellectual leader of the United Presbyterians, see MacEwen, *Life and Letters of John Cairns*. Writing to Sir William Hamilton, his old philosophy teacher, in 1848, Cairns declared: "Philosophy has been much to me, but it can never be all, never the most, and I have found the true good in another quarter – in the mysticism of the Bible – the mysticism of the conscious reconciliation and intimacy with the living persons of the Godhead." This is cited in Davie, *The Democratic Intellect*, 291. See also Brown, *Thomas Chalmers*, 165–6.

40 Hoeveler, *James McCosh*, 147–56.

41 For the agnostic implications of Hamilton's philosophy, see Hoeveler, *James McCosh*, and, more recently, Lightman, "Pope Huxley and the Church Agnostic," 150-63.

42 For Mansel's ideas and the influence of his extreme statement of the late Common Sense views of the relationship between religion and philosophy on the emerging views of scientific naturalism, see Lightman, "Pope Huxley and the Church Agnostic."

43 Rice, "An Attempt at Systematic Reconstruction," 179–83.

44 The phrase is Davie's. His final chapter of *The Democratic Intellect* offers a version of Scottish intellectual history intensely sympathetic to the program of Hamilton and his philosophical allies.

45 Masters, *Protestant Church Colleges in Canada*, 29, 81–2, and Nicholson,
"Michael Willis." The colonial situation was actually the reverse of
that in the metropolis. In Scotland, the Free Church contained only
one-third of the clergy and faithful; the Church of Scotland remained,
beyond doubt, the church of the people. In the Canadian provinces,
however, the Free Church comprised nearly two-thirds of the total
Presbyterian memebership. See Drummond and Bulloch, *The Church in
Victorian Scotland, 1843–1874*, 1–5, 11 and, for the Canadian scene,
Moir, *Enduring Witness*, 82, 105–6.

46 "German Preaching" [exchange paper], *The Ecclesiastical and Missionary
Record* [*E&MR*] (Toronto), 12, no. 6 (April 1856): 103. See also "Our
College Movement"[editorial], *The Presbyterian Witness*[*PW*] (Halifax)
(13 May 1848): 146; Omega, "On the Simple, Declarative Manner of
Apostolic Teaching," *Canada Christian Examiner and Presbyterian Review*
[*CCE&PR*] (Niagara), 1, no. 3 (May 1837): 65–70.

47 Lecture by the Rev. Dr Willis, "Introductory to the Studies of the Session," *E&MR*, 5, no. 2 (Dec. 1848): 17.

48 Willis, *Pulpit Discourses and College Addresses*, iv-v, 48. Born at Green-
ock in 1798, Willis graduated from the University of Glasgow with
high honours in Latin and Greek, entered the Seceder seminary, and
was called to the pulpit of Renfield Church, Glasgow, in 1821, where
he established himself, over the next two decades, as an active social
philanthropist and an uncompromising opponent of slavery. In 1835,
his personal balance of learning and forceful preaching, and his firm
devotion to the doctrines of Calvinism earned him the professorship
of theology at the Synod Divinity Hall, a position he held until 1839,
when he and his synod joined the Church of Scotland. At the time of
the Disruption of 1843, he followed Thomas Chalmers into the Free
Church. In 1844, Willis came to Canada as a Free Church deputy, and
in 1847, his reputation as a scholar ensured his call to the principalship of Knox College, a position he held until his retirement in 1870.
See, for the Scottish phase of Willis's career, Nicholson, "Michael Willis," *Presbyterian History* 17, no. 1 (June 1973).

49 "Opening of the Theological Hall of the Presbyterian Church of Nova
Scotia" [editorial], *PW* (11 Sept. 1848); the Rev. Professor King, "Inau-
gural Address delivered at the Opening of the Free Church College,
Nov. 2, 1848," *PW* (25 Nov. 1848): 370; "Knox's College: Opening of
Session," *E&MR*, 14, no. 1 (Nov. 1857): 3.

50 "On the Institution and Preparation of the Christian Ministry,"
CCE&PR, 1, no. 2 (April 1837): 41; Esson, *Statement Relative to the Educational System of Knox College*, 6; "Knox's College, The Opening,"
E&MR 4, no. 1 (Nov. 1847): 289; "Lecture by the Rev. Dr. Willis, Introductory to the Studies of the Session," *E&MR*, 5, no. 2 (Dec. 1848):

17. The curriculum of the Free Church College in Halifax was similar to that at Knox. See "Proceedings of the Synod of the Presbyterian Church of Nova-Scotia," *PW* (8 July 1848): 209–10; "Free Church College," *PW* (7 Oct. 1848): 314.

51 For the idealist influence in German religious thought, see Welch, *Protestant Thought in the Nineteenth Century*, vol. 1, 147–60; and Storr, *The Development of English Theology*, 167–70.

52 McCulloch, *The Nature and Uses of a Liberal Education*, 4; "A Lecture," 206; King, "Inaugural Address," 369. King's statement found an echo at Queen's University, the college of the Church of Scotland in Canada. There, the Rev. James George, the professor of philosophy, held that sin had deranged the nature of man, causing reason to work inharmoniously with the rest of his faculties. See George, "The Relation betwen Piety and Intellectual Labor. An Address Delivered at the Opening of the Fourteenth Session of Queen's College," cited in McKillop, *A Disciplined Intelligence*, 51.

53 "Knox's College, The Opening," *E&MR*, 4, no. 1 (Nov. 1847): 289.

54 See, for this attempt, Burns, *Life and Times of the Rev. Robert Burns*, 377–9. See, for the primacy of theology, McCulloch, "A Lecture," 200, 204.

55 McKillop, *A Disciplined Intelligence*, 44. Biographical details of Lyall's life have been drawn from this source.

56 Lyall, *The Philosophy of Thought*, 8–10.

57 Lyall, *Intellect, The Emotions, and The Moral Nature*, 3–4.

58 Ibid., 613–14.

59 "Opening of the Free Church College: Professor Lyall's Lecture," *PW* (6 Nov. 1858): 178.

60 Lyall, *The Philosophy of Thought*. "A Lecture delivered at the Opening of the Free Church College, Halifax, Nova Scotia, Session 1852–53, 8," cited in McKillop, *A Disciplined Intelligence*, 52.

61 Biographical details on George are provided by McKillop, *A Disciplined Intelligence*, 35–44.

62 According to Masters, the Church of Scotland believed in the union of arts and theology in a single institution, while the Free Church insisted on separate teaching. See *Protestant Church Colleges in Canada*, 37. For the foundation and early years of Queen's University, see Neatby, *Queen's University*.

63 George, *1 Cor. 1.23 – We Preach Christ Crucified –* a position that identified him as an adherent of the classically evangelical view of sin and redemption.

64 "University of Queen's College," *The Presbyterian* (Montreal) 7, no. 6 (June 1854): 83–4. See also "Queen's College, Annual General Examination," *The Presbyterian*, 1 no. 6 (June 1848): 77–8. See also "Address

of Principal Leitch at His Installation," *The Presbyterian* 13, no. 12 (Dec. 1860): 182–3.

65 Brown, *Thomas Chalmers*, 165–6.

66 "Review – *What Is Civilization?* A Lecture delivered in the City Hall, Kingston, by Rev. Professor James George, D.D. of Queen's College," *The Presbyterian* 12, no. 5 (May 1859): 78. This splendid statement has been curiously ignored by McKillop, who provides lengthy analysis of the other parts of the address.

67 "Suggestions for the Student," *The Ecclesiastical and Missionary Record of The Free Church of Nova Scotia* (Halifax) [*E&MR(N.S.)*] 3, no. 13 (Jan. 1855): 100. The earliest evidence of the use of Bacon's name in Canadian Methodist and Presbyterian colleges is found in an address by Thomas McCulloch. See McCulloch Papers, MG 1, vol. 552, no. 124, "Lecture on Philosophy," n.d.

68 There is an extensive literature on the cooperation of science and religion in the early Victorian period. See, for example, Young, "The Impact of Darwin on Conventional Thought," in Symondson, ed., *The Victorian Crisis of Faith*, 21; Cannon, *Science and Culture*, 2–3. For the American scene, see Daniels, *American Science in the Age of Jackson* and, for the Canadian aspect, Berger, *Science, God, and Nature*, lecture 1, and McKillop, *A Disciplined Intelligence*, chapter 3.

69 The emergence of Baconianism from the Common Sense philosophy has been discussed in the American context by Bozeman in *Protestants in an Age of Science*, and by Noll, "Common Sense Traditions and American Evangelical Thought." For the impact of the Baconian ideal in Britain, see Yeo, "An Idol of the Market-Place," 251–98. Noll insists, however, that Baconianism did not represent the entire Common Sense tradition. For Whewell and the Common Sense philosophers Reid and Stewart, see Yeo, "An Idol of the Market-Place," 261–73. Baden Powell, an influential High Anglican clergyman and Savilian professor of mathematics at Oxford, elaborated a philosophy of science on the basis of the Baconian principles enunciated by Dugald Stewart. See Corsi, *Science and Religion*.

70 For the impact of geological discoveries, see the older account by Gillispie, *Genesis and Geology*, which analyzes the possibility of conflict between Christian belief and uniformitarian geology. The effects of Chambers's work and its implications have been explored recently by Yeo, "Science and Intellectual Authority in Mid-Nineteenth Century Britain," 5–31. More general treatments of the problem of scientific discovery for Protestant Christians include Hovenkamp, *Science and Religion in America* and Heyck, "The Worlds of Science and the Universities" in Heyck, *The Transformation of Intellectual Life in Victorian England*.

71 Yeo, "An Idol of the Market-Place," 286–7.
72 McCulloch Papers, "Lecture on Philosophy."
73 "Review – *What Is Civilization?*" 76–7. See also "University of Queen's College," *The Presbyterian* 4, no. 6 (June 1851): 85–6; King, "Inaugural Address," 369.
74 McCulloch, *The Nature and Uses of a Liberal Education*, 16–18; "Lecture on Philosophy." See also "Suggestions for the Student," 99–101.
75 Jardine, *Outlines of Philosophical Education*. For the influence of Baconianism on the later Scottish philosphers, see Collini et al., *That Noble Science of Politics*, chapter 1.
76 For McCulloch's medical training and scientific interests, see *Life of Thomas McCulloch*, 7–9; McCulloch Papers, *Second Report of the Glasgow Society*, 14–15; ibid., MG 1, vol. 553, no. 7, McCulloch to the Rev. Mitchell, 29 May 1819; PANS, Records of the Pictou Academy, reel 1, "Memorial on Behalf of the Literary and Philosophical Institution."
77 This synopsis of Baconianism is drawn from Bozeman, *Protestants in an Age of Science*, xii-xiii, 3. For the broader impact of Baconian ideas, see Gauvreau, "Baconianism, Darwinism, Fundamentalism," 434–44.
78 Noll's seminal article provides a fresh perspective on the role of "Common Sense" in defining evangelical theology. His refined and subtle awareness of diverse strands within the Scottish intellectual heritage stands in marked contrast to the interpretations of the early nineteenth century advanced for the Canadian context by McKillop's *A Disciplined Intelligence* and for the United States by Marsden's *Fundamentalism and American Culture*.
79 Brown, *Thomas Chalmers*, 15.
80 For the Baconian inspiration of Chalmers's theology, see Rice, "An Attempt at Systematic Reconstruction." For the "taxonomic" emphasis of the inductive method, which limited reason to classification of given "facts," see Hovenkamp, *Science and Religion in America*, 24; and Bozeman, *Protestants in an Age of Science*, 159.
81 Knox's College, The Opening," *E&MR* 4, no. 1 (Nov. 1847): 289.
82 "New Theology" [*Nevins*], *PW* (25 Nov. 1848): 373. See also the Rev. Alexander Vinet, "Sermon," *The Monthly Record of the Church of Scotland in Nova Scotia and the Adjoining Provinces* (Halifax), [*MR*] 8, no. 11 (July 1861): 145–59.
83 "Knox's College – Opening of Session," *E&MR* 14, no. 1 (Nov. 1857): 3.
84 "Review," *E&MR* 7, no. 5 (March 1851): 76. See also "Suggestions for the Student."
85 "Knox's College – Opening of Session," 3; McCulloch, "A Lecture," in *Life of Thomas McCulloch*, 205–6.
86 "Theological College, Toronto – Prospectus of a Course of Lectures on

the Philosophy of the Human Mind, by Rev. Henry Esson, November 1845," *E&MR* 2, no. 12 (December 1845): 142.

87 This line of interpretation began with Leslie Stephen in the 1870s and has persisted in the work of E.P. Thompson in the 1960s. For a critique of this historiography, see Semmel, *The Methodist Revolution*, 3–22 and, more recently, Frederick Dreyer, "Faith and Experience in the Thought of John Wesley," *American Historical Review* 88, no. 1 (February 1983): 12–30.

88 There is no modern study of Canadian Methodism comparable to Moir's work, *Enduring Witness*, which provides a narrative history of Presbyterianism. Methodist political involvements have, however, been well documented in French, *Parsons and Politics* and Moir, *Church and State in Canada West*. Westfall's "Order and Experience" provides a welcome relief from politics and attempts a preliminary study of Methodist theology and its relation to the culture of Ontario in the early nineteenth century. The most complete modern study, though for a slightly later period of Methodist development, is Semple, "The Impact of Urbanization."

89 On Wesley's theology, the standard source remains Outler, ed., *John Wesley*. See vii, 28, 65, 93–4 for Wesley's concept of religious authority.

90 On the general context of the Methodist debate with the eighteenth century see Semmel, *The Methodist Revolution*. On Wesley's debt to Locke and Hume see Dreyer, "Faith and Experience."

91 "Experimental Religion Essential to a Minister of Christ," [Life of the Rev. Wm. Black, by the Rev. Matthew Richey, A.M., Principal of the Upper Canada Academy], *The Christian Guardian*, (Toronto) [*ChG*], 20 March 1839, 77; "Victoria College," [editorial], *ChG*, 10 May 1848, 118. This was an address given by Egerton Ryerson.

92 "Intellectual Religion and Religious Experience," [editorial], *ChG*, 5 July 1854, 152; "Victoria College," 118. For Wesley's emphasis on feeling tested by the authority of the Bible, see Dreyer, "Faith and Experience," 15–16.

93 "Education of the Ministry" [editorial], *ChG*, 5 Sept. 1855, 190; "Inaugural Address of the Rev. Egerton Ryerson, Principal of Victoria College," *ChG*, 13 July 1842, 149. According to Walter T. Brown, there were no Methodist universities in England to provide professors who might shape educational traditions in Canada. See his "Victoria and a Century of Education," in *On the Old Ontario Strand*, 115. For itinerancy and the hindrances it placed on the minister's ability to study, see Semple, "The Impact of Urbanization on the Methodist Church," 128, 132, 144.

94 Nelles Papers, "Religion and Learning," college address, 1857.

95 Nelles Papers, "Formation of Character," lecture, 18 Feb. 1854; ibid., "Address to Victoria College Students re: Love of Learning & Love of Goodness, Winter Session, 1854–55." For the ideas of Francis Wayland, see Meyer, *The Instructed Conscience*, chapter 2.

96 Nelles Papers, "Formation of Character"; ibid., "Address to Victoria College Students re: Love of Learning & Love of Goodness."

97 Details of Ryerson's life may be found in his autobiography, *The Story of My Life*.

98 The most complete account of Ryerson's life is Sissons, *Egerton Ryerson*. More recently, Ryerson's contribution to public education has been the subject of an extensive literature. See Prentice, *The School Promoters*, and McDonald and Chaiton, eds, *Egerton Ryerson and His Times*.

99 The best general description of the political and economic background is provided by J.M.S. Careless, *The Union of the Canadas, 1841–1857*. The 1840s also witnessed the attempt to found a system of common schools and a remarkable expansion of universities and church colleges. See Masters, *Protestant Church Colleges in Canada*.

100 Westfall, *Two Worlds*, chapter 3. For discussion of a similar process among American evangelicals, see Mathews, *Religion in the Old South*.

101 For the American background of the Millerites, see Cross, *The Burned-Over District*. The influence of this group on theological discussion in British North America is treated in Westfall, "The Sacred and the Secular," chapter 5. For the Methodist concern about the preachings and activities of this sect, see "The Last Day of Millerism – The Spiritual Reign of Christ," [*New York Observer*], *ChG*, 24 April 1844, 105; N. Levings, "A Caution to the Credulous, Who Are Exposed to the Delusions of Miller," [*N.Y. Christian Advocate and Journal*], *ChG*, 12 Oct. 1842, 201.

102 "Victoria College," 118; "Victoria College. Ceremony of Inauguration. Introductory Address of the Rev. Anson Green, President of the Conference – Inaugural Address of the Rev. Egerton Ryerson," *ChG*, 6 July 1842, 145.

103 Ryerson, "Inaugural Address on the Nature and Advantages of an English and Liberal Education ... June 21, 1842," cited in McKillop, *A Disciplined Intelligence*, 19. Although McKillop claims that "Moral Science was clearly fundamental to the idea of a liberal education as Ryerson conceived it," Ryerson himself only claimed that it should "constitute a leading feature in every system of sound education." Ryerson did not claim that it should be *the* leading feature.

104 For Wayland's ideas, and the place of *Elements of Moral Science* in nineteenth-century America, see Blau, "Introduction," in Wayland, *The Elements of Moral Science*. Ryerson's brother George had been a

classmate of Wayland's at Union College, and the connection be-
tween Ryerson and Wayland was close and personal. As late as 1871,
Ryerson, then chief superintendent of education, prepared a work
closely modelled on Wayland's text, entitled *First Lessons in Christian
Morals*, for use in the elementary schools of Ontario. See Ryerson,
The Story of My Life, 26, 431.

105 Ryerson, "Inaugural Address," quoted in McKillop, *A Disciplined Intelligence*, 20.

106 Pickard, *An Inaugural Address*, 10. For the early years of this Methodist institution, see Reid, *Mount Allison University*.

107 Nelles Papers, "Book of Random Thoughts, 1846–1849," "Philosophy," 9 Nov. 1848.

108 "Victoria College," 118; "Inaugural Address of Rev. Egerton Ryerson," 149.

109 Ryerson, "Inaugural Address," quoted in McKillop, *A Disciplined Intelligence*, 20. See also, M.N., "Theology. No.l," *ChG*, 10 Jan. 1838, 37;
"Theology. No.2," *ChG*, 17 Jan. 1838, 41.

110 Chiles, *Theological Transition in American Methodism*, 46–7, 88–93. In
1876 the minutes of the Toronto Methodist Conference listed Watson's *Institutes* as required reading in both second and third year of
the four year course of study for probationers. For Watson's influence on Ryerson's thought, see Fiorino, "The Moral Education," 59–
80.

111 See "Inaugural Address," quoted in McKillop, *A Disciplined Intelligence*, 20.

112 Nelles Papers, box 2, file 16, "Spirit of Inquiry, Address Delivered at
the First Annual Exhibition, Victoria College, 20 April 1843"; ibid.,
"Book of Random Thoughts, 1846–1849," "Mysteries," n.d.

113 "Science and Religion United," [*Zion's Herald*], *ChG*, 10 Dec. 1834, 17;
NDDR, "The Reasonableness of Christianity - Paper I. – On a Divine
Revelation," *ChG*, 14 Oct. 1835, 193. See also Nelles Papers, "Random Thoughts," entry for 13 Dec. 1859; "Book of Random Thoughts,
1846–1849," "Philosophy," n.d.

CHAPTER TWO

1 Ryerson, *The Story of My Life*, 56–7.

2 The study of the central role of the "historical" in nineteenth-century
culture is only beginning to receive attention from historians in Britain
and America. However, an excellent introduction is Heyck, *The Transformation of Intellectual Life in Victorian England*, chapter 5. Specific
studies include Jann, *The Art and Science of Victorian History*; Burrow, *A
Liberal Descent*; and, of more interest for the application of history to

the study of politics, Collini, Burrow, and Winch, *That Noble Science of Politics*, 183–205. American scholarship, more preoccupied with philosophical and scientific currents, has produced fewer general works on the relationship of history and culture in the early nineteenth century. See, however, a provocative article by Dorothy Ross, "Historical Consciousness in Nineteenth-Century America," *American Historical Review* 89, no. 4 (Oct. 1984): 909–15. To date, few Canadian scholars have participated in this rediscovery of the role of the "historical" and the historian in early Victorian culture. Berger's *The Writing of Canadian History* makes no reference to the period prior to 1870 – nor, more surprisingly, does McKillop's more synthetic intellectual history, *A Disciplined Intelligence*.

3 "The Reality of Evil" [*Treasury*], *E&MR(N.S.)* 5, no. 6 (June 1857): 41.

4 Berger, *Science, God, and Nature in Victorian Canada*, 31.

5 On the use of Paley in both Methodist and Presbyterian colleges, see McKillop, *A Disciplined Intelligence*, 63–4.

6 Mount Allison University Archives [MAUA], Charles Stewart Papers, 5/29(1), "Lectures by Rev. Thomas Jackson," n.d. This corresponds to the argument advanced by Neal Gillespie that "natural theology," in the sense of connection between religion and scientific practice, was a late addition to the classical tradition of natural theology. Gillespie also advances the provocative argument that the older "human" sense of natural theology was very compatible with "Baconian" or inductive forms of reasoning. See his "Natural History, Natural Theology, and Social Order," 2–3.

7 The relationship between reason, natural theology, and revelation so characteristic of the Enlightenment has been extensively treated by historians in Britain, America, and Canada. For the British scene, see the older account by Gillispie, *Genesis and Geology*, and more recently, the common context of religion and science has been explored by Cannon, *Science and Culture*; Young, "Natural Theology, Victorian Periodicals, and the Fragmentation of a Common Context," in Young, *Darwin's Metaphor*, Morrell and Thackray, *Gentlemen of Science*; Corsi, *Science and Religion*; and Livingstone, *Darwin's Forgotten Defenders*. For the American environment, see Hovenkamp, *Science and Religion in America* and Daniels, *American Science in the Age of Jackson*. The role of natural theology in the educational institutions and religious and scientific communities of English Canada has been extensively examined by McKillop, *A Disciplined Intelligence*, chapter 3, and more recently, by Berger, *Science, God, and Nature in Victorian Canada*.

8 See Hilton, *The Age of Atonement*, 4–5; Livingstone, *Darwin's Forgotten Defenders*, 4; Garland, *Cambridge Before Darwin*, 52–5. Garland describes Paley's *Principles of Moral and Political Philosophy* as "little more than a textbook on utilitarianism."

9 Livingstone, *Darwin's Forgotten Defenders*, 6–19; Desmond, *Archetypes and Ancestors*, chapter 1.

10 See Livingstone, *Darwin's Forgotten Defenders*, 8; Rice, "Natural Theology and the Scottish Philosophy," 22–46; Hoeveler, *James McCosh*, chapter 6.

11 See Hilton, *The Age of Atonement*, 170–1. According to Hilton, there were only seven editions of Paley's *Natural Theology* published after 1830.

12 Ibid., 165.

13 Pickard, *An Inaugural Address*, 5.

14 Butler, *Analogy of Religion*, 112–13, 200.

15 Ibid., 174–5.

16 Ibid., 186.

17 For Chalmers's scientific interests and promotion of natural theology, see Brown, *Thomas Chalmers and the Godly Commonwealth*, and Rice, "Natural Theology and the Scottish Theology."

18 Chalmers, *On Natural Theology*, vol. 2, 397, quoted in Rice, "Natural Theology and the Scottish Philosophy," 38.

19 Rice, "Natural Theology and the Scottish Philosophy," 43.

20 On this point, see Drummond and Bulloch, *The Scottish Church, 1688–1843*, 107.

21 The nature, assumptions, and methods of eighteenth-century Scottish inquiry have been treated by Burrow, *Evolution and Society*, chapters 1 and 2, and more recently by Donald Winch, "The system of the North: Dugald Stewart and his pupils," in Collini et al., *That Noble Science of Politics*, 25–61. A similar point is made by Sher in his study of the Whig-Presbyterian clergymen of the Edinburgh Enlightenment. Men such as William Robertson and Adam Ferguson wrote treatises on history and moral philosophy, not on science or natural theology. See *Church and University in the Scottish Enlightenment*. For the English emphasis on understanding the world of nature in the late eighteenth and early nineteenth centuries, see Cannon, *Science and Culture*; Gillispie, *Genesis and Geology*; and Burns, *The Great Debate on Miracles*, chapter 1.

22 "The Reality of Evil," 41; "Review. Evidences of Revealed Religion, by a Number of the Ministers of Glasgow. Lecture I. The Necessity of a Divine Revelation, and the Obligation and Responsibility of Examining Its Claims," *CCE&PR* 2, no. 9 (Sept. 1838): 257–61.

23 "Insufficiency of the Light of Nature," [Hooker], *CCE&PR* 2, no. 9 (Sept. 1838): 283–84.

24 "Victoria College" [editorial], *ChG*, 10 May 1848, 118; "Reviews – Butler's Analogy," *E&MR* 9, no. 1 (Nov. 1852): 11.

25 "Original Review – Theological Notices," *PW* (14 Dec. 1850): 394. This was a review of James McCosh's *Method of the Divine Government*,

Physical and Moral. McCosh, a disciple of Chalmers, tried to integrate evangelical theology and the Scottish philosophy. See also McCosh, *The Scottish Philosophy*, 393–9. McKillop noticed the difference in emphasis between natural theology and the Scottish Common Sense tradition. His awareness of the tensions, however, did not deflect him from his argument of the central importance of natural theology to Anglo-Canadian culture, nor did it induce him to explore the differences between Presbyterian and Methodist colleges and the Anglican colleges. See *A Disciplined Intelligence*, 87–8. For the mechanistic implications of natural theology, and the relationship of that theology to Darwin's evolutionary hypothesis, see Moore, *The Post-Darwinian Controversies*, 307–40.

26 "The Decision of Natural Religion," [*Sherlock's Sermons*], *ChG*, 21 Nov. 1829, 1. See also the Rev. Egerton Ryerson, "Inaugural Address on the Nature and Advantages of an English and Liberal Education," quoted in McKillop, *A Disciplined Intelligence*, 62.

27 Ryerson, "Inaugural Address," 17.

28 Ryerson, *The Story of My Life*, 298.

29 For this tension, see Fiorino, "The Moral Education of Egerton Ryerson's Idea of Education," in McDonald and Chaiton, eds, *Egerton Ryerson and His Times*, 59–80.

30 See Wayland, *Elements of Moral Science*, xli.

31 Ibid., 122–5.

32 "The Moral and Religious State of England at the Period of the Rise of Methodism," [*Edinburgh Review*], *ChG*, 6 Mar. 1839, 69. Among Canadian cultural historians, only William Westfall has recognized that the approaches to natural theology adopted by the Church of England in the colonies and by the evangelical churches were essentially different. See Westfall, "Order and Experience."

33 Ryerson, "Inaugural Address," quoted in McKillop, *A Disciplined Intelligence*, 62.

34 Nelles Papers, box 5, file 95, "Atonement of Christ Viewed as a Declaration of God's Righteousness," sermon, April 1851. See also ibid., "Random Thoughts and Mental Records," entry for 25 Oct. 1848 and "Random Thoughts and Mental Records," vol. 2, entry for 14 Feb. 1849. Examples of earlier Methodist comments on the superiority of revelation include: "The Gain of Exchanging *Revealed* for *Natural* Religion, or Christianity for Infidelity," [*Watson's Apology for Christianity*], *ChG*, 25 Sept. 1830, 353; Iota, "Religion and Science," *ChG*, 15 Nov. 1837, 3.

35 Marsden, *Fundamentalism and American Culture*, 14, 20. For Thornwell, Hodge, and the ideas of "Old School" Presbyterianism, see Bozeman, *Protestants in an Age of Science*, 138. For the more general impact of these ideas, see Hovenkamp, *Science and Religion in America*, 10–11,

and Holifield, *The Gentleman Theologians*. For the commitment of British clergymen and scientists to the unity of religious, moral, and scientific knowledge, see Young, "The Impact of Darwin on Conventional Thought," 21; Cannon, *Science and Culture*, 2–3.

36 In its most uncritical form, this view has been advanced in the recent study by Zeller, *Inventing Canada*, 147–9. Zeller attempts to prove that Egerton Ryerson, in particular, viewed "science" as a "cultural adhesive." If Ryerson's tenure as president of Victoria College is any indication, by "science" he meant the Baconian method applied to a variety of branches of knowledge, an emphasis pointing to the primacy of morality and religion, not science, in college education. His original curriculum did not mention natural philosophy. Wood's recent study, "Thomas McCulloch's Use of Science," more correctly insists that McCulloch was interested in encouraging among his students a habit of mind, not in promoting natural history per se.

37 The role of evangelical clergymen in the creation of English-Canadian society and institutions has received little attention from Canadian historians preoccupied with the growth of a political system. Masters's *Protestant Church Colleges in Canada* and McKillop's *A Disciplined Intelligence* testify to their importance in founding a system of higher education. For a specific study of Egerton Ryerson's part in the creation of social institutions, see Prentice, *The School Promoters*. The American literature on the role of evangelicals in the movements of mid-nineteenth-century reform is both rich and extensive. See, for example, Smith, *Revivalism and Social Reform* McLoughlin, *Revivals, Awakenings, and Reform*, and, for a survey of the literature of the relationship between evangelical religion and social reform, Smith, "Righteousness and Hope: Christian Holiness and the Millennial Vision in America, 1800–1900," *American Quarterly* 31, no. 1 (spring 1979): 22–45.

38 For Beaven and Bovell, see McKillop, *A Disciplined Intelligence*, 65–85. For the ideas of Sir William Dawson, see ibid., 99–100, and Berger, *Science, God, and Nature*, 39–40, 45–6.

39 For the popular culture of the study of natural history in Canada, see Berger, *Science, God, and Nature*, lectures 1 and 2. Significantly, Berger scarcely mentions Methodist and Presbyterian clergymen in this book.

40 The Rev. James Narraway, "An Address delivered at the Anniversary of Mount Allison Wesleyan Academy, June 4, 1856," *Mount Allison Academic Gazette* 2, no. 2 (June 1856): 6–7.

41 See the splendid study by Porter, *Edward Gibbon: Making History*, 17–20 for the religious uses of history in Georgian England.

42 For a general account of the cultural importance of history in Victorian England, see Heyck, *The Transformation of Intellectual Life in Victorian England*, chapter 5. For the American scene, see Ross, "Historical Con-

sciousness in Nineteenth Century America." The growing popularity of "anthropology" has been studied by Burrow, *Evolution and Society*, and, more recently, by Stocking, *Victorian Anthropology*. Facets of the popular interest in ancient peoples have been explored by Jenkyns, *The Victorians and Ancient Greece*.

43 My interpretation on this point diverges from the prevailing orientation of British and American scholarship. Chadwick's magisterial *The Secularization of the European Mind* includes the rise of historical study as one of the most important intellectual forces working for secularization. He acknowledges, however, the more ambiguous nature of the relationship by arguing that "the historical revolution was not so upsetting for religion as the scientific revolution; for the very reason that it often brought with it more understanding of the nature of religion." (226). Chadwick's work provides, however, no discussion of the evangelical movement, and is based on the idea of opposition, rather than of context.

44 Both evangelicalism and the rise of history have been recognized by historians as facets of the "romantic" movement in religious thought. For the religious implications of "romanticism," see Sydney Ahlstrom, "The Romantic Religious Revolution and the Dilemmas of Religious History," *Church History* 46 (1977): 149–70; Reardon, *From Coleridge to Gore*, introduction. American historians have to a greater degree acknowledged the cultural transformation occasioned by the evangelical Awakening in the early nineteenth century. According to James Turner, evangelicalism was the key to a "moralization" of Christian belief that occurred between 1790 and 1850. See his recent *Without God, Without Creed*, 73–113. See also Douglas, *The Feminization of American Culture*. Historians of the older English-speaking societies tend to separate "evangelicalism" and "the historical" by focusing on the challenge and opposition posed by history to "orthodox" Christian belief.

45 Heyck, *The Transformation of Intellectual Life*, 124. See also "All that glitters: political science and the lessons of history," in Collini et al., *That Noble Science of Politics*, 183–205. On the concept of Victorian history as art and science, see the recent work by Jann, *The Art and Science of Victorian History*, introduction, and her discussion of Thomas Arnold and Thomas Carlyle. On the writing of "Whig" history by Macaulay and Froude, see Burrow, *A Liberal Descent*.

46 "Victoria College. Ceremony of Inauguration – Inaugural Address of the Rev. Egerton Ryerson, Principal of the College," *ChG*, 6 July 1842, 145.

47 Dr Burns, "Church History, Concluding Address, 17th April, 1850," *E&MR* 6, no. 8 (June 1850): 115.

48 The Rev. Henry Esson of Knox College explicitly identified history

with moral philosophy. See Esson, *Statement Relative to the Educational Affairs of Knox College*, 11. See also "Opening of the Free Church College, Halifax," *E&MR(N.S.)* 3, no. 23 (Nov. 1855): 179; Nelles Papers, "History," n.d.

49 "Speech of the Hon. the Speaker of the House of Assembly of Upper Canada at the York Auxiliary Bible Society," *ChG*, 3 April 1830, 153. See also "Power and Success of Christianity, a Proof of Its Divine Origin"[Massillon], *ChG*, 21 Nov. 1829, 1; The Rev. Professor Willis, "Knox's College – Opening of Session," *E&MR* (Nov. 1857): 3.

50 The enduring idea of the Bible as "sacred" history has been analyzed by Richardson in *History Sacred and Profane*, 23–5. For the views of British evangelicals concerning the relationship of sacred and secular in historical study, see Rosman, *Evangelicals and Culture*, 228–9.

51 The best analysis of this tradition of commentary and interpretation is provided by Frei, *The Eclipse of Biblical Narrative*, 1–2. On the "literal" reading of the Bible in Christian culture, see the splendid essay by Auerbach, "'Figura,'" in Auerbach, *Scenes from the Drama of European Literature*, 50–3.

52 Chadwick, *The Secularization of the European Mind*, 191.

53 The arrival of idealism in America has been treated by Kuklick, *Churchmen and Philosophers*, 119–43. For the impact of German thought on the British religious scene, see Reardon, *From Coleridge to Gore*, introduction.

54 For the underlying ideas of "historicism," see Iggers, *The German Conception of History*, 7–13. The ideas of de Wette have been discussed in Rogerson, *Old Testament Criticism in the Nineteenth Century*. Ranke's ideas concerning historical study have been explored in Iggers, *The German Conception of History*, chapter 4. For a modern assessment of Strauss, see Welch, *Protestant Thought in the Nineteenth Century*, vol. 1, 147–60.

55 For the "Liberal Anglican" historians, see Forbes, *The Liberal Anglican Idea of History*. For the ideas of Bushnell and Smith, see Kuklick, *Churchmen and Philosophers*, 191–2; Marsden, *The Evangelical Mind*, 159–74. On the criticism of Baconianism among the Anglican "Broad Church" school, see Cannon, "Humboldtian Science," in *Science and Culture*, 104.

56 For the impact of "romanticism" on the religion of the English-speaking world, see Ahlstrom, "The Romantic Religious Revolution and the Dilemmas of Religious History," 149–70. For the German influence on British historians, see Burrow, *A Liberal Descent*. For Parkman and the American "romantic" school of history, see Levin, *History as Romantic Art*. Ross has recently argued in "Historical Consciousness in Nineteenth Century America" for a more limited acceptance of "histori-

cism" by the great "romantics" like Bancroft. Adhering to the Christian and republican imperatives of the culture, they presented history as only partially self-explanatory, and retained elements of the Christian theology of history.

57 For Hodge's defence of Calvinism based on the tenets of Common Sense, see Bozeman, *Protestants in an Age of Science.*

58 Charles Stewart Papers, "Lectures of Rev. Thomas Jackson."

59 H.F. Bland Papers, box 2, file 29, no. 44, "The Word of Truth," sermon, 14 Jan. 1844.

60 Rogerson, *Old Testament Criticism*, 27, 28–9, 34–5.

61 "Knox's College – Opening of Session," *E&MR* 6, no. 1 (Nov. 1849): 2. See also "Notice of Hengstenberg on the Revelation," *E&MR* 8, no. 12 (Oct. 1852): 184.

62 "Knox's College – Opening of Session," *E&MR*, 14, no. 1 (Nov. 1857): 2–4. See also "The Modern Tactics of Infidelity," *E&MR* 12, no. 3 (Jan. 1856): 42–3; "Selection – The Field and the Men for It – An Address delivered at the Close of the Session to the Divinity Students of Queen's College, and now Published at Their Request. By Professor George, D.D.," *The Presbyterian* 13, no. 6 (June 1860): 89–93.

63 Carman Papers, box 23, file 3, "All Scripture is given by inspiration of God," sermon, n.d.

64 McCulloch, "A Lecture delivered at the Opening of the First Theological Class," in *Life of Thomas McCulloch*, 207–8.

65 For a definition and discussion of "textual" criticism, see Dillenberger and Welch, *Protestant Christianity Interpreted*, 189–90.

66 Horne, *An Introduction to the Critical Study and Knowledge of the Holy Scriptures*. For a modern analysis of Horne, see Rogerson, *Old Testament Criticism* 182–4. At Queen's College in 1848, Horne's text was listed as one of the examination in requirements for graduation in Arts. See "Queen's College, Annual General Examination," *The Presbyterian* 1, no. 6 (June 1848): 77–8. In his unpublished autobiography, Chancellor Nathanael Burwash of Victoria College recalled that the reading of Horne was essential for Methodist probationers in the 1850s and 1860s. Burwash Papers, "Life and Labors of Nathanael Burwash," n.d.

67 McCulloch, "A Lecture," in *Life of Thomas McCulloch*.

68 "Lecture by the Rev. Dr. Willis, Introductory to the Studies of the Session," *E&MR* 5, no. 2 (Dec. 1848): 18; "Knox's College – Close of the Session of 1851–52" [editorial], *E&MR* 8, no. 7 (May 1852): 105. For similar expressions of Canadian Methodist opinion, see the address by Egerton Ryerson, "Victoria College," *ChG*, 10 May 1848, 118.

69 Strauss, *Life of Jesus.* For the English reception of Strauss's ideas, see Chadwick, *The Victorian Church*, part 1, 530–1.

70 H.F. Bland Papers, "The Word of Truth."

71 Butler, *Analogy*, 273–4.

72 Ibid., 184–5.

73 Butler, *Analogy*, 236. For the background of the eighteenth-century debate, see Burns, *The Great Debate on Miracles*.

74 McCulloch Papers, MG 1, vol. 555, no. 2, "Preface to a Work on Calvinism and the Fallen Man." Examples of this stricture abound in evangelical literature. See especially NDDR, "The Reasonableness of Christianity – Paper I," *ChG*, 14 Oct. 1835, 193; H.F. Bland Papers, box 2, file 59, no. 74, "Moses and the Prophets, or Sufficiency of the Gospel," sermon, 20 Aug. 1859; "Plenary Inspiration" [*Edinburgh Review*], PW, 13 April 1850, 113; "Selection – Divine Inspiration of the Scriptures" [*Pollok's Dissertation on Prophetic Language*], *The Presbyterian* 11, no. 9 (Sept. 1858): 51–2.

75 For Hodge, see Bozeman, *Protestants in an Age of Science*. For a more general interpretation of the transatlantic aspect of this movement, see Sandeen, *The Roots of Fundamentalism*, 105–6. The link between Fundamentalism, Common Sense, and millenarianism has been argued most perceptively by Marsden, *Fundamentalism and American Culture*, 43–62.

76 Esson, *Statement Relative to the Educational System of Knox College*, 6. See also "Notice of Books – *The Plenary Inspiration of the Holy Scriptures*, by S.R.L. Gaussen, Professor of Theology in Geneva, Switzerland," *The Presbyterian* 7, no. 4 (April 1854): 60–1. Though the issue was less discussed by Methodists, they clearly drew their ideas on the subject from John Wesley, who believed in the literal truth and infallibility of the Bible, and, in a more sustained form, from Richard Watson's theological works. See Outler, *John Wesley*, 28, 65; and Chiles, *Theological Transition in American Methodism*, 46–7.

CHAPTER THREE

1 H.F. Bland Papers, box 5, file 236, no. 331, "The Lord Reigneth," sermon, n.d.

2 Details concerning Henry Bland's life are provided in "Henry Flesher Bland," UCCA, biographical files. His activities before his arrival in Canada, particularly his role in forming a local mechanics' institute, are mentioned in a number of his sermons and addresses, for example, H.F. Bland Papers, box 5, file 266, "An Address delivered in the Primitive Methodist Chapel, Irkley, on the Opening of the Mechanics Institute," 3 June 1844; ibid., box 5, file 262, "Address *re* Repeal of Corn Laws, 1841."

3 The work of Egerton Ryerson stands as a partial exception to this general statement. True, Ryerson wrote no church history, but his two-

volume work, *The Loyalists of America and their Times* places the Loyalists within a "providential" structure of history that Ryerson derived
from his evangelical convictions.

4 This process has been described by Eric Hobsbawm as the "invention
of tradition," which he sees at work in many parts of Europe in the
nineteenth century. See his essay, "Introduction: Inventing Traditions," in Hobsbawm and Ranger, eds, *The Invention of Tradition*, 1–14.

5 Nelles Papers, "Random Thoughts," "History," entry for 13 Aug.
1850.

6 For the rise of these ideas in the late eighteenth century, see Pollard,
The Idea of Progress. A more complete account of the British scene can
be gained from Burrow, *Evolution and Society*, and the recent work by
Stocking, *Victorian Anthropology*.

7 For studies of the Christian interpretation of history, see Richardson,
History Sacred and Profane and Gay, *A Loss of Mastery*. For this sum-
mary I am indebted to the splendid and succinct discussion in Cohen,
The Revolutionary Histories, 23–53.

8 See Gay, *A Loss of Mastery*, 9–10. The importance of John Foxe's work
in shaping the idea of popular nationalism in England has been assessed by Haller in *Foxe's Book of Martyrs*.

9 See Fussner, *The Historical Revolution*. This tradition later gave rise to
the political and constitutional polemics of the period following 1688,
and to the "impartial" objectives of the eighteenth-century historians
David Hume, William Robertson, and Edward Gibbon. This tradition
of secular historical writing culminated with the nineteenth-century
"Whig" historians Macaulay, Stubbs, Freeman, and Froude. For the
Whigs, see Burrow, *A Liberal Descent*.

10 See Gay, *A Loss of Mastery*, and Cohen, *The Revolutionary Histories*, 23–
53.

11 For the Scottish economists and their idea of "conjectural history," see
Burrow, *Evolution and Society* and, more recently, Stocking, *Victorian
Anthropology*, 14–16. For Condorcet and his nineteenth-century succes-
sors, Auguste Comte and the French positivists, see Manuel, *The
Prophets of Paris*.

12 For a discussion of the themes of early Victorian historical writing in
English Canada, see Taylor, "The Writing of English Canadian History
in the Nineteenth Century." The separation of theology and history in
late eighteenth century America has been discussed by Cohen in *The
Revolutionary Histories*, 48–53. Cohen in particular notes that the term
"providence," although still employed, had been stripped of any overt
theological meaning, and was used as a metaphor to refer to causes
that could not be immediately explained. Christie, in "Prophecy and
'The Principles of Social Life'," has discerned a similar process in late
nineteenth-century historical writing in English Canada.

13 Heyck in *The Transformation of Intellectual Life in Victorian England,*
chapter 5 has recently questioned the commitment of the early Victorian historians to "scientific" history, which implies research in original documents. He argues that the common practice was to read
available secondary works and published collections of documents,
and to rely on the "imagination" to supply narrative power in historical writing.

14 For the limitations of the historical sense among British evangelicals,
see Rosman, *Evangelicals and Culture,* 228–9.

15 On the role of the "man of letters" in early Victorian culture, see
Heyck, *The Transformation of Intellectual Life in Victorian England,* "The
World of the Men of Letters." In the Canadian context, Christie has
coined the term "cultural mediator" to describe a group of popular
historians who wrote narrative history in the late nineteenth century.
See "Prophecy and the 'Principles of Social Life'," introduction. Although evangelical clergymen were members of one of the traditional
professions, they, too, occupied a similar position in culture through
the act of preaching.

16 Dr Burns, "'Introductory Lecture on Church History,' read in the Di-
vinity Hall of Knox's College, on Thursday, 3 November 1848," *E&MR*
5, no. 3 (Jan. 1849): 33. A similar definition was provided by Principal
King of Presbyterian College, Halifax. See "Opening of the Free
Church College, Halifax," *E&MR (N.S.),* 3, no. 23 (Nov. 1855): 179.
For biographical details on Burns see Burns, *The Life and Times of the
Rev. Robert Burns.*

17 Burns, "Introductory Lecture on Church History," 35.

18 McCulloch, "A Lecture," in *Life of Thomas McCulloch,* 212–14. See also
Dr Willis, "Lecture by Dr. Willis, Introductory to the Studies of the
Session," *E&MR* 5, no. 2 (Dec. 1848): 17; "Knox's College – Close of
the Studies of the Session of 1851–52" [editorial], *E&MR* 8, no. 7 (May
1852): 105.

19 Nelles Papers, "History," n.d.

20 See "The Christian Philosophy of History" [*N.Y. Methodist Quarterly*],
ChG, 14 Sept. 1842, 185; "Reviews – Bede's Ecclesiastical History of
England," *The Presbyterian,* 1, no. 10 (1848): 165; Nelles Papers, box 5,
file 74, "Providence – Narrative of Joseph," sermon, Toronto,
Dec. 1848. For the "moral" and "spiritual" emphases of Victorian his-
torical writing, see Jann, *The Art and Science of Victorian History,* xiii.

21 Nelles Papers, box 5, file 74, "Providence – Narrative of Joseph," sermon, Toronto, Dec. 1848.

22 Ryerson, "'Outlines of Lectures on the Mosaic History,' delivered on
Sabbath Mornings to the Students of Victoria College, By the Princi-
pal, Lecture III, Original Language of Mankind – Origins of Nations,"
ChG, 15 Nov. 1843, 13; Ryerson, "The Bible – Its Worth – Divisions –

Authenticity of the Writings of Moses – His Sources of Information,"
ChG, 27 Sept. 1843, 193.

23 This interpretation has been recently advanced by Stocking in *Victorian Anthropology*. See his discussion (43–4) on the re-emphasis on the
biblical account of human societies in early Victorian social thought,
which, he argues, involved a fundamental discontinuity between the
progressive views of the eighteenth century and post-Darwinian views
of man and society.

24 See Hovenkamp, *Science and Religion in America*, 149–50, 159–63. On
the scientific theory of "polygenism," see Gould, *The Mismeasure of
Man*, 30–72.

25 See Burrow, *Evolution and Society*, 115–17.

26 See Rogerson, *Old Testament Criticism*, 189–90. The most complete
statement of the sources of "Liberal Anglicanism" and its historical
and religious outlook can be found in Forbes, *The Liberal Anglican Idea
of History*. More recently, Jann's *The Art and Science of Victorian History*
has provided an assessment of the ideas and contribution of Thomas
Arnold to the culture of historical writing in early Victorian England.

27 The Rev. John M. Brooke, "Annual Address delivered before the
Members of the Fredericton Athenaeum, Feb. 23, 1857," *The Monthly
Record of the Church of Scotland in Nova Scotia and the Adjoining Provinces*.

28 Ryerson, "The Bible – Lecture II," 1; Burns Papers, box 4, "'Scripture'Lectures," 1857.

29 "Revivals illustriously Display the Glory of God" [editorial], *PW*, 6
Oct. 1849, 316.

30 The role of dispensational views of history in the shaping of varieties
of American Protestantism has been addressed by Marsden, *Fundamentalism and American Culture*, 48–62; Weber, *Living in the Shadow of
the Second Coming*, 13–42.

31 Burns Papers, "'Scripture' Lectures," 1857.

32 See my discussion of this tradition in chapter 2. For an analysis of this
prevalent method of "realistic" or "literal" interpretation, see Auerbach, "'Figura'," 50–3.

33 See "The Christian Philosophy of History," 185; "Lectures on the Mos-
aic History" [editorial], *ChG*, 20 Sept. 1843, 190; Ryerson, "The Bible –
Lecture II," *ChG*, 25 Oct. 1843, 1; Nelles Papers, "History," n.d. For
Horne, see *An Introduction to the Critical Study and Knowledge*, 655–71.

34 "Lectures on the Mosaic History," 190; Ryerson, "The Bible – Lecture
II," 1.

35 Nelles Papers, "Book of Random Thoughts on Speech," "Query?" entry for 12 Aug. 1849.

36 Young, *Miscellaneous Discourses and Expositions*, 10, 176, 217–30, 321.
Further biographical details on Young may be found in "George Paxton Young," UCCA, biographical files.

37 For a study of this current in its American context, see Davidson, *The Logic of Millennial Thought*, and the splendid study by Hatch, *The Sacred Cause of Liberty*. Through a study of Revolutionary War sermons, Hatch presents the view that such biblical images and concepts formed a principal intellectual basis of the American republican ideology.

38 The Rev. John M. Brooke, "Annual Address," 74; E.S.H., "The 70 Weeks, Danl. 9c 24–27v" [letter], *The Presbyterian* 3, no. 7 (July 1850): 101–102.

39 Butler, *Analogy of Religion*, 242.

40 For an analysis of the difficulties that uniformitarianism caused for British religious and scientific opinion in the decade before 1860, see Gillispie, *Genesis and Geology*.

41 For Bunsen's life and biblical studies, see Rogerson, *Old Testament Criticism*, 121–129.

42 The phrase is employed by Stocking, in *Victorian Anthropology*, to encapsulate the far-reaching implications of ethnological researches and the "history of civilization" in the 1850s. See 69–74.

43 For the importance of Bunsen and Muller in this movement, see Stocking, *Victorian Anthropology*, 56–77. Chapter 4 of Stocking's work provides an analysis of the "scientific" study of human civilization in the 1850s, in which the key figures were Sir Henry Maine and Herbert Spencer. For an assessment of these key Victorian thinkers, see the older account by Burrow, *Evolution and Society*.

44 Burns Papers, box 4, "Scripture Lectures, 1857." See also McLaren, *The Unity of the Human Race*.

45 See for example, the Rev. M. Harvey, "The Monuments of Egypt as illustrative of Scripture. Introductory Lecture delivered in Free St. Andrew's Church, on the 11th January, 1855," *PW*, 17 Feb. 1855, 25, and continued, *PW*, 24 Feb. 1855, 29. See also "Augmented Evidence for the Truth of the Bible" [*Lamp and Lantern, by Dr. James Hamilton*], *E&MR* 10, no. 1 (Nov. 1853): 14.

46 "Babylonian Discoveries" [editorial], *PW*, 3 June 1854, 86.

47 Burns Papers, box 4, "Standpoints in Church History," 19 Oct. 1859.

48 For the influence of Foxe's *Book of Martyrs*, see Haller, *Foxe's Book of Martyrs*. For the persistence of the theme of Protestant "purity" against papal "corruption" in seventeenth-century England, see Christianson, *Reformers and Babylon*. In Scotland there was a popular tradition of "church history," based on the work of Thomas Wodrow in the seventeenth century, which similarly emphasized the virtue of Protestantism and the corruption of Catholicism. See Drummond and Bulloch, *The Scottish Church*.

49 See the succinct and stimulating essay by Gay, *A Loss of Mastery*, 3–25.

50 See the discussion in Norman, *Anti-Catholicism in Victorian England*.

51 For the religio-political conflict in Canada in the 1850s, see Careless, *The Union of the Canadas*, chapters 10 and 11. The Protestant response has been treated in Miller, "Anti-Catholic Thought in Canada," *The Canadian Historical Review* 66, no. 4 (Dec. 1985).

52 "The Voice of History," *ChG*, 4 Aug. 1858, 173; "Advantages of Religion to Society" [editorial], *ChG*, 16 July 1834, 142.

53 The equation of Protestantism and liberty, and Catholicism and national decay was one of the important concepts characterizing British "Whig" history of the period 1800–1880. For an analysis and discussion, see Burrow, *A Liberal Descent*. Francis Parkman and his American contemporaries J.H. Motley and W.H. Prescott have been treated by Levin in *History as Romantic Art*.

54 "Opening of the Free Church College, Halifax," *E&MR(N.S.)* 3, no. 23 (Nov. 1855): 179. See also Burns, *The Life and Times of the Rev. Robert Burns*, 256; Burns Papers, box 4, "Popery," 6 Mar. 1865. The debate over episcopacy and apostolic succession was a perennial concern of the evangelical press. See, for example, "The Equality and Identity of Bishops and Presbyters in the Primitive Church," *E&MR* 10, no. 1 (Nov. 1853): 14; "Review," *MR* 1, no. 1 (Jan. 1855): 10. For Methodist opinion on this issue, see "The Fabulous Apostolical Succession – No. 1"[*English Wesleyan Methodist Magazine*], *ChG*, 6 Oct. 1841, 197; "Apostolic Succession"[*N.Y. Observer*], *ChG*, 28 May 1856, 133.

55 See Burns Papers, box 4, "Popery"; Burns, "Introductory Lecture on Church History," 34. For the use of Mosheim among Methodists and Presbyterians, see Burns Papers, box 4, "'Scripture' Lectures"; Carman Papers, "University Lecture Notes," n.d., "Mosheim's Church History."

56 For this debate and the Protestant response, see Chadwick, *From Bossuet to Newman*; Gay, *A Loss of Mastery*, 11–12.

57 See McCulloch, *Popery Condemned*, v, 13–45, 134–35, 137, 144. See also McCulloch Papers, MG 1, vol. 555, no. 3, "A handwritten work on the early church and church organization," n.d. See also "Past History of Presbyterianism" [editorial], *PW*, 14 April 1849, 116; "The Presbytery Proved from Scripture," [*Irish Tracts in Presbyterianism*], *E&MR* 15, no. 6 (April 1859): 89.

58 Watson, "The Origin of the Methodist Church," *ChG*, 9 July 1856, 157.

59 McCulloch Papers, MG 1, vol. 555, "A Written Work on the Early Church and Church Organization," n.d.; McCulloch, *Popery Condemned*, 144; "Primitive Christianity Existing and Propagated in the Dark Ages," *ChG*, 27 Feb. 1833, 61. Attempts to explain the cycle of decline had begun as early as the sixteenth century with the publication of Foxe's *Book of Martyrs*.

60 Watson, "The Origins of the Methodist Church," 157.

61 Examples of this growing body of literature are too numerous to cite. See, however, the important works by Tuveson, *Redeemer Nation*, and Hatch, *The Sacred Cause of Liberty*. For a more critical assessment of the literature, see the review article by Smith, "Righteousness and Hope," 21–45 for an exploration of recent works on the links between the the-ology of millennialism, social reform, nationalism, and politics in nineteenth-century America. Canadian historians have been most re-luctant to explore this powerful and fertile strand of ideas. To date, the most complete exploration remains the initial path-breaking work by Westfall, "The Sacred and the Secular," chapter 5.

62 For a discussion of the beliefs of these popular movements from the early Middle Ages to the seventeenth century, see Cohn, *The Pursuit of the Millennium*, xiii-xiv.

63 The followers of Joanna Southcott are discussed in Harrison's excel-lent work, *The Second Coming*. The Millerites have received extensive treatment by Arthur, "Millerism," in Gaustad, ed., *The Rise of Adven-tism*, 154–72.

64 For the wider impact of the catastrophist implications of dispensation-alism and premillennialism, see Sandeen, *The Roots of Fundamentalism*, and the seminal work by Marsden, *Fundamentalism and American Cul-ture*.

65 "The Seventh Vial" [*Free Church Magazine*], PW, 26 Aug. 1848, 268. See also "Review," *The Presbyterian* 10, no. 2 (Feb. 1857): 30–2; "Prophecy and Its Interpretation" [*English Eclectic Review*], ChG, 20 Oct. 1841, 203.

66 H.F. Bland Papers, box 3, file 138, no. 158, "The Millennium," ser-mon, 12 Mar. 1864.

67 Nelles Papers, "Conversion of the World," missionary address, n.d.; the Rev. William Snodgrass, "Sermon," MR 7, no. 2 (19 Jan. 1861): 13.

68 For the ideas of Edwards on the millennium, see Ernest Tuveson, *Re-deemer Nation*, 30. For the ambiguity of millennial ideas in the eigh-teenth century, see Davidson, *The Logic of Millennial Thought*.

69 H.F. Bland Papers, box 3, file 138, no. 158, "The Millennium," ser-mon, 12 Mar. 1864.

70 The Rev. Alexander Forrester, "'The Present War Viewed in the Light of Prophecy,' Being a Lecture delivered before the Halifax Young Men's Christian Association, March 27, 1854," PW, 15 April 1854, 53; "Modern Interpreters of Prophecy" [*Ed. C. Magazine*], MR 1, no. 12 (Dec. 1855): 182. See also Omicron, "Voice of Prophecy; Mode of In-terpreting Unfulfilled Prophecy – Letter II," ChG, 29 Aug. 1855, 185; "'Common Sense', End of the World – No. 1," ChG, 19 April 1843, 101.

71 Nelles Papers, "'Thoughts on the Great Exhibition,' Address delivered to the Hamilton Merchants Association, 14 April 1851"; ibid., "Essay

re: Relationship between the Old and New Worlds," n.d.; H.F. Bland Papers, box 4, file 162, no. 188, "Religion, the Well-Being of Nations, Communities, and Individuals," sermon, 9 Dec. 1861.

72 "Editorial," *ChG*, 13 Mar. 1830, 130. See also "Society and Religion," *MR* 3, no. 1 (Jan. 1857): 1; "Reality of Human Progress" [Rev. M. Harvey], *PW*, 17 Mar. 1855, 41.

73 See for example, H., "The Doctrine of Progress," *ChG*, 11 May 1853, 121.

74 Burns Papers, "'Scripture' Lectures," 1857. See also McCulloch Papers, vol. 552, no. 128, "The Total Extinction of Nations or Tribes Who Formerly Existed upon the American Continent," n.d.; H., "The Doctrine of Progress."

75 Hamburger, in *Macaulay and the Whig Tradition*, has argued forcefully that Macaulay valued social stability and harmony over progress. More recently Burrow's *A Liberal Descent* has warned present-day historians that the equation of Whiggism and the idea of progress is too facile. On the primacy of the moral in early Victorian historical writing see Jann, *The Art and Science of Victorian History*, introduction.

CHAPTER FOUR

1 Nelles Papers, "Random Thoughts," entry for 16 Dec. 1859.

2 Janes, "Evolution, The Modern Atheism," *Canadian Methodist Magazine* [*CMM*] 5 (April 1877): 305–6. See also the Rev. W.S. Blackstock, "The Doctrine of Descent and Darwinism," *CMM* 6 (July 1877): 85–6.

3 Grant Papers, vol. 19, "Notes – Sermons," "Matt. XIII, 31,32," n.d.

4 The idea of Darwinism as disjuncture and the metaphor of the decline of religion dominates the writings of English-Canadian historians. McKillop's *A Disciplined Intelligence*, chapter 4 focuses on the evolutionary assault on natural theology and the reaction by Christian apologists. Chapters 6 and 7 of this compelling work insist on the importance of philosophical idealism in resolving the "crisis of faith" experienced by educated Canadians after 1870. More recently, Cook's *The Regenerators* has explored the facets of "doubt," but insists on the conflict model of intellectual change. Cook's interpretation is centred on the decline of theology and the transfer of the Christian idea of "regeneration" into social action. A similar metaphor of conflict, decline, and secularization also characterizes the recent study by Marshall, "The Clerical Response to Secularization," 1–3. Significantly, Marshall's study begins in 1860.

5 This theme is present in the works of both McKillop and Cook, who advance the idea that clergymen of the period 1860–1890 were unwitting "precursors" of secular forms of social thought characteristic of

the twentieth century. See *The Regenerators*, 228–9, and *A Disciplined Intelligence*, chapter 7.

6 Nelles Papers, box 11, file 247, "Latest Advices," lecture, n.d.[ca 1875].

7 Carman Papers, box 23, file 208, "University Lecture Notes," n.d., "British Constitution." See also the Rev. H.A.M. Henderson, "Evolution – What Is It?," *CMM*, 10 (Oct. 1879): 375, 378; W. Dewar, "Biology and Theology," *Knox College Monthly* [*KCM*] 4, no. 4 (Feb. 1886): 150–156.

8 See Moore, *The Post-Darwinian Controversies*, 19–122 for a brilliant critique of the "military metaphor" employed by most interpreters of the relationship between religion and science. Moore's book is equally seminal in presenting the varieties of evolutionary thought open to late nineteenth-century thinkers, as well as a broad variety of Christian strategies, ranging from outright hostility to outright acceptance of Darwin's mechanism of natural selection. The stress throughout is on the interaction of theology and evolution, rather than the displacement of a religious outlook by a secular one.

9 For the Darwinian debate in the English-Canadian context and for the ideas of Dawson and Wilson, see McKillop, *A Disciplined Intelligence*, chapter 4, and a more lengthy treatment of Wilson, entitled "Evolution, Ethnology, and the Poetic Fancy," in McKillop, *Contours of Canadian Thought*. More recently, Berger's *Science, God, and Nature* has explored the Darwinian debate among Canadian naturalists. The importance of Sir William Dawson in the transatlantic debate has been acknowledged by Moore, who devotes a lengthy section to the English-Canadian scientist in *The Post-Darwinian Controversies*, 193–216.

10 This was noted by Berger, *Science, God, and Nature*, 56–9, and more forcefully stated by Moore, *The Post-Darwinian Controversies*, 205: "it was not primarily the Bible against which Darwin had offended, but against the methods and truths of established science."

11 See Johnston, "The Presbyterian College, Montreal,"66. For the view that Dawson's opinions on evolution were atypical of the reaction of the Canadian scientific community, see Berger, *Science, God, and Nature*, 69.

12 Campbell was born in Lanark County, Ontario, in 1835. After attending Queen's University, he was called to St Gabriel Presbyterian Church, Montreal, in 1869, a position he held until his retirement in 1909. A dedicated botanist, he was a close associate of Sir William Dawson in the Natural History Society of Montreal, and he became president of the society in 1895. Campbell edited *The Presbyterian* between 1867 and 1870, and contributed frequently to *The Canadian Record of Science*. In 1892 he became clerk of the general assembly of the

Presbyterian Church, and was moderator of the church in 1907. See Clifford, "Robert Campbell, the Defender of Presbyterianism," in Reid, *Called to Witness*; Berger, *Science, God, and Nature*, 11.

13 This is the central contention of Marsden's *Fundamentalism and American Culture*, and serves as the basis for his postulate of the "uniqueness" of American evangelicalism.

14 Moore insists on this point in *The Post-Darwinian Controversies*. The "Anti-Darwinians" Hodge and Dawson shared a commitment to Calvinist doctrine with men such as McCosh, who saw affinities between Darwin's theories and the Common Sense tradition. Asa Gray, another Calvinist, found it possible to reconcile Calvinism and Darwin's hypothesis of natural selection and transmutation of species without violating the central premises of either. See Moore, 193–216, 252–98. Although Canadian historians continually invoke the name of Sir William Dawson to illustrate the hostility of a wider segment of culture to evolutionary ideas, the fact remains that the principal of McGill was representative of a minority of scientists. According to a recent work by Peter Bowler, Dawson was perceived by many of his contemporaries as a "cultural fossil." See Bowler, "Scientific Attitudes to Darwinism in Britain and America," in Kohn, *The Darwinian Heritage*, 655.

15 "Infidelity Among the Masses," *ChG*, 6 Dec. 1865, 194. In the early 1860s, professors in the church colleges increasingly sounded alarms regarding new scientific and critical methods adopted by "infidelity," and the need for Christian ministers to combat these currents. See, for example, "Selection – The Field and the Men For It. An Address delivered at the Close of the Session to the Divinity Students of Queen's College, and Now Published at Their Request. By Professor George, D.D.," *The Presbyterian* 13, no. 6 (June 1860): 89–93.

16 Benjamin Jowett, "On the Interpretation of Scripture," in Frederick Temple et al., *Essays and Reviews* (London, 1861; fourth edition), 337, 348, 372–7. For the motives of the "Essayists" and their reception in England, see Chadwick, *The Victorian Church*, part 2, 3, 76–7.

17 See Chadwick, *The Victorian Church*, part 2, 1–3. The response to *Essays and Reviews* in Canada has been analyzed by McKillop, *A Disciplined Intelligence*, chapter 4. Significantly, McKillop places this discussion after his treatment of the anti-Darwinian pronouncements of Sir William Dawson and Sir Daniel Wilson. Moore's otherwise splendid *The Post-Darwinian Controversies* scarcely mentions the question of historical criticism, a serious oversight in his treatment of British and American evangelicals. More sensitive to the issue is Chadwick's later volume of lectures, *The Secularization of the European Mind*, 189–228.

18 "Modern German Infidelity: Its Invasion of England" [editorial], *PW*,

19 April 1862, 1; "Infidelity in the Anglican Church – the Essays and Reviews"[editorial], *ChG*, 24 April 1861, 66; "Inspiration and Revelation: What is the Present Question in England," *ChG*, 19 Oct. 1864, 170; "German Infidels in America"[*New York Evangelist*], *ChG*, 25 April 1866, 65; W.F. Warren, "David Friedrich Strauss" [*Zion's Herald*], *ChG*, 10 July 1867, 110; "The Word of God, No. 3," *The Home and Foreign Record*[*H&FR*](Toronto) 3, no. 2 (Dec. 1863): 35–7. For the evangelical hostility to German criticism in England, see Rogerson, *Old Testament Criticism*, 161, 180, 250.

19 "Renan's Life of Jesus"[editorial], *PW*, 5 Dec. 1863, 194. See also J.H., "The Changing Aspects of Infidelity," *The Presbyterian* 17, no. 11 (Nov. 1864): 335–7; the Rev. John Straith, *The Fidelity of the Bible! Being a Review of Colenso's Writings as Against the Pentateuch and the Book of Joshua* (Ingersoll, 1864) 62; "Unreasonableness of Rationalism" [editorial], *ChG*, 20 Feb. 1867, 30.

20 On the ideas of H.T. Buckle, see Christopher Parker, "English Historians and the Opposition to Positivism," *History and Theory* 22, no. 2 (1983): 123. See also Pollard, *The Idea of Progress*, 145–8. For Lecky's ideas, see Lecky, *The Rise and Influence of Rationalism in Europe*, vol. 1, vii–ix, xviii, 109, 118, 194. On the rise of agnosticism, see Annan, *Leslie Stephen* and, for the American scene, Turner, *Without God, Without Creed*.

21 McCulloch Papers, MG 1, vol. 552, no. 74, The Rev. William McCulloch, "Existing Church Thought and Activity in Relation to Revealed Character and Objects," a sermon preached before the Synod of the Presbyterian Church of the Lower Provinces of British North America, June 24, 1868. For a statement of this position by a leading Methodist, see Carman Papers, box 22, file 2, "Ms. Booklet of sermons of the Rev. Albert Carman," 1865–1870, "To the Law and to the Testimony," Isaiah 8th, 20th, n.d.

22 See Chadwick, *The Victorian Church*, part 2, 5. For the penetration of evolutionary ideas among clergymen and religiously-minded scientists, see the seminal work by Moore, *The Post-Darwinian Controversies*. For the wider sphere of British culture, see Heyck, *The Transformation of Intellectual Life in Victorian England*, chapter 4. The American scene has been analyzed by Russett in *Darwin in America: The Intellectual Response*, chapters 2, 4, 5 and 7. There is no comprehensive study of the impact of evolutionary thought on Canadian culture. By 1880, however, it was apparent that evolutionary thought had made inroads in university, scientific, and literary circles. See McKillop, *A Disciplined Intelligence*, chapters 5 and 6, where he discusses the career of the critic William Dawson LeSueur, and studies the rise of philosophical idealism in university faculties. More recently, Berger has suggested

that in the scientific community, "the idea of evolution made its way in Canada not through noisy debate over abstract theory but by subtle penetration into the practice and writing of natural history." See his *Science, God, and Nature*, 72. For the influence of strands of evolutionary thought on Canadian historians who wrote between 1880 and 1920, see the recent work by Christie, "Prophecy and 'The Principles of Social Life'," chapter 2.

23 The most complete analysis of the differences between Darwin and these Victorian social thinkers has been presented by Burrow, *Evolution and Society*, xv, 21.

24 Tylor, *Primitive Culture*, vol. 1, 1, 22–3; Burrow, *Evolution and Society*, 14.

25 See Tylor, *Primitive Culture*, vol. 1, 426, 500–2. For the connections between social thought, rationalism, and agnosticism in the 1870s, see Annan, *The Curious Strength of Positivism*, 11–12.

26 Wellhausen, *Prolegomena to the History of Israel*, v–x, 8–13, 182, 512–13. The three layers of narrative tradition are the "Jehovistic"(J), "Elohistic"(E), and the "Priestly Code"(P). For Wellhausen's place in the history and development of German criticism, see Rogerson, *Old Testament Criticism*, 259–60, 265.

27 An argument eloquently advanced by Cook in *The Regenerators*, chapters 2 and 3. Burrow's *Evolution and Society* has attempted to assess the "relativist" implications of the new social theory. While Burrows advanced the idea that Spencer, Tylor, and Sir Henry Maine preserved the hierarchy of "civilized" over "primitive" peoples, the fact remains that from a Victorian religious standpoint the notion of social development according to natural rather than theological laws was dangerously relativist in its implications.

28 The Rev. W.S. Blackstock, "The Higher Criticism," *Methodist Magazine and Review*[MM&R](Toronto) 43 (Feb. 1896): 176–7. This periodical was the successor to the *Canadian Methodist Magazine*.

29 Marsden has advanced this argument most recently in "Understanding Fundamentalist Views of Science," in Montagu, ed., *Science and Creation*, 108–9. Moore has directly attacked the notion of Darwinism as a "revolution" or as a fundamental shift in "paradigms," thus revising the views of Kuhn, whose *Structure of Scientific Revolutions* forms the basis for much of Marsden's interpretation. See *The Post-Darwinian Controversies*, 12–15.

30 See Marsden, *Fundamentalism and American Culture*, 55–68, 229.

31 The best analysis of the "modernist" position has been provided by Hutchison in *The Modernist Impulse*. More recently, Noll has reinforced the insights of George Marsden by insisting on the factors dividing liberals and conservatives. His "Common Sense Traditions and Ameri-

can Evangelical Thought," 235 posits a connection between the abandonment of Common Sense and the loss of evangelical convictions. For Horace Bushnell and the Yale theologians, see Kuklick, *Churchmen and Philosophers*, and for the educational ideals of Yale, particularly "Christian nurture" see Stevenson, *Scholarly Means to Evangelical Ends*, 5–6.

32 For an analysis of these divisions, see Marsden, *Fundamentalism and American Culture*, 18–39.

33 For the central role of Presbyterians, see Marsden, *Fundamentalism and American Culture*, 109–18. Support for this view comes from William Hutchison, who suggests that "modernism" found its greatest support among denominations like the Methodists, whose theology was non-Calvinist. See *The Modernist Impulse*, 114. By contrast, Presbyterians were resistant to "liberal" theology. Hutchison's work also contains an account of the celebrated heresy trials of David Swing and Charles Briggs.

34 This "accommodating spirit" seems to have been characteristic of the Canadian evangelical churches as a whole between 1850 and 1900. See the essays on Baptist institutions of higher learning, and in particular Barry Moody's paper on Acadia University in Rawlyk, ed., *Canadian Baptists and Christian Higher Education*).

35 W.G. Jordan, "The Higher Criticism in Canada. II. The Canadian Situation," *QQ* 36, no. 1 (winter 1929): 31.

36 Charles Hodge's *Systematic Theology* was widely used in Canadian Presbyterian colleges. As late as 1891, the "Report of the Senate of Knox College" still listed Hodge's work as a standard in the classroom. See *Acts and Proceedings of the Presbyterian Church in Canada*, 1891. Two prominent figures in the Canadian church attended Princeton between 1860 and 1890 – James Robertson, who later became superintendent of missions, and James Frederick McCurdy, a leading biblical scholar. See Gordon, *Life of James Robertson*; "James Frederick McCurdy," UCCA, biographical files. For further favourable impressions of Princeton by young Canadian Presbyterians, see Baird Papers, James Ballantyne to A.B. Baird, 24 Oct. 1881; J.C. to Baird, 27 Dec. 1881.

37 The most prominent included G.M. Grant, principal of Queen's University, who attended the University of Glasgow 1853–1857 and his younger Church of Scotland colleagues Daniel Miner Gordon, who eventually succeeded Grant, and Daniel James Macdonnell, minister of St Andrew's Church, Toronto, both of whom studied at Glasgow in the early 1860s. After the union of the Canadian branches of the Church of Scotland and the Free Church in 1875, a growing number of students studied in Scotland. These included Andrew Browning

Baird, long-time professor of church history at Manitoba College, R.Y. Thomson of Knox College, R.W. Kennedy, James and Robert Falconer (important figures in Maritime Presbyterianism), and Clarence Mackinnon, who later became principal of Presbyterian College, Halifax. If one includes a steady stream of immigrant professors and clergy such as Principal King of Manitoba College, J.E. McFadyen of Knox College, and W.G. Jordan of Queen's, the influence of Scottish university culture must be regarded as paramount. I have explored this aspect further in "Presbyterianism, Liberal Education, and the Social Sciences: Sir Robert Falconer and the University of Toronto, 1907–1932," paper presented to the Symposium on the Presbyterian Contribution to Canadian Life and Culture," Presbyterian College, Montreal, Oct. 13–15, 1988.

38 This development was represented by the important figures of Robert Flint, Henry Calderwood, and Alexander Campbell Fraser, professors associated with the University of Edinburgh. On their importance for the formulation of an ideal of liberal education and a new synthesis of modern thought, see Gauvreau, "Presbyterianism, Liberal Education, and the Social Sciences."

39 This is the revisionist interpretation advanced by Cheyne in *The Transforming of the Kirk*. Davie's *The Democratic Intellect*, 286–338 views the period between 1843 and 1870 in exclusively negative terms, as the destruction of Common Sense philosophy, the one distinctively Scottish contribution to European culture.

40 "Lecture by Principal Candlish on Inspiration," *H&FR* 3, no. 3 (Jan. 1864): 89–90. For an analysis of Candlish's position, see Cheyne, *The Transforming of the Kirk*, 37–8.

41 Quoted in Strahan, *Andrew Bruce Davidson*, 197. For Davidson's career, see the Rev. S.D.F. Salmond, "A.B. Davidson, D.D., L.L.D.," *The Westminster*(Toronto) 3, no. 2 (Aug. 1897): 65–8.

42 This summary of idealist philosophy is drawn from Passmore, *A Hundred Years of Philosophy*, 55. There is no systematic account of the impact of idealism in Scotland. Impressions must be gleaned from works such as Jones and Muirhead, *The Life and Philosophy of Edward Caird*, 74, 333–4, 347–8; and Warr, *Principal Caird*, 155, 175, 182, 229. See also Nettleship, *Memoirs of Thomas Hill Green*, 145–6, 153. Green, a close associate of Caird, argued that faith was absolutely independent of historical evidence.

43 See Macmillan, *The Life of Robert Flint*, 262–4; Rainy, *Delivery and Development of Christian Doctrine*, 35–6, 40.

44 Flint, *The Philosophy of History in France and Germany*, 1–2, 67; Rainy, *Delivery and Development of Christian Doctrine*, 67–8.

45 Flint, *Theism*, 26.

46 Flint, *The Philosophy of History*, 8, 22.

47 On the outlook of these "Spencerian" or "Lamarckian" evolutionists, see Moore, *The Post-Darwinian Controversies*, 217–51. Spencerian ideas of evolution were particularly popular in Edinburgh and wide sections of the Scottish church. See James Moore, "Evangelicals and Evolution: Henry Drummond, Herbert Spencer, and the Naturalisation of the Spiritual World," *Scottish Journal of Theology* 38 (Sept. 1985): 383–417. On the impact of Lamarckian concepts of evolution in the Canadian context, see Christie, "Prophecy and the 'Principles of Social Life'."

48 Mackinnon, *Reminiscences*, 61–2. See also Falconer, *Religion on My Life's Road*, 49–51. For the association of Drummond and Moody, see Moore, "Evangelicals and Evolution."

49 The Rev. Prof. Campbell, "Opening Lecture, Presbyterian College, Montreal," *The Canada Presbyterian*(Toronto)[*CP*], 2 Nov. 1877, 10–11.

50 W. Dewar, "Biology and Theology," *KCM* 4, no. 4 (Feb. 1886): 153–6. For a similar process of careful distinction between "Darwinism" and "evolution," see Norman H. Russell, "Critical Philosophy," *Manitoba College Journal*(Winnipeg)[*MCJ*] 5, no. 4 (Feb. 1890): 62–4; W.A. Hunter, "Evolution and the Church," *KCM* 20, no. 7 (May 1895): 591–602; F.R. Beattie, "The Design Argument: Scope and Import," *KCM* 4, no. 2 (Dec. 1885): 49–56.

51 For this aspect of William MacLaren's career, see Sandeen, *The Roots of Fundamentalism*, 202. Born in 1828 at Torbolton, Carleton County, Ont., MacLaren was educated at the Ottawa Grammar School and Toronto Academy, and studied arts and theology at Knox College. He was ordained in 1853 at Amherstburg, Ont., and in 1857 received a call to Knox Church, Boston, where he remained for a year, attempting to direct the congregation to unite with the Old School Presbyterians. In 1858 he was called to Belleville, Ontario, where he ministered for eleven years before moving to Knox Church, Ottawa. In 1872 he lectured briefly in Apologetics at Presbyterian College, Montreal, and in 1873 he was called to the chair of systematic theology at Knox College. In spite of his advanced age, he succeeded William Caven as principal of the college in 1904, a post he occupied until his retirement in 1908. MacLaren was moderator of the general assembly in 1884, and, from 1867 to 1883, was convenor of the Presbyterian committee on foreign missions, also serving as a delegate to the Pan-Presbyterian Councils held in Edinburgh in 1877 and in London in 1878. See "William MacLaren," UCCA, biographical files, and MacLaren Papers, "Diary of Rev. William McLaren, 1857–1870."

52 MacLaren, *Literature and Dogma*, 5. MacLaren became principal of Knox College on the death of William Caven in 1903. For a fuller explanation of his theological views, see MacLaren, *Sixty Years' Retro-*

spect. On the Baconian cast of theology, see also the Rev. Principal Willis, "A Standing Ministry; and the Relation of Systematic Theology to the Work of the Pulpit. A Lecture delivered at the Close of the Session of Knox College," *H&FR* 8, no. 7 (May 1869): 193–202; "The Necessity of Exegetical Study as a Preparation for the Work of the Ministry. A Lecture delivered by Rev. J.M. Gibson, M.A., at the Close of the Sesion in the Presbyterian College, Montreal," *H&FR* 8, no. 8 (June 1869): 230–40. For a similar statement by Principal MacVicar of Presbyterian College, Montreal, see MacVicar, *Life and Work of Donald Harvey MacVicar*, 198–200.

53 MacLaren, "The Witness of the Spirit in Relation to the Authority and the Inspiration of Scripture," reported in "Knox College," *The Presbyterian Review[PR]*(Toronto), 10 Oct. 1895, 322–3; "'The Variable and the Permanent in the Evidences of our Faith.' A Sermon preached in Bloor St. Presbyterian Church, on Sabbath, 7th June, 1903(Toronto, 1903)"; *Calvinism in Relation to Other Theistic Systems: A Lecture delivered at the Opening of the Session of Knox College, Toronto, on 3rd October, 1883*(Toronto, 1884).

54 See MacLaren, *Sixty Years' Retrospect*, 21. For the presence of Hodge's views in Canada as late as 1900, see Moir, *Enduring Witness*.

55 "Conservative," "Letter," *QJ*, 17 Mar. 1894, 149; The Rev. W.D. Armstrong, *The Christian Ministry and Modern Thought*(Toronto, 1896), 14–15; William Gregg, "Moses the Deuteronomist," in "William Gregg," UCCA, biographical files, article written in 1878; "'Fallacies of Higher Critics'"[editorial], *PW*, 9 Feb. 1895, 41.

56 MacLaren, *The Unity of the Human Race*, 8.

57 McLaren, *The Variable and the Permanent in the Evidences of Our Faith*, 9. See also "'The Rule of Faith and Private Judgment.' A Lecture delivered at the close of the Session of Knox College, Toronto, on 7th April, 1880(Toronto, 1880)," 6–7 in which he declared that "it is quite true that this persuasion of the infallible truth and divine authority of the Holy Scriptures, does not admit of being presented in the form of a demonstration of the inspiration of every separate verse of Scripture. In reality, it supersedes the necessity of such a demonstration."

58 William MacLaren, "The New Theology and Its Sources," *CP*, 13 Oct. 1886, 663. For the reconciliation of Darwinism and design among the Princeton theologians, MacLaren's close associates, see Livingstone, *Darwin's Forgotten Defenders*.

59 Baird Papers, reel 1, unnamed correspondent to Baird, 30 Dec. 1881; ibid., James Ballantyne to Baird, 24 Oct. 1881; J.C. to Baird, 27 Dec. 1881.

60 Baird Papers, reel 1, R.Y. Thomson to A.B. Baird, 17 Mar. 1880; ibid., Thomson to Baird, 24 Jan. 1883. For denunciations of Smith, see the

Rev. John Gray, "Modern Biblical Hyper-Criticism," *The British American Presbyterian*(Toronto)[*BAP*], 2 Mar. 1877, 1; 9 Mar. 1877, 1; 16 Mar. 1877, 1. For statements of support on behalf of Robertson Smith, see the Rev. William Snodgrass, "Modern Biblical Hyper-Criticism"[letter], *BAP*, 9 Mar. 1877, 5.

61 Biographical details on William Caven may be found in "William Caven," UCCA, biographical files.

62 "'Theology and Religion,' A Review of Dr. Caven's Lecture at the Opening of Knox College," *Queen's Journal*[*QJ*] 5, no. 1 (20 Oct. 1877): 2.

63 Here, my interpretation diverges from that of Brian J. Fraser, who advances the notion that the theology taught at Knox College was a "mirror image" of the Scottish "liberal evangelicalism" that developed between 1850 and 1890. See Fraser's "'The Christianization of Our Civilization'."

64 William Caven, "The Need of an Educated Ministry," *H&FR* 6, no. 1 (Nov. 1866): 4–5. For the curriculum at Knox College during Caven's principalship, see "Report of the Senate of Knox College, Session 1875–6," *Acts and Proceedings of the Second General Assembly of the Presbyterian Church in Canada, 1876*, 193–4. The report listed courses in exegesis and biblical criticism, apologetics and church history, systematic theology, church government, and pastoral theology.

65 "Knox College – Opening of Session," *H&FR* 8, no. 1 (Nov. 1868): 11–12.

66 William Caven, "Clerical Conservatism and Scientific Radicalism," *KCM* 14, no. 6 (Oct. 1891): 294.

67 "Clerical Conservatism and Scientific Radicalism," 294; "Knox College – Opening of Session," 11–12. For the subordination of biblical criticism to the art of preaching, see W.C., "Expository Preaching," *H&FR* 2, no. 11 (Sept. 1863): 290.

68 Principal Caven, "'Progress in Theology,' Address delivered at Knox College, at the Close of Session 1878–79," *CP* (Toronto), 8 April 1879, 386–7.

69 Ibid., 388–9.

70 Biographical data concerning King can be found in the Rev. John Mark King, *The Theology of Christ's Teaching*(Toronto, 1903), introduction by the Rev. James Orr.

71 The Rev. Principal King, "The Spirit in Which Theological Enquiry Should be Prosecuted," *Manitoba College Journal*,[*MCJ*] 8, no. 6 (July 1893): 127–9, 133. For King's views on the centrality of "biblical theology," see *The Theology of Christ's Teaching*, xviii. For a similar expression of caution in biblical and doctrinal research, see Caven, "Clerical Conservatism and Scientific Radicalism."

72 MacVicar, *Life and Work of Donald Harvey MacVicar*, 198–200; Principal MacVicar, "Dogma and Current Thought," *KCM* 17, no. 1 (May 1893): 690–1. For MacVicar's position, see also "The Bible and Modern Thought," *CP*, 8 Oct. 1884, 668. For Caven's balance of the critical and reverent tempers, see Caven, "Clerical Conservatism and Scientific Radicalism."

73 J. Thompson, "Doctrinal Preaching," *KCM* 5, no. 5 (Mar. 1887): 260; Vicanus, "Preaching, the Great Work of the Christian Ministry," *KCM* 1, no. 1 (Feb. 1883): 3; D.M. Ramsay, "The Relation of Biblical Theology to Systematic Theology," *KCM* 7, no. 5 (Mar. 1888): 272–6.

74 The Rev. John Scrimger, "Is the Bible a Revelation?" in *Questions of the Day, Lecture delivered in the David Morrice Hall, Presbyterian College, Montreal, in 1883–84*(Montreal, 1885), 167, 188–90; John Scrimger, "Certainties and Uncertainties in Biblical Introduction," *PCJ* 10, no. 2 (Dec. 1890): 96. See also J.F. McCurdy, "The Prophecies of Isaiah by T.K. Cheyne"[book review], *KCM* 6, no. 6 (Oct. 1887): 363–6; R.Y. Thomson, "The Evolution in the Manifestation of the Supernatural," *KCM* 12, no. 6 (Oct. 1890): 318.

75 "Dr. Caven's Sermon," *KCM* 17, no. 3 (July 1893): 121–34.

76 This is the interpretation of the Canadian biblical criticism advanced by Moir in *A History of Biblical Studies in Canada*, 9.

77 The Rev. Professor Campbell, "'The Phenomenal God,' Opening Lecture delivered Oct. 1886," *PCJ* 6, no. 1 (Oct. 1886): 9–12; John Campbell, "The Search for God; the Theme of the Christian Apologist – Opening Lecture, II," *PCJ* 2, no. 2 (Nov. 1881): 16–17.

78 Campbell, *The Hittites*, vol. 1, vi-vii; *The Horites*, 37–8. See also Campell, *The Lost Tribes*, and "The Search For God; The Theme of the Christian Apologist – Opening Lecture, II," *PCJ* 2, no. 2 (Nov. 1881): 16.

79 McKillop has recently explored the genesis of the "research ideal" at the University of Toronto in the late 1880s. See "The Research Ideal and the University of Toronto" in *Contours of Canadian Thought*, 78–95.

80 John Scrimger, "Certainties and Uncertainties in Biblical Introduction," *PCJ* 10, no. 2 (Dec. 1890): 96; "Induction of Prof. Scrimger," *PCJ* 3, no. 1 (Oct. 1882): 4.

81 As Cook has explained in *The Regenerators*, 7–25. See also Marshall, "The Clerical Response to Secularization," chapter 3.

82 These definitions have been analysed by Hutchison in *The Modernist Impulse in American Protestantism*, 2–4. By contrast, students of the Canadian churches tend to use these terms imprecisely. For example, Cook in *The Regenerators*, chapter 3 conflates the terms, and defines as "liberal" or "modernist" anyone who attempted to accommodate evangelical theology and elements of the higher criticism. More recently

Marshall, in "The Clerical Response to Secularization," chapter 2, has adopted a similar view of attempts to reconcile Christianity, evolutionary thought, and biblical criticism. For Hutchison's strictures against the conflation of the terms, see *The Modernist Impulse in American Protestantism*, 4, in which he argues that not all "liberals" adopted a favourable view of modern culture – many hoped to use their theology to resist the inroads of "modernism."

83 Nelles Papers, box 1, file 4, G.M. Grant to S.S. Nelles, 23 Sept. 1881.

84 For an estimate of John Watson's thought and influence, see McKillop, *A Disciplined Intelligence*, chapters 6 and 7. More recently, George Rawlyk and Kevin Quinn have noted the profound impact of Watson's philosophy on students of theology at Queen's. See Rawlyk and Quinn, *The Redeemed of the Lord Say So*, 3–7.

85 For this estimate of Grant, see McKillop, *A Disciplined Intelligence*, 216–18; Cook, *The Regenerators*, 18–20, 184–7. McKillop has even enlisted Grant as a central figure in a strand of thought he terms the "idealist tradition," which, he argues, dominated Canadian churches and universities between 1880 and 1920. See "The Idealist Legacy," in McKillop, *Contours of Canadian Thought*, 98–110.

86 Watson Papers, box 1, file "J. Watson; Material re Queen's," quoted in Kiesekamp, "Community and Faith," 78–84.

87 Grant Papers, vol. 11, "Memoranda and Reports-Presbyterian Church"; "Extracts from, and notes of the Record of the Church of Scotland in Nova Scotia and the Adjoining Provinces, 1855–1875"; "The Free Kirk – Establishment Controversy." For further details on Grant's stay in Scotland see Grant and Hamilton, *Principal Grant*.

88 Oliphant, *Memoir of the Life of John Tulloch*, 114–15.

89 See McLeod, *Memoirs of Norman McLeod*, 214, 217–8. See also *"Religion in Common Life. A Sermon preached at Crathie Church, 14th Oct. 1855 before Her Majesty the Queen and Prince Albert by the Rev. John Caird, M.A., Minister of Errol, Scotland, published by Her Majesty's Command," The Presbyterian*, 4 May 1856, 73–7.

90 McCurdy, ed., *Life and Work of D.J. Macdonnell*, 25–7. See also Gordon Papers, box 10, "Reminiscences, Vol. I." The practical, unspeculative temper of Canada's evangelical clergymen has been similarly noted by Kiesekamp "Community and Faith," 78–84.

91 Grant and Hamilton, *The Life of Principal Grant*, 77–8.

92 The Rev. G.M. Grant, "Laon on Messrs. Moody and Sankey and Revivalism," *The Canadian Monthly and National Review*[CMNR] 8, no. 3 (Sept. 1875): 252. See also Laon, "Messrs. Moody and Sankey and Revivalism," *CM, NR* 7, no. 6 (June 1875): 510–13. For a close and lucid study of LeSueur's ideas, see McKillop, *A Disciplined Intelligence*, chapter 5.

93 Macdonnell Papers, box 1, "Toronto Presbytery: Rev. Mr. Macdonnell's Case," *The Daily Globe*, 5 Dec. 1875.

94 Grant Papers, negative of G.M. Grant's "Queen's Letters," Grant to Principal William Snodgrass, 4 May 1876. See also McCurdy, *Life and Work of D.J. Macdonnell*, 98–9; Grant and Hamilton, *The Life of Principal Grant*, 152–4.

95 "Impressions of the Alumni Conference," *QJ* 20, no. 20 (1 April 1893): 154–5; Rev. J. Lindsay, "The Theological Student – His Work and Destination," *QJ* 27, no. 10 (17 Mar. 1900): 188–9.

96 Grant Papers, vol. 12, "Inaugural Address," Queen's University, 1877. For the close friendship between Grant and Robert Flint, see Grant and Hamilton, *The Life of Principal Grant*, 23.

97 "Convocation Day," *QJ* 6, no. 12 (3 May 1879): 139; Grant Papers, vol. 15, "Notebooks," "Systematic Theology," "Introductory Lecture, 8 Nov. 1880."

98 Grant Papers, vol. 16, "Notes on Theology, etc.," "Notes on a Course of Lectures on 'Higher Criticism' delivered in Ottawa, during the University Session of 1891–92, under the auspices of the Queen's University Extension Association of Ottawa"; Grant, *The Religions of the World*, 6; D.M. Gordon, "The Spirit of Theological Enquiry," *The Theologue* [*Theol.*] 6, no. 1 (Nov. 1894).

99 Grant Papers, vol. 14, "Exams and Lectures for Session 1892–93," "Inspiration"; vol. 13, "Notebook," "Apologetics," lecture 9, "History and a Moral Purpose," n.d.

100 King Papers, reel 1, "Inaugural Lecture," MCJ (1893): 133. For other criticisms of Hegelian idealism by Canadian Presbyterians, see J. Seth, "*An Introducton to the Philosophy of Religion*, by John Caird"[book review], *Theol.* (Halifax) 1, no. 1 (Dec. 1889): 51–61; F.R. Beattie, "Apologetic …, von J.H.A. Ebrard"[book review], *KCM* 5, no. 1 (Nov. 1886): 55–6; "Knox College – Celebration of the Semi-Centenary," *The Presbyterian Review*(Toronto) (1894): 250–60.

101 This biographical information on the Rev. Samuel Nelles is drawn from the Nelles Papers, box 1, Alfred H. Reynar, "Samuel Sobieski Nelles," *ChG*, 27 July 1904, 6–7.

102 See Cross, *The Burned-Over District*.

103 See, for example, Nelles Papers, "Random Thoughts and Mental Records," entry for 22 Nov. 1848; "Book of Random Thoughts on Speech," "Transcendentalism," entry for 1 Aug. 1849; "Formation of Character," lecture, 18 Feb. 1854.

104 Nelles Papers, "Random Thoughts and Mental Records," entries for 22 Nov. 1848, 25 Nov. 1848, and 28 Nov. 1848.

105 Nelles Papers, "Random Thoughts and Mental Records," entries for 25 Oct. 1848 and 28 Nov. 1848.

106 Nelles Papers, "Random Thoughts," "Intensity," 21 Nov. 1858; "Reli-

gious Meditations," "On Feeling," 28 Dec. 1866; and 3 Feb. 1848, Port Hope.

107 See Semple, "The Impact of Urbanization on the Methodist Church," chapter 5, "The Decline of Revival: The Extraordinary Means of Grace." According to Semple, revival acquired a new meaning between 1854 and 1884, and lost its central place in Methodism. Gradual growth of grace within an evolutionary framework appeared as legitimate and more rational that enthusiastic conversion. For an analysis of the impact on the American colleges of the change from "revival" to "Christian nurture," see Stevenson, *Scholarly Means to Evangelical Ends.*

108 Nelles Papers, "Book of Random Thoughts," 1846–1849, "Christianity a Germ," n.d.; see also ibid., "Christianity Progressive," Port Hope, early 1848; box 5, file 65, "Progressive Piety," sermon, Toronto, 20 Oct. 1848.

109 Nelles Papers, "Book of Random Thoughts on Speech," Entry for 5 Mar. 1850.

110 Nelles Papers, "Random Thoughts and Mental Records," entries for 24 Nov. 1848, and 25 Nov. 1848; box 5, file 63, "For the Redemption of their Soul is Precious," sermon, Cobourg, 9 Jan. 1848.

111 Nelles Papers, "Taught of God," "Intellectual Age," address, n.d.; "Preaching and Teaching," undated and untitled manuscript, in file "Essays", etc.; "Book of Random Thoughts," "Harmony of Truth – Philosophy and Religion," Sept. 1848.

112 Nelles Papers, "Book of Random Thoughts," "Philosophy Eclectic," 8 Feb. 1848.

113 Nelles Papers, "Book of Random Thoughts on Speech," "Probable and Necessary," entry for 25 Aug. 1849. For a critique of the speculative method in theology, see ibid., "Cant and Technical Divinity," 25 July 1849.

114 Nelles Papers, "Book of Random Thoughts," 1846–1849, "Scripture Interpretation – Is The Bible Exhausted," n.d.; ibid., "Moral and Religious Lectures," 1864.

115 Nelles Papers, "Random Thoughts and Mental Records," entry for 28 Nov. 1848.

116 Nelles Papers, "Random Thoughts," entry for Dec. 16, 1859.

117 Burwash Papers, "The Life and Labors of Nathanael Burwash," typescript of an unpublished autobiography. A more complete study of Burwash's life and achievements is provided by Van Die, *An Evangelical Mind.*

118 Biographical details on Burwash are contained in "Nathanael Burwash," UCCA, biographical files, F.H. Wallace, "Rev. Chancellor Burwash," *ChG*, 15 Oct. 1913.

119 Nelles Papers, "Doubting," address, n.d.

120 See Nelles Papers, box 2, file 9, "Diary Jan. 1, 1866–Jan. 13, 1867," entry for 21 Jan. 1866 and entry for 24 June 1866; ibid., "Rowsell's Diary, Jan. 30, 1867–Dec. 31, 1867," entries for 2 Feb. 1867 and 14 Dec. 1867. Though lauding Butler as the greatest of all ethical writers because of his unsectarian spirit and "Baconian" outlook, Nelles criticized the great Christian apologist for lacking imagination or fancy. See Nelles Papers, "Notebook of Lectures on Butler's *Sermons, 1866.*"

121 Nelles Papers, box 2, file 18, "Essay for Ministerial Association of Cobourg on Farrar's *Free Thought*," 6 Dec. 1869.

122 Nelles propounded his views on the principles of biblical criticism in a series of lectures given between 1865 and 1869. See Nelles Papers, "Sunday Lectures," "Progressive Character of Religious Truth," 17 Dec. 1865; ibid., "Notebook of Ethical Lectures," "'Questions and Prelections on Westcott's Introduction to the Study of the Gospels,' 7 Aug. 1866, for Sunday Class of Session 1866–7"; ibid., "Bible Lecture," 12 Sept. 1869 and 10 Oct. 1869.

123 This is particularly true of Fisher's *Essays on the Supernatural Origin of Christianity,* 579–80. Fisher's work was used at Mount Allison University throughout the 1870s. See *Catalogue of Mount Allison Wesleyan College, 1875*. More recently, Van Die's *An Evangelical Mind,* 102–3 has noted that the appearance of Farrar's *History of Interpretation* in 1886 marked a turning point in the reception of higher criticism by Nathanael Burwash. However, the common Butlerian mind-set shared by this leading Canadian Methodist and the Anglican cleric ensured that this "revolution" was accomplished with minimal need for serious readjustment.

124 Burwash Papers, box 16, file 444, "Introductory Lecture on Natural History," Victoria College, Aug. 1867.

125 H.F. Bland Papers, box 5, file 270, "Evidences of Christianity," and "Inspiration of the Bible," 1867–68; Carman Papers, box 22, file 2, "Ms Booklet of Sermons of the Rev. Albert Carman," 1865–1870, "To the Law and to the Testimony," Isaiah 8th 20th, n.d.; ibid., box 23, file 208, "University Lecture Notes," "Rule and Principle," n.d. The works of Butler continued to be read by young probationers long after they ceased to be used at Victoria College. See, for example, Salem Bland Papers, box 9, no. 807, "Notes on Butler's Analogy," 1879.

126 Nelles Papers, "Religious Meditations," "Practicality," 4 July 1865; H.F. Bland Papers, box 5, file 248, no. 353, "Christian Experience," sermon, 19 Nov. 1890.

127 See Burwash Papers, box 14, file 382, "Address on the Development of Methodist Theology and Mission," 1899; "Education of Candidates

for the Ministry", *Acta Victoriana*[*AV*] 9, no. 5 (Feb. 1888): 5. For the background to the creation of the faculty of theology, see Burwash, *History of Victoria College*, 235–68.

128 "Modern Skepticism"[editorial], *ChG*, 23 May 1870, 45; "University and Theological Education"[editorial], *ChG*, 10 Feb. 1875, 44; "The Study of the Scriptures"[editorial], *CMM* (Toronto) 2, (July 1875): 75–6.

129 The Rev. J.B. Clarkson, "The Harmony of Science and Religion," *CMM* 5 (March 1877): 250; S.H. Janes, "Evolution, The Modern Atheism," *CMM* 5 (April 1877): 305–6; The Rev. W.S. Blackstock, "The Doctrine of Descent and Darwinism," *CMM* 6 (July 1877): 85–6. On the separation of revelation and natural science, see Burwash, "Divine Revelation of the Creation," in Phillips, *The Methodist Pulpits*, 90–1; The Rev. W. Harrison, "The Religious Faculty: – Its Nature, Scope, and Satisfaction," *Canadian Methodist Quarterly*[*CMQ*](Toronto) 1 (Jan. 1889): 12–39.

130 The Rev. W.S. Blackstock, "The Theistic Conception of the World," *CMM* 5 (March 1877): 198–9.

131 The Rev. S.S. Nelles, "The Place of Theology Among the Sciences," *CMM* 8 (Oct. 1878): 368–9.

132 The Rev. E.H. Dewart, "The Development of Doctrine: A Lecture delivered before the Theological Union of Victoria University, May 19, 1879," in *Lectures and Sermons, Theological Union, Victoria University, 1878–1882*, 32–3, 40; Carman Papers, box 24, file 39, "Address on the three main points of attack at present upon our system of Christian doctrine," n.d.

133 Nelles Papers, box 10, file 235, "Lectures to Candidates for the Ministry," Feb.-April, 1872, lecture 2, 5 Mar. 1872; ibid., "Bible Lecture," 10 Oct. 1869.

134 For the substance of Yale scholarship, see the recent work by Stevenson, *Scholarly Means to Evangelical Ends, 1–4, 89–92*.

135 A copy of the examination can be found in the McLaughlin Papers, box 2, file 46, "Contracts, Certificates, Agreements." For the curriculum see also Burwash Papers, box 14, file 382, "Address on the Development of Methodist Theology and Mission," 1899, 6. See "Report of the Board of Examiners, 1897," in *Minutes of Conferences, 1897* for a listing of the requirements for ministerial candidates.

136 Burwash Papers, box 12, file 197, "Untitled Sermon," ca 1890.

137 Burwash Papers, box 12, file 197, "The Commission and Spirit of the Christian Ministry," sermon delivered May 1890; box 12, file 201, "College Sermons, 1896–97," "The Permanent Elements of Religion." For the Methodist strictures on speculative philosophy, see, for example, the Rev. E.I. Badgley, "'Faith vs. Knowledge,' being the tenth

annual lecture delivered before the Theological Union of Victoria University in 1887," in *Lectures and Sermons delivered before the Theological Union of The University of Victoria College*, 28; The Rev. J. Burwash, "The Limits of Religious Thought," in Phillips, ed., *The Methodist Pulpits*, 188; Burwash, *Manual of Christian Theology on the Inductive Method*, vol. 1, 4–7.

138 Burwash Papers, box 17, file 449, "The Poetical Book of the Old Testament," introductory lecture, 1880; "Bricks and the Bible," *CMM* 24 (Oct. 1886): 338.

139 Burwash, *A Handbook of the Epistle of St. Paul to the Romans*, vii; Burwash Papers, box 12, file 181, "All Scripture is given by inspiration of God," sermon delivered July 1881; ibid., box 19, file 484, "Lecture Series III. Apocalyptics. Section I. History of Revelation," n.d.

140 Wallace Papers, box 4, "Memories of the Manse, the Parsonage, and the College," vol. 1, 119, 237, 295. See also "The Preacher's Place," *AV* 8 (April 1895): 9–12; F.H. Wallace, "The Message and the Man," *AV* 17, no. 7 (April 1894): 227–31. A large number of Victoria graduates went to Germany for postgraduate studies. In addition to Wallace, George Coulson Workman, A.P. Misener, L.E. Horning, and A.H. Reynar attended German universities.

141 "Prof. Robertson Smith"[editorial], *ChG*, 6 July 1881, 212; "Destructive Critics of the Old Testament"[editorial], *ChG*, 5 Oct. 1887, 623. See also "The Old Testament in the Jewish Church – Twelve Lectures on Biblical Criticism by W. Robertson Smith"[book review], *CMM* 14 (Oct. 1881) 382.

142 Nelles Papers, box 1, file 6, G.C. Workman to Nelles, 4 Feb. 1886. For the development of Delitzsch's opinions, see Rogerson, *Old Testament Criticism*, 112, 140, 271.

143 See McKillop, "The Research Ideal and the University of Toronto." The background to federation has been treated in Burwash, *History of Victoria College*, 271–396.

144 See Boyle, "Higher Criticism and the Struggle for Academic Freedom in Canadian Methodism"; Lawrence Burkholder, "Canadian Methodism and Higher Criticism, 1860–1910," history research paper, University of Toronto, 1975; Tom Sinclair-Faulkner, "Theory Divided from Practice: The Introduction of the Higher Criticism into Canadian Protestant Seminaries," Canadian Society of Church History, *Papers*, 1980, 33–75. See also Cook, *The Regenerators*, for the now standard view of higher criticism and the Workman Case as the source conflict between rival theological parties of "conservatives" and "modernists."

145 G.C. Workman, "Messianic Prophecy," *CMQ* 2, no. 4 (Oct. 1890): 407–78.

146 Wallace Papers, box 4, "Memories of the Manse, the Parsonage, and the College"; McLaughlin Papers, box 2, file 21, "Diary 1892," entry for 16 July 1892.

CHAPTER FIVE

1 Grant Papers, vol. 19, "Notes – Sermons," "The Evolution of Canada and the Outlook," n.d.

2 Burwash Papers, box 17, file 456, "Lectures on the History of Christian Doctrine," 1897.

3 For a well-balanced synthesis exploring the social and industrial transformation of Canada between 1890 and 1920, see Brown and Cook, *Canada 1896–1921*. More recently, historians have sought to explore the intellectual transition from nineteenth-century individualism to the welfare state, identifying the years between 1890 and 1910 as the crucial period for the penetration and acceptance of "collectivism," in the form of either liberalism or socialism, into the Canadian intellectual community. See also the recent study by Owram, *The Government Generation*, chapters 1–3. For an exploration of the impact of "collectivist" ideas on an influential group of historians, see Christie, "Prophecy and the 'Principles of Social Life'," chapter 6.

4 See Allen, *The Social Passion*; Magney, "The Methodist Church and the National Gospel"; Fraser, "Theology and the 'social gospel'." More recent studies, though disagreeing with Allen's positive estimate of the social gospel, agree that social activism dominated the intellectual life of the Canadian churches. See, for example, Cook, *The Regenerators*; McKillop, *A Disciplined Intelligence*, chapter 7; Marshall, "The Clerical Response to Secularization."

5 See Allen, *The Social Passion*, 355–6. The "social gospel" influence in Canadian radical politics has been traced by McNaught, *A Prophet in Politics*, and by Allen, "The Social Gospel and the Reform Tradition."

6 This represents the substance of the conclusions advanced by Cook in *The Regenerators*, 228–32. The secularization thesis has been applied most thoroughly and uncritically in the recent work by David Marshall, who argues that the dominant activity of the Protestant churches between 1860 and 1940 was "the adjustment of the Church to a society growing more secular, not a march of progress towards the Kingdom of God." "Clergymen" he concludes, "unwittingly contributed to the process of secularization in their quest to make religion conform to the needs and demands of the modern world." See "The Clerical Response to Secularization," 18–19.

7 Richard Allen's study is described as a "history of ideas." The intellectual aspect of religion and social reform plays, however, a minor role

in *The Social Passion*, which tends to focus on Methodist and Presbyterian social action. The defenders of the secularization thesis fail to link social action to any precise or coherent body of ideas. Perhaps the most interesting attempt to remedy this gap is McKillop's *A Disciplined Intelligence*, chapter 7, which identifies philosophical idealism as an important source of ideas for the social gospel. The idealist legacy is accorded similar importance by Brian Fraser in his study "'The Christianization of Our Civilization,' Presbyterian Reformers and their Defence of a Protestant Canada, 1875–1914."

8 G.M. Grant, "The Pulpit in Scotland as It Is, and As It Was Forty or Fifty Years Ago," *QQ* 7, no. 3 (Jan. 1900): 197–9.

9 Grant Papers, vol. 12, "Speeches – Notes," "Practical Preaching," n.d.; ibid., vol. 23, "Speeches, Notes, & Drafts," "Christianity in Relation to Social Problems and the Wage Question," n.d.

10 For this interpretation of Grant, see McKillop, *A Disciplined Intelligence*, 216–19; Cook, *The Regenerators*, 184–6.

11 Grant Papers, "Practical Preaching."

12 The fact that a prominent evangelical spokesman like Principal Grant could make such statements during the 1890s calls into serious question the interpretation advanced by Cook and McKillop. Far from surrendering to "liberalism" and watering down his creed into a vague form of social ethics, Grant was firmly admonishing his students to hold fast to the traditions of an earlier age.

13 Grant Papers, "Practical Preaching."

14 Burwash Papers, box 12, file 188, "The Church and the Nation," sermon delivered 25 Aug. 1884.

15 For Davidson's ideas on the subject of the Old Testament, see Davidson, *Old Testament Prophecy*, 1–3, 8. This is a collection of lectures delivered to students at Edinburgh throughout Davidson's career.

16 Davidson, *Old Testament Prophecy*, 8–11; Robertson Smith, *The Prophets of Israel*, 18, 63. Smith was Davidson's disciple, and advanced similar claims for the centrality of the prophets in the history of Israel.

17 Davidson, *Old Testament Prophecy*, 16–18.

18 Ibid., 98–9.

19 Ibid., 71–2.

20 Burwash Papers, box 16, file 447, "Lecture Notes on Isaiah," Victoria College, 1877; ibid., box 17, file 449, "The Poetical Book of the Old Testament," introductory lecture, 1880. See also the Rev. Prof. Scrimger, "The Prophets and Their Work, A Lecture delivered at the Opening of the Session, 1882–83," *PCJ* 3, no. 1 (Oct. 1883): 6–9; Grant Papers, vol. 13, "Notebook," "Notes for Lectures to Junior Divinity Class, 1884–85," "Notes on Isaiah"; Grant, *The Religions of the World*, 159–64.

21 Biographical details on McCurdy may be found in "James Frederick McCurdy," UCCA, biographical files. For the Princeton attempt to reconcile Calvinism and Darwinism, see the recent work by Livingstone, *Darwin's Forgotten Defenders*.

22 McCurdy, *History, Prophecy, and the Monuments*, vol. 1, vi, 9, 75–6; ibid., vol. 3, 35. McCurdy's central role in shaping the course of Canadian biblical studies is discussed in Moir, *A History of Biblical Studies*, 16, 23.

23 Ibid., vol. 1, 2–3.

24 Ibid., 13–14.

25 The view of history as a "spiral" was also characteristic of groups who more enthusiastically adopted prevailing forms of Lamarckian evolutionary thought. For the "Lamarckian" structure of popular histories written in Canada between 1880 and 1920, see Christie, "Prophecy and 'The Principles of Social Life'."

26 McCurdy, *History, Prophecy, and the Monuments*, vol. 3, 430–1.

27 See Allen, *The Social Passion*, 3–17; Magney, "The Methodist Church and the National Gospel"; Fraser, "Theology and the 'social gospel'." Recent studies of the labour movement by Gregory Kealey and Brian Palmer suggest the importance of the 1880s in the creation of working-class organizations. See Kealey, *Toronto Workers Respond to Industrial Capitalism* and Palmer, *A Culture in Conflict*. The 1880s and 1890s witnessed the rise of movements devoted to urban reform. See Rutherford, "Tomorrow's Metropolis: The Urban Reform Movement in Canada, 1880–1920," in Stelter and Artibise, eds, *The Canadian City*, 368–92. Living standards among the Canadian working class at this time have been discussed in Copp's *The Anatomy of Poverty*. A recent and provocative study of the difficulties of transition to urban life has been provided by Walden in "Respectable Hooligans."

28 McCurdy, *History, Prophecy, and the Monuments*, vol. 3, 430–1; Professor J.F. McCurdy, "Modern Old Testament Criticism: A Study for Preachers and Teachers," *The Westminster*(Toronto) 11, no. 1 (6 July 1901): 25–7.

29 McLaughlin Papers, box 2, file 32, "Homiletic Use of Old Testament History," n.d.; ibid., "The Prophets of the Old Testament: Berwick Studies, Aug. 1910," delivered at Albert College, Belleville.

30 Scrimger, "The Prophets and Their Work," 6–9.

31 The Rev. Septimus Jones, "Prophets, the Need of the Church," *CMM* 40 (July 1894): 46–7. See also Burwash Papers, box 19, file 488, "Introduction to a Treatise on Messianic Prophecy," Cobourg, 11 Nov. 1890; George C. Workman, "Messianic Prophecy," *CMQ* 2 (Oct. 1890): 419; W.G. Elmslie, "The Prophet Hosea," *KCM* 14, no. 2 (June 1891): 57; W. Wylie, "The Modern Prophetical Office," *KCM* 8, no. 2 (June

1888): 103; Carman Papers, box 24, file 12, "The School of the Prophets," address at the Wesleyan College Convocation, Montreal, 26 April 1892; The Rev. Eber Crummy, "The Prophet and the Book – Past and Present," Theological Union Lecture, Victoria University, *ChG*, 28 Nov. 1900, 754; Prof. J.F. McLaughlin, "The Living and Abiding Word. VI. The Prophets and their Message," *ChG*, 21 March 1900, 178.

32 McCurdy, *History, Prophecy, and the Monuments*, vol. 2, 230–1.

33 The Rev. C.B. Ross, "Hoseah, Amos, and Micah," *PCJ* 16, no. 5 (March 1897): 345–9; The Rev. O. Armstrong, "The Age of Amos and Hosea," (Toronto) 44 (Nov. 1906): 423–4; John W. Currie, "Dynasty of Omri and Jehu," M.A. thesis, University of Toronto, 1906, 15; G.A. McIntosh, "The Relation of the Prophecy of the Assyrian Period to the Formal Religious Worship of the Time," *AV* 18, no. 7 (April 1895): 228–87; R.J. Hutcheon, "The Origin and Early Growth of Hebrew Prophecy," *QQ* 5, no. 2 (Oct. 1897): 89–103, paper read at the conference in Queen's University in February, 1897. See also Irwin Papers, box 2, no. 296, "Isaiah the Prophet Statesman," n.d.; ibid., box 1, no. 51, "Isaiah and God's Poor," n.d.

34 For the writings of Andrew Macphail and James Cappon, see Shortt, *The Search for an Ideal*.

35 Chown Papers, box 13, file 366, "The Prophets as Preachers to their Own Times: With their Influence on the Social Ethics of Christendom," Address, n.d. Biographical details on Chown may be found in his unpublished autobiography, entitled *My Life*. See Chown Papers, box 16, files 455, 456, 457, "Manuscript. *My Life*."

36 For this estimate of Chown, see Cook, *The Regenerators*, 229–30; McKillop, *A Disciplined Intelligence*, 224–8 and "The Idealist Legacy" in McKillop, *Contours of Canadian Thought*.

37 Jordan, *Prophetic Ideas and Ideals*, 11–13. Jordan was born in 1852 and ordained in the United Methodist Free Church in England, but in 1886 he was admitted to the Presbyterian Church. He emigrated to Canada in 1889 and was minister of St Andrew's Church, Strathroy, before his call to the Chair of Old Testament at Queen's in 1899. For biographical material on Jordan, see McCree, "William George Jordan," in Wallace, ed., *Some Great Men of Queen's*, 96–113. Jordan's emphasis on the social message of Hebrew prophecy was echoed by his colleague at Knox College, John Edgar McFadyen, in his inaugural address. See the Rev. J.E. McFadyen, "The Place of the Old Testament in the Faith and Teaching of the Church," *The Westminster* (8 Oct. 1898): 373.

38 Jordan, *Prophetic Ideas and Ideals*, 20.

39 McCurdy, *History, Prophecy, and the Monuments*, vol. 3, 371; the Rev. C.B. Ross, "Hoseah, Amos, and Micah," 350–1; J.F. McLaughlin, "He-

brew Prophecy in the Assyrian Period," *AV* 19, no. 7 (April 1896): 338–9; W.G. Watson, "Some Aspects of the Prophetic Doctrine of God," *AV* 19, no. 5 (Feb. 1896): 247–52.

40 Grant Papers, vol. 23, "Speeches, Notes, & Drafts," "Christianity in Relation to Social Problems, and the Wage Question," n.d.; "Practical Preaching," n.d.

41 Grant, "Presbyterian Union and Reformation Principles," *QQ* (Jan. 1894): 181. Allan Smith's "The Thought of George Monro Grant," *Canadian Literature* no. 83 (winter 1979), has advanced a similar interpretation of Grant's ideas based on a consideration of his nationalist ideas and social criticism. Brian Fraser also supports an individual emphasis in "'The Christianization of Our Civilization'," a study of six Free Church Canadian clergymen. Although influenced by the idealist outlook, they preserved an individualist bias in interpreting the relationship between individual and community.

42 J.A.M., "Looking Backward"[review], *KCM* 10, no. 4 (Aug. 1889): 12. See also Thomas Ritchie, "The Church and the Labour Question," *KCM* 12, no. 1 (May 1890): 30; A.K. Birks, "Society and Religion," *AV* 10, no. 6 (March 1887): 8–9. For a fuller study of Macdonald's career, which included editorship of the Presbyterian journal *The Westminster* and, eventually, of the influential Toronto *Globe*, see Brian Fraser, "'The Christianization of our Civilization'," unpublished PH.D. thesis, York University, 1982.

43 Macdonald figures in Cook's *The Regenerators*. Cook describes Macdonald as one of a growing number of Protestant clergymen for whom "the ethical" took precedence over "the theological." See 184–5. Macdonald's thought, however, expressed a basic confidence that the Bible and theology would eventually prevail intellectually over the new forms of social thought.

44 S.D. Chown, "Moral Reform Notes – The Duty of the Hour," *ChG*, 20 Jan. 1904, 8.

45 See Chown Papers, "The Prophets as Preachers to their Own Times." See also ibid., box 3, file 66, "The Burden of Habakkuk and the Prophets," Hab. 3:2, ordination sermon preached at Peterborough, to the Bay of Quinte Conference, 5 June 1904; box 6, file 165, "The Enthronement of Christ in the Industrial Life of the Nation," James 5:2–3, sermon, 1899.

46 Robertson Smith, *The Prophets of Israel*, 82, 49–52, 58–9.

47 Grant Papers, vol. 26, "Clippings," "Pan-Presbyterian Council," *Weekly Witness*, 5 Oct. 1892. See also W.G. Watson, "Christian Socialism," *AV* 17, no. 5 (Feb. 1894): 159; Nathanael Burwash, "The Problem of Social Salvation," *MM&R* 55 (May 1902): 463–4; F.L. Farewell, "The Church and Social Problems," *AV* 27, no. 1 (Oct. 1903): 31–8; The Rev. Ernest

Thomas, "The Social Mission of Christianity," *ChG*, 12 May 1897, 290; W.H. "The Social Law of Service – by Richard T. Ely"[book review], *ChG*, 3 Feb. 1897, 67; "The Duty of the Church in the Matter of Social Reform"[editorial], *ChG*, 5 Mar. 1902, 152; The Rev. C.B. Ross, "Hoseah, Amos, and Micah"; The Rev. Principal MacVicar, "The Study of Sociology," *PCJ* 18, no. 3 (Jan. 1898): 175–88.

48 Grant Papers, vol. 26, "Clippings," "Political Partyism," *The Toronto Mail*, 14 Feb. 1887; ibid., vol. 19, "Righteousness Exalteth a Nation"; Burwash Papers, box 15, file 388, "The Evolution and Degeneration of Party. A Study in Political History," address to the Royal Society of Canada, section 2, 1903. See also S.D. Chown, "Moral Reform Notes"; "The Christianization of Politics"[editorial], *ChG*, 3 Feb. 1904, 5; "Not Party but Purity"[editorial], *ChG*, 18 Jan. 1905, 5. The critique of "partyism" was a general concern of other reformist groups in Canadian society. See, for the attitude of Canadian "imperialists," Berger, *The Sense of Power*, chapters 7 and 8. Like the imperialists, clergymen such as Grant, Burwash, and Chown insisted on education and leadership, rather than institutional modification, as a cure for the evils of party. The rise of a powerful non-partisan tradition oriented to national efficiency and service has been explored by English in *The Decline of Politics*. English's analysis is weakened, however, by lack of systematic attention to the intellectual beginnings of the movement, in which Protestant clergymen played a leading part.

49 See the recent interpretation by Christie of how late nineteenth-century historians combined idealism and Darwinian science into an explanation promoting the balance between cooperation and individualism in new societies. See "Prophecy and the 'Principles of Social Life'," chapter 6.

50 See Owram *The Government Generation*, 4–5. A debate continues both in Canada and abroad over the precise character of late nineteenth-century "social science," particularly varieties of the "New Liberalism" that were influenced both by Darwinian biology and by currents of idealist philosophy. A recent work on the social thought of Canadian historians has indicated a similar tension, and provides an interpretation of collectivism that stresses its fulfillment of the potential of the individual. See Christie, "Prophecy and the 'Principles of Social Life'." For the traditional interpretation, that idealism led directly to a collectivist outlook, see McKillop, *A Disciplined Intelligence*, chapter 7.

51 Burwash Papers, box 12, file 207, "Now unto him that is able to do exceedingly abundantly," sermon, 1899. See also W. Robertson Nicoll, "The Revival of Religion," *ChG*, 8 Nov. 1899, 712.

52 Grant Papers, "Practical Preaching." See also "The Principal of Queen's," *KCM* 18, no. 4 (Feb. 1893): 578; R. Milliken, "Hastening the

Prophetic Vision," *Vox Wesleyana* [*VW*] (Winnipeg) 9, no. 4 (Feb. 1905): 104; The Rev. W. Harrison, "The Victorian Era," *CMM* 25 (June 1887): 531–6; Dr Kilpatrick, "The Victorian Era," *VW* 4, no. 2 (Nov. 1899): 42–5; "Christ the True Horoscope of Humanity"[editorial], *ChG*, 11 Jan. 1899, 24; Edward A. Wicher, "The Place of the Missionary Enterprise in the General Development of the Race," *AV* 18, no. 1 (Oct. 1894): 20–3; Burwash Papers, box 14, file 375, "The Bible in the Life of the Christian Citizen," address given to the Provincial Sabbath School Association, Oct. 1895; Pidgeon Papers, box 32, no. 522, "The Victorian Era," sermon delivered at Streetsville, 27 Jan. 1901.

53 This is the argument advanced in chapter 10 of Cook's *The Regenerators*.

54 Robert Falconer, "Christ the Personal Source of Religion and Theology," *Theol.* (Halifax) 5, no. 1 (Dec. 1893): 4.

55 For the impact of the Ritschlian theology on the American religious scene, see Hutchison, *The Modernist Impulse in American Protestantism*, 112–13. For the British context, see Reardon, *Coleridge to Gore*. Canadian scholars have been notoriously imprecise concerning the impact of this important strand of religious thought. Allen argues in *The Social Passion*, 4–5, however, that "Ritschl's thought, usually unsystematically appropriated, provided the implicit theological foundations of much of the social gospel,"but he offers no analysis of this theme in the Canadian context. The text of Cook's *The Regenerators* contains no mention of Ritschl, despite his approving mention in a footnote of H.R. Mackintosh 's view that Ritschl stripped the Kingdom of God "of the eschatological transcendence that belongs to it in the Gospels," making it "hardly more than ... a realm of moral ends, a purely present and mundane commonwealth." (*The Regenerators*, 242n15).

56 Harnack, *History of Dogma*, vol. 1, 16; Harnack, *What Is Christianity?* 51, 199–214. For Harnack's views, see Reardon, *Liberal Protestantism*, 17. For a modern study of Harnack, see Glick, *The Reality of Christianity*.

57 Wallace Papers, box 4, "Memories of the Manse, the Parsonage, and the College," vol. 1, 74–5. See also Prof. R.A. Falconer, "Christian Theology Spiritually Discerned," *PCJ* 15, no. 3 (Jan. 1896): 176–7; Robert Falconer, "My Memory of Harnack," *The Canadian Journal of Religious Thought CJRT* 7, no. 5 (Nov.-Dec. 1930): 376–80; James W. Falconer, "Religious Factor in Ritschl's Theology," *PCJ* 16, no. 4 (Feb. 1897): 263–9.

58 John Currie, "The Theology of Ritschl," *KCM* 20 (Jan. 1896): 427–43. A lecture originally delivered at the opening of Presbyterian College, Halifax, Nov. 1895.

59 The prominent example of Salem Bland is particularly instructive. Al-

len's *The Social Passion* is based on the dubious generalization that the intellectual currents that influenced Salem Bland also determined the wider social outlook of the Canadian churches.

60 Nathanael Burwash, "History of Dogma"[book review], *MM&R* 43 (April 1896): 371–2.

61 Burwash Papers, box 17, file 456, "Lectures on the History of Christian Doctrine," Victoria College, Oct. 1897. For a similar assessment of Harnack's views on doctrine, see Herbert Symonds, "Harnack's History of Dogma," *QQ* 3, no. 2 (Oct. 1895): 132–3; The Rev. E.A. Wicher, "What Is Christianity?" *The Westminster* (20 Dec. 1901): 792–3; "'What Is Christianity'," *ChG*, 7 Aug. 1901, 497; Wallace Papers, box 1, file 1, Wallace to Nathanael Burwash, 21 Dec. 1910.

62 For A.B. Bruce's views, see J.E. McFadyen, "Alexander Balmain Bruce: An Appreciation," *The Westminster* (7 April 1900): 394. Henry Drummond was professor of natural science at New College, Edinburgh. For his life and influence, see Smith, *The Life of Henry Drummond*.

63 Fairbairn, *The Place of Christ in Modern Theology*, viii, 3, 47–9, 187–8. The copy consulted in the John P. Robarts Research Library, University of Toronto, was Robert Falconer's personal copy. For impressions of Fairbairn by a young Canadian Methodist student, see McLaughlin Papers, box 1, file 3, "Correspondence 1890–1892," J.F. McLaughlin to "Dear Uncle." McLaughlin found Fairbairn "inspiring."

64 Fairbairn, *The Philosophy of the Christian Religion*, vii. See the admiring review by Samuel McComb, "The Meaning of Christianity," *QQ* 10, no. 4 (April 1903): 431–9.

65 Falconer, "Christ the Personal Source of Religion and Theology," 8. See also Principal MacVicar, "Dogma and Current Thought," *KCM* 17, no. 1 (May 1893): 691; King Papers, reel 1, "Inaugural Lecture," *The Manitoba College Journal*, 1893, 127–34.

66 Professor Samuel McComb, "Do We Need Dogma?" *The Westminster* 9, no. 19 (10 Nov. 1900): 569–70.

67 Burwash Papers, box 14, file 382, "Address on the Development of Methodist Theology and Mission." See also the Rev. C.S. Eby, "Modern Evangelism vs. Modern Scholarship – VIII. Wesley's Methodism," *ChG* 11 Oct. 1899, 650.

68 Burwash, *Manual of Christian Theology* vol. 1, 88–9. See also "Methodism and Religious Thought" [editorial], *ChG*, 3 Jan. 1900, 8; Ministers of the Church, "Letters to Young Ministers. 4. The Thinker above the Student," *ChG* 14 Feb. 1900; The Rev. J. Munro Gibson, "The Relation of Faith to Expanding Knowledge," *ChG* 21 Aug. 1901, 531.

69 Falconer, "Christ the Personal Source of Religion and Theology," 1–2, 9.

70 This historical outlook was often presented in the college journals and weekly newspapers of both the Presbyterian and Methodist Churches. See, for example, Robert Falconer, "The Church and Unity According to the New Testament," *PW*, 3 June 1905, 170; "The Church and its Unity According to the New Testament, II – The Earlier Apostolic World," *PW*, 10 June 1905, 178. See also "From Apostle to Priest" [review of the Rev. James W. Falconer's *From Apostle to Priest*], *The Westminster* (23 Feb. 1901): 223–5; the Rev. Prof. Scrimger, "The Ethical Development of Christianity – III. Early Experiences," *PCJ* 20, no. 4 (Feb. 1901): 271–5; Robert Falconer, "Early Christian Art," *QQ* 11, no. 3 (Jan. 1904): 236–42; Burwash Papers, "An Inner View of Early Christianity, A.D. 53–64," n.d.; ibid., "Conference Sermon," Niagara, 3 June 1906, "The Unity of Believers"; Grant Papers, vol. 14, "Exams and Lectures for Session 1892–93," "Inspiration."

71 "The Fact of Christ"[editorial], *The Westminster* (30 Mar. 1901): 363. See also "A New Rallying Point"[editorial], *The Westminster* 8, no. 19 (12 May 1900): 543; Chown Papers, box 14, file 416, "The Methodist Attitude Towards the Person of Christ," article, n.d.; Grant Papers, "Practical Preaching"; "Principal MacVicar's Address," *PCJ* 16, no. 6 (April 1897): 468; J. Thompson, "The Character of Christ: The Proof of Christianity," *KCM* 12, no. 3 (July 1890): 140–8; the Rev. S.J. Allin, "Christ the Unit of Theology," paper read before the Methodist Ministerial Association of London, *ChG*, 15 May 1901, 360.

72 Falconer, "Christ the Personal Source of Religion and Theology," 5; Rev. S.J. Allin, "Christ the Unit of Theology II," *ChG*, 22 May 1901, 322; J.W.F., "Lectures on the Incarnation, by Charles Gore," *Theol.* 3, no. 4 (May 1892): 182–3; F.H. Wallace, "The Principles, Methods, and Results of the Biblical Theology of the New Testament," *AV* 19, no. 3 (Dec. 1895): 95–6.

73 Chown Papers, box 6, file 147, "Beloved if God so loved us we ought to love one another," John 4:11, sermon, n.d.

74 Nathanael Burwash, "Current Tendencies in Religious Thought," *MM&R* 43 (Jan. 1896): 83. See also Burwash Papers, box 16, file 415, "Note on Personality and Morality," n.d.; ibid., box 12, file 201, "The Permanent Elements of Religion"; ibid., box 12, file 180, "The Atonement," sermon preached July 1881; ibid., box 17, file 453, "Lecture on the Atonement," Oct. 1888.

75 Gordon Papers, box 3, file 2, "The Fatherhood of God in Recent Theology"; the Rev. Prof. Scrimger, "The Presentation of the Gospel," *PCJ* 19, no. 5 (March 1900): 365–6.

76 For the impact of ethical humanism on the Canadian churches between 1880 and 1900, see Cook, *The Regenerators*. Although Cook does not specifically discuss views of sin, the implications are clear. Allen's

The Social Passion insists that "social gospel" clergymen such as Salem Bland and J.S. Woodsworth came to view sin not as a personal matter but as a social matter requiring the salvation of an entire society. McKillop's *A Disciplined Intelligence*, chapter 7, examines the impact of philosophical idealism on Christian doctrine through the eyes of John Watson, G.M. Grant, and George John Blewett.

77 The Rev. S.D. Chown, "The Place of Fear in Religion," *ChG*, 20 Jan. 1897, 34.

78 Burwash, *Manual of Christian Theology*, vol. 2, 68. See also Burwash Papers, box 20, file 505, "Biblical Data on the Doctrine of Sin," essay, n.d.; *Manual of Christian Theology*, vol. 2, 44; and A.C. Courtice, "'Future Punishment,' An Extract from the Inaugural Address Read before the Jackson Society," *AV* 8, no. 4 (Jan. 1885): 12–14.

79 R.A. Falconer, "Sin as a Religious Concept," *Theol.* 18 (Feb. 1907): 64, 66–7. See also J.A. Macdonald, "Principal Caven," *KCM* 11 (1891): 3; the Rev. E.H. Dewart, "What Should Ministers Preach?" *MM&R* 44 (July 1896): 73–4; Pidgeon Papers, box 32, no. 523, "The New Birth," sermon delivered at Streetsville, 11 Nov. 1900; Gordon Papers, box 5, file 76, "Spiritual Diagnosis," n.d.; King Papers, reel 1, "'The Purely Ethical Gospel Examined," a Lecture delivered by the Rev. Principal King, D.D. at the Opening of the Theological Classes in Manitoba College, 30 Mar. 1897."

80 S. Bland Papers, box 1, no. 28, "The Social Ideal," sermon delivered 13 Feb. 1905. See also Irwin Papers, box 1, no. 111, "The Kingdom of God," n.d.

81 See S. Bland Papers, box 4, no. 356, "The Kingdom of God realized only in Individual Regeneration," sermon, 18 Jan. 1899. For Bland's early career, see Allen, "Salem Bland – The Young Preacher," and his earlier treatment of Bland in "Salem Bland and the Social Gospel in Canada." For the influence of Queen's University and philosophical idealism on Bland, see McKillop, "The Idealist Legacy," in McKillop, *Contours of Canadian Thought*.

82 Chown Papers, box 6, file 159, "And the disciples were called Christians first in Antioch," Acts 11:26, sermon, n.d.

83 Chown Papers, "The Enthronement of Christ in the Industrial Life of the Nation."

84 Caven, "The Purpose of the Bible," in *Christ's Teachings Concerning the Last Things*, 107–8; Burwash Papers, box 12, file 207, "And if Christ is in you the body is dead," sermon, n.d.; Burwash, *Manual of Christian Theology on the Inductive Method*, vol. 2, 18.

85 Bruce, *The Kingdom of God*, 40–1, 59–60.

86 Watson, "Christian Socialism," 157–8. See also Robert Falconer, "Preaching to the Times," *Theol.* 14, no. 1 (Nov. 1902): 466; Farewell,

"The Church and Social Problems," 32–3; Gandier Papers, box 2, "A Sermon for the New Year," preached in St James Square Church, Toronto, Sunday morning, 31 Dec. 1905; A.E. Vrooman, "The Relation of the Church to Social Problems," *VW* 6, no. 2 (Nov. 1901): 27–9; the Rev. Prof. Scrimger, "The Ethical Development of Christiantity – V. The Present and the Future," *PCJ* 20, no. 6 (April 1901): 441–6; Burwash Papers, "The Map and History of the Twentieth Century."

87 The Rev. Principal MacVicar, "The Study of Sociology," *PCJ* 18, no. 3 (Jan. 1898): 176–9.

88 See McLoughlin's provocative and stimulating work, *Revivals, Awakenings, and Reform*, 141–78, which posits a conjunction between religion and the rising social sciences. For the British scene, see Jones, *Social Darwinism and English Thought*. The origin of the American social sciences has been treated in Haskell, *The Emergence of Professional Social Science*. The intellectual vitality of the American churches in this period is documented in Hutchison's *The Modernist Impulse in American Protestantism*.

89 See S. Bland Papers, box 1, file 18, "Four Steps and A Vision," lecture, Smith's Falls, 19 Oct. 1898. This address refers to popular evolutionary works by Henry Drummond, Benjamin Kidd, Arnold Toynbee, and Edward Bellamy. Such an acquaintance with evolutionary social thought was not typical of Canadian preachers at this time.

90 The link between history and the "evangelical" outlook remained strong, particularly in England, until the 1880s. See Parker, "English Historians and the Opposition to Positivism." For the late development of "professional" history in the English universities, see Heyck, *The Transformation of Intellectual Life in Victorian England*, chapter 5. More recently, Christie's work on late nineteenth-century historians in Canada and Australia has suggested the importance of the evolutionary paradigm to the interpretation of social life in these societies. This paradigm was, however, not acceptable to most evangelical clergymen.

91 For this emphasis of pre-1860 revivalism, see Smith, *Revivalism and Social Reform in America*, 7–8; Cole, *The Social Ideas of the Northern Evangelists*; and, most recently, Howe, *The Political Culture of the American Whigs*, chapter 7. For the Scottish scene, see Brown, *Thomas Chalmers*; and for the "perfectionist" emphasis of American religious figures before 1860, see McLoughlin, *Revivals, Awakenings, and Reform*, 122–31.

CHAPTER SIX

1 Burwash Papers, box 15, file 408, "Our Need of a Great Revival," address to the Nova Scotia Conference, June 1914.

2 Chown Papers, box 11, file 295, "The Present Need," address delivered January 1912.

3 Although not overtly stated, this is the implicit thesis of Cook's *The Regenerators*. Cook's secularization thesis touches upon the clergy, but concentrates on the thought and activity of individuals on the fringes of the evangelical churches. More recently, Cook's argument has been applied to clergymen themselves by Marshall in "The Clerical Response to Secularization." Marshall concentrates on Methodist and Presbyterian ministers in the period just before 1914, explaining that the "crisis" was brought about by the perpetual dichotomy between the monolithic categories of "other-worldly religion" and "identification with the dominant political, social, and economic ethos of the nation."

4 For the British scene, see Cox, *The English Churches in a Secular Society*, chapter 7, and Yeo, *Religion and Voluntary Organizations in Crisis*. For the American churches, see Marsden, *Fundamentalism and American Culture*, 124–38.

5 Cox, *English Churches in a Secular Society*, 221–7. In the Canadian context, Marshall's recent thesis has strongly emphasized the perception of Canadian church leaders that their numbers were declining. Clinging to the secularization thesis advanced by Cook, Marshall undercuts his own case by refusing to consider the problem of numbers, on the grounds that statistical evidence of church attendance tells us little about the problem of secularization.

6 Marsden, *Fundamentalism and American Culture*, 124–5.

7 For the European scene, see Hughes, *Consciousness and Society*. More recently, Kloppenberg's *Uncertain Victory* presents the "pragmatic revolution" in its European, American, and British manifestations. See also John Higham, "The Reorientation of American Culture in the 1890's", in Higham, *Writing American History*, 73–102. The literature on this reorientation of social thought is critically assessed in Haskell, *The Emergence of Professional Social Science*, 1–23.

8 Gordon Papers, box 5, file 77, "Inaugural Address of Principal Gordon, 1903." See also the Rev. A.H. Reynar, "Christian Culture," *CMM* 40 (Oct. 1894): 397–8; the Rev. Principal MacVicar, "The Church and the College," *PCJ* 16, no. 4 (Feb. 1897): 270–6; Gandier Papers, box 2, "The Moral Ideal – Greek and Christian," n.d.; Burwash Papers, box 20, file 510, "Moral and Religious Spirit of the Greek Tragedy," essay, n.d.

9 See the Rev. Principal MacVicar, "The Holy Ghost the Author and Interpreter of the Scriptures," *PCJ* 15, no. 2 (Dec. 1895): 108; the Rev. Prof. G.L. Robinson, "'The Place of Deuteronomy in Hebrew Literature,' lecture delivered at Knox College," *The Westminster* (Oct. 1896): 201–6; Prof. J.F. McLaughlin, "'Critical Views of the Mosaic Religion

and Literature,' paper read at the Theological Conference, Nov. 1896, *AV* 20, no. 5 (Feb. 1897): 242–5; John Scrimger, "Recent Discussions in Old Testament Criticism," *PCJ* 17, no. 1 (Nov. 1897): 5–8.

10 See, for example, Ross, "Historical Consciousness in Nineteenth Century America" Heyck, *The Transformation of Intellectual Life in Victorian England*, chapter 5; Christie, "Prophecy and the 'Principles of Social Life'," chapter 2. Both Ross and Heyck, however, make the point that the 1870s and 1880s mark a time of transition for historical writing in the United States and Britain – from history as a study of immutable moral principles to history studied for its own sake. According to Christie, the older outlook in Canada did not succumb to "historicism" until well into the twentieth century.

11 Christie's "Prophecy and the 'Principles of Social Life'," offers an example of this contrast. It examines the uses of history by more secular writers, journalists, educators, and historians to formulate a nationalism based on bio-social evolutionary assumptions – a goal that evangelical clergymen, with their overtly theological interpretation of history, would almost certainly not have condoned.

12 McFadyen, *Old Testament Criticism and the Christian Church*, 46–7.

13 Prof. J.F. McCurdy, "The Drawbacks of Criticism," *The Westminster* (2 Nov. 1901): 526; "Is the Bible a Fixed Authority" [editorial], *ChG*, 16 Mar. 1904, 5.

14 See Antoni, *From History to Sociology*, introduction by Hayden White. See also Iggers, *The German Conception of History*, 13–14, 26. For the British scene, see Parker, "English Historians and the Opposition to Positivism." Burrow's *Evolution and Society* contains a fine discussion of how evolutionary thinkers like Spencer, Tylor, Maine, and Lubbock avoided the perils of relativism.

15 See Iggers, *The German Conception of History*, 124–5.

16 Kloppenberg's recent study of transatlantic intellectual currents, *Uncertain Victory*, insists upon the "revolutionary" nature of the period after 1890, as well as the study of history, the record of human experience, as the point uniting thinkers such as William James, John Dewey, Wilhelm Dilthey, Alfred Fouillee, and T.H. Green. The impact of pragmatism on American historical writing has been the subject of several studies. See, especially, White, *Social Thought in America*, and Strout, *The Pragmatic Revolt in American History*.

17 For the Canadian pilgrimage to Germany after 1900, see Moir, *A Sense of Proportion*, 108.

18 For the definition of form criticism, see Bultmann and Kundsin, *Form Criticism*.

19 Gibert, *Une theorie de la legende*, 253, 263, 260–6, 271–2, 362. This work contains the complete 1910 edition of Gunkel's *The Legends of Genesis*.

The most extreme statement of the "Babylonian theory" was provided by Delitzsch, in his celebrated *Babel and Bible*.

20 Troeltsch, "The Dogmatics of the Religiongeschichtliche Schule." Antoni's *From History to Sociology* contains a fine essay on Troeltsch.

21 Iggers, *The German Conception of History*, 182–4; Antoni, *From History to Sociology*, xvii, 48–51. See also Troeltsch, "Historiography," in Hastings, ed., *Encyclopedia of Religion and Ethics*, vol. 6, 721. Hastings's *Encyclopedia* was a widely consulted work of reference to which Canadian evangelical scholars contributed.

22 Weiss, *Jesus' Proclamation of the Kingdom of God*, 4–5, 129–33, 135–6.

23 Schweitzer, *The Quest of the Historical Jesus*, vi, xv, 396–7.

24 "Manitoba College Opening" [editorial], *The Presbyterian* (Toronto) (12 July 1902): 57. See also "Our Westernmost College," *The Presbyterian*, 6 Jan. 1910, 3; J.W. Macmillan, "Theological Education," *The Presbyterian*, 31 Oct. 1912, 478–9; McCree, "William George Jordan," in R.C. Wallace, ed., *Some Great Men of Queen's* (Toronto, 1941), 107.

25 Burwash Papers, box 1, file 5, A.P. Misener to Burwash, 27 July 1906. See also McFadyen, *Old Testament Criticism and the Christian Church*, 22.

26 "A New Method of New Testament Study," *Theol.* 18, (Dec. 1906): 13.

27 Prof. J.M. Shaw, "The Incarnation and Modern Thought," *Theol.* 26 (Dec. 1914): 7–8, 10–11; Principal Ross, "Theological Education," *The Presbyterian*, 19 Feb. 1914, 233.

28 Jordan, *Biblical Criticism and Modern Thought*, 127–8, 178, 247–8.

29 Biographical details on Gordon can be found in "Alexander Reid Gordon," UCCA, biographical files.

30 Gordon, *The Early Traditions of Genesis*, 36, 43–5, 54.

31 Ibid., 89–90.

32 Denney, *Jesus and the Gospel*, vii-viii; 383.

33 Scott, *The Kingdom and the Messiah*, vi, 252–7; *The Beginnings of the Church*, 258–61. Scott attended the University of Glasgow and Balliol College, Oxford, and preached in Scotland before assuming the New Testament chair at Queen's in 1908. In 1919, he left Queen's to join the theological faculty at Union Theological Seminary, New York. For biographical details on Scott's years at Queen's see Rawlyk and Quinn, *The Redeemed of the Lord Say So*.

34 See Owram, *The Government Generation*, chapter 3, for a discussion of the quest for authority among political economists and social scientists. Significantly, Owram's periodization of 1906–1916 almost exactly parallels the impact of historical relativism on the theological faculties, but he does not make the connection between this movement and changes in the international climate of philosophical and historical discussion.

35 See Scott, *Office to Profession*, for a fine discussion of the New England

clergy between 1790 and 1850. Scott presents the paradox that during an age of religious revival the cultural and social authority of the clergy actually declined. He links this process to social changes unleashed by the American Revolution, and to the nineteenth-century evangelical revival.

36 For a recent exploration of this cultural shift, see the stimulating essay by Lears, "From Salvation to Self-Realization: Advertising and the Therapeutic Roots of the Consumer Culture, 1880–1930," in Fox and Lears, *The Culture of Consumption*, 1–38. I thank George Rawlyk for having called this important issue to my attention. This problem has not been addressed so far by students of Canadian history. See, however, the provocative essay by Rawlyk on McMaster University in the early twentieth century in Rawlyk, ed., *Canadian Baptists and Christian Higher Education*.

37 James Wilkins, "Study of the Old Testament," *VW* 17, no. 3 (Jan. 1913): 7. See also Prof. H.A. Kent, "The Old Testament," *Theol.* 23 (Feb. 1912): 44–52; A.H. Mackay, "Modern Views of Miracle in the Gospels," *Theol.* 17 (March 1906): 87–96; James Moffatt, D.D., "Considering Jesus," *The Presbyterian*, 4 Jan. 1912, 76–7; "We Know"[editorial], *ChG*, 6 Mar. 1907, 6.

38 R.P. Bowles, "The Bible and Revelation," *ChG*, 11 Jan. 1911, 11–12, 30.

39 E.F. Scott, "The Place of Theology," *QQ* 16, no. 3 (Jan. 1909): 209–12.

40 The Rev. Alfred E. Lavell, "Theological Education and the Methodist Church," *ChG*, 14 Nov. 1906, 7; Lavell, "Theological Education and the Methodist Church," *ChG*, 21 Nov. 1906, 11–12. See also the Rev. Principal Mackinnon, untitled article in *Theol.* 23 (April 1912): 113–16; Gandier Papers, box 2, "Predestination and the Historical Decision," article in *The Presbyterian*, 1906; Prof. A.H. Abbott, "Essential Christianity," *VW* 34, no. 4 (Jan. 1911): 212–18; Bowles, "The Bible and Revelation," 30; "Editorial," *PCJ* 26, no. 4 (March 1907): 63–4; W. Lashley Hall, "Present-Day Conditions and the Kingdom of God. II. Intellectual and Religious Unrest," *ChG*, 6 Oct. 1907, 8–9.

41 John Dall, "The Study of History," *QQ* 19, no. 3 (Jan. 1912): 256–63.

42 Ibid., 263.

43 Ibid., 268.

44 "Religious Thought"[editorial], *The Presbyterian*, 4 Aug. 1910, 99. See also Gandier Papers, box 2, "Inaugural Address," delivered at Convocation Hall, 19 Nov. 1908; J.W.A. Nicholson, "Ministers and Ministry," *Theol.* 21 (Dec. 1909): 9–11. This equation of Christianity and progress was sufficiently widespread for Robert Falconer, then president of the University of Toronto, to issue a critique and warning. See R.A. Falconer, "Progress," *Theol.* 22 (Feb. 1911): 61.

45 On industrialization and its attendant difficulties in Canada, see the

discussion by Brown and Cook in *Canada 1896–1921*, chapters 5 and 6.
On the problem of intellectual authority and the social sciences, see
Owram, *The Government Generation*, chapters 1–3; and on consumer-
ism, see Fox and Lears, *The Culture of Consumption*.

46 My interpretation of the concept of "ritual of consensus" is derived
from Bercovitch, *The American Jeremiad*. In this analysis of modes of
rhetoric, Bercovitch argues that the jeremiad, a mode of public exhor-
tation favoured by the New England Puritans, was a "ritual designed
to join social criticism to spiritual renewal, public to private identity,
and shifting 'signs of the times' to certain traditional metaphors,
themes, and symbols,"(ix). Given the central role of the study of history in the Canadian evangelical creed, and the prominence of prophetic and millennial symbols and metaphors, which confirmed and
ordered the Protestant vision of the past, the alliance of theology and
history served as a modernized analogue of the jeremiad among Canadian Methodists and Presbyterians.

47 Machen, "Christianity and Culture," address delivered at the opening
of the Princeton Theological Seminary, and originally published in *The
Princeton Theological Review*. Machen's address was reprinted in two in-
stallments in *The Presbyterian*, 27 Feb. 1913, 268–70, and 6 Mar. 1913,
300–2.

48 Machen, "Christianity and Culture," 27 Feb. 1913, 268.

49 For Machen's historical views, see Marsden, "J. Gresham Machen,
History, and Truth," *Westminster Theological Journal* 42, no. 1 (Fall
1979): 157–75. For Machen's place in the debate over the relationship
between "Christianity" and "culture," and his role in the fundamentalist movement that emerged in the 1920s, see Marsden, *Fundamentalism
and American Culture*, 135–8, 173–95.

50 James Mills, "The Condition of Methodism in Canada," *ChG*, 9 Nov.
1898, 706. For the number of college-trained ministers in 1900, see
Burwash Papers, "Address on the Development of Methodist Theology and Mission."

51 Accounts of the Carman-Jackson affair are provided by Prang in *N.W.
Rowell*, 70–88; and by Sinclair-Faulkner, "Theory Divided from Practice: The Introduction of the Higher Criticism into Canadian Protestant Seminaries," *Papers*, 1980, 33–75.

52 Carman Papers, box 24, file 45, "Authority in Religion," n.d.

53 Jackson Papers, box 1, the Rev. George Jackson, "The Early Narratives
of Genesis," lecture at the Young Men's Christian Association, Toronto, 16 Feb. 1909.

54 Jackson Papers, box 1, "A.R. Carman's Letter to *The Globe*," 26 Feb.
1909. See also Carman Papers, box 24, file 98, "The Higher Criticism
and the Lower Socialism," n.d.

55 Burwash Papers, "The Life and Labors of Nathanael Burwash," "Inductive Theology," 2; W.R. Harper, "The Rational and the Rationalistic Higher Criticism," *CMQ* 4 (Oct. 1892): 442.

56 Burwash's dealings with Workman were indeed curious. He continued to write Workman letters of recognition, but privately he complained that "Dr. Workman is the kind of material out of which martyrs are made and his best friends are at a loss to know what can be done ... I did my best for him ... and if he had been at all willing to cooperate with me, he might have been in Victoria still, but he is unfortunate in his way of putting things. Other men would teach probably the most of what he desires to teach without giving any offence or without putting it in any way before the public that it would to appear to contradict doctrines which are held to be essential by the Methodist Church." See Burwash Papers, box 7, file 58, Burwash to the Rev. William Philp, 6 Feb. 1909. For the rules governing biblical scholarship at Victoria College, particularly the ambiguous insistence that academic freedom must not conflict with the essential beliefs of the church, see Sinclair-Faulkner, "Theory Divided from Practice," 53–6.

57 Lavell, "'The Popularization of the Old and New Testament Literature and History, and the History and Institutions of th Christian Church.' Prepared for use in Connection with the Institutes for the Extension of University Teaching in Old and New Testament Literature and History ... under the auspices of the Educational Society of the Methodist Church and the General s.s. and e.l. Board, Series no. 2, issued 22 May 1905."

58 Carman Papers, box 18, file 123, May R. Thornley to the Rev. C.T. Scott, 23 Feb. 1906. The impact of the London Institute is also noted by Prang, *N.W. Rowell*, 74.

59 Burwash Papers, box 1, file 7, Morley Pettit to Burwash, 11 Feb. 1908.

60 For the resolution of the controversy, and the drafting of a statement ostensibly guaranteeing academic freedom to the college faculty, see Prang, *N.W. Rowell*, 79; Burwash Papers, box 1, file 7, Morley Pettit to Burwash, 11 Feb. 1908; ibid., box 2, file 14, Elizabeth McNaughton to Burwash, 19 May 1909. See also Jackson Papers, box 1, John Carlisle to Carman, 12 Oct. 1910; W.J. Kellogg to Carman, 6 Aug. 1910; Carman papers, box 5, file 100, Millie Magwood to A.R. Carman. 7 June 1912.

61 Burwash Papers, box 7, file 59, C.A. Jones to Burwash, 5 April 1909. For letters voicing similar opinions see in Carman Papers, Anna Ross to the editor of *The Globe*, copy given to A.R. Carman, 8 Mar. 1909; W.J. Kellogg to Albert Carman, 16 Aug. 1910; John Carlisle to A.R. Carman, 12 Oct. 1910.

62 Wm. H. Hincks[letter], *ChG*, 25 Jan. 1905, 8–9; the Rev. C.S. Eby, "The Methodist Note," *ChG*, 19 April 1906, 6–7; Carman Papers, box 18, file 123, the Rev. C.T. Scott to Carman, 28 Feb. 1906; Jackson Papers, box 1, Dr J.N. Hutchison to Carman, 10 Mar. 1909; ibid., M. McGregor to Carman, 26 May 1911.

63 S. Bland Papers, box 1, no. 51, "Fragments on Christianity and Science," 18 Oct. 1908; ibid., box 5, no. 443, "Christianity the Completion of All Things," university sermon, Oct. 1908.

64 S. Bland Papers, box 3, file 227, "The Fourth Gospel, 1900–1907."

65 S. Bland Papers, box 3, no. 231, "Pre-Eminence of Christ in Relation to the Bible," lecture 2, 1914.

66 In 1910–11 some Manitoba Methodists accused Bland of Unitarianism and efforts were made to try him for heresy. Despite the intervention of General Superintendent Carman, these proceedings failed. See S. Bland papers, box 11, no. 897a, "Charge of Unsound Doctrine," 1911. See also Carman Papers, box 14, file 86, the Rev. H. Kenner to Albert Carman, 10 Feb. 1910; Kenner to Carman, 24 Feb. 1910; Carman to Salem Bland, 16 Feb. 1910.

67 Jackson Papers, box 1, C.T. Scott to A.R. Carman, 14 Mar. 1910.

68 See Charles H. Huestis, "Theological Education and the Work of the Ministry," *ChG*, 17 Feb. 1909, 7–8. The Board of Regents' statement is quoted in Prang, *N.W. Rowell*, 79. See also Sinclair-Faulkner, "Theory Divided from Practice," 52. While Sinclair-Faulkner agrees that a division between college teaching and preaching occurred, my assessment traces the problem to a more fundamental cultural problem than the skirmish between Carman and Jackson.

69 The Rev. A.K. Birks, "The Theological School and the Faith of the Student: A Reply to Mr. Huestis," 11 Aug. 1909, 11–12.

70 Armstrong, *The Christian Ministry and Modern Thought*, 6–8.

71 Baird Papers, reel 6, J.N. Maclean to A.B. Baird, 11 Dec. 1901.

72 See Moir, *Enduring Witness*, 176, 201–2. For the dialogue between the Princeton theology and Darwinian evolution, see Livingstone, *Darwin's Forgotten Defenders*.

73 MacLaren, *Sixty Years' Retrospect*, a lecture delivered at the opening of Knox College, 8 Oct. 1907. MacLaren's views paralleled a hardening of the Princeton theology against evolution and higher criticism after 1905. See Livingstone, *Darwin's Forgotten Defenders*, and Marsden, *Fundamentalism and American Culture*.

74 Mrs J.W. Van Norman, "Present-Day Preaching"[letter], *The Presbyterian*, 20 Oct. 1910, 446–7; William R. Woods, "The Cause of Our Ineffectiveness," *The Presbyterian*, 21 Sept. 1905, 363.

75 Baird Papers, reel 20, D. Macleod to Baird, 5 May 1908.

76 See Paul Peel, "Getting Rid of Mysticism," *The Westminster* (8 April 1902): 430–1; the Rev. H. Gracey, "The Scientific Method of Biblical

Criticism," *The Presbyterian* (6 Feb. 1904): 170–1; J.F. McLaren, "The Decrease in the Number of Students for the Ministry – II," *The Presbyterian*, 18 Oct. 1906, 448; the Rev. H. Gracey, "'Criticism's Mark'"[letter], *The Presbyterian*, Nov. 24, 1910, 594; George Hanson, "'The Pentateuch – A Study'" [letter], *The Presbyterian*, 9 April 1914, 475–8.

77 "The Value of Biblical Controversy"[editorial], *The Presbyterian*, 23 Jan. 1908, 99. See also "Controversy"[editorial], *The Presbyterian*, 18 Mar. 1909.

78 McFadyen, *Old Testament Criticism and the Christian Church*, 25–7; Jordan, *Biblical Criticism and Modern Thought*, 237.

79 On the question of church union, which eventually split the Presbyterian Church, see the recent study by Clifford, *The Resistance to Church Union in Canada*. The troubles over the secularization of Queen's University have been explored by Rawlyk and Quinn in *The Redeemed of the Lord Say So*, chapter 1. There is no modern study of the intense debate over theological education that exercised church opinion between 1910 and 1914, but its general tenor can be gained from the following: Gandier Papers, box 2, C.W. Gordon to Gandier, 8 Aug. 1910; ibid., box 2, Reply to Gordon's letter, n.d.; ibid., box 1, file "Correspondence 1911," J.W. Macmillan to Gandier, 17 Jan. 1911. See also articles in *The Presbyterian* by Principal Ross, 19 Feb. 1914, 233–5; "Greek, Hebrew, and English"[editorial], 12 Sept. 1912, 251–2; W.L. Grant, "Education for the Ministry," 3 Oct. 1912, 350; Logie Macdonnell, "Greek and Hebrew in Theological Education"[letter], 12 Sept. 1912, 270–1; "Study the Originals," 5 Feb. 1914, 168; Daniel Strachan, "That Interview with Ralph Connor," 19 Mar. 1914, 359.

80 Consider the examples of John Watson and his disciple Samuel Dyde, who eventually headed Queen's Theological College. Both men opposed the secularization of the university, against Principal Gordon, whose theological position was more "traditional" in nature. See the analysis by Rawlyk and Quinn in *The Redeemed of the Lord Say So*.

81 Chown Papers, box 11, file 295, "The Present Need," address delivered January 1912.

82 Chown Papers, box 12, file 338, "What Methodism Stands For," Ottawa address, n.d. My interpretation of Chown's soul-searching differs fundamentally from that posited by Marshall in "The Clerical Response to Secularization." Marshall argues that, prior to World War I, Chown held to a naïve faith in theological "liberalism" and "sociology," and that shocked him into a return to a more "evangelical" position.

83 Gordon Papers, box 5, file 83, "Gordon's Address at the Induction of Professor William Morgan, October 23, 1912." See also Gandier Papers, box 2, "Predestination and the Historical Decision. II," *The Pres-*

byterian, 1906; "Transcendent as Well as Immanent"[editorial], *ChG*, 27 Feb. 1907, 5; "The Passion For God"[editorial], *The Presbyterian*, 2 May 1912, 547; the Rev. William Morgan, "Divine Revelation," *The Presbyterian*, 7 Nov. 1912, 513–14.

84 See Hutchison, *The Modernist Impulse in American Protestantism*, 222–5. For the European scene, see Richardson, *History Sacred and Profane*, 131.

85 Worries concerning the loss of evangelistic power were expressed from time to time in the pages of *The Christian Guardian*. See the Rev. W. McMullen, "The Dangers and Needs of To-Day," *ChG*, 4 Jan. 1905, 6, 10; Wm. H. Hincks[letter], *ChG*, 25 Jan. 1905, 8–9; the Rev. C.S. Eby, "The Methodist Note," *ChG*, 19 April 1906, 6–7.

86 Chown Papers, "What Methodism Stands For."

87 Chown Papers, "The Present Need." For the impact of James's ideas and pragmatism on Canadian Methodism, see A.B. Macallum, "Pragmatism, Religion, Politics, and Morals," *AV* 37, no. 3 (Dec. 1912): 134–6.

88 Chown Papers, box 11, file 294, "The Adaptation of the Church to the Needs of Modern Life," Address delivered at the Ecumenical Conference, Toronto, 10 Oct. 1911. See also ibid., box 15, file 428, "Report re Course of Study for Ministry," n.d.; S.D. Chown, "Reorganization of Theological Training," *ChG*, 11 Feb. 1914, 8; ibid., 18 Feb. 1914, 8–9; ibid., 25 Feb. 1914, 8–9; J.W. Magwood, "A Change in our Theological Curriculum Imperative," *ChG*, 3 June 1914, 8–9.

89 Chown Papers, box 13, file 377, "The Sociological Man," address, n.d.; ibid., "The Present Need."

90 McKillop, *A Disciplined Intelligence*, 226.

91 The Rev. S.D. Chown, "Christianity and Socialism," *ChG*, 9 Jan. 1907, 10; Chown Papers, box 13, file 379, "Sociological Course. Lecture I. Importance of the Study of Sociology," delivered at Wesley College, Winnipeg, 1914.

92 Chown Papers, box 13, file 380, "Sociological Course. Lecture II. The Relation of Sociology to the Kingdom of Heaven," 1914; ibid., box 13, file 381, "Sociological Course. Lecture III. Socialism and the Social Teachings of Jesus," 1914. Works cited by Chown during the course of these addresses included Henry Churchill King, *The Ethics of Jesus*; John Spargo, *Socialism*; Le Rossignol, *Orthodox Socialism*; Walter Rauschenbusch, *Christianity and the Social Crisis*; Professor Peabody, *Jesus Christ and the Social Question*. For the independent position of sociology in major American research schools by 1914, see Haskell, *The Emergence of Professional Social Science*. Chown belonged, according to Haskell's logic, not to the world of Albion Small, John Dewey, or Max Weber, who claimed to offer a value-free, objective "science of soci-

ety," but to the world of the 1870s and 1880s, where an intense moral-
ism dominated the reform discussions of the American Social Science
Association. See 100–4.

93 This is McKillop's dictum on Chown's place in the strand of moral
thinking examined in *A Disciplined Intelligence*.

CHAPTER SEVEN

1 Chown Papers, box 14, file 408, *Some Causes of the Decline of the Earlier
Typical Evangelism*, (Toronto, 1930), 3.

2 Ibid., 5.

3 Ibid., 5–6.

4 For the wartime reform activities of Canada's Protestant clergymen,
see Allen, *The Social Passion*, chapters 3 and 4. See also Bliss, "The
Methodist Church and World War I," and the regional study by
Thompson, *The Harvests of War*. For the impact of the "ideal of service" on Canadian politics, see English, *The Decline of Politics*. For the
discussions and tensions surrounding church union, see Clifford, *The
Resistance to Church Union in Canada*.

5 Allen, *The Social Passion*. Allen's dichotomy was, however, a source of
optimism for his commitment to democratic socialism. Although the
churches failed to hold the two elements in balance, they were able to
influence the wider culture and political tradition through the "social
gospel." Allen's interpretation has assumed the status of historical
"orthodoxy," as it has found its way into the most recent survey of
the period. See Thompson with Seager, *Canada 1922–1939*, 58–61. In
the 1980s, however, it has been given a pessimistic twist by historians
who see the abandonment of the "old evangelism" as an indication of
outright defeat, and an expression of the intellectual bankruptcy of
Canadian Protestantism. For this "neo-conservative" interpretation,
see Bliss, "The Methodist Church and World War I," and the more
recent work by Marshall, "The Clerical Response to Secularization."

6 Chown, *Some Causes of the Decline of the Earlier Typical Evangelism*, 8.

7 Professor Alexander R. Gordon, "The Prophets as Models for the
Preacher," *The Presbyterian and Westminster*[*P&W*](Toronto), 5 April
1917, 382–3. See also J.E. Todd, "Through History to God," *Theol.* 27
(Dec. 1916): 5–19; F.N. Stapleford, "Prophets: True and False," *ChG*,
11 Sept. 1918, 7–8; McLaughlin Papers, box 2, file 35, "Interpretation
of Prophecy in Light of Modern Events," ca 1918.(The folder containing this address also includes a 1918 article entitled "Bolshevism.")

8 Chown Papers, box 5, file 119, "Thou hast set me at large when I was
in distress," Psa. 4:1, sermon ca 1914–1918. See also Mackinnon Papers, reel 1, "Gal. 5:1, sermon delivered to the North British Society,

Dec. 31, 1916"; Gandier Papers, box 2, "The Challenge of this War to the Church," lecture delivered at the opening of the 1916–17 session of Knox College, 28 Sept. 1916.

9 Allen, *The Social Passion*, chapters 3 and 4; Bliss, "The Methodist Church and World War I."

10 Chown Papers, box 2, file 30, "A New Year's Message," 30 Dec. 1920; ibid., box 2, file 43, "Letter to the Editor *re* National Campaign: Winning 100,000 Souls for Christ – The Method: Personal Evangelism," 8 Mar.1920. See also Pidgeon Papers, box 33, file 577, "The Test of True Religion," sermon delivered at Bloor St Church, Toronto, 28 May 1916; Norman Ritcey, "The Two-Fold Work of Christianity," *ChG*, 16 Aug. 1916, 9–10; Principal S.W. Dyde, "The War, the Church, and Spiritual Life," *P&W*, 1 Mar. 1917, 242–3; "Religion, Personal and Social"[editorial], *P&W*, 13 Mar. 1919, 243–4..

11 Allen, *The Social Passion*, chapters 5, 6, and 7; Bliss, "The Methodist Church and the First World War"; Thompson, *The Harvests of War*.

12 Oliver Papers, reel 1, file 6a, sermon/address, ca 1916.

13 Dr E.F. Scott, "A Living Sacrifice," *The Canadian Student*[CS] 1, no. 4 (Dec. 1918): 9. See also Mackinnon Papers, reel 1, "Gal. 5:1"; Gandier Papers, "The Challenge of this War to the Church"; Law, "Optimism," in *Optimism and Other Sermons*, 32–3; Chown Papers, box 14, file 406, "The Mission of the Church after the War." One recent analysis has suggested that similar themes dominated the preaching of the chaplains at the battlefront. See Marshall, "Methodism Embattled," 55–6.

14 Wohl, *The Generation of 1914*, 200–1. Canadian historians have lagged behind in assessing the effects of the war on the common soldier and on popular culture. See, however, the article by Martel, "Generals Die in Bed," 6. British and European discussions on the impact of war on the common soldier have provoked exciting research. See, for example, Keegan, *The Face of Battle*; Fussell, *The Great War and Modern Memory*; Leed, *No Man's Land*.

15 This type of analysis is represented by Marshall, "Methodism Embattled." In an attempt to force the wartime experience into the categories established nearly twenty years ago by Allen and Bliss, Marshall misses a chance to probe the ideas and the context of the activities of wartime chaplains.

16 E.A. Corbett, "Religion in the Army," *CS* 1, no. 1 (March 1918): 21.

17 C. Wellesley Whittaker, "When the Boys Return," *ChG*, 6 Feb. 1918, 8–9. See also Theo. R.W. Lunt, "The Soldiers and the Church," *P&W*, 26 July 1917, 88–9; Capt. D. Wallace Christie, Chaplain, "A Soldiers' Meeting and Some Reflections," *ChG*, 27 June 1918, 620.

18 The Rev. John Kelman, "Religion at the Front," *P&W*, 12 July 1917, 39; Christie, "A Soldiers' Meeting," 620.

19 Martel, "Generals Die in Bed," 5. In Christian tradition, Christ is, of course, identified with the shepherd.

20 Law, "The Hope of our Calling," in Law, *The Hope of Our Calling*, 16. Other sermons dealt with Resurrection, Judgment, and the Eternal Life.

21 See Cook, *The Regenerators*, for the classic expression of such a belief. Apart from looking at a rather small though certainly vocal community of late-Victorian "secularists," Cook fails to provide evidence that the belief in Christ's divinity was called into question in either the colleges or the pulpits of the evangelical churches.

22 Mackinnon Papers, reel 1, "Acts 26:19," sermon, n.d.

23 E.A. Corbett, "The Student and the Church," *CS* (July 1918): 17–20.

24 Capt. the Rev. A.E. Lavell, "The Returning Soldier and the Church. V. Some Theological Suggestions," *ChG*, 15 May 1918, 9–10. See also S.H. Hooke, "The Student Movement and the Church," *CS* 1, no. 2 (Oct. 1918): 21–4; Frank N. Stapleford, "The Creeds and their Critics," *ChG*, 30 Jan. 1918, 8–9.

25 Pidgeon Papers, box 33, file 593, "Moral Responsibility," sermon delivered at Bloor St Church, 8 Oct. 1916. See also Mackinnon Papers, reel 1, "John 1:29," sermon, n.d.; the Rev. James Barber, "Prayer and National Defence," *P&W*, 12 July 1917, 44–5; "What Life is For"[editorial], *P&W*, 18 Jan. 1917, 71–2.

26 On the idea of comradeship and community, see Wohl, *The Generation of 1914*, 220; Leed, *No Man's Land*, 213.

27 Roberts Papers, box 4, file 112, "The Scope of Theology," lecture, 1927.

28 See Allen, *The Social Passion*, 347–56. This interpretation has also influenced the analysis of Thompson and Seager, *Decades of Discord* (see the chapter entitled "An End to Idealism," where the disillusionment of the churches is emphasized).

29 Pidgeon Papers, box 20, file 339c, G.C. Pidgeon to Charles J. Stephens, 23 Dec. 1929; Allen, *The Social Passion*, 283; Marshall, "The Clerical Response to Secularization."

30 On revivals in the 1920s and 1930s, see Marshall, "The Clerical Response to Secularization," the chapter "Why No Revival?" especially.

31 Richard Roberts was born in Wales in 1874. He had a distinguished career as an English Methodist minister, but resigned from his parish in 1915, because of his pacifist stand, and became secretary of the Fellowship of Reconciliation. In 1917 he was called to the Church of the Pilgrims (Congregational) in Brooklyn, New York. In 1921 he moved to Canada, and was inducted as minister of the American Presbyterian Church, Montreal. In 1927 he moved to Sherbourne St United Church, Toronto, and lectured occasionally at Emmanuel College. In 1938 he retired from Sherbourne St and assumed a lectureship at Pine

Hill College (the former Presbyterian College, Halifax), before returning to the United States, where he died in 1945. See "Richard Roberts," UCCA, biographical files.

32 Roberts Papers, "The Scope of Theology."

33 See Schorske's splendid work entitled *Fin-De-Siecle Vienna*, xvii. The
rejection of history has also been noted by Wood, "The Twentieth-
Century Revolt Against Time," in Wagar, ed., *The Secular Mind*, 197–
217. This definition of "modernism" is quite distinct from that offered
in the fine study of the American theological context by William R.
Hutchison, who holds that "modernism" preserved its links with historical study, and attempted to adjust religion to the fruits of modern
culture, not to remove the Bible to some absolute realm beyond history. See Hutchison, *The Modernist Impulse in American Protestantism*.

34 Barth, *The Word of God*. For the affinities of neo-orthodoxy and "Comparative Religion," see Richardson, *History Sacred and Profane*, 134–5,
139.

35 The phrase was first used as the title of Brunner's *The Theology of Crisis*.

36 The most sensitive recent analysis of the "fundamentalist controversies" of the 1920s has been provided by Marsden's *Fundamentalism and
American Culture*, 141–95.

37 See Clifford, *Resistance to Church Union in Canada*.

38 For details of Pidgeon's life and theological outlook, see Grant, *George
Pidgeon*.

39 For the revivalistic emphasis in Pidgeon's thought, see Marshall, "The
Clerical Response to Secularization."

40 Pidgeon Papers, box 40, file 1097, "What Has Science to Teach Religion?" sermon delivered at Bloor St Church, 4 Nov. 1928; ibid.,
box 40, file 1056, "The Need of the United Church of Canada," sermon delivered at Bloor St Church, 4 Dec. 1927. For echoes of Pidgeon's position, see S.D. Chown, "Modernism and Fundamentalism,"
ChG, 15 Aug. 1923, 4–5; "Theological Unrest"[editorial], *ChG*, 23 Aug.
1922, 6. For the position articulated within the theological colleges, see
Shaw, *Essentials and Non-Essentials of the Christian Faith*.

41 See "John Dow," UCCA, biographical files. The British impact was evi-
c ent through other faculty members. Both Alfred Gandier, the principal, and John Fletcher McLaughlin, the dean of theology, had
received their basic theological training in the "historical" or "inductive" theology of the 1890s, and they actively recruited professors of
similar views. Scottish-born William Manson, Dow's predecessor in
the New Testament chair, was appointed in the 1920s. Richard Roberts, who occasionally lectured to the students, had spent most of his
life in Britain, and was closely attuned to British theological debates.

42 See Cheyne, *The Transforming of the Kirk*, for a discussion of the themes of post-World War I Scottish theology. The emphasis remained on the preservation of the close links already established between history and theology.

43 See, for example, The Editor[E.A. Betts], "Karl Barth and the Message of his Theology," *The Pine Hill Messenger* 1, no. 3 (yearbook 1929): 5, 18; John Line, "Barth and Barthianism," *Canadian Journal of Religious Thought* [*CJRT*] 6, no. 1 (Jan.-Feb. 1929): 98–104; D.L. Ritchie, "Barth and Barthianism," *CJRT* 6, no. 5 (Sept.-Oct. 1929): 317–25; Jenkin H. Davies, "The Ideas of Karl Barth," *CJRT* 7, no. 4 (Sept.-Oct. 1930): 325–34. According to Sydney Ahlstrom, Barth's wartime theological works, such as *The Epistle to the Romans*(1919), were not translated until 1928. See Ahlstrom, *A Religious History of the American People*, 947.

44 S.H. Hooke, "Quo Vadis?" *AV* 40, no. 3 (Dec. 1915): 161–7.

45 On the importance of Bergson in French and European thought before 1914, see Hughes, *Consciousness and Society*, chapter 4. For a recent and discerning portrayal of William James and the central ideas of pragmatism, see Hollinger, "William James and the Culture of Inquiry," in Hollinger, *In the American Province*.

46 See McKillop, *A Disciplined Intelligence*, chapter 7 for his claim that absolute idealism was the dominant Canadian philosophy between the turn of the century and World War I.

47 A.B. Macallum, "Pragmatism, Religion, Politics, and Morals," *AV* 37, no. 3 (Dec. 1912): 134–6. For a discussion of some of the ideas in William James's *The Varieties of Religious Experience*, see the Rev. R.G. Strathie, "Psychology and Prayer," *Theol.* 16 (Nov. 1904): 1–6.

48 For the ideas of Bowne, see Chiles, *Theological Transition in American Methodism*, 63–4; Hutchison, *The Modernist Impulse in American Protestantism*, 208–9. For the use of *The Philosophy of Theism* at Victoria College, see "Report of the Board of Examiners," minutes of the Toronto Methodist Conference, in *Minutes of Conference, 1891*, 39–40. In 1891, the fourth year of college study at Victoria listed under mental philosophy the requirement of John Dewey's *Psychology*. I am aware that this evidence is counter to McKillop's assertion in *A Disciplined Intelligence* that Hegelian idealism, so forcefully represented by John Watson at Queen's, was the ruling philosophy of both Presbyterian and Methodist Churches in Canada.

49 See Chown Papers, box 11, file 295, "The Present Need," address delivered Jan. 1912.

50 See Watson, *The Philosophical Basis of Religion*, 100, 156–8; and *The Interpretation of Religious Experience*. part second. constructive. The Gifford Lectures, 1910–1912, 33, 37. This dynamic element of debate between speculative idealism and pragmatism is neglected in McKillop's

final chapter of *A Disciplined Intelligence*. McKillop claims that the impact of pragmatism was felt in Canada only after World War I, but there is considerable evidence in Watson's own writings that, even before 1914, he believed that his philosophical enterprise was beleaguered.

51 For the influence of Spencerianism and Comtean positivism on Le-Sueur, see McKillop, *A Disciplined Intelligence*, chapter 5, which is a lengthy and perceptive essay on this late Victorian man of letters. More recently, Cook's *The Regenerators* has examined a radical "fringe" of theosophists, agnostics, and secularists who inhabited a late Victorian demi-monde. I do not agree with Professor Cook that this group constituted a major and influential current of relgous thought in late Victorian English Canada, but their ideas provide insight into a fascinating and little-known corner of late nineteenth-century intellectual life.

52 For a definition of the "culture of Victorianism," see Howe, "American Victorianism as a Culture."

53 J. Davidson Ketchum, "The Saving of God," *The Canadian Forum*[CF], April 1923, 204–6. For an analysis of the positions taken by *The Canadian Forum* on the political, social, and religious questions of the 1920s, see McKillop, "Science, Authority, and the American Empire." According to Richard Allen, the *Canadian Forum* group offered what he terms "the theology of radical reform" in the early 1920s. See Allen, *The Social Passion*, 302–12.

54 S.H. Hooke, "A Modern Lay Apologia,"*CF*, Aug. 1923, 335–6.

55 Margaret Fairley, "Creative Evolution," *CF*, Jan. 1922, 493–5. The title of this article copied, significantly, that of Bergson's *Creative Evolution*, published before World War I.

56 Hooke, *Christ and the Kingdom of God*, 5–6.

57 Hooke, *Christianity in the Making*, 140–2.

58 Allen, *The Social Passion*, 303.

59 "A Revived Interest in Theology," *CJRT* 1, no. 1 (Jan.-Feb. 1924): 3. See also Professor J.M. Shaw, "Some Recent Books on Theology," *PW*, 10 Nov. 1921, 8; Professor T.B. Kilpatrick, "The Mystery of the Atonement," *PW*, 3 Feb. 1921, 13; Gandier Papers, box 2, "Theological Professors in Conference," ca 1928; ibid., box 2, "Essential Elements in an Effective Ministry," delivered at Colgate-Rochester Theological Seminary, N.Y., ca 1925–1929.

60 The revival of theology was obliquely noted by Richard Allen when he declared that "the titles of Canadian religious writings in general became more theological after 1922 and remained so for the rest of the decade," (*The Social Passion*, 230). This he attributes, mistakenly I believe, to the decline in the application of the "social gospel" and to the

recession of the church's presence in society. He does not address the influence of pre-war intellectual difficulties, the battlefront experience, or the presence of new philosophical currents. A more recent study of the 1920s by Marshall, "The Clerical Response to Secularization," does not even mention the revival of theology.

61 Law, *Optimism and Other Sermons*, 26. See also Kilpatrick, *The Redemption of Man*, 3–4; "The Christian Attitude"[editorial], *PW*, 24 Feb. 1921, 3. Other telling criticisms of the easy identification of progress and Christianity appeared in the post-war years. The Methodist Richard Roberts declared in 1921 that progress could only be regarded as conditional, for it was based on the premise of human free will. See Roberts Papers, box 3, file 71, "A Modern Religious Outlook," 1921. For a discussion of the more widespread critique of progress in English Canada, see McKillop, "Science, Authority, and the American Empire."

62 "Has Historical Study Failed?"[editorial], *CJRT* 5, no. 3, (May-June 1928): 175; "The Limits of Historical Study"[editorial], *CJRT* 5, no. 3, (May-June, 1928): 175. See also F. Platt, "III. The Value of History," *The New Outlook* [*NO*], 5 Aug. 1925, 11.

63 See Wohl, *The Generation of 1914*, 223–5. Wohl argues that the dream of political and cultural renewal did not die among European intellectuals. For the vitality of the EnglishCanadian cultural scene in the 1920s, see Vipond, "National Consciousness in English-speaking Canada in the 1920s."

64 Fairbairn, *The Appeal to Reality*, 5.

65 Baillie, *The Place of Jesus Christ*, 119–20. See also Gandier, *The Son of Man Coming in His Kingdom*, 116–17; Chown Papers, box 5, file 113, "The Abolition of War," sermon, n.d.; Mackinnon Papers, reel 1, "John 12:24," sermon, n.d.

66 Baillie, *The Interpretation of Religion*, 123–7.

67 Ibid., 126–7.

68 Whitehead, *Religion in the Making*. For discussion of Whitehead's ideas in the United Church, see Roberts Papers, box 3, file 77, "Wheels and Systems, A Plea for Another Theology," ca 1929; ibid., box 4, file 112, "The Scope of Theology"; H.A. Macleod, "What the Church Expects of Science," *NO*, 26 Feb. 1930, 200.

69 This summary of the neo-Kantian outlook is drawn from the recent study by Willey, *Back to Kant*, 51–3.

70 Whitehead, *Religion in the Making*, 75–6.

71 The concepts of personality, community, and the Cross of Christ dominated the theological writing of the period. See Baillie, *The Interpretation of Religion*, 446; Dow, *Jesus and the Human Conflict*, 81, 322; Morgan, *The Nature and Right of Religion*, 229; Graham, *The Meaning of*

the Cross. It was no coincidence that most of these books were dedicated to comrades who had been killed in "trenchland."

72 Willey, *Back to Kant*, 144–8.
73 Baillie, *The Interpretation of Religion*, 3–6, 11, 37, 107; Morgan, *The Nature and Right of Religion*, 60–1.
74 Baillie, *The Interpretation of Religion*, 122–3, 129, 131–2.
75 For a recent study of the thought of George Sidney Brett, see Gauvreau, "Philosophy, Psychology, and History," 209–36.

CONCLUSION

1 This argument is most strongly advanced in Cook's *The Regenerators*. Though less intensely presented, the progression of "Orthodoxy – Liberalism – Social Science," with social science as secular theology, also informs the conclusions of McKillop in *A Disciplined Intelligence*, and the older study by Allen, *The Social Passion*. Recent studies by American and British historians have questioned the extent to which social science was secular theology. See, for example, the seminal work by Haskell, *The Emergence of Professional Social Science*, and, for a British view, Collini's *Liberalism and Sociology*. Both suggest that social scientists in the late nineteenth century were preoccupied with a broader range of questions than those involving "regeneration."
2 See Moore, *The Post-Darwinian Controversies*, 12–16.
3 See Marsden, *Fundamentalism and American Culture*, 55–71.
4 See Braudel, "History and the Social Sciences," in Braudel, *On History*, 25–54.
5 There are, however, prominent exceptions to this general statement. See, for example, Walden's *Visions of Order*, which examines the existence of just such a mental "structure" in histories, novels, and films. For a provocative application of the "longue durée" to Canadian religious history, see the final section of Rawlyk's *Ravished by the Spirit*, which analyses the continued cultural and religious force of revivalism among Maritime Baptists.

Bibliography

MANUSCRIPT SOURCES

MOUNT ALLISON UNIVERSITY ARCHIVES
Charles Stewart Papers

PRESBYTERIAN CHURCH OF CANADA ARCHIVES
William MacLaren Papers

PUBLIC ARCHIVES OF CANADA
George Monro Grant Papers

PUBLIC ARCHIVES OF NOVA SCOTIA
Clarence Mackinnon Papers
Thomas McCulloch Papers
Records of the Pictou Academy

QUEEN'S UNIVERSITY ARCHIVES
Daniel Miner Gordon Papers
George Monro Grant Papers
John Watson Papers

UNITED CHURCH OF CANADA ARCHIVES
Andrew Browning Baird Papers
Henry Flesher Bland Papers
Salem Bland Papers
Robert Burns Papers

Nathanael Burwash Papers
Albert Carman Papers
Samuel Dwight Chown Papers
Alfred Gandier Papers
Alexander James Irwin Papers
George Jackson Papers
John Mark King Papers
Daniel James Macdonnell Papers
John Fletcher McLaughlin Papers
John Hugh Michael Papers
Samuel Sobieski Nelles Papers
Edmund Henry Oliver Papers
George Campbell Pidgeon Papers
Richard Roberts Papers
Edward Wilson Wallace Papers
Francis Huston Wallace Papers

BIOGRAPHICAL FILES
Nathanael Burwash
John Campbell
Albert Carman
William Caven
John Dow
Alexander Reid Gordon
William Gregg
Alexander James Irwin
Robert Law
John Line
James Frederick McCurdy
John Edgar McFadyen
William MacLaren
Samuel Nelles
Edmund Henry Oliver
Richard Roberts
John Scrimger
Michael Willis
Irwin Roberta M. "John Fletcher McLaughlin, Scholar Pilgrim"
Rose, William John. "Brief Pilgrimage of George John Blewett"

OFFICIAL SOURCES

Acts and Proceedings of the General Assembly of the Presbyterian Church of Canada (1876–1914)

Minutes of the Methodist General Conference (1876–1914)

NEWSPAPERS AND PERIODICALS

METHODIST

Acta Victoriana (Toronto, 1878–1939)
The Canadian Methodist Magazine (Toronto, 1874–1896)
The Canadian Methodist Quarterly (Toronto, 1889–1892)
The Canadian Methodist Review (Toronto, 1892–1895)
The Christian Guardian (Toronto, 1829–1925)
The Methodist Magazine and Review (Toronto, 1896–1906)
Vox Wesleyana (Winnipeg, 1896–1915)
The Wesleyan Mirror (Montreal, 1921–1925)

PRESBYTERIAN

The British American Presbyterian (Toronto, 1872–1877)
The Canada Christian Examiner and Presbyterian Review (Niagara, 1837–1842)
The Canadian Presbyterian (Toronto, 1877–1888)
The Ecclesiastical and Missionary Record (Toronto, 1844–1861)
The Ecclesiastical and Missionary Record of the Free Church of Nova Scotia (Halifax, 1852–1875)
The Home and Foreign Record (Toronto, 1861–1875)
Knox College Monthly (Toronto, 1883–1896)
The Monthly Record of the Church of Scotland in Nova Scotia and Adjoining Provinces (Halifax, 1854–1875)
The Presbyterian (Montreal, 1848–1875)
The Presbyterian (Toronto, 1902–1916)
The Presbyterian and Westminster (Toronto, 1917–1920)
Presbyterian College Journal (Montreal, 1881–1907)
The Presbyterian Review (Toronto, 1886–1898)
The Presbyterian Witness (Halifax, 1848–1921; Toronto 1921–1925)
Queen's Journal (Kingston, 1874–1900)
The Theologue (Halifax, 1889–1916)
The Westminster (Toronto, 1896–1902)

UNITED CHURCH

The New Outlook (Toronto, 1925–1939)

OTHER

The Canadian Monthly and National Review (Toronto, 1872–1878)
Queen's Quarterly (Kingston, 1893–1939)
University of Toronto Quarterly (Toronto, 1932–1945)
Mount Allison Academic Gazette

BOOKS AND PAMPHLETS

Armstrong, W.D. *The Christian Ministry and Modern Thought*. Toronto, 1896.

Baillie, John. *The Interpretation of Religion: An Introductory Study of Theological Principles*. New York: Charles Scribner's Sons, 1928.

– *The Place of Jesus Christ in Modern Christianity*. New York: Charles Scribner's Sons, 1929.

Barth, Karl. *The Word of God and the Word of Man*. London: Hodder and Stoughton, 1928.

Berdyaev, Nicolas. *The Meaning of History*. London: Geoffrey Bles, 1936.

Black, John Sutherland and George Chrystal. *The Life of William Robertson Smith*. London: Hodder and Stoughton, 1912.

Bland, Salem. *James Henderson, D.D.* Toronto: Ryerson Press, *The New Christianity*. Toronto: University of Toronto Press, 1973. Original edition, 1920. New introduction by Richard Allen.

Blewett, George John. *The Christian View of the World*. Toronto: William Briggs, 1912.

– *The Study of Nature and the Vision of God*. Toronto: William Briggs, 1907.

Bousset, Wilhelm. *What is Religion?* London: T. Fisher Unwin, 1911.

Bruce, Alexander Balmain. *The Kingdom of God; or Christ's Teaching According to the Synoptical Gospels*. Edinburgh: T. & T. Clark, 1890. First edition, 1889.

Brunner, Emil. *The Theology of Crisis*. New York: Charles Scribner's Sons, 1931.

Bryden, Walter Williamson. *Why I Am a Presbyterian*. Toronto: The Thorn Press, 1934.

– *The Christian's Knowledge of God*. Toronto: The Thorn Press, 1940.

Bultmann, Rudolf. *The History of the Synoptic Tradition*. Oxford: The Clarendon Press, 1963. First edition, 1921.

Bultmann, Rudolf, and Karl Kundsin. *Form Criticism: A New Method of New Testament Research*. Tr. by Frederick C. Grant. New York: Harper, 1966.

Burns, R.F. *The Life and Times of the Reverend Robert Burns, D.D.* Toronto: J. Campbell and Sons, 1873.

Burwash, Nathanael. *A Handbook of the Epistle of St. Paul to the Romans*. Toronto: William Briggs, 1887.

– *History of Victoria College*. Toronto: Victoria College Press, 1927.

– *Manual of Christian Theology on the Inductive Method*, 2 vols. London: H. Marshall and Son, 1900.

Butler, Joseph. *The Analogy of Religion Natural and Revealed to the Constitution and the Course of Nature*. London: Routlege, 1884. First edition, 1736.

Campbell, John. *The Hittites: Their Inscriptions and Their History.* 2 vols. Toronto: Williamson and Company, 1891.

Caven, William. *Christ's Teaching Concerning the Last Things and Other Papers.* London: Hodder and Stoughton, 1908.

Christianizing the Social Order. A Statement Prepared by the Board of Evangelism and Social Service. Toronto: 1934.

Cochrane, Charles Norris. *Thucydides and the Science of History.* London: Oxford University Press, 1929.

– *Christianity and Classical Culture: A Study in Thought and Action from Augustus to Augustine.* London: Oxford University Press, 1940.

Cunningham, John. *The Church History of Scotland,* vol. 1. Edinburgh: C. Black, 1859.

Davidson, Andrew Bruce. *Biblical and Literary Essays.* London: Hodder and Stoughton, 1903.

– *Old Testament Prophecy.* Edinburgh: T. & T. Clark, 1905.

Delitzsch, Friedrich. *Babel and Bible.* London: Williams and Norgate, 1903.

Denny, James. *Jesus and the Gospel: Christianity Justified in the Mind of Christ.* London: Hodder and Stoughton, 1909.

Dewart, E.H. *The Bible Under Higher Criticism.* Toronto: William Briggs, 1900.

Dods, Marcus. *An Introduction to the New Testament.* London: Hodder and Stoughton, 1895.

Dow, John. *Jesus and the Human Conflict.* London: Hodder and Stoughton, 1928.

Driver, Samuel R. *An Introduction to the Literature of the Old Testament.* Edinburgh: T. & T. Clark, 1892.

Esson, The Reverend Henry. *Statement Relative to the Educational System of Knox College, Toronto; with Suggestions for Its Extension and Improvement.* Toronto, 1848.

Fairbairn, Andrew Martin. *The Philosophy of the Christian Religion.* London: Hodder and Stoughton, 1902.

– *The Place of Christ in Modern Theology.* London: Hodder and Stoughton, 1893.

Fairbairn, R. Edis. *The Appeal to Reality.* New York: Abingdon Press, 1927.

Falconer, James W. *From Apostle to Priest: A Study of Early Church Organization.* Edinburgh: T. & T. Clark, 1900.

Falconer, Robert. *Religion on My Life's Road.* The Rockwell Lectures Delivered at the Rice Institute, April 1938.

– *The Truth of the Apostolic Gospel.* New York: The International Committee of the Young Men's Christian Association, 1904.

Farrar, Adam Storey. *A Critical History of Free Thought in Reference to the Christian Religion.* Bampton Lectures, 1862. New York: D. Appleton & Co., 1888.

Farrar, F.W. *History of Interpretation*. Bampton Lectures, 1885. New York: E.P. Dutton, 1886.

Fisher, George P. *Essays on the Supernatural Origin of Christianity, with special reference to the Theories of Strauss, Renan, and the Tubingen School*. New York: Scribner, Armstrong & Co., 1877.

Flint, Robert. *The Philosophy of History in France and Germany*. Edinburgh: W. Blackwood and Sons, 1874.

Frazer, James G. *The Golden Bough: A Study in Magic and Religion*. London: Macmillan, 1922. First edition, 1889.

Gandier, Alfred. *The Son of Man Coming in His Kingdom*. New York: George H. Doran Company, 1922.

George, James. *"1 Cor. 1.23 – We Preach Christ Crucified," A Sermon*. Toronto, 1837.

Gordon, Alexander Reid. *The Early Traditions of Genesis*. Edinburgh: T. & T. Clark, 1907.

Gordon, C.W. *Life of James Robertson, D.D.* Westminster, 1909.

Graham, William Creighton. *The Meaning of the Cross*. Toronto: Ryerson Press, 1923.

Grant, George Munro. *The Religions of the World*. London: A. & C. Black, 1895.

Grant, William L. and C.F. Hamilton. *Principal Grant*. Toronto: Morang, 1904.

Harnack, Adolf von. *History of Dogma*, vol. 1. London: Williams and Norgate, 1887. First edition, 1885.

– *What is Christianity?* London: Williams and Norgate, 1901.

Hodge, Charles. *Systematic Theology*. Grand Rapids, Mich.: William Eerdmans, 1952.

Hooke, S.H. *Christ and the Kingdom of God*. London: Student Christian Movement, 1922.

– *Christianity in the Making: A Critical and Historical Summary of the First Three Centuries*. Toronto: Macmillan, 1927.

Horne, Thomas Hartwell. *An Introduction to the Critical Study and Knowledge of the Holy Scriptures*, vol. 2. Fifth edition. London: Cadell, 1825.

James, William. *The Varieties of Religious Experience*. New York: Random House, 1920. First edition, 1902.

Jardine, George. *Outlines of Philosophical Education, Illustrated by the Method of Teaching the Logic, or First Class of Philosophy, in the University of Glasgow*. Glasgow: Andrew and James Duncan, 1818.

Jones, Sir Henry and John Henry Muirhead. *The Life and Philosophy of Edward Caird*. Glasgow: Maclehose, 1921.

Jordan, William George. *Biblical Criticism and Modern Thought*. Edinburgh: T. & T. Clark, 1909.

– *Prophetic Ideas and Ideals*. Toronto: Fleming H. Revell, 1902.

Kilpatrick, T.B. *The Redemption of Man*. Edinburgh: T. & T. Clark, 1920.

Law, Robert. *The Hope of Our Calling*. Toronto: McLelland and Stewart, 1918.

– *Optimism and Other Sermons*. Toronto: McLelland and Stewart, 1919.

Lecky, William E.H. *History of the Rise and Influence of Rationalism in Europe*, vol. 1. London: Longmans, Green, 1865.

Lyall, William. *Intellect, The Emotions, and the Moral Nature*. Edinburgh: Thomas Constable, 1855.

Lyall, William. *The Philosophy of Thought: A Lecture delivered at the Opening of the Free Church College, Halifax, Nova Scotia*. Halifax: James Barnes, 1853.

McCosh, James. *The Scottish Philosophy*. New York: R. Carter, 1874.

McCulloch, Thomas. *The Nature and Uses of a Liberal Education Illustrated, Being a Lecture Delivered at the Opening of the Building, Erected for the Accommodation of the Classes of the Pictou Academical Institution*. Halifax, 1819.

– *Popery Condemned by Scripture and the Fathers: Being a Refutation of the Principal Popish Doctrines and Assertions Maintained in the Remarks on the Rev. Mr. Stanser's Examination of the Rev. Mr. Burke's Letter of Instruction to the Catholic Missionaries of Nova Scotia and in the Reply to the Rev. Mr. Cochran's Fifth and Last Letter to Mr. Burke, &c*. Edinburgh, 1808.

McCulloch, William. *The Life of Thomas McCulloch*. 1920.

McCurdy, James Frederick. *History, Prophecy, and the Monuments*, vol. 1. New York: Macmillan, 1895.

– *History, Prophecy, and the Monuments*, vol. 2. New York: Macmillan, 1896.

– *History, Prophecy, and the Monuments*, vol. 3. New York: Macmillan, 1901.

– *Life and Work of D.J. Macdonnell*. Toronto: William Briggs, 1897.

MacEwen, Alexander Robertson. *Life and Letter of John Cairns, D.D., L.L.D.* London: Hodder and Stoughton, 1896.

McFadyen, John Edgar. *Old Testament Criticism and the Christian Church*. New York: Charles Scribner's Sons, 1903.

Mackenzie, Robert. *John Brown of Haddington*. London: Hodder and Stoughton, 1918.

McIntyre, Alasdair. *Secularization and Moral Change*. London, 1967.

Mackinnon, Clarence. *Reminiscences*. Toronto: Ryerson Press, 1938.

MacLaren, William. *Calvinism In Relation to Other Theistic Systems*. A Lecture delivered at the Opening of the Session of Knox College, Toronto, on 3 October 1883. Toronto: Presbyterian Printing House, 1884.

– *Literature and Dogma: An Inaugural Lecture*. Delivered in Knox Church, Toronto, 1 October 1873.

– *The Romish Doctrine of the Rule of Faith Examined*. A Lecture delivered at the Close of the Session of Presbyterian College, Montreal, 4 April 1872.

– *The Rule of Faith and Private Judgment*. A Lecture delivered at the close of the Session of Knox College, Toronto, on 7 April 1880. Toronto: C. Blackett Robinson, 1880.

– *Sixty Years' Retrospect*. Toronto: 1908.

– *The Variable and the Permanent in the Evidences of our Faith*. A Sermon preached in Bloor Street Presbyterian Church, on Sabbath, 7 June 1903. Toronto: Fleming H. Revell Co., 1903.

– *The Unity of the Human Race*. A Lecture Delivered Before the Members of the Belleville Young Men's Christian Association, 19 March 1860.

McLeod, Donald. *Memoirs of Norman McLeod*. Toronto: Belford, 1876.

Macmillan, Donald. *The Life of Robert Flint*. London: Hodder and Stoughton, 1914.

MacMurray, John. *Reason and Emotion*. London: Faber, 1935.

MacVicar, John H. *Life and Work of Donald Harvey MacVicar*. Toronto: The Westminster Co., 1904.

Maritain, Jacques. *The Degree of Knowledge*. London: Geoffrey Bles, 1937. First edition, 1932.

– *True Humanism*. London: Geoffrey Bles, 1946. First edition, 1938.

Morgan, William. *The Nature and Right of Religion*. Edinburgh: T. & T. Clark, 1926.

Muller, F. Max. *Introduction to the Science of Religion*. Four Lectures Delivered at the Royal Institution in February and May 1870. London: Longmans, Green, 1873.

Nettleship, R.L. *Memoirs of Thomas Hill Green*. London: Macmillan, 1906.

Niebuhr, Reinhold. *Moral Man and Immoral Society*. New York: Charles Scribner's Sons, 1932.

– *Reflections on the End of an Era*. New York: Charles Scribner's Sons, 1936.

Oliphant, Mrs. *A Memoir of the Life of John Tulloch, D.D., L.L.D.* Edinburgh: W. Blackwood and Sons, 1888.

Paley, William. *The Evidences of Christianity*. London: Parker, 1959. First edition, 1794.

– *Principles of Moral and Political Philosophy*, vol. 4, of William Paley, *The Works of William Paley, With Additional Sermons*. 7 vols. London: 1825.

Phillips, S.G., ed. *The Methodist Pulpits*. Toronto: William Briggs, 1884.

Pickard, Humphrey. *An Inaugural Address delivered at the Opening of the Wesleyan Academy, Mount Allison, Sackville, N.B.* Saint John: Henry Chubb, 1843.

Rainy, Robert. *Delivery and Development of Christian Doctrine*. Edinburgh: A. and C. Black, 1874.

Ryerson, Egerton. *The Loyalists of America and Their Times: From 1620 to 1816*. 2 vols. Toronto: William Briggs, 1880.

– *The Story of My Life*. Edited by J. George Hodgins. Toronto: William Briggs, 1883.

Saunders, J.B. *Some Mistakes and Perils of Higher Criticism From a Preacher's Standpoint*. Toronto, 1901.

Schweitzer, Albert. *The Quest of the Historical Jesus*. London: A. & C. Black, 1954. First edition, 1906.

– *The Kingdom and the Messiah*. Edinburgh: T. & T. Clark, 1911.

Scott, Ernest F. *The Beginnings of the Church*. New York: Charles Scribner's Sons, 1914.

– *The Kingdom and the Messiah*. Edinburgh: T. and T. Clark, 1911.

Scott, R.B.Y. and Gregory Vlastos, eds. *Towards the Christian Revolution*. Chicago: Willett, Clark and Co., 1936.

Shaw, John Mackintosh. *Essentials and Non-Essentials of the Christian Faith*. Edinburgh: T. & T. Clark, 1928.

Simpson, P. Carnegie. *The Life of Principal Rainy*, vol. 1. London: Hodder and Stoughton.

Smith, George Adam. *The Life of Henry Drummond*. Edinburgh: T. & T. Clark, 1899.

Smith, Goldwin. *Guesses at the Riddle of Existence*. New York: Macmillan Co., 1897.

Smith, W. Robertson. *Lectures on the Religion of the Semites*. London: Hodder and Stoughton, 1923. First edition, 1889.

– *The Prophets of Israel and their Place in History to the Close of the Eighth Century, B.C.* London: Hodder and Stoughton, 1907. First edition, 1882.

Strahan, James. *Andrew Bruce Davidson*. London: Hodder and Stoughton, 1917.

Straith, John. *The Fidelity of the Bible! Being a Review of Colenso's Writings as Against the Pentateuch and the Book of Joshua*. Ingersoll, 1864.

Strauss, David Freidrich. *Life of Jesus*. Fourth edition. London: Chapman Brothers, 1846.

Temple, Frederick, et al. *Essays and Reviews*. Fourth edition. London: Longmans, Green, 1861.

Tylor, Edward B. *Primitive Culture*, vol. 1. London: J. Murray, 1920. First edition, 1871.

Warr, Charles L. *Principal Caird*. Edinburgh: T. & T. Clark, 1926.

Watson, John. *Christianity and Idealism*. Glasgow: James Maclehose, 1897.

– *The Interpretation of Religious Experience*. First and second parts. Constructive. The Gifford Lectures, 1910–1912. Glasgow: James Maclehose, 1912.

– *The Philosophical Basis of Religion: A Series of Lectures*. Glasgow: James Maclehose, 1907.

Watson, Richard. *Theological Institutes: or, A View of the Evidences, Doctrines, Morals and Institutions of Christianity.* London: J. Mason, 1829.

Wayland, Francis. *The Elements of Moral Science.* Ed. by Joseph L. Blau. Cambridge, Mass.: Belknap Press, 1963.

Weiss, Johannes. *Jesus' Proclamation of the Kingdom of God.* Translated, edited, and with introduction by Richard H. Hiers and David L. Holland. Philadelphia: Fortress Press, 1971.

Wellhausen, Julius. *Prolegomena to the History of Israel.* Edinburgh: T. & T. Clark, 1885. First German edition, 1878.

Whitehead, Alfred North. *Religion in the Making.* New York: Macmillan, 1926.

Willis, Michael. *Pulpit Discourses Expository and Practical, and College Addresses, &c.* London: James Nisbet & Co., 1873.

Young, George Paxton. *Miscellaneous Discourses and Expositions of Scripture.* Edinburgh: Johnston and Hunter, 1854.

– *The Nature of Freedom.* Notes selected, translated, and arranged by his pupil, James Gibson Hume. Toronto: University Press, 1911.

ARTICLES AND PARTS OF BOOKS

Burwash, J. "The Limits of Religious Thought." In S.G. Phillips, *The Methodist Pulpits.* Toronto: William Briggs, 1884.

Burwash, Nathanael. "Divine Revelation of the Creation." In S.G. Phillips, *The Methodist Pulpits.* Toronto: William Briggs, 1884.

Badgley, E.I. "Faith vs. Knowledge, being the tenth annual lecture delivered before the Theological Union of Victoria University in 1887." In *Lectures and Sermons, Theological Union, Victoria College.* Toronto: William Briggs. 1888.

Dewart, E.H. "The Development of Doctrine: A Lecture delivered before the Theological Union of Victoria University, May 19, 1879." In *Lectures and Sermons, Theological Union, Victoria University, 1878–1882.* Toronto: William Briggs, 1883.

McCree, W.T. "William George Jordan." In R.C. Wallace, ed., *Some Great Men of Queen's.* Toronto: Ryerson Press, 1941.

Scrimger, John. "Is the Bible a Revelation?". In *Questions of the Day, Lectures delivered in the David Morrice Hall, Presbyterian College, Montreal, in 1883–84.* Montreal, 1885.

Troeltsch, Ernst. "The Dogmatics of the Religiongeschictliche Schule." *American Journal of Theology* 17 (January 1913).

– "Historiography." In James Hastings, ed., *Encyclopedia of Religion and Ethics,* vol. 6 (1913).

Woodhouse, A.S.P. "Charles Norris Cochrane." In *Proceedings and Transactions of the Royal Society of Canada,* 40 (1946).

SECONDARY SOURCES

BOOKS

Ahlstrom, Sydney. *A Religious History of the American People*. New Haven: Yale University Press, 1972.

Allen, Richard. *The Social Passion: Religion and Social Reform in Canada, 1914–1928*. Toronto: University of Toronto Press, 1973.

Annan, Noel Gilroy. *The Curious Strength of Positivism in English Political Thought*. London: Oxford University Press, 1959.

– *Leslie Stephen*. London: MacGibbon and Kee, 1951.

Antoni, Carlo. *From History to Sociology: The Transition in German Historical Thinking*. Detroit: Wayne State University Press, 1959. First edition, 1940.

Bedford, A.G. *The University of Winnipeg: A History of the Founding Colleges*. Toronto: University of Toronto Press, 1976.

Bender, Thomas. *New York Intellect: A History of Intellectual Life in New York City, from 1750 to the Beginnings of Our Own Time*. New York: Alfred A. Knopf, 1987.

Bercovitch, Sacvan. *The American Jeremiad*. Madison: University of Wisconsin Press, 1978.

Berger, Carl. *Science, God, and Nature in Victorian Canada*. The 1982 Joanne Goodman Lectures. Toronto: University of Toronto Press, 1983.

– *The Sense of Power*. Toronto: University of Toronto Press, 1970.

– *The Writing of Canadian History*. Toronto: Oxford University Press, 1976.

Boyer, Paul. *Urban Masses and Moral Order in America, 1820–1920*. Cambridge, Mass.: Harvard University Press, 1978.

Bozeman, Theodore Dwight. *Protestants in an Age of Science: The Baconian Ideal and Antebellum American Religious Thought*. Chapel Hill: University of North Carolina Press, 1977.

Braudel, Fernand. *On History*. Chicago: University of Chicago Press, 1983.

Brown, R.C. and Ramsay Cook, *Canada 1896–1921: A Nation Transformed*. Toronto: McLelland and Stewart, 1974.

Brown, Stewart J. *Thomas Chalmers and the Godly Commonwealth in Scotland*. Oxford: Oxford University Press, 1982.

Burns, R.M. *The Great Debate on Miracles*. Lewisburg, Pa.: Bucknell University Press, 1981.

Burrow, J.W. *Evolution and Society: A Study in Victorian Social Theory*. Cambridge: Cambridge University Press, 1966.

– *A Liberal Descent*. Cambridge: Cambridge University Press, 1981.

Butterfield, Herbert. *The Whig Interpretation of History*. Harmondsworth: Penguin Books, 1973. First edition, 1931.

Cannon, Susan Faye. *Science and Culture: The Early Victorian Period*. New York: Dawson and Science History Publications 1978.

Chadwick, Owen. *From Bossuet to Newman: The Idea of Doctrinal Development*. Second edition. New York: Cambridge University Press, 1987.

– *The Secularization of the European Mind in the Nineteenth Century*. Cambridge: Cambridge University Press, 1975.

– *The Victorian Church*, part 1. London: Oxford University Press, 1966.

– *The Victorian Church*, part 2. London: Oxford University Press, 1970.

Cheyne, Alexander. *The Transforming of the Kirk: Victorian Scotland's Religious Revolution*. Edinburgh: University of Edinburgh Press, 1983.

Chiles, Robert E. *Theological Transition in American Methodism, 1790–1935*. New York: Abingdon Press, 1965.

Christianson, Paul K. *Reformers and Babylon: Apocalyptic and Millennial Thought in Seventeenth Century England*. Toronto: University of Toronto Press, 1977.

Clifford, N. Keith. *The Resistance to Church Union in Canada*. Vancouver: University of British Columbia Press, 1985.

Cohen, Lester H. *The Revolutionary Histories*. Ithaca: Cornell University Press, 1983.

Cole, C.C. *The Social Ideas of the Northern Evangelists*. New York: Columbia University Press, 1954.

Collini, Stefan. *Liberalism and Sociology: L.T. Hobhouse and Political Argument in England, 1880–1914*. Cambridge: Cambridge University Press, 1979.

Collini, Stefan, et al. *That Noble Science of Politics: A Study in Nineteenth-Century Intellectual History*. Cambridge: Cambridge University Press, 1983.

Cook, Ramsay. *The Maple Leaf Forever*. Toronto: McLelland and Stewart, 1971.

Cook, Ramsay. *The Regenerators: Social Criticism in Late Victorian English Canada*. Toronto: University of Toronto Press, 1985.

Copp, Terry. *The Anatomy of Poverty: The Condition of the Working Class in Montreal, 1897–1929*. Toronto: McClelland and Stewart, 1974.

Corsi, Pietro. *Science and Religion: Baden Powell and the Anglican Debate, 1800–1860*. Cambridge: Cambridge University Press, 1988.

Cox, Jeffrey. *The English Churches in a Secular Society: Lambeth, 1870–1930*. Oxford: Oxford University Press, 1982.

Cragg, Gerald R. *Reason and Authority in the Eighteenth Century*. Cambridge: Cambridge University Press, 1964.

Cross, Whitney R. *The Burned-Over District: The Social and Intellectual History of Enthusiastic Religion in Western New York, 1800–1850*. Ithaca: Cornell University Press, 1950.

Daniels, George H. *American Science in the Age of Jackson*. New York: Columbia University Press, 1968.

Davidson, James West. *The Logic of Millennial Thought: Eighteenth Century New England*. New Haven: Yale University Press, 1977.

Davie, George Elder. *The Democratic Intellect: Scotland and Her Universities in the Nineteenth Century*. Edinburgh: Edinburgh University Press, 1961.

Desmond, Adrian. *Archetypes and Ancestors: Palaeontology in Victorian London, 1850–1875*. Chicago: University of Chicago Press, 1982.

Dillenberger, John and Claude Welch. *Protestant Christianity Interpreted Through Its Development*. New York: Charles Scribner's Sons, 1954.

Douglas, Ann B. *The Feminization of American Culture*. New York: Alfred A. Knopf, 1977.

Drummond, Andrew and James Bulloch. *The Scottish Church, 1688–1843: The Age of Moderates*. Edinburgh: Edinburgh University Press, 1973.

– *The Church in Victorian Scotland, 1843–1874*. Edinburgh: Edinburgh University Press, 1975.

English, John. *The Decline of Politics: The Conservatives and the Party System, 1901–1920*. Toronto: University of Toronto Press, 1977.

Falconer, J.W. and W.G. Watson. *A Brief History of Pine Hill Divinity Hall and the Theological Department at Mount Allison University*. Halifax: 1946.

Forbes, Duncan. *The Liberal Anglican Idea of History*. Cambridge: Cambridge University Press, 1952.

Fox, Richard W. and Jackson Lears, eds. *The Culture of Consumption: Critical Essays in American History, 1880–1980*. New York: Pantheon Books, 1983.

Frank, Douglas W. *Less than Conquerors: How Evangelicals Entered the Twentieth Century*. Grand Rapids: William B. Eerdmans Publishing Co., 1986.

Fraser, Brian. *The Social Uplifters: Presbyterian Progressives and the Social Gospel in Canada, 1875–1915*. Waterloo: Wilfrid Laurier University Press, 1988.

Frei, Hans W. *The Eclipse of Biblical Narrative: A Study in Eighteenth and Nineteenth Century Hermeneutics*. New Haven and London: Yale University Press, 1974.

French, Goldwin. *Parsons and Politics: The Role of The Wesleyan Methodists in Upper Canada and the Maritimes from 1780 to 1855*. Toronto: The Ryerson Press, 1962.

Fussell, Paul. *The Great War and Modern Memory*. New York: Oxford University Press, 1975.

Fussner, F. Smith. *The Historical Revolution: English Historical Writing and Theory, 1580–1640*. London: Routledge and Paul, 1962.

Garland, Martha McMacken. *Cambridge Before Darwin: The Ideal of a Liberal Education, 1800–1860*. Cambridge: Cambridge University Press, 1980.

Gaustad, Edwin S., ed. *The Rise of Adventism: Religion and Society in Mid-Nineteenth Century America*. New York: Harper and Row, 1974.

Gay, Peter. *A Loss of Mastery: Puritan Historians in Colonial America*. New York: Vintage Books, 1968. First edition, 1966.

Gillespie, Neal C. "Natural History, Natural Theology, and Social Order: John Ray and the 'Newtonian Ideology'." *Journal of the History of Biology* 20, no. 1 (spring 1987): 1–49.

Gillispie, Charles Coulson. *Genesis and Geology*. Cambridge: Cambridge University Press, 1951.

Gibert, Pierre. *Une theorie de la legende: Hermann Gunkel et les legendes de la Bible*. Paris: Flammarion, 1979.

Glick, G. Wayne. *The Reality of Christianity: A Study of Adolf von Harnack as Historian and Theologian*. New York: Harper and Row, 1967.

Grant, John Webster. *George Pidgeon*. Toronto: Ryerson Press, 1962.

Haller, William. *Foxe's Book of Martyrs and the Elect Nation*. London: Jonathon Cape, 1963.

Hamilton, William B. "Education, Politics, and Reform in Nova Scotia, 1800–1848." Unpublished PH.D. thesis, University of Western Ontario, 1970.

Hamburger, Joseph. *Macaulay and the Whig Tradition*. Chicago: University of Chicago Press, 1976.

Harrison, J.F.C. *The Second Coming: Popular Millenarianism 1780–1850*. London: Routledge and Kegan Paul, 1979.

Haskell, Thomas L. *The Emergence of Professional Social Science: The American Social Science Association and the Nineteenth-Century Crisis of Authority*.

Hatch, Nathan O. *The Sacred Cause of Liberty: Republican Thought and the Millennium in Revolutionary New England*. New Haven: Yale University Press, 1977.

Heyck, T.W. *The Transformation of Intellectual Life in Victorian England*. London: Croom Helm, 1982.

Hilton, Boyd. *The Age of Atonement: The Influence of Evangelicalism on Social and Economic Thought, 1795–1865*. Oxford: Clarendon Press, 1988.

Hobsbawm, Eric, and Ranger, Terence, eds. *The Invention of Tradition*. Cambridge: Cambridge University Press, 1983.

Hoeveler, J. David. *James McCosh and the Scottish Intellectual Tradition*. Princeton: Princeton University Press, 1981.

Holifield, E. Brooks. *The Gentlemen Theologians: American Theology in Southern Culture, 1795–1860*. Durham, N.C.: Duke University Press, 1978.

Hollinger, David. *In the American Province*. Baltimore: Johns Hopkins University Press, 1985.

Hovenkamp, Herbert. *Science and Religion in America, 1800–1860*. Philadelphia: University of Pennsylvania Press, 1978.

Howe, Daniel Walker. *The Political Culture of the American Whigs*. Chicago: University of Chicago Press, 1979.

Hughes, H. Stuart. *Consciousness and Society: The Revolution in European Social Thought, 1890–1930*. Brighton: Hassock, Harvester Press, 1979. First edition, 1958.

Hutchison, William R. *The Modernist Impulse in Amerian Protestantism.* Cambridge, Mass.: Harvard University Press, 1976.

Iggers, Georg G. *The German Conception of History.* Middletown, Conn.: Wesleyan University Press, 1968.

Jann, Rosemary. *The Art and Science of Victorian History.* Columbus: Ohio State University Press, 1985.

Johnson, Paul E. *A Shopkeeper's Millennium: Society and Revivals in Rochester, New York, 1815–1837.* New York: Hill and Wang, 1978.

Jenkyns, Richard. *The Victorians and Ancient Greece.* Cambridge, Mass.: Harvard University Press, 1980.

Kealey, Gregory S. *Toronto Workers Respond to Industrial Capitalism, 1867–1892.* Toronto: University of Toronto Press, 1980.

Keegan, John. *The Face of Battle: A Study of Agincourt, Waterloo and the Somme.* Harmondsworth: Penguin Books, 1975.

Kloppenberg, James T. *Uncertain Victory: Social Democracy and Progressivism in European and American Thought, 1870–1920.* New York: Oxford University Press, 1986.

Kohn, David, ed. *The Darwinian Heritage.* Princeton: Princeton University Press, 1985.

Krieger, Leonard. *Ranke: The Meaning of History.* Chicago: University of Chicago Press, 1977.

Kuhn, Thomas. *Structure of Scientific Revolutions.* Princeton: Princeton University Press, 1962.

Kuklick, Bruce. *Churchmen and Philosophers: From Jonathan Edwards to John Dewey.* New Haven and London: Yale University Press, 1985.

Leed, Eric J. *No Man's Land: Combat and Identity in World War One.* Cambridge: Cambridge University Press, 1979.

Levin, David. *History as Romantic Art.* Stanford: Stanford University Press, 1959.

Lightman, Bernard. *The Origins of Agnosticism: Victorian Unbelief and the Limits of Knowledge.* Baltimore and London: Johns Hopkins University Press, 1987.

Livingstone, David N. *Darwin's Forgotten Defenders: The Encounter Between Evangelical Theology and Evolutionary Thought.* Grand Rapids: William B. Eerdmans Publishing Co., 1987.

Manuel, Frank E. *The Prophets of Paris.* Cambridge, Mass.: Harvard University Press, 1962.

Marsden, George M. *Fundamentalism and American Culture: The Shaping of Twentieth-Century Evangelicalism, 1870–1925.* New York: Oxford University Press, 1980.

– *The Evangelical Mind and the New School Presbyterian Experience: A Case Study of Thought and Theology in Nineteenth-Century America.* New Haven and London: Yale University Press, 1970.

Marty, Martin E. *Righteous Empire: The Protestant Experience in America*. New York: Dial Press, 1970.

Masters, D.C. *Protestant Church Colleges in Canada*. Toronto: University of Toronto Press, 1966.

Mathews, Donald G. *Religion in the Old South*. Chicago: University of Chicago Press, 1977.

May, Henry F. *The Enlightenment in America*. Oxford: Oxford University Press, 1976.

– *Ideas, Faiths, and Feelings*. New York: Oxford University Press, 1983.

McDonald, Neil and Alf Chaiton, eds. *Egerton Ryerson and His Times: Essays on the History of Education*. Toronto: Macmillan Co., 1978.

McIntyre, Alasdair. *Secularization and Moral Change*. London, 1967.

McKillop, A.B. *Contours of Canadian Thought*. Toronto: University of Toronto Press, 1987.

– *A Disciplined Intelligence: Critical Inquiry and Canadian Thought in the Victorian Era*. Montreal: McGill-Queen's University Press, 1979.

McLoughlin, William G. *Revivals, Awakenings, and Reform: An Essay on Religion and Social Change in America, 1607–1977*. Chicago: University of Chicago Press, 1978.

McNaught, Kenneth. *A Prophet in Politics*. Toronto: University of Toronto Press, 1959.

Meyer, D.H. *The Instructed Conscience: The Shaping of the American National Ethic*. Philadelphia: University of Pennsylvania Press, 1972.

Miller, Perry. *The Life of the Mind in America*. New York: Harcourt, Brace and World, 1965.

– *The New England Mind: The Seventeenth Century*. New York: Macmillan Co., 1939.

Moir, J.S. *Church and State in Canada West: Three Studies in The Relation of Denominationalism and Nationalism, 1841–1867*. Toronto: University of Toronto Press, 1959.

– *Enduring Witness: A History of the Presbyterian Church in Canada*. Toronto: Presbyterian Press, 1976.

– *A History of Biblical Studies in Canada: A Sense of Proportion*. Society of Biblical Literature, Centennial Studies, no. 7. Chico, Calif.: Scholars Press, 1982.

Moore, James R. *The Post-Darwinian Controversies: The Protestant Struggle to Come to Terms with Darwin in Britain and America, 1870–1900*. Cambridge: Cambridge University Press, 1979.

Morell, J.B. and Arnold Thackray. *Gentlemen of Science: Early Years of the British Association for the Advancement of Science*. Oxford: Clarendon Press, 1981.

Norman, E.R. *Anti-Catholicism in Victorian England*. London: Allen and Unwin, 1968.

Outler, Albert C., ed. *John Wesley*. New York: Abingdon Press, 1964.

Owram, Doug. *The Government Generation*. Toronto: University of Toronto Press, 1986.

Palmer, Bryan D. *A Culture in Conflict*. Montreal: McGill-Queen's University Press, 1979.

Passmore, John. *A Hundred Years of Philosophy*. Harmondsworth: Penguin Books, 1966.

Pollard, Sydney. *The Idea of Progress: History and Society*. Harmondsworth: Penguin Books, 1971.

Porter, Roy. *Edward Gibbon: Making History*. London: Weidenfeld and Nicolson, 1988.

Prang, Margaret. *N.W. Rowell: Ontario Nationalist*. Toronto: University of Toronto Press, 1975.

Prentice, Alison. *The School Promoters*. Toronto: McClelland and Stewart, 1976.

Rawlyk, George. *Ravished by the Spirit: Revivals, Baptists, and Henry Alline*. Montreal: McGill-Queen's University Press, 1985.

Rawlyk, George, ed. *Canadian Baptists and Christian Higher Education*. Montreal: McGill-Queen's University Press, 1988.

Rawlyk, George, and Kevin Quinn. *The Redeemed of the Lord Say So: A History of Queen's Theological College, 1912–1972*. Kingston: Queen's Theological College, 1980.

Reardon, Bernard M.G. *From Coleridge to Gore: A Century of Religious Thought in Britain*. London: Longman, 1971.

Reardon, Bernard M.G., comp. *Liberal Protestantism*. Stanford: Stanford University Press, 1968.

Reid, John G. *Mount Allison University: A History, to 1963, vol. 1*. Toronto: University of Toronto Press, 1984.

Reid, W. Stanford. *Called to Witness: Profiles of Canadian Presbyterians. A Supplement to Enduring Witness*. Toronto: Presbyterian Publications, 1975.

Richardson, Alan. *History Sacred and Profane*. London: SCM Press, 1964.

Rogerson, John. *Old Testament Criticism in the Nineteenth Century: England and Germany*. London: Fortress Press, 1985.

Rosman, Doreen. *Evangelicals and Culture*. London and Canberra: Croom Helm, 1984.

Russett, Cynthia Eagle. *Darwin in America: The Intellectual Response*. New York: W.H. Freeman, 1976.

Sandeen, Ernest R. *The Roots of Fundamentalism: British and American Millenarianism, 1800–1930*. Chicago and London: University of Chicago Press, 1970.

Scott, Donald M. *Office to Profession*. Philadelphia: University of Pennsylvania Press, 1978.

Semmel, Bernard. *The Methodist Revolution*. New York: Free Press, 1973.

Sher, Richard B. *Church and University in the Scottish Enlightenment: The Moderate Literati of Edinburgh*. Edinburgh: Edinburgh University Press, 1985.

Schorske, Carl. *Fin-de-Siècle Vienna: Politics and Culture*. New York: Vintage Books, 1980.

Shortt, S.E.D. *The Search for an Ideal*. Toronto: University of Toronto Press, 1976.

Sissons, C.B. *Egerton Ryerson: His Life and Letters, vol. 1*. Toronto: The Ryerson Press, 1937.

Sloan, Douglas. *The Scottish Enlightenment and the American College Ideal*. New York: Teacher's College Press, Columbia University, 1971.

Smith, Timothy L. *Revivalism and Social Reform in Mid-Nineteenth Century America*. New York: Abingdon Press, 1957.

Smith, Wilson. *Professors and Public Ethics: Studies of Northern Moral Philosophers before the Civil War*. Ithaca: Cornell University Press, 1956.

Stevenson, Louise, L. *Scholarly Means to Evangelical Ends: The New Haven Scholars and the Transformation of Higher Learning in America, 1830–1890*. Baltimore and London: Johns Hopkins University Press, 1986.

Stocking, George. *Victorian Anthropology*. New York: Free Press, 1987.

Storr, Vernon F. *The Development of English Theology in the Nineteenth Century, 1800–1860*. London: Longman, Green and Company, 1913.

Strout, Cushing. *The Pragmatic Revolt in American History: Carl Becker and Charles Beard*. New Haven: Yale University Press, 1958.

Sweet, L.I. *The Evangelical Tradition in America*. Macon, Ga.: Mercer University Press, 1984.

Symondson, Anthony, ed. *The Victorian Crisis of Faith*. London: SPCK, 1970.

Thompson, John Herd. *The Harvests of War: The Prairie West 1914–1928*. Toronto: McLelland and Stewart, 1976.

Thompson, John H. and Allen Seager. *Canada 1922–1939: Decades of Discord*. Toronto: McClelland and Stewart, 1986.

Turner, Frank Miller. *The Greek Heritage in Victorian Britain*. New Haven: Yale University Press, 1981.

Turner, James. *Without God, Without Creed: The Origins of Unbelief in America*. Baltimore: Johns Hopkins University Press, 1985.

Tuveson, Ernest L. *Redeemer Nation: The Idea of America's Millenial Role*. Chicago: University of Chicago Press, 1968.

Van Die, Marguerite. *An Evangelical Mind: Nathanael Burwash and the Methodist Tradition in Canada, 1839–1918*. Kingston and Montreal: McGill-Queen's University Press, 1989.

Wagar, W. Warren, ed. *The Secular Mind*. New York: Holmes and Meier, 1982.

Walden, Keith. *Visions of Order: The Mounties in Symbol and Myth*. Toronto: Butterworths Press, 1983.

Wallace, Elisabeth. *Goldwin Smith: Victorian Liberal*. Toronto: University of Toronto Press, 1950.

Weber, Timothy, P. *Living in the Shadow of the Second Coming: American Premillennialism, 1875–1982*. New York: Oxford University Press, 1979.

Welch, Claude. *Protestant Thought in the Nineteenth Century, vol. 1*. New Haven: Yale University Press, 1972.

Westfall, William. *Two Worlds: The Protestant Culture of Nineteenth Century Ontario*. Kingston and Montreal: McGill-Queen's University Press, 1989.

White, Morton. *Social Thought in America: The Revolt Against Formalism*. Boston: Beacon Press, 1957.

Willey, Thomas E. *Back to Kant: The Revival of Kantianism in German Social and Historical Thought, 1860–1914*. Detroit: Wayne State University Press, 1978.

Wohl, Robert. *The Generation of 1914*. Cambridge, Mass.: Harvard University Press, 1979.

Yeo, Stephen. *Religion and Voluntary Organizations in Crisis*. London: Croom Helm, 1976.

Young, R.M. *Darwin's Metaphor: Nature's Place in Victorian Culture*. Cambridge: Cambridge University Press, 1985.

Zeller, Suzanne. *Inventing Canada: Early Victorian Science and the Idea of a Transcontinental Nation*. Toronto: University of Toronto Press, 1987.

ARTICLES AND PARTS OF BOOKS

Ahlstrom, Sydney. "The Romantic Religious Revolution and the Dilemmas of Religious History." *Church History* 46, no. 2 (1977)

Allen, Richard. "The Social Gospel and the Reform Tradition in Canada, 1890–1928." *Canadian Historical Review* 49, no. 4 (Dec. 1968).

Auerbach, Erich. "Figura." In Auerbach, *Scenes from the Drama of European Literature*. Gloucester, Mass.: Peter Smith, 1973.

Bainton, Roland H. "The Bible in the Reformation." In *The Cambridge History of the Bible: The West from the Reformation to the Present Day*. Cambridge: Cambridge University Press, 1976.

Bliss, Michael. "The Methodist Church in World War I." *Canadian Historical Review* 49, no. 3 (September 1968).

Brown, Walter T. "Victoria and a Century of Education." In *On the Old Ontario Strand, Victoria's Hundred Years*. Toronto, 1936.

Buggey, Susan and Gwendolyn Davies. "Thomas McCulloch." *Dictionary of Canadian Biography*, vol. 7. Toronto: University of Toronto Press, 1988.

Dreyer, Frederick. "Faith and Experience in the Thought of John Wesley." *American Historical Review* 88, no. 1 (February 1983).

Fiorino, Albert S. "The Moral Education of Egerton Ryerson's Idea of Education." In Neil McDonald and Alf Chaiton, eds, *Egerton Ryerson and His Times*. Toronto: Macmillan Co., 1978.

Fraser, Brian. "Theology and the 'social gospel' among Canadian Presbyterians: A Case Study." *Studies in Religion* 8, no. 1 (winter 1979).

French, Goldwin. "The Evangelical Creed in Canada." In W.L. Morton, ed., *The Shield of Achilles*. Toronto: McLelland and Stewart, 1968.

Frye, Northrop. "Conclusion." In C.F. Klinck et al., eds, *Literary History of Canada*, vol. 2. Toronto: University of Toronto Press, 1976.

Gauvreau, Michael. "Baconianism, Darwinism, Fundamentalism: A Transatlantic Crisis of Faith." *Journal of Religious History* 13, no. 4 (1985).

– "The Taming of History: Reflections on the Canadian Methodist Encounter with Biblical Criticism, 1830–1900." *Canadian Historical Review* 65, no. 3 (Sept. 1984).

– "Philosophy, Psychology, and History: George Sidney Brett and the Quest for a Social Science at the University of Toronto, 1910–1940." Canadian Historical Association, *Historical Papers* (1988).

– "War, Culture, and the Problem of Religious Certainty: The Methodist and Presbyterian Church Colleges, 1914–1930." *Journal of the Canadian Church Historical Society* 22, no. 1 (spring 1987).

Higham, John. "The Reorientation of American Culture in the 1890's." In Higham, *Writing of American History: Essays on Modern Scholarship*. Bloomington: Indiana University Press, 1970.

Lightman, Bernard. "Pope Huxley and the Church Agnostic: The Religion of Science." Canadian Historical Association, *Historical Papers* (1983).

Magney, William H. "The Methodist Church and the National Gospel, 1884–1914." United Church Archives, *The Bulletin* 20 (1968).

Marsden, George. "J. Gresham Machen: History and Truth." *Westminster Theological Journal* 42, no. 1 (fall 1979).

– "Understanding Fundamentalist Views of Science." In Ashley Montagu, ed., *Science and Creationism*. New York: Oxford University Press, 1984.

Marshall, David B. "Methodism Embattled: A Reconsideration of The Methodist Church and World War I." *Canadian Historical Review* 66, no. 1 (March 1985)

Martel, Gordon. "Generals Die in Bed: Modern Warfare and the Origins of Modernist Culture." *Journal of Canadian Studies* 16 (fall/winter 1981): 3–4.

McMullin, Stanley. "In Search of the Liberal Mind: Thomas McCulloch and the Impulse to Action." *Journal of Canadian Studies* 23 (1988)

Meacham, Standish. "The Evangelical Inheritance." *Journal of British Studies* 3, no. 1 (Nov. 1963).

Moore, James R. "Evangelicals and Evolution: Henry Drummond, Herbert Spencer, and the Naturalisation of the Spiritual World." *Scottish Journal of Theology* 38 (Sept. 1985): 383–417.

Noll, Mark A. "Common Sense Traditions and American Evangelical Thought." *American Quarterly* 37, no. 2 (summer 1985).

Parker, Christopher. "English Historians and the Opposition to Positivism." *History and Theory* 22, no. 2 (1983).

Phillipson, Nicholas. "Culture and Society in the 18th Century Province: The Case of Edinburgh and the Scottish Enlightenment." In Lawrence Stone, ed., *The University in Society*, vol. 2. Princeton: Princeton University Press, 1974.

Rice, Daniel F. "Natural Theology and the Scottish Philosophy in the Thought of Thomas Chalmers." *Scottish Journal of Theology* 24, no. 9 (Feb. 1971).

– "An Attempt at Systematic Reconstruction in the Theology of Thomas Chalmers." *Church History* 48, no. 2 (June 1979).

Ross, Dorothy. "Historical Consciousness in Nineteenth Century America." *American Historical Review* 89, no. 4 (Oct. 1984).

Rutherford, Paul. "Tomorrow's Metropolis: The Urban Reform Movement in Canada, 1880–1920." In G.A. Stelter and Alan Artibise, eds., *The Canadian City: Essays in Urban History*. Toronto: McClelland and Stewart, 1977.

Sinclair-Faulkner, Tom. "Theory Divided from Practice: The Introduction of the Higher Criticism in Canadian Protestant Seminaries." Canadian Society of Church History, *Papers* (1980).

Smith, The Reverend Dr A. Lloyd, "III. Victoria and a Century of Theological and Religious Life." In *On the Old Ontario Strand*.

Smith, Timothy L. "Righteousness and Hope: Christian Holiness and the Millennial Vision in America." *American Quarterly* (1979).

Sykes, Norman. "The Religion of Protestants." In *The Cambridge History of the Bible*.

Walden, Keith. "Respectable Hooligans: Male Toronto College Students Celebrate Hallowe'en, 1884–1910." *Canadian Historical Review* 68, no. 1 (March 1987).

Westfall, William. "The Dominion of the Lord: An Introduction to the Cultural History of Protestant Ontario in the Victorian Period." *Queen's Quarterly* 83, no. 1 (spring 1976).

– "Order and Experience: Patterns of Religious Metaphor in Early Nineteenth Century Upper Canada." *Journal of Canadian Studies* 20, no. 1 (spring 1985).

Wise, S.F. "Sermon Literature and Canadian Intellectual History." In J.M.

Bumsted, ed., *Canadian History before Confederation*. Georgetown: Irwin-Dorsey, 1972.

Wood, B. Anne. "Thomas McCulloch's Use of Science in Promoting a Liberal Education." *Acadiensis* 17 (1987).

Yeo, Richard. "William Whewell, Natural Theology, and the Philosophy of Science in Mid-Nineteenth Century Britain." *Annals of Science* 36 (1979).

– "Science and Intellectual Authority in Mid-Nineteenth Century Britain: Robert Chambers and Vestiges of the Natural History of Creation." *Victorian Studies* 28, no. 1 (autumn 1984).

– "An Idol of the Market-Place: Baconianism in Nineteenth-Century Britain." *History of Science* 23 (1985).

THESES

Allen, A. Richard. "Salem Bland – the Social Gospel in Canada." Unpublished M.A. thesis, University of Saskatchewan, 1961.

Christie, Nancy J. "Prophecy and the 'Principles of Social Life': Historical Writing and the Making of New Societies in Canada and Australia, 1880–1920." Unpublished PH.D. thesis, University of Sydney, 1986.

Fraser, Brian J. "'The Christianization of Our Civilization': Presbyterian Reformers and their Defence of a Protestant Canada, 1875–1914." Unpublished PH.D. thesis, York University, 1982.

Gauvreau, Michael. "Presbyterianism, Idealism, and the Social Sciences: Sir Robert Falconer and the University of Toronto, 1907–1932." Paper presented to the Symposium on the Presbyterian Contribution to Canadian Life and Culture, Montreal, October 1988.

Johnston, J.A. "The Presbyterian College, Montreal, 1865–1915." Unpublished M.A. thesis, McGill University, 1951.

Kiesekamp, Burkhard. "Community and Faith: The Intellectual and Ideological Bases of the Church Union Movement in Victorian Canada." Unpublished PH.D. thesis, University of Toronto, 1974.

Nicholson, D.R. "Michael Willis: Missionary Statesman, Social Activist, Christian Educator, and Reformed Theologian." Unpublished M.TH. thesis, Toronto School of Theology, 1973.

Marshall, D.B. "The Clerical Response to Secularization: Canadian Methodists and Presbyterians, 1860–1940." Unpublished PH.D. thesis, University of Toronto, 1986.

Schwartz, E.R. "Theological Education Policies of the Congregational, Presbyterian, and Methodist Churches to 1925." Unpublished PH.D. thesis, University of Alberta, 1975.

Semple, Neil. "The Impact of Urbanization on the Methodist Church in Central Canada, 1854–1884." Unpublished PH.D. thesis, University of Toronto, 1979.

Taylor, M. Brook. "The Writing of English Canadian History in the Nine-teenth Century." Unpublished PH.D. thesis, University of Toronto, 1984.

Vipond, Mary. "National Consciousness in English-speaking Canada in the 1920's: Seven Studies." Unpublished PH.D. thesis, University of Toronto, 1974.

Westfall, William. "The Sacred and the Secular: Studies in the Cultural History of Protestant Ontario in the Victorian Period." Unpublished PH.D. thesis, University of Toronto, 1976.

Index

agnosticism, 132. *See also* Buckle, Henry Thomas; Common Sense, Scottish; Hamilton, Sir William; Mansel, Henry

Allen, Richard, 256, 276, 361 n.5; on the "social gospel," 183, 259–60, 266

Analogy of Religion (Butler), 62–4, 87–8. *See also* Butler, Bishop Joseph

anti-Catholicism, 112–17

archaeology, 108–9, 111

Armstrong, Rev. W.D., 248

Arnold, Rev. Thomas: on idea of sacred history, 101–2. *See also* liberal Anglicans, 74, 80, 81

"Back to Christ" movement, 205

Baconianism, 38–9, 41–4, 53–5, 69, 74, 83, 90, 107, 111, 137–8, 144–6, 148–9, 152, 170–1, 180, 240, 258, 279–80, 288, 328 n.31. *See also* inductive method, Scottish Common Sense

Baillie, Rev. John, 270, 278–82

Baird, Rev. Andrew Browning, 143, 146, 154, 248

Barth, Karl, 267, 271

Beaven, Rev. James, 70

Beecher, Henry Ward, 138

Beecher, Lyman, 216

Beginnings of the Church, The (Scott), 233. *See also* Scott, Rev. E.F.

Berger, Carl, 60

Bergson, Henri, 272, 274

Bible: historical criticism of the, 4, 57–9, 77–90; idea of degeneration in the, 101, 123. *See also* higher criticism, 3, 4, 50, 82, 87, 101–3, 107, 108, 118, 131, 145, 151–3, 173, 223, 225

Biblical Criticism and Modern Thought, 230. *See also* Jordan, Rev. William George

biblical theology, 148, 150, 153–4, 184–5; definition of, 148. *See also* historical theology, inductive theology

Birks, Rev. A.K., 247

Blackstock, Rev. W.S., 136, 173

Bland, Rev. Henry Flesher, 82, 87, 91–2, 117, 120–1, 170, 171

Bland, Rev. Salem, 3–4, 9, 10, 183–4, 204, 211–12, 215, 216, 245–6, 259. *See also* social gospel, Wesley College

Bliss, Michael, 259–60

Book of Martyrs. See Foxe, John

Bousset, Wilhelm, 226

Bovell, Rev. James, 70

Bowles, Rev. R.P., 236

Bowne, Borden Parker, 274

Brett, George Sidney, 282

Bridgewater Treatises, The, 63

Brooke, Rev. John, 102–3, 108

Brown, Rev. John, 22

Brown, Thomas, 17

Bruce, Rev. Alexander Balmain, 205, 213

Bruce, Rev. Archibald, 22

Brunner, Emil, 267–8

Buckle, Henry Thomas, 132

Bultmann, Rudolf, 267–8
Bunsen, Baron Christian,
109–10
Burns, Rev. Robert, 32,
34, 75, 97–9, 104, 110,
112, 115, 123–4, 135,
151. *See also* Knox Col-
lege
Burwash, Rev. Nathan-
ael, 10, 127, 166–7, 169,
170, 175–7, 180, 182,
184–5, 187–8, 189–90,
193, 200, 201, 204–8,
209, 212, 215, 218, 220–
1, 225, 228, 229, 242–3,
246–7, 273, 357 n.56
Bushnell, Rev. Horace,
80, 138, 161
Butler, Bishop Joseph, 17,
62–3, 71, 87–8, 108,
118, 170. *See also Anal-
ogy of Religion*

Caird, Edward, 140–1,
273. *See also* Hegelian-
ism
Caird, John, 140, 156, 157
Cairns, Rev. John, 29
Calvinism, 20–22
Campbell, Rev. John, 143,
153
Campbell, Robert, 325
n.12
Canadian Forum, The, 274–
6
*Canadian Journal of Reli-
gious Thought,* 276–8
Candlish, Rev. Robert,
139–40
Cappon, James, 195
Carlyle, Thomas, 74, 76,
81
Carman, Rev. Albert, 83–
4, 126, 170–1, 173, 176,
220–1, 241–7, 250, 283
Caven, Rev. William, 10,
127, 144, 147–9, 150,
151, 152–3, 154, 158,
159, 212, 225, 228, 247,
265
Chadwick, Owen, 4, 72,

79, 131, 314 n.43, 326
n.17
Chalmers, Rev. Thomas,
17, 28–31, 42, 44, 61,
63–4, 139, 216, 228
Chown, Rev. Samuel
Dwight, 10, 193, 195–6,
199–200, 209–12, 215,
218–21, 225, 228, 250–2,
252–3, 253–4, 255–7,
259, 260, 271, 272, 274,
282, 289, 349 n.76
*Christ and the Kingdom of
God* (Hooke). *See*
Hooke, S.H. 276
church colleges, 8–9, 32,
36–7, 51–2, 70, 73, 80–
1, 127, 130, 140, 144,
153, 223–4, 225, 233,
235–6, 270–1, 276–83,
277, 366–7 n.60. *See also*
Emmanuel College,
Knox College, Mount
Allison Wesleyan Col-
lege, Pictou Academy,
Presbyterian College
Halifax, Presbyterian
College Montreal,
Queen's University,
Victoria College, Wes-
ley College
Church of Scotland, 27–
31, 150, 156–7. *See also*
Presbyterian Church
Clarke, Dr Adam, 81
Clarkson, Rev. J.B., 173
clergymen-professors,
9–10, 119–20, 138, 143–
4, 170, 174, 182, 186,
193–4, 200, 205–7, 213–
14, 234–5, 257–8, 280–
3, 290, 354–5 n.35
Colenso, Bishop, 129,
130, 132, 166
Coleridge, Samuel Taylor,
80
Common Sense. *See* Scot-
tish Common Sense,
Scottish Enlightenment
"comparative religion,"
226–8, 267

Cook, Ramsay, 274
Corbett, E.A., 262, 264
*Critical History of Free
Thought* (Farrar). *See*
Farrar, Rev. A.S.
Crummy, Rev. Eber, 9,
244
Cunningham, Rev. Wil-
liam, 139–40
Currie, Rev. John, 204

Dall, Rev. John, 236–8
Darby, John Nelson, 89
Darwin, Charles, 71, 125,
146
Davidson, Rev. A.B., 140,
143, 146, 188–9, 244
Dawson, Sir William, 70,
127–9
Delitzsch, Franz, 178, 190
Denney, Rev. James,
232–3
Dewart, Rev. Edward
Hartley, 172, 173–4,
176, 177–9
de Wette, W.M.L., 79
Dilthey, Wilhelm, 225
dispensationalism, 103–4,
115–16, 120, 323 n.64.
See also fundamental-
ism, premillennialism
Dow, Rev. John, 270
Drummond, Henry, 143,
205
Dyde, Rev. Samuel, 260

*Early Traditions of Genesis,
The* (Gordon), 231–2.
See also Gordon,
Rev. Alexander Reid
Ecclesiastical History
(Mosheim). *See* Mosh-
eim, Johann Lorenz
von
Edwards, Rev. Jonathan,
11, 21, 108, 113, 121
*Egypt's Place in Universal
History* (Bunsen). *See*
Bunsen, Baron Christian
Elements of Moral Science
(Wayland). *See* Way-

land, Rev. Francis, 51, 67

Emerson, Ralph Waldo, 80

Emmanuel College, 270. *See also* church colleges

Enlightenment, 15–16, 64. *See also* Scottish Common Sense

Essays and Reviews, 130, 132. *See also* Jowett, Benjamin; liberal Anglicans

Essays on the Supernatural Origins of Christianity (Fisher). *See* Fisher, George P.

Evidences of Christianity (Paley). *See* Paley, Rev. William, 87

evolutionary thought, 4, 101, 125–31, 133–4, 142, 144–6, 150, 166–74, 215, 287, 324 n.4

Fairbairn, Rev. Andrew Martin, 205–6

Fairbairn, Rev. R. Edis, 278

Falconer, Rev. Robert, 10, 143, 202–4, 206–9, 211, 228, 247

Farrar, Rev. F.W., 170

Ferguson, Adam, 26

Ferrier, J.F., 30

Finney, Charles Grandison, 216

Fisher, George P., 170

Flint, Rev. Robert. *See* historical theology, 141–2, 143

form-criticism, 226

Forrester, Rev. Alexander, 121–2

Foxe, John, 94, 112, 321 n.48

Free Church, 143, 150, 151. *See also* Presbyterian Church

French, Goldwin, 8

Frye, Northrop, 15

fundamentalism, 89, 268–70, 277. *See also* dispensationalism, premillennialism

Gandier, Rev. Alfred, 228, 247, 270, 278

George, Rev. James, 17, 36, 37, 40

Gladden, Rev. Washington, 216

Gliddon, George, 101, 108

Gordon, Rev. Alexander Reid, 231, 258–9, 260

Gordon, Rev. Daniel Miner, 157, 158, 209, 223, 228, 251

Graham, Rev. William Creighton, 280

Grant, Rev. George Monro, 10, 125, 127, 150, 155–60, 181, 184–5, 185–7, 193, 197–8, 200, 201, 215, 225, 228, 247, 265, 283, 284

Gray, Asa, 129

Great Disruption. *See* Presbyterian Church, 139

Green, T.H., 198

Green, William Henry, 190

Gregg, Rev. William, 146

Gunkel, Hermann, 226, 230

Hamilton, Sir William, 17, 30, 38, 64

Hare, Julius, 80, 101

Harnack, Adolf von, 203–5, 206, 227, 233

Hegel, G.W.F., 79

Hegelianism, 140–1, 157, 204, 272–3. *See also* Idealism

Hilton, Boyd, 63

Hincks, William, 245

historical criticism, 11, 78–90, 105, 135–40, 144, 149, 150–4, 223, 225–6. *See also* Bible, higher criticism

historical study, 58–9, 72, 74–5, 79, 89–90, 93–6, 99–101, 114–17, 149, 176, 278, 286–7

historical theology, 140–3, 147–8, 156–7, 159, 192–3, 197–8, 201–6, 210, 215–16, 220, 233–4, 238–41, 248, 257–8, 260–3, 273, 287–9, 351 n.90. *See also* biblical theology, inductive theology

historicism, 79–81, 101, 224–5

History of Dogma (Harnack). *See* Harnack, Adolf von, 204–5

History of Interpretation (Farrar). *See* Farrar, Rev. F.W.

History, Prophecy and the Monuments (McCurdy). *See* McCurdy, Rev. James Frederick, 190, 192

Hodge, Rev. Charles, 11, 21, 69, 80, 81, 89, 128–9, 138, 139, 144. *See also* Princeton theology

Hooke, S.H., 271, 274–6, 279

Horne, Thomas Hartwell, 85, 105

Hume, David, 46, 64, 68

Hutcheson, Francis, 26–7, 64

idealism, 5, 79–81. *See also* Hegelianism.

inductive theology, 166–74, 175, 241–3. *See also* biblical theology, historical theology, Baconianism

Innis, Harold, 282

Institutes of Theology (Chalmers). *See* Chalmers, Rev. Thomas, 31

Intellect, the Emotions and Man's Moral Nature

(Lyall). *See* Lyall, Rev. William, 34
Interpretation of Religion, The (Baillie). *See* Baillie, Rev. John, 279
Introduction to the Critical Study and Knowledge of the Holy Scriptures (Horne). *See* Horne, Thomas Hartwell, 85
Irving, Edward, 89
Irwin, Rev. A.J., 9, 244

Jackson, Rev. George, 242. *See also* Carman, Rev. Albert
Jackson, Rev. Thomas, 81
James, William, 215, 225, 252, 254, 272, 274, 279. *See also* Pragmatism
Janes, Rev. S.H., 125
Jardine, George, 41
Jones, Rev. Septimus, 194
Jordan, Rev. William George, 139, 197, 230, 247, 344 n.37
Jowett, Benjamin. *See Essays and Reviews*; liberal Anglicans

Kant, Immanuel, 79, 168
Kelman, Rev. John, 262
Ketchum, J. Davidson, 274–6
Kilpatrick, Rev. T.B., 249–50
King, Rev. Andrew, 32–4, 54, 114
King, Rev. John Mark, 8, 147, 150–2, 154, 158, 247
Kingdom and the Messiah, The (Scott). *See* Scott, Rev. E.F., 233
Knox College, 9, 19, 32–3, 43, 60, 86, 107, 146, 147, 248–9. *See also* church colleges

Laon (pseud.). *See* LeSueur, William Dawson

Lavell, Rev. A.E., 244, 264–5
Law, Rev. Robert, 263, 277
Law, Rev. William, 17
Layard, Austen Henry, 110
Lecky, William, 132
Legends of Genesis, The (Gunkel). *See* Gunkel, Hermann, 226
LeSueur, William Dawson, 157, 274, 316 n.51
liberal Anglicans, 80, 82, 101–2, 105. *See also* Arnold, Thomas; Jowett, Benjamin
Life of Jesus (Strauss). *See* Strauss, David Friedrich, 87
Lyall, Rev. William, 17, 34–6
Lyell, Charles, 39, 108

Macallum, A.B., 273
Macaulay, Thomas, 75, 76, 81
McComb, Rev. Samuel, 207
McCosh, Rev. James, 28, 30, 61, 128–9, 190
McCulloch, Thomas, 10, 14–15, 18, 20–9, 34, 40–1, 57, 69, 79, 84–7, 89, 92, 96–7, 116–17, 151, 182, 284, 300 n.25
McCulloch, William, 133
McCurdy, Rev. James Frederick, 190–5
MacDonald, Rev. J.A., 198–9, 208–9, 247
Macdonnell, Rev. Daniel James, 157–9
McFadyen, Rev. John Edgar, 223–4, 250
McGill University, 70
Machen, J. Gresham, 239–41, 268–9
McKillop, A.B., 15, 28, 29
Mackinnon, Clarence, 143, 264, 280

MacLaren, Rev. William, 10, 127, 144–6, 159, 248–9, 331 n.51
McLaughlin, Rev. John Fletcher, 193, 247
Maclean, Rev. J.N., 248
Macleod, Rev. D.D., 248
McLeod, Rev. Norman, 156–7, 198
McLoughlin, William, 214–15
Macphail, Andrew, 195
MacVicar, Rev. Donald Harvey, 127, 147, 150–2, 154, 158, 214, 247, 269–70
Malthus, Thomas, 65
Manitoba College, 9, 151. *See also* church colleges
Mansel, Henry, 30
Marsden, George, 11, 137–8, 220–1, 240, 268, 288
Marshall, D.B., 261, 362 n.15
Methodist Church, 8, 45–8, 66, 68–9, 105–8, 116–17, 121–2, 160–3, 166–75, 207–8, 241–7, 273, 365 n.48
millennialism, 118–19. *See also* premillennialism, postmillennialism
Miller, William, 50
Millerites, 50, 53, 19, 161
Miscellaneous Discourses and Expositions of Scripture (Young). *See* Young, Rev. George Paxton
Misener, Rev. A.P., 229
modernism, 126, 138, 154, 267–8, 338 n.84, 364 n.33
Moody, Dwight, 138, 143, 205
Moore, James R., 127, 142, 287, 325 n.8
Morgan, Rev. William, 280
Mosheim, Johann Lorenz von, 115

Mount Allison Wesleyan College, 9, 169–170, 172. *See also* church colleges
Muller, Max, 109–10, 134
Munger, Theodore, 146
Murray, Walter, 247

Narraway, Rev. James, 72
natural theology, 60, 61, 65, 69. *See also* Butler, Bishop Joseph; Paley, Rev. William
Natural Theology (Paley). *See* Paley, Rev. William, 60, 70
Nelles, Rev. Samuel, 10, 17, 18, 46, 48–9, 52, 55, 68–9, 71, 92–4, 96–7, 99–100, 106–7, 121–2, 126–7, 155, 161–9, 171, 173–4, 228, 265, 273, 337 n.107
neo-Kantianism, 280
neo-Orthodoxy, 267–8, 270–1, 277
new theology, 138, 146
Noll, Mark, 17
Nott, Josiah, 101, 108

Oliver, Rev. Edmund Henry, 260–1, 262, 281
On Natural Theology (Chalmers). *See* Chalmers, Rev. Thomas, 63
Origin of Species (Darwin), 71, 125, 130. *See also* Darwin, Charles

Paley, Rev. William, 60–3, 70–1, 87–8, 108. *See also* natural theology
Philosophy of the Christian Religion, The (Fairbairn). *See* Fairbairn, Rev. Andrew Martin, 206
Philosophy of Thought, The (Lyall). *See* Lyall, Rev. William, 35
Pickard, Rev. Humphrey, 51–2

Pictou Academy, 13–15, 19–20. *See also* church colleges
Pidgeon, Rev. George Campbell, 266, 269–70
Place of Christ in Modern Theology, The (Fairbairn). *See* Fairbairn, Rev. Andrew Martin, 206
post-millennialism, 121–2, 191–2, 201–2. *See also* millennialism, premillennialism
Powell, Rev. Baden, 39
pragmatism, 272–3. *See also* James, William
premillennialism, 119–20. *See also* fundamentalism, millennialism, post-millennialism
Presbyterian Church (Canada), 8, 20–2, 23, 27–8, 31–8, 38–45, 64–6, 69, 85–6, 107–8, 121–2, 138–42, 147–50, 154, 247–50, 269
Presbyterian Church (Scotland), 63–4
Presbyterian College, Halifax, 9, 19, 34–6
Presbyterian College, Montreal, 9, 143, 152–3
Princeton theology, 139, 144, 146, 148, 248–9. *See also* Hodge, Rev. Charles
Prolegomena to the History of Israel (Wellhausen). *See* Wellhausen, Julius, 135
Prophets of Israel and their Place in History, The (Smith). *See* Smith, Robertson, 199
Puritan, 95, 113

Queen's University, 9, 19, 60, 155, 250, 260

Rainy, Rev. Robert, 140–3

Ranke, Leopold von, 223
Reformation, 94–5
Reid, Thomas, 17, 27, 38–9, 64
relativism, 221–2, 232, 257–8, 290
Religion in the Making (Whitehead). *See* Whitehead, Alfred North, 280
Renan, Ernest, 130
Richey, Rev. Matthew, 47
Ritschl, Albrecht, 203–5, 207–8
Robb, Rev. James, 43
Roberts, Rev. Richard, 265–6, 267–8, 363–4 n.31
Robertson, William, 26, 64
Roman Catholicism, 112–17
Ross, Rev. C.B., 195
Ryerson Rev. Egerton, 10, 17, 18, 46, 49–54, 57–8, 66–9, 75, 79, 87, 89, 92, 96–7, 100, 103–4, 106, 123, 162, 164–5, 182, 273, 284, 317 n.3

Schorske, Carl, 266, 364 n.33
Schweitzer, Albert, 233–4, 276
Scott, C.T., 246
Scott, Donald, 234–5
Scott, Rev. E.F., 233, 236–7, 261, 354 n.33
Scottish Common Sense, 17–18, 26, 27–31, 62, 64, 95–6, 139, 287. *See also* Scottish Enlightenment; Common Sense; Baconianism
Scottish Enlightenment. *See* Scottish Common Sense; Scottish Enlightenment
Scrimger, Rev. John, 152–3, 154, 193–4, 247
Second Great Awakening, 216

secularization, 4–6, 79, 181, 183–4, 200–1, 218–20, 256, 285, 288, 341–2 n.7, 352 n.3, 361 n.5, 368 n.1
Seeley, J.R., 130
Sermons (Butler). See Butler, Bishop Joseph, 62
Shaw, Rev. J.M., 229
Smith, Adam, 64
Smith, George Adam, 151, 231, 244
Smith, Goldwin, 3
Smith, Henry B., 80
Smith, Robertson, 140, 146, 188, 199–200
Snodgrass, Rev. William, 121, 150, 158
social gospel, 5, 9, 183–4, 215–16, 259–60, 341 n.4, 341 n.6
social sciences, 5, 110–11, 200–1, 213–17, 224–5, 253–4, 257–8, 271–2, 288–9
Southcott, Joanna, 23, 119
Spencer, Herbert, 110, 142, 214
Stanley, Arthur, 101
Stephen, Leslie, 132
Stewart, Dugald, 17, 27, 38–9, 64
Stewart, Rev. Charles, 169
Strauss, David Friedrich, 79, 87, 129
Strong, Augustus, 268
Student Christian Movement, 275

Text of Jeremiah, The (Workman). See Workman, Rev. George Coulson, 178

Theological Institutes (Watson). See Watson, Rev. Richard, 54
theological liberalism, 126, 154, 203, 334 n.82
"theology of crisis," 268
theology of history, 94–6, 100–5, 108–9, 110–11, 112–17, 118–24, 127, 130, 153, 182, 191–2, 258–9, 260, 277–8
Thomson, Rev. R.Y., 146–7
Thornwell, James, 69
Trinity College, Toronto, 70
Troeltsch, Ernst, 225, 238, 279
Tulloch, Rev. John, 156

uniformitarianism, 101, 109. See also Lyell, Charles
United Church of Canada, 8, 268–70, 270–1, 276–83

Varieties of Religious Experience, The. See James, William
Victoria College, 9, 49–51, 60, 68, 163, 166, 169–70, 172, 175–7, 178–80, 244–5, 273–4, 340 n.140, 377 n.107, See also church colleges
vitalism. See pragmatism

Wallace, Rev. Francis Huston, 177, 202, 203–4, 208–9
Warfield, Benjamin, 190
Watson, John, 155, 160, 244, 273, 365–6 n.50

Watson, Rev. Richard, 54, 81, 116, 162, 164
Watson, Rev. W.G., 213
Wayland, Rev. Francis, 48, 51, 67
Weiss, Johannes, 226–7
Wellhausen, Julius, 135–6, 154
Wesley College, 9, 172, 245–6. See also church colleges
Wesley, Rev. John, 17, 45–6, 53, 66, 228
Wesleyan College, Montreal, 172. See also church colleges
Westcott, B.F., 168
What is Civilization? (George). See George, Rev. James, 37
Whewell, William, 39, 109–10
Whitefield, George, 21
Whitehead, Alfred North, 279, 280
Whittaker, Rev. C. Wellesley, 262
Willis, Rev. Michael, 10, 18, 32–3, 44, 54, 83, 86, 87, 90, 92, 303 n.48
Wilson, Sir Daniel, 129
Withrow, William, 172, 176–7
Woodsworth, Rev. James S., 183–4, 259
Workman, Rev. George Coulson, 178–80, 243
World War I, 258–65, 274, 278, 362 n.14, 367 n.63

Yale University, 175
Young, Rev. George Paxton, 107–8